FIFTH EDITION

3

P9-DVQ-496

GRAMMAR *in* CONTEXT

SANDRA N. ELBAUM

The cover photo shows the MacArthur Causeway over Biscayne Bay in Miami, Florida.

HEINLE
CENGAGE Learning

Australia • Brazil • Japan • Korea • Mexico • Singapore • Spain • United Kingdom • United States

HEINLE
CENGAGE Learning

Grammar in Context 3, Fifth Edition
Student Book
Sandra N. Elbaum

Publisher: Sherrise Roehr

Acquisitions Editor: Tom Jefferies

Development Editor: Sarah Sandoski

Senior Technology Development Editor:
 Debie Mirtle

Director of Global Marketing: Ian Martin

Director of US Marketing: Jim McDonough

Product Marketing Manager: Katie Kelley

Marketing Manager: Caitlin Driscoll

Content Project Manager: Andrea Bobotas

Senior Print Buyer: Susan Spencer

Project Manager: Chrystie Hopkins

Production Services: Nesbitt Graphics, Inc.

Interior Design and Cover Design:
 Muse Group, Inc.

Library of Congress Control Number: 2009936999

ISBN 13: 978-1-4240-7902-5

ISBN 10: 1-4240-7902-0

Heinle
20 Channel Center Street
Boston, Massachusetts 02210
USA

Cengage Learning is a leading provider of customized learning solutions with office locations around the globe, including Singapore, the United Kingdom, Australia, Mexico, Brazil, and Japan. Locate our local office at international.cengage.com/region

Cengage Learning products are represented in Canada by Nelson Education, Ltd.

Visit Heinle online at **elt.heinle.com**

Visit our corporate website at **www.cengage.com**

Printed in the United States of America.
7 8 9 10 — 14

Contents

Lesson 3

Lesson 4

Lesson 5

Lesson 6

Lesson 7

Lesson 8

Lesson 9

Lesson 10

Appendices

Index

Acknowledgments

Many thanks to Dennis Hogan, Sherrise Roehr, and Tom Jefferies from Heinle Cengage for their ongoing support of the *Grammar in Context* series. I would especially like to thank my development editor, Sarah Sandoski, for her patience, sensitivity, keen eye to detail, and invaluable suggestions.

And many thanks to my students at Truman College, who have increased my understanding of my own language and taught me to see life from another point of view. By sharing their observations, questions, and life stories, they have enriched my life enormously.

This new edition is dedicated to the millions of displaced people in the world. The U.S. is the new home to many refugees, who survived unspeakable hardships in Burundi, Rwanda, Sudan, Burma, Bhutan, and other countries. Their resiliency in starting a new life and learning a new language is a tribute to the human spirit.—*Sandra N. Elbaum*

Heinle would like to thank the following people for their contributions:

Elizabeth A. Adler-Coleman
Sunrise Mountain High
    School
Las Vegas, NV

Dorothy Avondstondt
Miami Dade College
Miami, FL

Judith A. G. Benka
Normandale Community
    College
Bloomington, MN

Carol Brutza
Gateway Community
    College
New Haven, CT

Lyn Buchheit
Community College of
    Philadelphia
Philadelphia, PA

Charlotte M. Calobrisi
Northern Virginia
    Community College
Annandale, VA

Gabriela Cambiasso
Harold Washington College
Chicago, IL

Jeanette Clement
Duquesne University
Pittsburgh, PA

Allis Cole
Shoreline Community
    College
Shoreline, WA

Fanshen DiGiovanni
Glendale Community
    College
Glendale, CA

Antoinette B. d'Oronzio
Hillsborough Community
    College-Dale Mabry
    Campus
Tampa, FL

Rhonda J. Farley
Cosumnes River College
Sacramento, CA

Jennifer Farnell
University of Connecticut
    American Language
    Program
Stamford, CT

Gail Fernandez
Bergen Community College
Paramus, NJ

Irasema Fernandez
Miami Dade College
Miami, FL

Abigail-Marie Fiattarone
Mesa Community College
Mesa, AZ

John Gamber
American River College
Sacramento, CA

Marcia Gethin-Jones
University of Connecticut
    American Language
    Program
Stamford, CT

Kimlee Buttacavoli Grant
The Leona Group, LLC
Phoenix, AZ

Shelly Hedstrom
Palm Beach Community
    College
Lake Worth, FL

Linda Holden
College of Lake County
Grayslake, IL

Sandra Kawamura
Sacramento City College
Sacramento, CA

Bill Keniston
Normandale Community
    College
Bloomington, MN

Michael Larsen
American River College
Sacramento, CA

Bea C. Lawn
Gavilan College
Gilroy, CA

Rob Lee
Pasadena City College
Pasadena, CA

Oranit Limmaneeprasert
American River College
Sacramento, CA

Linda Louie
Highline Community
    College
Des Moines, WA

Melanie A. Majeski
Naugatuck Valley
    Community College
Waterbury, CT

Maria Marin
De Anza College
Cupertino, CA

Michael I. Massey
Hillsborough Community
    College-Ybor City Campus
Tampa, FL

Marlo McClurg-Mackinnon
Cosumnes River College
Sacramento, CA

Michelle Naumann
Elgin Community College
Elgin, IL

Debbie Ockey
Fresno, CA

Lesa Perry
University of Nebraska at
    Omaha
Omaha, NE

Herbert Pierson
St. John's University
Queens, NY

Dina Poggi
De Anza College
Cupertino, CA

Steven Rashba
University of Bridgeport
Bridgeport, CT

Mark Rau
American River College
Sacramento, CA

Maria Spelleri
State College of Florida
    Manatee-Sarasota
Venice, FL

Eva Teagarden
Yuba College
Marysville, CA

Colin S. Ward
Lone Star College-North
    Harris
Houston, TX

Nico Wiersema
Texas A&M International
    University
Laredo, TX

Susan Wilson
San Jose City College
San Jose, CA

A word from the author

My parents immigrated to the U.S. from Poland and learned English as a second language. Born in the U.S., I often had the task as a child to explain the intricacies of the English language. It is no wonder that I became an English language teacher.

When I started teaching over forty years ago, grammar textbooks used a series of unrelated sentences with no context. I knew instinctively that there was something wrong with this technique. It ignored the fact that language is a tool for communication, and it missed an opportunity to spark the student's curiosity. As I gained teaching experience, I noticed that when I used interesting stories that illustrated the grammar, students became more motivated, understood the grammar better, and used it more effectively.

In 1986, I published the first edition of *Grammar in Context* and have continued to search for topics that teach grammar in contexts that are relevant to students' lives. The contexts I've chosen each tell a story: practical ones about technology (eBay and Freecycle), interesting people, whether well-known or not, recent events that made history (Hurricane Katrina), science (travel to Mars), and more. Whether the task is a fill-in grammar exercise, a listening activity, an editing exercise, an interactive conversation activity, or free writing, the context is reinforced throughout the lesson.

I hope you enjoy the new edition of *Grammar in Context!*

Sandra N. Elbaum

In memory of
Meyer Shisler
Teacher, Scholar, Inspiration

Welcome to *Grammar in Context,*
Fifth Edition

Grammar in Context presents grammar in interesting contexts that are relevant to students' lives and then recycles the language and context throughout every activity. Learners gain knowledge and skills in both the grammar structures and topic areas.

The new fifth edition of *Grammar in Context* engages learners with updated readings, clear and manageable grammar explanations, and a new full-color design.

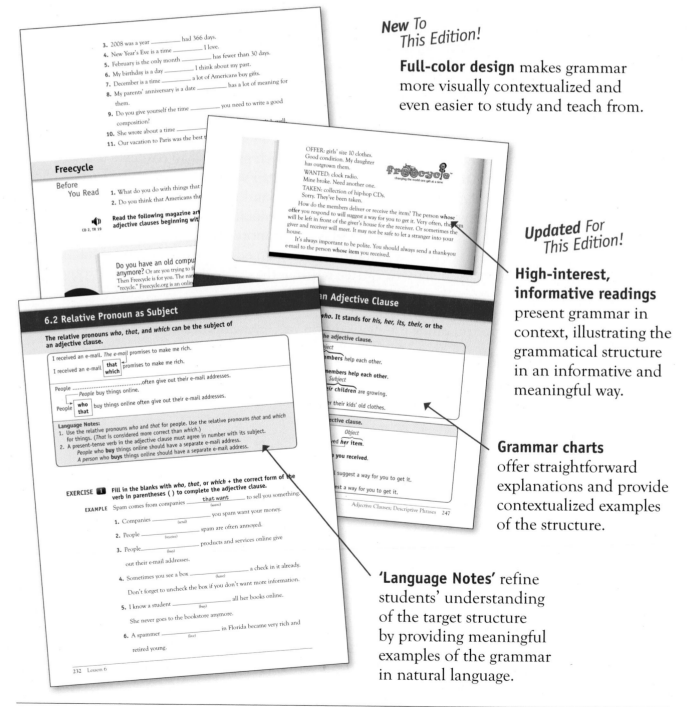

New To This Edition!

Full-color design makes grammar more visually contextualized and even easier to study and teach from.

Updated For This Edition!

High-interest, informative readings present grammar in context, illustrating the grammatical structure in an informative and meaningful way.

Grammar charts offer straightforward explanations and provide contextualized examples of the structure.

'Language Notes' refine students' understanding of the target structure by providing meaningful examples of the grammar in natural language.

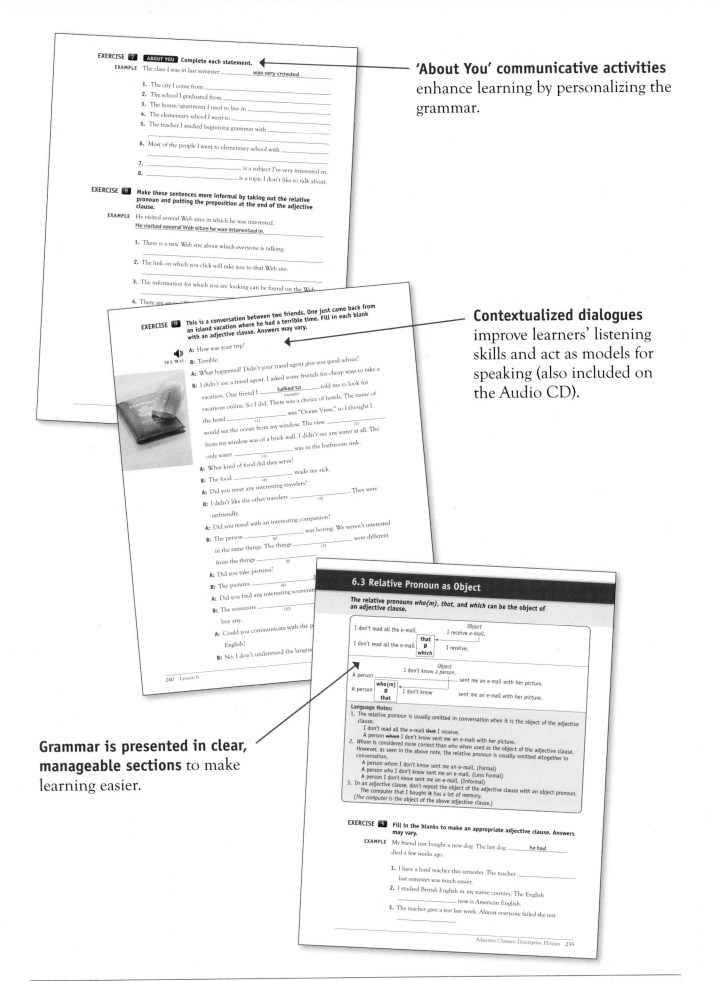

EXERCISE 7 **ABOUT YOU** Complete each statement.

EXAMPLE The class I was in last semester _____ *was very crowded.*

1. The city I come from _____
2. The school I graduated from _____
3. The house/apartment I used to live in _____
4. The elementary school I went to _____
5. The teacher I studied beginning grammar with _____
6. Most of the people I went to elementary school with _____
7. _____ is a subject I'm very interested in.
8. _____ is a topic I don't like to talk about.

EXERCISE 8 Make these sentences more informal by taking out the relative pronoun and putting the preposition at the end of the adjective clause.

EXAMPLE He visited several Web sites in which he was interested.
He visited several Web sites he was interested in.

1. There is a new Web site about which everyone is talking.
_____

2. The link on which you click will take you to that Web site.
_____

3. The information for which you are looking can be found on the Web.

4. There are

'About You' communicative activities enhance learning by personalizing the grammar.

EXERCISE 9 This is a conversation between two friends. One just came back from an island vacation where he had a terrible time. Fill in each blank with an adjective clause. Answers may vary.

🔊
CD 2, TR 17

A: How was your trip?

B: Terrible.

A: What happened? Didn't your travel agent give you good advice?

B: I didn't use a travel agent. I asked some friends for cheap ways to take a vacation. One friend I _____ *talked to* _____ told me to look for
(example)
vacations online. So I did. There was a choice of hotels. The name of
the hotel _____ was "Ocean View," so I thought I
(1)
would see the ocean from my window. The view _____
(2)
from my window was of a brick wall. I didn't see any water at all. The
only water _____ was in the bathroom sink.
(3)

A: What kind of food did they serve?

B: The food _____ made me sick.
(4)

A: Did you meet any interesting travelers?

B: I didn't like the other travelers _____. They were
(5)
unfriendly.

A: Did you travel with an interesting companion?

B: The person _____ was boring. We weren't interested
(6)
in the same things. The things _____ were different
(7)
from the things _____.
(8)

A: Did you take pictures?

B: The pictures _____
(9)

A: Did you find any interesting souvenir

B: The souvenirs _____
(10)
buy any.

A: Could you communicate with the p
English?

B: No. I don't understand the langua

240   Lesson 6

Contextualized dialogues improve learners' listening skills and act as models for speaking (also included on the Audio CD).

6.3 Relative Pronoun as Object

The relative pronouns *who(m)*, *that*, and *which* can be the object of an adjective clause.

```
                                    Object
I don't read all the e-mail.   I receive e-mail.
                     ┌─ that ─┐
I don't read all the e-mail ─┤ ø     ├─ I receive.
                     └─ which ┘
```

```
                                    Object
                        I don't know a person.
A person ·········································· sent me an e-mail with her picture.
          ┌─ who(m) ─┐
A person ─┤ ø        ├─ I don't know ─ sent me an e-mail with her picture.
          └─ that    ┘
```

Language Notes:
1. The relative pronoun is usually omitted in conversation when it is the object of the adjective clause.
    I don't read all the e-mail ~~that~~ I receive.
    A person ~~whom~~ I don't know sent me an e-mail with her picture.
2. *Whom* is considered more correct than *who* when used as the object of the adjective clause. However, as seen in the above note, the relative pronoun is usually omitted altogether in conversation.
    A person *whom* I don't know sent me an e-mail. (Formal)
    A person *who* I don't know sent me an e-mail. (Less Formal)
    A person I don't know sent me an e-mail. (Informal)
3. In an adjective clause, don't repeat the object of the adjective clause with an object pronoun.
    The computer that I bought ~~it~~ has a lot of memory.
    (*The computer* is the object of the above adjective clause.)

EXERCISE 5 Fill in the blanks to make an appropriate adjective clause. Answers may vary.

EXAMPLE My friend just bought a new dog. The last dog _____ *he had* _____
died a few weeks ago.

1. I have a hard teacher this semester. The teacher _____
last semester was much easier.
2. I studied British English in my native country. The English _____
_____ now is American English.
3. The teacher gave a test last week. Almost everyone failed the test
_____

Adjective Clauses; Descriptive Phrases   235

Grammar is presented in clear, manageable sections to make learning easier.

Editing Advice

1. Never use *what* as a relative pronoun.
   > She married a man ~~what~~ who has a lot of money.
   > Everything ~~what~~ that you did was unnecessary.

2. You can't omit a relative pronoun that is the subject of the adjective clause.
   > I know a man who speaks five languages.

3. If the relative pronoun is the object of the adjective clause, don't put an object after the verb.
   > The car that I bought ~~it~~ has a stick shift.

4. Make sure you use subject-verb agreement.
   > I know several Engli...

Editing Quiz

Some of the shaded words and phrases have mistakes. Find the mistakes and correct them. If the shaded words are correct, write C.

Last semester I took a photo editing class that has helped me a lot.
(example) C

The teacher what taught the class is an expert in photo editing.
(example) who

This teacher, whose name is Mark Ryan, is patient, helpful, and fun.
(1)

A lot of the photos I took were too dark. I learned how to lighten the
(2)

parts what needed lightening without lightening the whole photo. I also
(3)

learned to cut out parts I don't want them. For example, I have a family
(4)

picture, but it has one person who's not in the family. It's a woman
(5)

who live next door to us. She came right at the time when
(6)

was taking the picture my friend and she wanted to be in it. It's a great
(7)

photo, except for her. I tried scanning it and editing it at home, but I

didn't do a good job. My teacher, who his scanner is much better than
(8)

mine, scanned the photo and showed me how to cut the neighbor out. I

learned many things in this class. Everything what I learned is very helpful.
(9)

I started to take another photo class this semester. The teacher

whose class I'm taking now is not as good as last semester's teacher. Who
(10) *(11)*

wants to learn a lot about photo editing should take Mark Ryan's class.

---

7. My mother who lives in Miami has a degree in engineering.
8. I have two sisters. My sister who lives in New Jersey has three children.
9. Our parents who live with us now are beginning to study English.
10. I often use Freecycle.org which has communities in most big cities.
11. The city where I was born has beautiful museums.
12. St. Petersburg where I was born has beautiful museums.

Expansion

Classroom Activities

❶ **Make a sentence with each of the following phrases. Discuss your answers in a small group.**

a. children who use the Internet a lot
b. people who don't have a computer
c. Web sites that have a lot of ads
d. the spam I get in my mailbox
e. people who work with computers all day
f. schools that don't have modern computer equipment

❷ **Fill in the blanks and discuss your answers:**

a. _____ is one of my favorite Web sites.
b. One thing I really like about the Web is _____
c. One thing I don't like about the Web is _____

Talk About It

❶ In what ways does the computer make life better? In what ways does it make life worse?

❷ One way to get rid of things you don't need is by using Freecycle. What do you do with things you have no more use for?

Adjective Clauses; Descriptive Phrases **273**

Write

About It

❶ Write a paragraph telling the different ways you use your computer.

❷ Write about an important person you know of who did something great but isn't well-known (like Tim Berners-Lee).

❸ Write about some type of technology that you use today that you didn't use ten years ago.

EXAMPLE

> ### Using Facebook
>
> A few years ago I started using Facebook, and I love it. I can see what my friends are doing. Also I can make new friends by seeing whom my friends have included as their friends. Any of my friends who want to know what I'm doing can see my page ...

💻 For more practice using grammar in context, please visit our Web site.

Enhanced For This Edition!

Enhanced editing section guides students to first identify and then correct common grammatical errors in context.

Updated For This Edition!

Comprehensive 'Expansion' section for each lesson provides opportunities for students to interact with one another and further develop their speaking and writing skills.

More Writing Models In This Edition!

Writing models provide additional writing practice using the grammar structure for that lesson.

---

xiv Welcome to *Grammar in Context*

Additional resources for each level

FOR THE STUDENT:

New To This Edition!

- **Online Workbook** features additional exercises that learners can access in the classroom, language lab, or at home.

- **Audio CD** includes dialogues and all readings from the student book.

- Student Web site features a review unit and additional practice: http://elt.heinle.com/grammarincontext.

FOR THE TEACHER:

New To This Edition!

- **Online Lesson Planner** is perfect for busy instructors, allowing them to create and customize lesson plans for their classes, then save and share them in a range of formats.

Updated For This Edition!

- **Assessment CD-ROM with Exam*View*®** lets teachers create and customize tests and quizzes easily and includes many new contextualized test items.

- **Teacher's Edition** offers comprehensive teaching notes including suggestions for more streamlined classroom options.

- Instructor Web site includes a printable Student Book answer key.

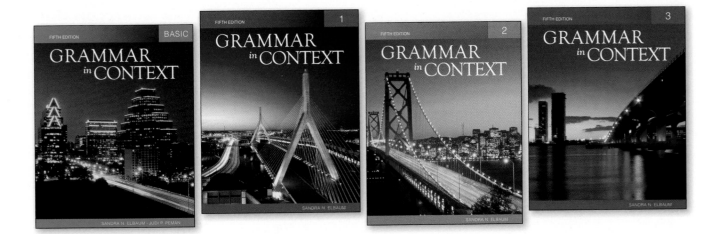

Grammar
The Present Perfect Tense

The Present Perfect Continuous Tense[1]

Context
Jobs

[1]The present perfect continuous is sometimes called the present perfect progressive.

Cover Letter and Job Résumé

Before
You Read

1. Do you have a résumé?

2. Do you have a job now? What do you do?

CD 1, TR 01

Read the following cover letter and résumé. Pay special attention to the present perfect and present perfect continuous tenses.

6965 Troy Avenue
Chicago, Illinois 60659
773-555-1946
dmendoza99@e*mail.com

Mr. Ray Johnson, General Manager
Paradise Hotel
226 West Jackson Boulevard
Chicago, Illinois 60606

Dear Mr. Johnson:

I would like to apply for the job of hotel office manager at the Paradise Hotel.

I come from Mexico City, where my family owns a hotel. I worked in the family business part-time when I was in high school. After high school, I studied hotel and restaurant management at the National University of Mexico. I came to the U.S. in 1998 because I wanted to continue my education and learn about managing larger hotels. Since I came to the U.S., I **have worked** in several American hotels. Over the years my English **has improved**, and I now consider myself bilingual. I am fluent in both Spanish and English, and this is a plus in the hotel business. I **have** also **studied** French and can speak it fairly well. I **have been** a U.S. citizen for the past five years.

I received my bachelor's degree from the University of Illinois in 2002 and my master's degree from Northwestern University in 2004. For the past few years, I **have been working** at the Town and Country Hotel. As you can see from my résumé, I **have had** a lot of experience in various aspects of the hotel business. Now that I have my degree in business administration, I am ready to assume² more responsibilities.

If you **have** already **filled** the manager's position, I would like you to consider me for any other position at your hotel. I **have** always **loved** the hotel business, and I know I can be an asset³ to your hotel.

Enclosed is my résumé for your review. Thank you for considering my application. I look forward to meeting with you soon.

Sincerely,

Daniel Mendoza

Daniel Mendoza

---

²Assume means *take on* or *accept.*

³To be an *asset* to a company means to have a talent or ability that will help the company.

DANIEL MENDOZA

6965 Troy Avenue
Chicago, Illinois 60659
773-555-1946
dmendoza99@e*mail.com
www.mendozahotel.com

SUMMARY: Hotel professional with proven management skills and successful experience in improving operations, upgrading properties, building teams, and improving customer relations.

PROFESSIONAL EXPERIENCE
- Developed sales/marketing plans geared towards business travelers
- Handled customer relations, correspondence, and communication
- Coordinated, organized, and supervised front desk operations and food service
- Assisted guests and groups in planning tours and arranging transportation, restaurant accommodations, and reservations
- Designed and maintained hotel Web site
- Managed hotel bookkeeping

EMPLOYMENT HISTORY

2007–Present	Town and Country Hotel, Front Office Manager	Chicago, IL
2002–2007	Mid-Town Hotel, Bookkeeper (part-time)	Evanston, IL
1998–2002	Travel Time Hotel, Front Desk Clerk (part-time)	Champaign, IL
1994–1998	Hotel Mendoza, Front Desk Clerk	Mexico City, Mexico

TECHNICAL PROFICIENCIES
- Microsoft Office (Word, Excel, Access, PowerPoint); Quicken; Photoshop; Dreamweaver; Flash; Fireworks; FrontPage; HTML

EDUCATION
- Master of Science: Business Administration, Northwestern University, 2004
- Bachelor of Science: Business Administration, University of Illinois, 2002
- Degree in Hotel Management: National University of Mexico, 1998

PROFESSIONAL AFFILIATIONS
- Travel & Tourism Research Association (TTRA)
- Association of Travel Marketing Executives (ATME)
- International Association of Convention & Visitor Bureaus (IACVB)

True or False. Based on the cover letter and résumé, decide if the statement is true (*T*) or false (*F*).

EXAMPLES   Daniel has worked for his parents.   T

Daniel has worked in California.   F

1. Daniel has never worked in a factory.

2. Daniel has had experience with computers.

3. He has been in the U.S. for less than two years.

4. He has included information about his education.

5. He has studied a foreign language.

6. He has had experience in several hotels.

7. He has already met with Mr. Johnson.

8. He has included his age and marital status in his résumé.

1.1 The Present Perfect Tense—Forms

Affirmative

Subject	*Have*	Past Participle	Complement	Explanation
I	have	been	in the U.S. for a year.	To form the present perfect tense, use: *I, you, we, they, there,* or a plural noun + *have* + past participle.
You	have	had	a lot of experience.	
We	have	written	a job résumé.	
They	have	seen	the application.	
My parents	have	given	me encouragement.	
There	have	been	many interviews.	

Subject	*Has*	Past Participle	Complement	Explanation
My sister	**has**	**been**	a doctor for two years.	To form the present perfect tense, use: *he, she, it, there*, or a singular noun + *has* + past participle.
She	**has**	**had**	a lot of experience.	
My father	**has**	**visited**	me in the U.S.	
It	**has**	**been**	hard to find a job.	
There	**has**	**been**	a lot of unemployment.	

Negative

Subject	*Have/ Has*	*Not*	Past Participle	Complement	Explanation
He	**has**	**not**	**found**	a job.	To form the negative, put *not* between the auxiliary verb (*has/have*) and the past participle.
Mr. Johnson	**has**	**not**	**seen**	the résumé yet.	
We	**have**	**not**	**had**	an interview.	
I	**have**	**not**	**applied**	for a job.	

With an Adverb

Subject	*Have/ Has*	Adverb	Past Participle	Complement	Explanation
You	**have**	**never**	**worked**	in a factory.	You can put an adverb between the auxiliary verb (*have/has*) and the past participle.
We	**have**	**always**	**wanted**	to learn English.	
They	**have**	**already**	**found**	a job.	
He	**has**	**just**	**had**	an interview.	
The manager	**has**	**probably**	**interviewed**	a lot of people.	

EXERCISE **2** Read the following student composition. Underline all present perfect tense verbs.

Looking for a Job

I am looking for a job. I <u>have been</u> an electrical engineer for the past eight years. I arrived in the U.S. a few months ago, so I have not had much experience with American job interviews. I don't think my English is a problem because I have studied English since I was a child. In my country, I found a job right after I graduated from college. I stayed at the same job until I came here. The process of finding a job in the U.S. is a bit different. To learn about this process, I have used the Internet. I have also taken a course at a nearby college on how to prepare for an interview. So far, I have had three interviews, but I have not done well on them. I hope that each interview will help me do better on the next one, and soon I hope to find a good job.

1.2 The Past Participle

The past participle is the third form of the verb. We use it to form the present perfect tense.

Regular Verbs—Past and past participle are the same.

FORMS			EXPLANATION
Base Form	**Past Form**	**Past Participle**	The past participle of regular verbs ends in
work	worked	worked	-ed. The past form and the past participle
improve	improved	improved	of regular verbs are the same.

Irregular Verbs—Past and past participle are the same.

FORMS			EXPLANATION
Base Form	**Past Form**	**Past Participle**	The past participle of many irregular verbs
have	had	had	is the same as the past form.
buy	bought	bought	
leave	left	left	
make	made	made	
put	put	put	

Irregular Verbs—Past and past participle are different.[4]

BASE FORM	PAST FORM	PAST PARTICIPLE
become	became	become
come	came	come
run	ran	run
blow	blew	blown
draw	drew	drawn
fly	flew	flown
grow	grew	grown
know	knew	known
throw	threw	thrown
swear	swore	sworn
tear	tore	torn
wear	wore	worn
break	broke	broken
choose	chose	chosen
freeze	froze	frozen
speak	spoke	spoken
steal	stole	stolen
begin	began	begun
drink	drank	drunk
ring	rang	rung
sing	sang	sung
sink	sank	sunk
swim	swam	swum
bite	bit	bitten
drive	drove	driven
hide	hid	hidden
ride	rode	ridden
rise	rose	risen
write	wrote	written
be	was/were	been
do	did	done
eat	ate	eaten
fall	fell	fallen
forget	forgot	forgotten
forgive	forgave	forgiven
get	got	gotten
give	gave	given
go	went	gone
lie	lay	lain
mistake	mistook	mistaken
prove	proved	proven (or proved)
see	saw	seen
shake	shook	shaken
show	showed	shown (or showed)
take	took	taken

[4]Note: For an alphabetical list of irregular past tenses and past participles, see Appendix M.

EXERCISE 3   Fill in the blanks with the past participle of the verb shown.

EXAMPLE   shake _____shaken_____

1. eat _____
2. go _____
3. read _____
4. drive _____
5. work _____
6. see _____
7. believe _____
8. swim _____
9. drink _____
10. steal _____
11. find _____
12. listen _____
13. think _____
14. live _____
15. make _____

16. write _____
17. grow _____
18. begin _____
19. be _____
20. study _____
21. ride _____
22. hide _____
23. look _____
24. leave _____
25. fall _____
26. feel _____
27. choose _____
28. lose _____
29. do _____
30. understand _____

EXERCISE 4   Fill in the blanks with the correct form of the verb in parentheses ( ) to form the present perfect tense.

EXAMPLE   Daniel _____has sent_____ three résumés this week.
                              (send)

1. He _____ several interviews.
           (have)

2. Mr. Johnson _____ a letter from Daniel.
                    (get)

3. There _____ many applicants for the job.
             (be)

4. Daniel's parents _____ in the hotel business.
                        (always/be)

5. Daniel _____ from college.
             (already/graduate)

6. I _____ Daniel's résumé.
       (read)

7. Daniel _____ as a programmer.
             (never/work)

8. He _____ his résumé to many companies.
          (send)

9. The company _____ 20 applicants so far.
                    (interview)

1.3 The Present Perfect—Contractions

EXAMPLES	EXPLANATION
I've had a lot of experience. **It's** been hard to find a job. **There's** been a change in my plans.	We can make a contraction with subject pronouns and *have* or *has*. I have = I've He has = He's You have = You've She has = She's We have = We've It has = It's They have = They've There has = There's
My father**'s** taught me a lot about the hotel business. The manager**'s** had many job applications.	Most singular nouns can contract with *has*.
I **haven't** had experience in the restaurant business. Mr. Johnson **hasn't** called me.	Negative contractions: have not = haven't has not = hasn't

Language Note: The *'s* in *he's, she's, it's,* and *there's* can mean *has* or *is*. The verb form following the contraction will tell you what the contraction means.
He**'s** working. = He **is** working.
He**'s** worked. = He **has** worked.

EXERCISE 5   Contract *have* or *has* with the subject for affirmative statements. Use *hasn't* or *haven't* for negative statements.

EXAMPLE   You <u>'ve</u> already sent your application.

1. I _____ applied for many jobs.

2. We _____ seen Daniel's résumé.

3. His father _____ never come to the U.S.

4. It _____ been hard for Daniel to find a job.

5. Daniel _____ had several jobs so far.

6. Mr. Johnson (not) _____ looked at all the résumés.

7. They (not) _____ made a decision yet.

1.4 The Present Perfect—Question Formation

Compare affirmative statements and questions.

Wh- Word	Have/Has	Subject	Have/Has	Past Participle	Complement	Short Answer
		He	has	had	hotel experience.	
	Has	he		had	restaurant experience?	No, he hasn't.
Where	has	he		had	hotel experience?	In Mexico and the U.S.
		You	have	worked	in the U.S.	
	Have	you		worked	in Mexico?	Yes, I have.
How long	have	you		worked	in the U.S.?	For six years.
		Someone	has	read	the résumé.	
		Who	has	read	the résumé?	
		Something	has	happened.		
		What	has	happened?		

Compare negative statements and questions.

Wh- Word	Haven't/Hasn't	Subject	Haven't/Hasn't	Past Participle	Complement
		He	hasn't	found	a job yet.
Why	hasn't	he		found	a job?
		You	haven't	seen	my résumé.
Why	haven't	you		seen	my résumé?

EXERCISE **6** **Read the job interview with Daniel. Write the missing words in the blanks.**

CD 1, TR 02

A: I've ___looked at___ your résumé. I see you work in a hotel.
(example)

B: Yes, I do.

A: How long _____ you _____ this job?
(1)   (2)

B: I' _____ had this job for several years. But I
(3)

_____ a lot of experience in the hotel business.
(4)

In fact, my parents own a hotel in Mexico.

A: How long _____ your parents _____ a hotel?
                          (5)   (6)

B: Most of their lives.

A: _____ you seen your parents recently?
     (7)

B: My mother _____ _____ to the U.S. a few times to see me.
                 (8)   (9)
But my father _____ never _____ here because someone
               (10)   (11)
has to stay at the hotel all the time. He's _____ me
                             (12)
many times, "When you are an owner of a business, you don't have
time for vacations." But I don't want to be an owner now. I just want a
job as a manager. _____ you filled the position yet?
              (13)

A: No, I haven't. I' _____ already _____ several
            (14)   (15)
people and will interview a few more this week. When we make our
decision, we'll let you know.

1.5 Uses of the Present Perfect Tense—An Overview

EXAMPLES	EXPLANATION
Daniel **has been** in the U.S. since 1998. He **has had** his present job for several years. He **has** always **loved** the hotel business.	The action started in the past and **continues** to the present.
He **has sent** out 20 résumés so far. He **has had** three interviews this month.	The action **repeats** during a period of time that started in the past and continues to the present.
Mr. Johnson **has received** Daniel's letter. He **hasn't made** his decision yet. **Has** Daniel ever **worked** in a restaurant? Daniel **has studied** French, and he speaks it fairly well.	The action occurred at an **indefinite time** in the past. It still has importance to a present situation.

EXERCISE **7** **Fill in the blanks with appropriate words to complete each statement. In some cases, answers may vary. (Refer to the résumé and cover letter on pages 2–3.)**

EXAMPLE   Daniel has included ___his phone number___ in his résumé.

1. Daniel has been _____ since 1998.

2. He has had his job at the Town and Country Hotel for _____.

3. He has studied at _____ universities.

4. He has never worked in _____.

5. He has had a lot of experience in _____.

6. In his résumé, he has not included _____.

7. So far, he has worked in _____ hotels.

8. He hasn't _____ a job yet.

9. Why _____ a job yet?

10. _____ ever organized group transportation?

11. Daniel has _____ a hotel bookkeeper.

12. _____ finished his master's degree yet? Yes, he _____.

13. How long _____ a member of a travel association? He's been a member for several years.

14. How many times _____ worked with business travelers?

15. He has lived in _____ cities in Illinois. He has never _____ in New York.

16. He has _____ French and speaks it fairly well.

1.6 The Present Perfect with Continuation from Past to Present

We use the present perfect tense to show that an action or state started in the past and continues to the present.

past ◄————— 1998 —————————— now ‑‑‑‑‑‑‑‑‑‑‑‑‑‑‑‑‑‑‑‑‑‑► future

He **has been** in the U.S. since 1998

EXAMPLES	EXPLANATION
a. Daniel *has been* a U.S. citizen **for two years**. b. His parents *have been* in the hotel business **all their lives**. c. He *has had* his job **for the past few years**.	a. Use *for* + amount of time. b. Omit *for* with an expression beginning with *all*. c. You can say *for the past / last* + time period.
Daniel *has been* in the U.S. **since 1998**. I *have been* a citizen **since last March**.	Use *since* + date, month, year, etc. to show when the action began.
He *has had* a car **since he *came* to the U.S.** He *has wanted* to manage hotels **ever since he *was* a teenager**.	Use *since* or *ever since* to begin a clause that shows the start of a continuous action. The verb in the *since* clause is in the simple past tense.
Daniel went to Chicago in 2002. He *has been* there **ever since**. 从那时危，此后一直 His father started to work in the hotel when he was twenty years old. He *has worked* there **ever since**.	You can put *ever since* at the end of the sentence. It means "from the past time mentioned to the present."
How long *have* you *been* in the U.S.? **How long** *has* your family *owned* a hotel?	Use *how long* to ask an information question about length of time.
Daniel *has* **always** *loved* the hotel business. I *have* **always** *wanted* to start my own business. I *have* **never** *worked* in a restaurant. Daniel *has* **never** *written* to Mr. Johnson **before**.	We use the present perfect with *always* and *never* to show that an action began in the past and continues to the present. We often use *before* at the end of a *never* statement.

EXERCISE **8**   **Fill in the blanks to complete the sentences. Not every sentence needs a word.**

EXAMPLE   I'_ve_____ been in the U.S. for three years.

1. Daniel has _____ in Chicago _____ 2004.
2. How _____ has he been in the U.S.? He'_____ been in the U.S. _____ many years.
3. He found a good job in 2004. He _____ worked at the same job ever _____.
4. He's worked at a hotel ever _____ he _____ from high school.
5. His parents have lived in Mexico _____ all their lives.
6. Daniel has had his apartment for the _____ ten months.
7. _____ you always worked in a hotel?
8. _____ long have you had your job?
9. Daniel _____ been in the U.S. since he _____ from college.
10. He's wanted to manage a hotel _____ since he was a child.

EXERCISE **9**   **ABOUT YOU** **Make statements with *always*.**

EXAMPLE   Name something you've always thought about.
           I've always thought about my future.

1. Name something you've always disliked.
2. Name something you've always liked.
3. Name something you've always wanted to own.
4. Name something you've always wanted to do.
5. Name something you've always believed in.

EXERCISE **10**   **ABOUT YOU** **Write four true sentences telling about things you've always done or ways you've always been. Share your answers with the class.**

EXAMPLES   I've always worked very hard.

            I've always been very thin.

1. _____
2. _____
3. _____
4. _____

EXERCISE **11** **ABOUT YOU** Make statements with *never*.

EXAMPLE   Name a machine you've never used.

I've never used a sewing machine.

1. Name a food you've never tried.
2. Name something you've never drunk.
3. Name something you've never owned.
4. Name something you've never done.
5. Name something your teacher has never done in class.
6. Name a job you've never had.

EXERCISE **12** **ABOUT YOU** Write four true sentences telling about things you've never done but would like to. Share your answers with the class.

EXAMPLES   I've never gone to Paris, but I'd like to.

I've never flown in a helicopter, but I'd like to.

1. _____

2. _____

3. _____

4. _____

1.7 Negative Statements with *Since*, *For*, and *In*

We can use *since*, *for*, and *in* with negative statements.

EXAMPLES	EXPLANATION
Daniel hasn't worked in Mexico **since** 1998.	He worked in Mexico until 1998. He stopped in 1998.
Daniel hasn't seen his parents **for** three years. OR Daniel hasn't seen his parents **in** three years.	He saw his parents three years ago. That was the last time. In negative statements, you can use either *for* or *in*.
Language Note: We often say *in ages* to mean "in a long time." Hi Daniel! I haven't seen you **in ages**!	

EXERCISE 13 [ABOUT YOU] Name something.

EXAMPLES Name something you haven't eaten in a long time.

I haven't eaten fish in a long time.

1. Name someone you haven't seen in a long time.
2. Name a place you haven't visited in a long time.
3. Name a food you haven't eaten in a long time.
4. Name a subject you haven't studied since you were a child.
5. Name a game you haven't played since you were a child.
6. Name something you haven't had time to do since you started to study English.

1.8 The Present Perfect vs. the Simple Present

EXAMPLES	EXPLANATION
I **am** in the U.S. now. I **have been** in the U.S. *for* two years.	The simple present refers only to the present time. The present perfect with *for*, *since*, *always*, or *never* connects the past to the present.
He **has** a car. He **has had** his car *since* March.	
I love my job. I **have** *always* **loved** my job.	
I **don't like** to wake up early. I **have** *never* **liked** to wake up early.	

EXERCISE 14 Fill in the blanks to complete the following conversations. Some answers may vary.

EXAMPLES **A:** Do you have a computer?

B: Yes, I do.

A: How long _____have you_____ had your computer?

B: I __'ve had_____ my computer for three years.

1. **A:** Do you have a car?

   B: Yes, I do.

   A: How long _____ your car?

   B: I _____ my car for six months.

2. **A:** Is your sister married?

   B: Yes, she is.

   A: How long _____ married?

   B: She _____ since 2005.

3. **A:** Do you have a bike?

   B: Yes, I _____.

   A: How long _____ your bike?

   B: I _____ my bike _____ the past _____.

4. **A:** Do you want to learn English?

   B: Of course I do.

   A: _____ long _____ to learn English?

   B: I _____ to learn English ever since I _____ a child.

5. **A:** Does your mother have a driver's license?

   B: Yes, she _____.

   A: How _____ her driver's license?

   B: She _____ her driver's license since _____.

6. **A:** _____ Ms. Foster your teacher?

   B: Yes, she is.

   A: How long _____ your teacher?

   B: For _____.

7. **A:** Does your school have a computer lab?

   B: Yes, it _____.

   A: _____ long _____ a computer lab?

   B: It _____ a computer lab since _____.

8. **A:** Do you know your friend Mark very well?

   B: Yes, I _____.

   A: How long _____ each other?

   B: We _____ each other ever _____ we _____ in elementary school.

   (continued)

---

9. **A:** _____ your son _____ a laptop?

   B: Yes, he _____.

   A: How long _____?

   B: He bought one when he started going to college and he

   _____ it ever _____.

10. **A:** Does your mother like to dance?

    B: Yes, she _____.

    A: _____ she always _____ to dance?

    B: Yes. She's always liked to dance. But my father

    _____ never _____ to dance.

EXERCISE 15 **Read each statement about your teacher. Then ask your teacher a question beginning with the words given. Include *always* in your question. Your teacher will answer.**

EXAMPLE You're a teacher. Have you _always been a teacher?_
No. I was a nurse before I became a teacher. I've only been a teacher for five years.

1. You teach grammar. Have you _____

2. You work with ESL students. Have you _____

3. You're a teacher at this school. Have you _____

4. You think about grammar. Have you _____

5. English is easy for you. Has English _____

6. Your last name is _____. Has your last name _____

   _____

7. You live in this city. Have you _____

8. You like teaching. Have you _____

EXERCISE 16 **ABOUT YOU Ask a present tense question. Another student will answer. If the answer is *yes*, ask *Have you always . . .?***

EXAMPLE **A:** Are you interested in learning English?
B: Yes, I am.
A: Have you always been interested in learning English?
B: Yes. I've been interested in learning English since I was a small child.

1. Are you a good student?

2. Do you wear glasses?

3. Do you like to travel?

4. Are you interested in politics?

5. Do you like American movies?

6. Are you an optimist?

7. Do you think about your future?

8. Do you live in an apartment?

9. Are you a friendly person?

10. Do you use credit cards?

11. Do you work hard?

12. Do you want a college degree?

Where Have All the Jobs Gone?

Before You Read

1. Do you know anyone who has lost a job?

2. Do you think some jobs are more secure than others? Which ones?

CD 1, TR 03

Read the following magazine article. Pay special attention to the present perfect and present perfect continuous tenses.

Have you ever **called** an American company for service and **gotten** an answer from someone in another country? Many American companies **have been moving** customer service and technology jobs overseas. Using workers in other countries is called  "outsourcing." India, the Philippines, and China are the leading countries used in outsourcing. Why these countries? Because they have a high level of information technology (IT) workers who are fluent in English.

Why **has** this shift[5] **occurred?** By using lower wages[6] overseas, U.S. companies can cut labor costs. In addition, service is available to customers 24 hours a day by phone or online.

[5]A *shift* is a change.
[6]*Wages* means pay for doing a job.

(continued)

Years ago, American companies started using foreign labor for manufacturing jobs. But college-educated workers thought they had nothing to worry about. Then companies started to move call centers abroad[7] to cut costs. But more and more of the jobs going abroad today go to highly skilled, educated people.

Many American workers who **have been working** at the same company for years are losing their jobs. Many educated workers **have had** to take jobs for lower pay or get more training or education. While U.S. companies **have been benefiting** from outsourcing, American workers **have been losing**. While some American workers in some fields **have become** more insecure about their jobs, educated, skilled workers abroad **have become** more confident.

The U.S. government **has been studying** the impact of outsourcing on the American economy.

1.9 The Present Perfect Continuous

Forms

Subject	Have/ Has	Been	Present Participle	Complement
I	have	been	working	in a call center.
Workers	have	been	losing	their jobs.
You	have	been	getting	more job experience.
Companies	have	been	moving	jobs overseas.
The U.S.	has	been	studying	the effects of outsourcing.
Daniel	has	been	working	at a hotel.
He	has	been	living	in the U.S.

Language Notes:
1. To form the negative, put *not* between *have* or *has* and *been*.
   You **have *not* been** studying.   She **has *not* been** working hard.
2. We can make contractions for negative forms.
   have not = haven't   has not = hasn't

---

[7]*Abroad* means beyond the boundaries of one's country.

Uses

EXAMPLES	EXPLANATION
I **have been working** at the same job *since* 2007. American companies **have been using** workers in foreign countries *for* many years.	We use the present perfect continuous to talk about an action that started in the past and continues to the present. We use *for* and *since* to show the time spent at an activity.
He **has been working** as a programmer for the past few years. OR He **has worked** as a programmer for the past few years.	With some verbs, we can use either the present perfect or the present perfect continuous with actions that began in the past and continue to the present. There is very little difference in meaning.
He's working now. → He **has been working** for the past eight hours.	If the action is still happening, use the present perfect continuous, not the present perfect.
I **have** *always* **worked** as a programmer. I **have** *never* **had** another career.	Do not use the continuous form with *always* and *never*.
Americans **have become** insecure about their jobs. I **have had** my job for ten years.	We do not use a continuous tense with nonaction verbs. *Wrong:* Americans *have been becoming* insecure. *Wrong:* I *have been having* my job for ten years. (See Language Notes below for a list of nonaction verbs.)
Action: I **have been thinking** *about* starting a new career. Nonaction: I **have** always **thought** *that* an educated person can find a good job.	*Think* can be an action or nonaction verb, depending on its meaning. *Think about* = action verb *Think that* = nonaction verb
Nonaction: Daniel **has had** a lot of experience in hotels. Action: Daniel **has been having** problems finding a job.	*Have* is usually a nonaction verb. However, *have* is an action verb in these expressions: *have a problem, have a hard time, have a good time, have difficulty, have trouble.*

Language Notes:
1. The following are usually nonaction verbs.

like	want	know	own	see	think (that)
love	need	believe	understand	hear	care (about)
hate	prefer	cost	remember	seem	have (for possession)

2. When used as sense-perception verbs, the following are nonaction verbs.

smell	taste	feel	look	sound

EXERCISE 17   **Fill in the blanks with the present perfect continuous form of the verb in parentheses ( ).**

EXAMPLE Bob <u>has been working</u> as a programmer for the past ten years.

(work)

1. His company _____ jobs to India since 2005.

(send)

2. He and his coworkers _____ about losing their jobs.

(worry)

3. Bob _____ classes for the past two years to get retrained.

(take)

4. He _____ a lot of articles about outsourcing.

(read)

5. He _____ on his résumé for the past two days.

(work)

6. His friends _____ him to see a job counselor.

(advise)

EXERCISE 18   **Fill in the blanks in the following conversations. Some answers may vary.**

EXAMPLE **A:** Do you <u>play</u> a musical instrument?

B: Yes. I play the guitar.

A: How long <u>have</u> you <u>been playing</u> the guitar?

B: I <u>'ve been playing</u> the guitar since I <u>was</u> 10 years old.

1. **A:** Do you work with computers?

   B: Yes, I do.

   A: How long _____ you _____ with computers?

   B: I _____ with computers since 2004.

2. **A:** _____ your father study English?

   B: Yes, he does.

   A: How long _____ he been _____ English?

   B: He _____ since he _____ to the U.S.

3. **A:** Does your teacher have a lot of experience?

   B: Yes, she _____.

   A: How long _____ teaching English?

   B: She _____ English for 20 years.

4. **A:** Do you wear glasses?

   B: Yes, I _____.

   A: How long _____ glasses?

   B: I _____ glasses since I _____ in
high school.

5. **A:** _____ your parents live in this city?

   B: Yes, they _____.

   A: How long _____ in this city?

   B: For _____.

6. **A:** Is your roommate preparing to take the TOEFL[8] test?

   B: Yes, he _____.

   A: How long _____ to take this test?

   B: Since _____.

7. **A:** _____ you studying for your chemistry test?

   B: Yes, I _____.

   A: How long _____ for your chemistry test?

   B: I _____ all week.

8. **A:** _____ your roommate using the computer now?

   B: Yes, he _____.

   A: How long _____ it?

   B: He started to use it when he woke up and _____
it ever _____.

9. **A:** _____ it raining now?

   B: Yes, it _____.

   A: How long _____?

   B: It _____ since _____.

10. **A:** _____ she talking about her children again?

   B: Yes, she _____.

   A: How long _____ about them?

   B: For the past _____.

[8]The *TOEFL*™ is the Test of English as a Foreign Language. Many U.S. colleges and universities require foreign students to take this test.

EXERCISE **19** **ABOUT YOU** Fill in the blanks to make a true statement about the present. Then make a statement that includes the past by changing to the present perfect continuous form with *for* or *since*.

EXAMPLE   I'm studying ___French.___

I've been studying French for two semesters.

1. I work in / as _____

2. I live _____

3. I attend _____

4. I'm trying to _____

5. I'm wearing _____

6. The teacher is explaining _____

7. I'm thinking about _____

8. I'm using _____

9. I'm studying _____

10. We're using _____

1.10 The Present Perfect Tense vs. the Simple Past Tense

EXAMPLES	EXPLANATION
How long have you **had** your current car? I've **had** my current car *for* three months. *How long* have you **been working** at your current job? I've **been working** at my current job *for* two years.	Use *how long* and *for* with the present perfect tense or present perfect continuous tense to include the present.
How long **did** you **have** your last car? I **had** my last car *for* six years. *How long* **did** you **work** at your last job? I **worked** at my last job *for* five years.	Use *how long* and *for* with the simple past tense when you are not including the present.
When **did** you **come** to the U.S.? I **came** to the U.S. a few years *ago*.	A question that asks *when* usually uses the simple past tense. A sentence that uses *ago* uses the simple past tense.
I **came** to this city on January 15. I **have been** in this city since January 15. I **have been living** in this city since January 15.	Use the simple past tense to refer to a past action that does not continue. Use the present perfect (continuous) tense to show the continuation of an action from past to present.

EXERCISE 20 **ABOUT YOU** Fill in the blanks with the simple past, the present perfect, or the present perfect continuous, using the words in parentheses ( ). Another student will answer the question.

EXAMPLES How long ___have you had___ your present computer?
(you/have)

When ___did you buy___ your computer?
(you/buy)

1. How long _____ your last computer?
(you/own)

2. How long _____ at this school?
(you/study)

3. How long _____ at your last school?
(you/study)

4. How long _____ in this city?
(you/be)

5. How long _____ at your last address?
(you/live)

6. How long _____ your dictionary?
(you/have)

7. When _____ your dictionary?
(you/buy)

8. When _____ for this class?
(you/register)

(continued)

9. When _____?
   (the semester/begin)

10. When _____ today?
    (the teacher/arrive)

EXERCISE 21 Two friends meet on the street. Fill in the blanks in their conversation below. Use the present perfect, the present perfect continuous, or the simple past. Fill in any other necessary words.

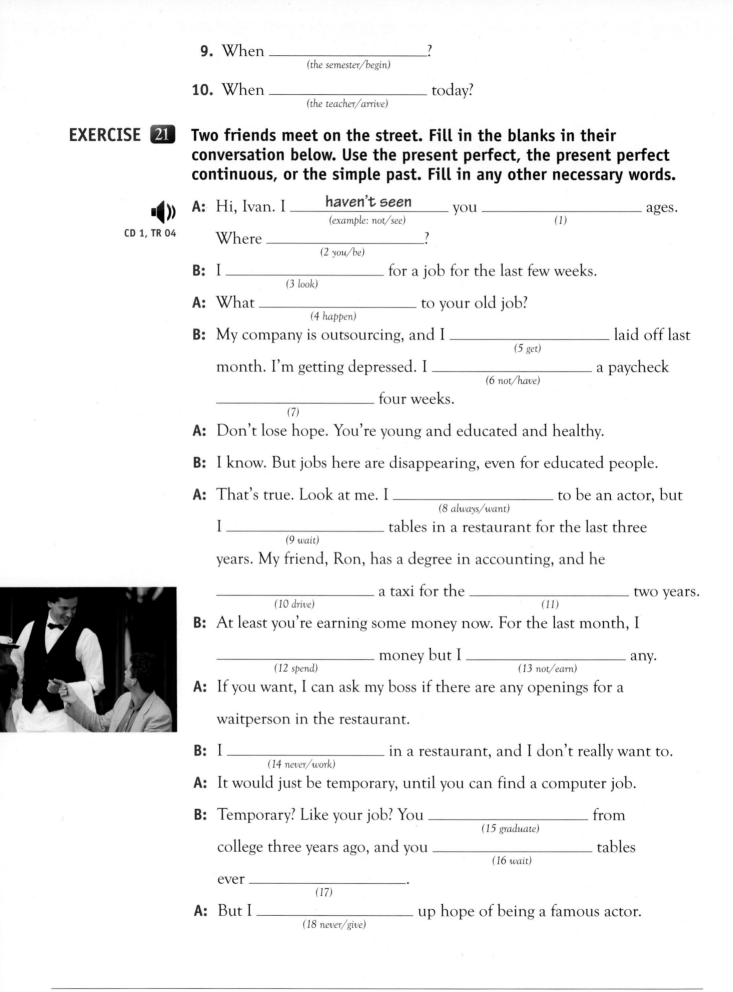

CD 1, TR 04

A: Hi, Ivan. I ___**haven't seen**___ you _____ ages.
   (example: not/see) _____ *(1)*
   Where _____?
   (2 you/be)

B: I _____ for a job for the last few weeks.
   (3 look)

A: What _____ to your old job?
   (4 happen)

B: My company is outsourcing, and I _____ laid off last
   (5 get)
   month. I'm getting depressed. I _____ a paycheck
   (6 not/have)
   _____ four weeks.
   (7)

A: Don't lose hope. You're young and educated and healthy.

B: I know. But jobs here are disappearing, even for educated people.

A: That's true. Look at me. I _____ to be an actor, but
   (8 always/want)
   I _____ tables in a restaurant for the last three
   (9 wait)
   years. My friend, Ron, has a degree in accounting, and he

   _____ a taxi for the _____ two years.
   (10 drive) _____ *(11)*

B: At least you're earning some money now. For the last month, I

   _____ money but I _____ any.
   (12 spend) _____ *(13 not/earn)*

A: If you want, I can ask my boss if there are any openings for a

   waitperson in the restaurant.

B: I _____ in a restaurant, and I don't really want to.
   (14 never/work)

A: It would just be temporary, until you can find a computer job.

B: Temporary? Like your job? You _____ from
   (15 graduate)
   college three years ago, and you _____ tables
   (16 wait)
   ever _____.
   (17)

A: But I _____ up hope of being a famous actor.
   (18 never/give)

1.11 The Present Perfect with Repetition from Past to Present

now

past ←————————— ✕ ✕ ✕ ————————————————→ future

He **has had** three interviews this month.

EXAMPLES	EXPLANATION
Daniel is looking for a job. He **has had** three interviews *this month*. Mr. Johnson **has interviewed** two people *today*.	We use the present perfect tense to talk about the repetition of an action in a time period that includes the present. The time period is open, and there is a possibility for more repetition to occur. Open time periods include: *today, this week, this month, this year, this semester*.
My company is sending some jobs to India. It **has sent** 50 jobs to India *so far*. *Up to now* 50 workers in my company **have lost** their jobs.	*So far* and *up to now* mean "including this moment." We use these expressions with the present perfect to show that another repetition may occur. These expressions can come at the beginning or the end of the sentence.
Daniel **has worked** at *several* hotels. You **have had** *a lot of* experience with computers. I **have learned** *many* new skills at my job. Daniel **has had** *four* jobs so far.	We can use *several, many, a lot of,* or a number to show repetition from past to present.
How many interviews **have** you **had** this year? *How much* money **have** you **spent** on career counseling so far? I **haven't spent** *any* money *at all* on career counseling.	We can ask a question about repetition with *how many* and *how much*. A negative statement with *"any . . . at all"* means the number is zero.
We**'ve studied** two lessons so far.	Do not use the continuous form for repetition. *Not: We've been studying* two lessons so far.

EXERCISE **22** **Fill in the blanks in the following conversations.**

EXAMPLE **A:** How many pages have we ___done___ in this book so far?

B: We _'ve_ _____ done 27 pages so far.

1. **A:** How many tests _____ we had so far this semester?

   B: So far we _____ two tests this semester.

2. **A:** How many compositions have we _____ this semester?

   B: We _____ two compositions this semester.

3. **A:** How many times have you _____ absent this semester?

   B: I _____ absent one time this semester.

4. **A:** How many times _____ the teacher been absent this semester?

   B: The teacher _____ absent at all this semester.

5. **A:** How _____ lessons _____ the teacher _____ so far?

   B: She _____ only one lesson so far.

6. **A:** How _____ time has the teacher _____ on the present perfect?

   B: He _____ about three hours on the present perfect.

7. **A:** How _____ students _____ the computer lab today?

   B: More than 100 students _____ the computer lab so far today.

8. **A:** How _____ exercises _____ so far?

   B: We _____ done about 22 exercises so far.

EXERCISE **23** **ABOUT YOU** **Write a statement to tell how many times you have done something in this city. (If you don't know the exact number, you may use _a few_, _several_, or _many_.)**

EXAMPLES live in / apartment(s)

I've lived in one apartment in this city.
_____

get lost / time(s)

I've gotten lost a few times in this city.
_____

1. have / job(s)

_____

2. have / job interview(s)

_____

3. have / out-of-town visitor(s)

_____

4. buy / car(s)

_____

5. attend / school(s)

_____

6. live in / apartment(s)

_____

7. go downtown / time(s)

_____

EXERCISE **24**   **ABOUT YOU** Ask a question with *How much . . . ?* or *How many . . . ?* and the words given. Talk about today. Another student will answer.

EXAMPLES   coffee / have

A: How much coffee have you had today?
B: I've had three cups of coffee today.

glasses of water / drink

A: How many glasses of water have you drunk today?
B: I haven't drunk any water at all today.

1. tea / have
2. juice / drink
3. cookies / eat
4. glasses of water / have
5. times / check your e-mail
6. miles / walk or drive
7. money / spend
8. text messages / receive
9. text messages / send
10. photos / take
11. times / use your dictionary

1.12 The Present Perfect Tense vs. the Simple Past Tense with Repetition

EXAMPLES	EXPLANATION
How many interviews **have** you **had** *this month*? I **have had** two interviews *so far this month*. How many times **have** you **been** absent *this semester*? I **have been** absent twice *so far*.	To show that there is possibility for more repetition, use the present perfect. *This month* and *this semester* are not finished. *So far* indicates that the number given may not be final.
How many interviews **did** you **have** *last month*? I **had** four interviews *last month*. How many times **were** you absent *last semester*? I **was** absent four times *last semester*.	To show that the number is final, use the simple past tense with a past time expression (*yesterday, last week, last year, last semester,* etc.).
Compare: a. I **have seen** my counselor twice *this week*. b. I **saw** my counselor twice *this week*. a. I **have made** five phone calls *today*. b. I **made** five phone calls *today*.	With a present time expression (such as *today, this week,* etc.), you may use either the present perfect or the simple past tense. a. The number may not be final. b. The number seems final.
Compare: a. My grandfather died in 1998. He **had** several jobs in his lifetime. b. My father is a programmer. He **has had** five jobs so far.	a. If you refer to the experiences of a deceased person, you must use the simple past tense because nothing more can be added to that person's experience. b. A living person can have more of the same experience.
Compare: a. In my country, I **had** five jobs. b. In the U.S., I **have had** two jobs.	a. To talk about a closed phase of your life, use the simple past tense. For example, if you do not plan to live in your native country again, use the simple past tense to talk about your experiences there. b. To talk about your experiences in this phase of your life, you can use the present perfect tense.

EXERCISE 25 **In the conversation below, fill in the blanks with the correct form of the verb in parentheses ( ).**

CD 1, TR 05

A: I'm very frustrated about finding a job. I ___**have sent**___ out
(example: send)

100 résumés so far. And I _____ dozens of phone calls
(1 make)

to companies.

B: Have you _____ any answers to your letters and calls?
(2 have)

A: Yes. Last week I _____ six interviews. But so far, nobody
(3 have)
_____ me a job.
(4 offer)

B: You should call those companies.

A: I know I should. But this week, I _____ very busy
(5 be)
getting career counseling. I _____ my counselor
(6 see)
several times in the past few weeks.

B: Has your counselor _____ you any advice about looking
(7 give)
for a job?

A: Yes. Last week she _____ me a lot of advice. But looking
(8 give)
for a job is so strange in the U.S. I feel like I have to sell myself.

B: Don't worry. You _____ much work experience in
(9 not/have)
the U.S. so far. I'm sure you'll get used to the process of finding a job.

A: I don't know. I _____ to a lot of other people
(10 talk)
looking for work. Even though English is their native language, they
_____ much luck either.
(11 not/have)

B: _____ easy for you to find a job when you lived
(12 it/be)
in your native country?

A: In my native country, I _____ this problem. After I
(13 never/have)
_____ from college, I _____ a job
(14 graduate)   (15 find)
immediately and _____ in the same place for many years.
(16 work)

B: In the U.S., people change jobs often. Take me, for example.

I _____ six jobs, and I'm only 28 years old.
(17 have)

A: I'm 40 years old. But when I lived in my native country,

I _____ the same job for ten years. And
(18 have)
I _____ in the same apartment for many years until I
(19 live)
came to the U.S. My parents _____ in the same
(20 live)
apartment from the time they got married until the time they died.

B: Get used to it! Life today is about constant change.

The *Occupational Outlook Handbook*

Before
You Read

1. Have you ever seen a counselor about finding a job?

2. What careers interest you? What are some jobs you wouldn't want to have?

CD 1, TR 06

Read the following conversation between a college student (S) and her counselor (C). Pay special attention to the present perfect tense and the present perfect continuous tense.

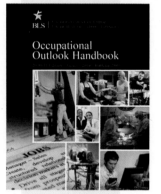

C: I see you're majoring in art. **Have** you **thought** about a career yet for your future?

S: I've **thought** about it, but I'm still not sure what I'm going to do when I graduate. I've always **loved** art, but my parents are worried that I won't be able to make a living as an artist. Lately **I've been thinking** about changing majors.

C: What major **have** you **been considering**?

S: Graphic design or commercial art.

C: **Have** you **taken** any courses in these fields?

S: I've already **taken** a course in graphic design. But I don't know much about the future of this career. Are there a lot of jobs for graphic artists?

C: **Have** you ever **used** the *Occupational Outlook Handbook*?

S: No, I **haven't**. I've never even **heard** of it. What is it?

C: It's a government publication that gives you a lot of information about jobs in the U.S. You can find it in the library or on the Internet. If you look up "graphic designer" in this publication, it will tell you the nature of the work, where the jobs are, what salary you can expect, what kind of training you need, what the future will be for graphic designers, and much more.

S: Thanks for the information. Can I come back and see you in a few weeks after I have a chance to check out the *Occupational Outlook Handbook*?

C: Yes, please come back.

(A few weeks later)

C: Hi. **Have** you **looked** at the *Occupational Outlook Handbook* yet?

S: Yes. Thanks for telling me about it. I**'ve looked** at many jobs in the art field, but so far I **haven't decided** on anything yet. But I have some ideas.

C: **Have** you **talked** to your parents lately? **Have** you **told** them that you're planning on changing majors?

S: Oh, yes. They're very happy about it. They don't want me to be a starving artist.[9]

1.13 The Present Perfect Tense with Indefinite Past Time—An Overview

We use the present perfect tense to refer to an action that occurred at an indefinite time in the past and that still has importance to a present situation.

QUESTIONS	SHORT ANSWERS	EXPLANATION
Has she *ever* **visited** a counselor? **Have** you *ever* **used** the *Occupational Outlook Handbook*? **Have** you *ever* **taken** an art history course?	Yes, she **has.** No, I never **have.** No, I **haven't.**	A question with *ever* asks about any time between the past and the present. Put *ever* between the subject and the main verb in a question.
Have you **decided** on a major *yet*? **Has** she **told** her parents about her decision *yet*?	No, not *yet.* Yes, she *already* has.	*Yet* and *already* refer to an indefinite time in the near past. There is an expectation that an activity took place a short time ago.
Have you **talked** to your parents *lately*? **Have** you **seen** your counselor *recently*?	No, I **haven't.** Yes, I **have.**	Questions with *lately* and *recently* refer to an indefinite time in the near past.

[9]A *starving artist* is an artist who does not make enough money to support him or herself.

EXERCISE 26   **Read the following conversation. Underline the present perfect tense and circle the present perfect continuous tense.**

EXAMPLE   **A:** There's going to be a job fair at the college next week. <u>Have</u> you ever <u>gone</u> to one?

     B: What's a job fair?

     A: Representatives from different companies come to one place. You can meet these people, find out about their companies, and give them your résumé. Lately I've been going to a lot of job fairs. And I've been looking for jobs online. I've just rewritten my résumé too. I haven't found a job yet, but I'm hopeful.

     B: But you have a good job as an office manager.

     A: I'm going to quit in two weeks. I've already given my employer notice. I've worked there for two years, and I haven't had a raise yet. I've realized that I can make more money doing something else. I've talked to a career counselor and I've taken a test to see what I'm good at. I've also taken more courses to upgrade my skills.

     B: Have you decided what you want to do?

     A: Yes. I've decided to be a legal assistant.

1.14 Questions with *Ever*

EXAMPLES	EXPLANATION

Have you *ever* **seen** a job counselor?
  Yes, I **have**. I**'ve seen** a job counselor a few times.
Have you *ever* **used** the Internet to find a job?
  Yes, I**'ve used** the Internet many times.
Have you *ever* **worked** in a restaurant?
  No, I never **have**.
	We use *ever* to ask a question about any time in the past.

Have you *ever* **written** a résumé?
  a. Yes, I **have**.
    OR
  b. Yes. I **wrote** my résumé two weeks ago.
Has he *ever* **taken** a design course?
  a. Yes. He **has taken** several design courses.
    OR
  b. Yes. He **took** one last semester.
	You can answer an *ever* question with the present perfect or the simple past.
	a. Use the **present perfect** to answer with no reference to time.
	b. Use the **simple past** to answer with a definite time (*last week, last semester, last Friday, two weeks ago*, etc.).

EXERCISE 27 **ABOUT YOU** Ask a question with *Have you ever . . . ?* and the words given. Use the past participle of the verb. Another student will answer. If the answer is *yes*, ask for more specific information. To answer with a specific time, use the simple past tense. To answer with a frequency response, use the present perfect tense.

EXAMPLE eat a hot dog

A: Have you ever eaten a hot dog?
B: Yes, I have.
A: When did you eat a hot dog?
B: I ate one at a picnic last summer.

1. find money on the street
2. go to a garage sale
3. meet a famous person
4. study art history
5. bake bread
6. be on television
7. win a contest or a prize
8. lend money to a friend
9. lose your keys
10. break an arm or a leg
11. go to a football game
12. go to court
13. hear of[10] Martin Luther King Jr.
14. eat in a Vietnamese restaurant
15. order products over the Internet
16. get lost in this city
17. tell a lie
18. go to Canada
19. travel by train
20. eat pizza
21. act in a play
22. see a play in this city
23. eat Chinese food
24. see a job counselor
25. go camping
26. use a scanner

EXERCISE 28 Work with a partner. Use *ever* to write four questions to ask your teacher. Your teacher will answer.

EXAMPLES Have you ever eaten raw fish? _____

Have you ever written a poem? _____

1. _____

2. _____

3. _____

4. _____

---

[10]*Hear of* means to recognize a name.

EXERCISE 29   Fill in the blanks with the present perfect tense or the simple past tense to complete each conversation. Sometimes part of the verb (phrase) has already been supplied.

1. **A:** Have you ever ___studied___ algebra?
   (example)

   B: Yes. I studied it in high school.

   A: I like math a lot. Do you?

   B: No, I _____ never _____ math.

2. **A:** Have you ever _____ to Canada?

   B: No, I never have. But I would like to go there some day.

   A: _____ you ever gone to Mexico?

   B: Yes. I _____ there two years ago.

3. **A:** Have you ever broken your arm or leg?

   B: Yes. I _____ my leg when I was ten years old. I was climbing a tree.

   A: Which leg _____ you _____?

   B: I broke my left leg.

4. **A:** _____ your parents ever come here to visit you?

   B: No, they never _____. But last year my brother _____ to visit me for three weeks.

5. **A:** _____ you ever _____ an Italian movie?

   B: No, I haven't. But I _____ seen many French movies.

   A: I _____ never _____ a French movie.

6. **A:** _____ you ever _____ to the public library in this city?

   B: Yes. I _____ gone there many times. Last Monday I _____ there and checked out a novel by Mark Twain. I've never _____ Mark Twain's books in English.

   A: _____ you ever _____ his books in translation?

   B: Oh, yes. In high school, I _____ two of his novels in Spanish.

EXERCISE 30 **ABOUT YOU** Interview a student who has a job. Ask a question with *Have you ever . . . ?* and the words given.

EXAMPLE   ask your boss for a raise

A: Have you ever asked your boss for a raise?
B: No, I never have.

1. get job counseling at this school
2. use the Internet to find a job
3. fill out a job application online
4. use the *Occupational Outlook Handbook*
5. go to a state employment office
6. use a résumé writing service
7. take courses to train for a job
8. read a book about finding a job
9. attend a job fair
10. use a computer on a job
11. work in a restaurant
12. have a problem with a coworker
13. work for a family member
14. work in a hotel
15. think about owning your own business
16. be unemployed
17. quit a job

1.15 Yet, Already

Use *yet* with the present perfect tense with an expected action. Use *already* for a recent action at an indefinite time.

EXAMPLES	EXPLANATION
I **have talked** to my job counselor *already*. I **have** *already* **talked** to my job counselor.	For an affirmative statement, use *already*. You can put *already* at the end of the verb phrase or between the auxiliary verb and the main verb.
I **haven't written** my résumé *yet*. The counselor **hasn't answered** my e-mail *yet*.	For a negative statement, use *yet*. Put *yet* at the end of the verb phrase.
Have you **talked** with your counselor *yet*? 　No, I **haven't**. **Have** you **written** your résumé *yet*? 　No, **not** *yet*. **Have** you **filled** out the application *yet*? 　Yes, I *already* **have**.	For questions, use *yet*. You can use *yet* in a negative answer. You can use *already* in an affirmative answer.
Has he **found** a job *yet*? 　Yes, he **found** a job *two weeks ago*. **Have** you **gotten** a raise *yet*? 　Yes, I **got** a raise *last month*.	You can answer a *yet* question with a specific time. If you do so, you must use the simple past tense.

Language Note: You often hear the simple past tense in questions and negatives with *yet* and statements with *already*. There is no difference in meaning between the present perfect and the simple past tense.
> **Have** you **eaten** dinner *yet*? = **Did** you **eat** dinner *yet*?
> No, I **haven't eaten** dinner yet. = No, I **didn't eat** dinner yet.
> I **have eaten** dinner *already*. = I **ate** dinner *already*.

EXERCISE **31**　Ask a student who has recently moved here questions with the words given and *yet*. The student who answers should use the simple past tense if the answer has a specific time.

EXAMPLE　go downtown
> **A:** Have you gone downtown yet?
> **B:** Yes. I went downtown three weeks ago.

1. buy a map of this city
2. find an apartment
3. get a library card

4. use public transportation
5. visit any museums
6. meet any of your neighbors

EXERCISE 32 **Ask a question with the words given and *yet*. The student who answers should use the simple past tense if the answer has a specific time.**

EXAMPLES   the teacher / take attendance

A: Has the teacher taken attendance yet?
B: Yes, he has. He took attendance at the beginning of the class.

the teacher / return the homework

A: Has the teacher returned the homework yet?
B: No, he hasn't. OR No, not yet.

1. we / have an exam
2. we / study modals
3. you / learn the irregular past tense forms
4. the teacher / learn the students' names
5. you / learn the other students' names
6. the teacher / teach the past perfect tense

EXERCISE 33 **Daniel is preparing for his job interview. He has made a list of things to do. He has checked those things he has already done. Make sentences about Daniel's list using the present perfect tense with *yet* or *already*.**

EXAMPLES   ___✓___ prepare his résumé
He has already prepared his résumé.

_____ send his suit to the cleaner's
He hasn't sent his suit to the cleaner's yet.

1. ___✓___ buy a new tie
2. ___✓___ wash his white shirt
3. _____ iron his white shirt
4. ___✓___ get a haircut
5. ___✓___ rewrite his résumé
6. _____ take his résumé to a copy center
7. ___✓___ see a job counselor
8. _____ put his papers in his briefcase
9. ___✓___ send for his transcripts
10. ___✓___ get letters of recommendation

EXERCISE **34** **Fill in the blanks to complete each conversation.**

EXAMPLE **A:** Have you bought your textbook yet?

    B: No. I ___*haven't*___ bought it yet.

1. **A:** Have you _____ dinner yet?

   B: No, I haven't. I _____ lunch at 2:30, so I'm not hungry now.

2. **A:** _____ your sister gotten married yet?

   B: Yes. She _____ married two weeks ago. She _____ a beautiful wedding.

   A: Has she _____ back from her honeymoon yet?

   B: Yes. She _____ back last Thursday.

3. **A:** Have your parents _____ an apartment yet?

   B: No. They _____ found one yet. They're still looking.

4. **A:** I'm going to rent the movie *Spider-Man*. Have you _____ it yet?

   B: Yes, I _____ it a couple of years ago, but I'd like to see it again.

5. **A:** What are you going to do during summer vacation?

   B: I haven't _____ about it yet. It's only April.

   A: I've already _____ plans. I'm going to Mexico. I _____ my ticket last week.

6. **A:** Has the movie _____ yet? I want to buy some popcorn before it begins.

   B: Shhh! It _____ ten minutes ago.

7. **A:** Do you want to go to the museum with me on Saturday?

   B: Sorry. I _____ already _____ other plans for Saturday.

8. **A:** _____ your brother _____ back from Mexico yet?

   B: No, he hasn't. We're expecting him to arrive on Tuesday.

9. **A:** I'd like to talk to the teacher, please.

   B: I'm sorry. She's already _____ for the day.

   A: But she told me to call her before four o'clock and it's only 3:30.

   B: She _____ at two o'clock because her son was sick.

10. **A:** Is that a good book?

    B: Yes, it is. I haven't _____ it yet, but when I finish it, you can have it.

1.16 Questions with *Lately* and *Recently*

Questions with *lately* and *recently* ask about an indefinite time in the near past. We can answer a *lately* or *recently* question with the present perfect tense or the simple past tense.

EXAMPLES	EXPLANATION
Have you **seen** your parents *lately*? No, I **haven't**. **Have** you **gotten** a raise *recently*? No. I **haven't gotten** a raise *recently*.	When the answer is *no*, we usually use the present perfect tense.
Have you **had** any interviews *lately*? Yes. I **had** an interview *last week*. **Have** you **seen** a job counselor *recently*? Yes. I **saw** one *two days ago*.	When the answer is *yes*, we usually give a specific time and use the simple past tense.

EXERCISE 35 **ABOUT YOU** Ask a *yes/no* question with the words given. Another student will answer. A past tense statement may be added to a *yes* answer.

EXAMPLE   go swimming recently

   A: Have you gone swimming recently?
   B: Yes, I have. I went swimming yesterday.

1. write to your family lately
2. go to the library recently
3. go to the zoo lately
4. see any good movies lately
5. receive any letters lately
6. be absent lately
7. have a job interview lately
8. read any good books recently
9. make any international calls lately
10. take any tests recently

EXERCISE 36 Work with a partner. Write three questions to ask your teacher about what he or she has done lately. Your teacher will answer.

EXAMPLE   <u>Have you taken a vacation lately (or recently)?</u>

1. _____
2. _____
3. _____

EXERCISE 37 **Fill in the blanks with the correct verb forms.**

EXAMPLE **A:** Have you ___gotten___ a letter from your parents lately?
(get)

B: Yes. I ___got___ a letter from them yesterday.

1. **A:** Have you _____ any pictures lately?
(take)

   B: No, I _____. My camera is broken.

2. **A:** Have you _____ any good movies lately?
(see)

   B: Yes. I _____ a great movie last weekend.

3. **A:** Have you _____ for a walk lately?
(go)

   B: Yes. I _____ for a walk yesterday.

4. **A:** Have you _____ yourself a gift lately?
(buy)

   B: Yes. I _____ myself a new CD player last week.

5. **A:** Have you _____ a good conversation with a friend lately?
(have)

   B: No. I _____ time to talk with my friends lately.

6. **A:** Have you _____ the art museum lately?
(visit)

   B: No. I _____ never _____ the art museum.

7. **A:** Have you _____ the laundry lately?
(do)

   B: Yes. I _____ it this morning.

8. **A:** Have you _____ to any parties lately?
(go)

   B: No, I _____. I've been too busy lately.

9. **A:** Have you _____ any compositions lately?
(write)

   B: Yes. I _____ a composition last night.

10. **A:** Have you _____ any good books lately?
(read)

    B: No, I _____. I'm too busy with my schoolwork.

1.17 The Present Perfect Continuous Tense with Ongoing Activities

EXAMPLES	EXPLANATION
Many American companies **have been sending** jobs abroad. American companies **have been benefiting** from outsourcing. Lately I **have been thinking** about changing majors. My English **has been improving** a lot lately.	We use the present perfect continuous to show that an activity has been ongoing or in progress from a time in the near past to the present. Remember, do not use the continuous form with nonaction verbs: She **has been** absent a lot lately.

EXERCISE 38   **ABOUT YOU** Fill in the blanks with *have* or *haven't* to tell about your experiences lately. (You may add a sentence giving more information.)

EXAMPLE   I __haven't__ been reading a lot lately.
I haven't had much time.

1. I _____ been getting a lot of sleep recently.
2. I _____ been getting together with my friends lately.
3. I _____ been watching the news a lot lately.
4. I _____ been studying a lot lately.
5. I _____ been learning a lot about English grammar lately.
6. I _____ been worrying a lot lately.
7. I _____ been looking for a job recently.
8. I _____ been watching a lot of TV recently.
9. I _____ been sending a lot of text messages lately.
10. I _____ been spending a lot of money recently.
11. I _____ been absent a lot lately.
12. I _____ been using a computer a lot lately.

EXERCISE 39   **ABOUT YOU** Fill in the blanks to make true statements about yourself.

EXAMPLES   __My pronunciation__ has been getting better.
__My eyesight__ has been getting worse.

1. _____ has been improving.
2. _____ has been getting worse.
3. _____ has been increasing.   *(continued)*

4. _____ has been helping me with my studies.

5. _____ has been making me tired.

1.18 The Present Perfect Tense with No Time Mentioned

EXAMPLES	EXPLANATION
A: I'm changing my major. **B: Have** you **told** your parents about it? **A:** The job situation is bad these days. **B:** I know. Many workers **have lost** their jobs. **A:** Her uncle has a taxicab business. **B:** Really? **Has** he **made** a lot of money in his business? **A:** Are there a lot of call centers in India? **B:** Yes, there are. A lot of jobs **have moved** overseas.	We can use the present perfect to talk about the past without any reference to time. The time is not important or not known or imprecise. Using the present perfect, rather than the past, shows that the past is relevant to a present situation or statement.

EXERCISE 40 **ABOUT YOU** **Fill in the blanks to make a true statement about yourself.**

EXAMPLE   I've eaten _____ _pizza_ _____, and I like it a lot.

1. I've visited _____, and I would recommend it to others.

2. I've tried _____, and I like this food a lot.

3. I've seen the movie _____, and I would recommend it to others.

4. The teacher has said that _____, but some of us forget.

5. I've studied _____, and it has really helped me a lot.

6. I've had a lot of experience with _____ and can help you with it, if you need me to.

EXERCISE **41**   **ABOUT YOU** Place a check mark (✓) next to the work-related experiences you've had. Then at the bottom, write three more things you've done at your present or former job. Write things that would impress an interviewer.

1. _____ I've worked on a team.

2. _____ I've taken programming courses.

3. _____ I've had experience talking with customers on the phone.

4. _____ I've worked overtime when necessary to finish a project.

5. _____ I've worked and gone to school at the same time.

6. _____ I've helped my family financially.

7. _____ I've given oral presentations.

8. _____ I've done research.

9. _____ I've created a Web site.

10. _____ I've done physical labor.

11. _____ I've been in charge of a group of workers.

12. _____ I've traveled as part of my job.

13. _____

14. _____

15. _____

EXERCISE **42**   **Fill in the blanks with the present perfect tense (for no time mentioned) or the simple past tense (if the time is mentioned). Use the verb in parentheses ( ). Answers may vary.**

CD 1, TR 07

I ___**have had**___ many new experiences since I moved
    (example: have)

here. I _____ some foods for the first time in my
    (1 try)

life. I _____ pizza, but I don't like it much.
    (2 eat)

Yesterday, I _____ Chinese food for the first
    (3 try)

time and thought it was delicious.

    I _____ a lot of new people and have some new
    (4 meet)

friends. I _____ some new behaviors. For example,
    (5 see)

there's a guy in my math class who wears torn jeans every day. Yesterday

I _____ him if he needs money for new clothes, but he
    (6 ask)

just laughed and said, "Torn clothes are in style."

(continued)

I _____ (7 visit) some interesting places. I

_____ (8 go) to the art museum and the science museum.

I _____ (9 take) a boat ride on a nearby river. I

_____ (10 even/go) to the top of the tallest building.

I _____ (11 learn) about looking for a job. I

_____ (12 write) résumés and I _____ (13 have) job

interviews. I _____ (14 go) to job fairs. I _____ (15 even/use)

the Internet for my job search. Last week I _____ (16 go)

to see a job counselor at my college, and she _____ (17 give)

me some help with interviewing techniques.

1.19 The Present Perfect Tense vs. the Present Perfect Continuous Tense with No Time Mentioned

We can use both the present perfect tense and the present perfect continuous tense with no time mentioned.

EXAMPLES	EXPLANATION
a. My counselor **has helped** me with my résumé. b. My family **has been helping** me a lot.	The (a) examples are present perfect. They refer to a single occurrence at an indefinite time in the past.
a. I **have applied** for a job in New York. b. I **have been applying** for jobs all over the U.S.	The (b) examples are present perfect continuous. They refer to an ongoing activity that is not finished. The activity is still in progress.
a. **Have** you **used** the Internet in your job search lately? b. I'**ve been using** the Internet a lot lately.	

EXERCISE 43 Check (✓) the sentence or clause that best completes the idea.

EXAMPLE I can't concentrate. The people in the next apartment . . .

_____ have made a lot of noise.

_✓_ have been making a lot of noise.

1. My boss has been sick all week.

_____ She's stayed in bed.

_____ She's been staying in bed.

2. My friend is unhappy.

_____ She has just lost her job.

_____ She has been losing her job.

3. She lost her job three weeks ago. She hasn't had much free time lately because . . .

_____ she has looked for a new job.

_____ she has been looking for a new job.

4. My résumé writing skills have been improving a lot because . . .

_____ I have practiced with my counselor.

_____ I have been practicing with my counselor.

5. At first my sister planned to move, but she found a job here. So . . .

_____ she has changed her mind.

_____ she has been changing her mind.

6. I meet new people everywhere: in my neighborhood, at my job, at school.

_____ I have met new people.

_____ I have been meeting new people.

7. Now I can buy a new computer because I . . .

_____ have found a job.

_____ have been finding a job.

8. Every week I put 20 percent of my salary in the bank. I hope I'll have enough to buy a new TV soon.

_____ I have saved my money.

_____ I have been saving my money.

9. I'm going to become an engineer.

_____ I have made my decision.

_____ I have been making my decision.

10. I need to finish my résumé soon.

_____ I've worked very hard on it.

_____ I've been working very hard on it.

EXERCISE 44 Fill in the blanks with the simple past, the present perfect, or the present perfect continuous tense of the verb in parentheses ( ). In some cases, more than one answer is possible.

EXAMPLE I _____worked_____ as a cashier when I was in high school.
(work)

1. I think I'm qualified for the job of driver because I

   _____ as a driver before.
   (work)

2. I _____ as a pilot many years ago. My job as a pilot
   (work)

   _____ me away from home much of the time.
   (take)

3. I don't like the sight of blood, so I _____ about
   (never/think)

   becoming a doctor.

4. I'm a hair stylist. I _____ people's hair for six years.
   (cut)

5. I'm afraid of the interview process because I

   _____ a job interview before.
   (never/have)

6. Many years ago, I _____ as a kindergarten
   (work)

   teacher. Now I have my own day-care center.

7. I'm a car mechanic. I _____ a mechanic for three
   (be)

   years. I _____ a lot of experience working with
   (have)

   American cars, but I _____ much experience with
   (not/have)

   foreign cars.

8. I'm 62 years old and I like my job as a lab technician, but lately I

   _____ a lot about retirement.
   (think)

9. When I was in my native country, I _____ an
   (be)

   engineer, but now I'm a salesperson.

10. People _____ me why I want to be a funeral
            (often/ask)

director when I graduate.

11. Lately I _____ the Internet a lot to get
            (use)

information about jobs.

Summary of Lesson 1

Compare the simple present and the present perfect tenses.

SIMPLE PRESENT	PRESENT PERFECT
She **has** a job. She **is** a lab technician.	She **has had** her job for six months. She **has been** a lab technician since May.

Compare the present continuous and the present perfect continuous tenses.

PRESENT CONTINUOUS	PRESENT PERFECT CONTINUOUS
He **is working** now. She **is using** the Internet now.	He **has been working** for three hours. She **has been using** it for two hours.

Compare the simple past and the present perfect tenses.

SIMPLE PAST	PRESENT PERFECT
Daniel **worked** in Mexico City from 1994 to 1998.	He **has worked** in the U.S. since 1998.
He **found** a job in 2004.	He **has had** his present job since January 2004.
He **bought** his car when he came to Chicago.	He **has had** a car since he came to Chicago.
When **did** he **come** to Chicago?	How long **has** he **been** in Chicago?
He **had** three interviews last month.	He **has had** two interviews this month.
He **studied** business in college.	He **has studied** French and speaks it well.
He **went** to New York in July.	He **has gone** to Los Angeles many times.
Did you **go** to the job fair last week?	**Have** you ever **gone** to a job fair?

Compare the present perfect and the present perfect continuous tenses.

PRESENT PERFECT	PRESENT PERFECT CONTINUOUS
Ron **has worked** as a programmer for the past five years. (*This sentence has the same meaning as the one on the right.*)	Ron **has been working** as a programmer for the past five years. (*This sentence has the same meaning as the one on the left.*)
I **have lived** in three American cities. (*This sentence refers to a repetition from past to present.*)	I **have been living** in this city for the past two years. (*This sentence shows a continuation from past to present.*)
How many apartments **have** you **had** in this city? (*This question asks about a repetition from past to present.*)	How long **have** you **been living** in your current apartment? (*This question asks about a continuation from past to present.*)
Dan **has studied** French. (*This sentence shows only past activity, with no indication of a continuation.*)	The U.S. government **has been studying** the effect of outsourcing. (*This sentence shows an activity that is still in progress.*)
I **have thought** about changing majors. (*This sentence tells about an indefinite time in the past.*)	I **have been thinking** a lot about my future. (*In this sentence, the phrase "a lot" indicates that this activity is still in progress.*)

Editing Advice

1. Don't confuse the *-ing* form and the past participle.

   taking
   I've been ~~taken~~ English courses for several years.

   been
   Have you ever ~~being~~ to Texas?

2. Don't confuse *for* and *since*.

   for
   He's been in Chicago ~~since~~ three years.

3. Use the simple past, not the present perfect, with a specific past time and in questions and statements with *when*.

   wrote
   He ~~has written~~ a book five years ago.

   She ~~has~~ bought a car when she ~~has~~ found a job.

   did he get
   When ~~has he gotten~~ his driver's license?

4. Use the present perfect (continuous), not the present tense, if the action started in the past and continues to the present.

have been
I'm working in a factory for six months.

have   had
How long ~~do~~ you ~~have~~ your computer?

5. Don't use the continuous form for repetition.

eaten
How many times have you ~~been eating~~ pizza?

6. Use the simple past in a *since* clause.

came
He's had three jobs since he ~~has come~~ to the U.S.

7. Use the correct word order.

never been
He has ~~been never~~ late to class.

ever eaten
Have you ~~eaten ever~~ Chinese food?

8. Use *yet* in negative statements. Use *already* in affirmative statements.

yet
I haven't finished the book ~~already~~.

already
I've finished the book ~~yet~~.

9. Use *how long* for a question about length of time. Don't include the word *time*.

How long ~~time~~ have they been working in a restaurant?

10. If the main verb is *have*, be sure to include the auxiliary verb *have* for the present perfect.

has
He had his job since March.

Editing Quiz

Two women, Karen (K) and Lucy (L), meet by chance in a shopping mall. Here's their conversation. Some of the shaded words and phrases have mistakes. Find the mistakes and correct them. If the shaded words are correct, write *C*.

L: Hi, Karen. I <u>haven't seen</u> ^C you since high school. How are you? Tell me
    (example)
    about your life. What ~~you have~~ **have you** been doing <u>lately</u>?
    (example)   *(1)*

K: Well, I <u>got</u> married after high school.
         (2)

L: Really? How long <u>time</u> have you <u>being</u> married?
                        (3)   *(4)*

K: <u>For</u> about four years. And <u>I've had</u> a baby six months ago.
       (5)   *(6)*

L: That's wonderful. Did you marry your high-school boyfriend, Steve?

K: Oh, no. I <u>haven't seeing</u> Steve since <u>we've been</u> in high school. I married
                 (7)   *(8)*
    Robert Kanter. You've <u>met him never</u>. What about you? What
                          (9)
    <u>you have been doing</u> since high school? Did you marry your old
       (10)
    boyfriend, Greg?

L: Oh, no. I <u>haven't seen</u> Greg <u>since</u> four years. I'm not married. I
                 (11)   *(12)*
    <u>haven't meet</u> the right guy <u>yet</u>. I <u>started</u> college right after high school. I
       (13)   *(14)*   *(15)*
    <u>graduated</u> last year with a degree in teaching.
       (16)

K: That's great! <u>I've always have</u> a great respect for the teaching profession.
                    (17)
    Where do you teach?

L: <u>I've had</u> many interviews for teaching jobs, but I <u>haven't find</u> one
       (18)   *(19)*
    <u>yet</u>. But <u>I been working</u> at a day-care center <u>since</u> the last three
    (20)   *(21)*   *(22)*
    months. I was so happy when <u>I've found</u> this job. I was worried that I'd
                                (23)
    never find a job.

K: Are you still living in Ridgeland?

L: No. I'm living in Oakwood since I graduated from college. Here's my
(24)   (25)   (26)

phone number. Call me when you have more time and we can talk.

K: Thanks. I'd love to.

Lesson 1 Test/Review

PART 1 **Fill in the blanks with the simple present, simple past, present perfect, or present perfect continuous tense of the verb in parentheses ( ). In some cases, more than one answer is possible.**

A: Hi, Ben. I ___*haven't seen*___ you in a long time. How
(example: not/see)

___*have you been*___ ?
(example: you/be)

B: I'm okay. But I _____ a job now, so I feel
(1 not/have)

pretty depressed about it. I _____ for a job for the
(2 look)

past three months, but so far I _____ any success.
(3 not/have)

A: My best friend _____ from college last year, and
(4 graduate)

he _____ a job yet. A lot of American jobs
(5 not/find)

_____ in recent years. Many jobs
(6 disappear)

_____ to India and other countries.
(7 go)

B: That's terrible. My family _____ to the U.S. last
(8 come)

year to find better jobs, but it's not easy anymore.

A: But it's not impossible. _____ the
(9 you/ever/use)

Occupational Outlook Handbook?

B: No, I never _____ .
(10 have)

A: You can find it on the Web. It lists information about professions in

the U.S. My counselor _____ me about it when I
(11 tell)

_____ taking courses. I _____ a
(12 start)   *(13 have)*

good job now. I _____ as a dental assistant.
(14 work)

B: How long _____ at that job?
(15 you/work)

(continued)

The Present Perfect Tense; The Present Perfect Continuous Tense   **53**

A: Since I _____ my certificate two years ago. I don't
(16 get)

have to worry about outsourcing. You can't look in people's mouths

from another country.

B: You're lucky to have such a good job.

A: It's not luck. I _____ this job carefully before I started
(17 choose)

taking courses. And I _____ hard when I was
(18 study)

in the dental program. Now when I _____ to work
(19 go)

every day, I _____ good because I'm helping people
(20 feel)

and making good money. Also I _____ good benefits.
(21 have)

In addition, I _____ two salary increases so far.
(22 get)

B: That's wonderful! _____ about becoming a dentist?
(23 you/ever/think)

Dentists make good money.

A: I _____ about it, but I don't want to spend so much
(24 think)

time studying for a new career. It takes a long time to become a dentist.

And you need to study a lot of science. I _____
(25 never/be)

very good in science.

B: Well, when you have time, will you show me how to find the

Occupational Outlook Handbook online?

A: I'd be happy to.

Expansion

❶ Walk around the room. Find one person who has done each of these things. Write that person's name in the blank.

a. _____ has been exercising a lot lately.

b. _____ has been watching a lot of TV lately.

c. _____ has never gone to an art museum.

d. _____ has traveled to more than five countries.

e. _____ has never owned a car.

f. _____ hasn't bought the textbook yet.

g. _____ has been in this city for less than six months.

h. _____ has just found a job.

i. _____ has worked in a restaurant.

j. _____ has never used public transportation in this city.

k. _____ has eaten raw fish.

l. _____ has worked out in a gym several times this month.

m. _____ has never shopped online.

n. _____ has never sent a text message.

o. _____ has been looking for a job.

❷ Role Play: Find a partner. Pretend that one of you is looking for a job and the other one is the interviewer. Ask and answer questions about your experience, education, interests, talents, etc. Here are some sample questions that interviewers sometimes ask:

- Why did you leave your last job?

- Why are you applying for this position?

- Where would you like to be five years from now?

- What are your strengths?

- What are your weaknesses?

- Why should we hire you?

- How many years experience have you had in this field?

- Have you had experience with computers?

❸ Game—True-True-False: Form a small group. On a piece of paper, write two unusual things you have done in the past. Write one false statement about your past. (Use the present perfect with no mention of time.) Read your statements to the other members of your group. Your classmates have to guess which is the false statement.

EXAMPLES   I've flown in a helicopter.

I've worked on a farm.

I've met the president of my native country.

❹ Fill in the blanks and discuss your answers.

a. I've learned _____ from my experiences in the U.S.

b. I've thought a lot about _____.

c. Most people in my native country have never _____.

d. In the U.S., it's been hard for me to _____.

Talk
About It

❶ How is looking for a job in the U.S. different from looking for a job in other countries?

❷ How is the work environment in your present job different from the work environment in a previous job you had?

❸ In other countries, how do people usually select a career? Are there career counselors to help people make a decision?

❹ Have you ever used the Internet to search for jobs? Has it been helpful?

❺ In your native country, do high school students ever have a part-time job? If so, what kinds of jobs do they do?

6 **Look at the following list of jobs. Which ones do you think are interesting and why? What do you think are some good or bad aspects of these jobs?**

airplane pilot	funeral director	librarian
architect	gardener	musician
bus driver	immigration officer	newspaper reporter
circus clown	lawyer	police officer
firefighter	letter carrier	veterinarian

Write
About It

1 **Write about a career that you think is interesting. Explain why you think this career is interesting.**

2 **Write about a job you would never want to have. Tell why.**

3 **Write an article giving advice to somebody looking for a job.**

4 **Write about your past work experience.**

EXAMPLE

My Job Experience

I've been in the U.S. for only five years, but I have already had several jobs. When I arrived, I didn't know much English and I started to work as a dishwasher in a restaurant. I didn't like this job and quit after four months...

For more practice using grammar in context, please visit our Web site.

Grammar

The Passive Voice

Participles Used as Adjectives

Get + Participles and Adjectives

Context

Hollywood

2.1 The Passive Voice—An Overview

We use the passive voice when the subject of the sentence is the receiver of the action.

EXAMPLES	EXPLANATION
Popcorn **is sold** in movie theaters. Old movies **were filmed** in black and white. Many movies **have been made** in Hollywood.	Passive verb = a form of *be* + past participle
Active: subject verb object The children **saw** the movie. **Passive:** subject verb by agent The movie **was seen** *by* the children.	Compare active and passive. The object of the active sentence (*movie*) is the subject of the passive sentence. If the agent of the action (the person who performs the action) is mentioned, it follows *by*.

The Oscars

Before You Read

1. Who is your favorite actor? Who is your favorite actress?

2. What movies have you seen recently?

CD 1, TR 08

Read the following magazine article. Pay special attention to verbs in the passive voice.

Did You
Know?

Walt Disney has won the most Oscars ever: 26.

The Academy Awards **are given** out every year to recognize outstanding work of movie actors, directors, and others who are part of the movie-making industry. These awards, called Oscars, **are presented** in a formal ceremony in Hollywood. Several people **are nominated** in specific categories, such as Best Movie, Best Actor, Best Music, and Best Costumes. One nominee **is chosen** to receive an award in each category.

When the awards ceremony started in 1929, 15 awards **were presented** and the ceremony **was attended** by only 250 people. Tickets cost $10, and anyone who could afford a ticket could attend. Today about two dozen Oscars **are presented**. Tickets **are** no longer **sold** to the general public; invitations **are sent** only to people involved in making the movies and to their guests. Today the awards **are presented** in the 3400-seat Kodak Theatre in Hollywood.

Until 1941, the winners' names **were** already **known** before the ceremony and **published** in newspapers the night before the ceremony. Now the winners' names are placed in sealed envelopes and the envelopes **are** not **opened** until the night of the ceremony.

Since 1953, Oscar night **has been televised** and **broadcast** all over the world. This show **is seen** by hundreds of millions of people. Viewers watch as their favorite movie stars arrive looking beautiful and hopeful.

2.2 The Passive Voice—Form

Compare active voice and passive voice in different tenses.

Tense	Active	Passive = *Be* + Past Participle
Simple Present	A committee **chooses** the winner.	The winner **is chosen** by a committee.
Present Continuous	They **are presenting** an award now.	An award **is being presented** now.
Future	They **will pick** the best movie. They **are going to pick** the best movie.	The best movie **will be picked**. The best movie **is going to be picked**.
Simple Past	They **announced** the winner's name.	The winner's name **was announced**.
Past Continuous	They **were interviewing** the winners.	The winners **were being interviewed**.
Present Perfect	They **have chosen** the best movie.	The best movie **has been chosen**.
Modal	You **can see** the movie on DVD.	The movie **can be seen** on DVD.

Language Notes:
1. Both the active voice and the passive voice can be used with different tenses and with modals. The tense of the passive sentence is shown in the verb *be*. Use the past participle with every tense.
2. If two verbs in the passive voice are connected with *and*, do not repeat *be*.
   The Oscar ceremony **is televised** *and* **seen** by millions of people.

(continued)

EXAMPLES	EXPLANATION
Before 1941, the winners' names **were *already* known** before the ceremony. Today the winners **are *never* announced** ahead of time.	An adverb can be placed between the auxiliary verb and the main verb.
Affirmative: The movie **was filmed** in the U.S. **Negative:** It **wasn't filmed** in Canada. ***Yes/No* Question: Was** it **filmed** in Hollywood? **Short Answer:** No, it **wasn't**. ***Wh-* Question:** Where **was** it **filmed**? **Subject Question:** Which movie **was filmed** in Canada?	Observe affirmative statements, negative statements, and questions with the passive voice. Never use *do*, *does*, or *did* with the passive voice. (*Wrong:* The movie **didn't** filmed in Canada.)
Active: **She** saw **him**. **Passive:** **He** was seen *by* **her**. **Active:** **They** helped **us**. **Passive:** **We** were helped *by* **them**.	Notice the difference in pronouns in an active sentence and a passive sentence. After *by*, the object pronoun is used.

EXERCISE 1 **Read the following sentences. Decide if the underlined verb is active (A) or passive (P).**

EXAMPLES   The actress <u>received</u> an Oscar.   **A**

The actress <u>was given</u> an Oscar.   **P**

1. The actress <u>wore</u> a beautiful gown.
2. Halle Berry <u>presented</u> an Oscar.
3. Halle Berry <u>has been seen</u> in many movies.
4. The director <u>has been nominated</u> many times.
5. Old movies <u>were filmed</u> in black and white.
6. Many actors <u>live</u> in California.
7. Many movies <u>are made</u> in Hollywood.
8. The names of the winners <u>will be printed</u> in tomorrow's newspaper.
9. The actress <u>thanked</u> all the people who helped her win.
10. The actress <u>was driven</u> to the ceremony in a white limousine.
11. Hollywood <u>was built</u> at the beginning of the twentieth century.
12. Hollywood <u>has become</u> the movie capital of the U.S.

EXERCISE 2 **Fill in the blanks with the passive voice of the verb in parentheses. Use the tense or modal given.**

EXAMPLE   (simple present: *give*)

The best actor ___is___ ___given___ an Oscar.

1. (simple present: *see*)

   The awards ceremony _____ _____ by millions of people.

2. (future: *choose*)

   Which actor _____ _____ _____ next year?

3. (modal: *can / see*)

   The movie _____ _____ _____ at many theaters.

4. (present perfect: *make*)

   Many movies _____ _____ _____ about World War II.

5. (simple past: *give*)

   Kate Winslet _____ _____ the best actress award in 2009.

6. (present continuous: *show*)

   A good movie _____ _____ _____ at a theater near
   my house.

7. (simple past: *make*)

   Star Wars _____ _____ in 1977.

8. (present perfect: *show*)

   The movie _____ _____ _____ on TV many times.

9. (present perfect: *give*)

   Over 2,000 Academy Awards _____ _____ _____ out
   since 1929.

10. (simple past: *give*)

    In 1929, only one award _____ _____ to a woman.

11. (simple past: *add*)

    When _____ sound _____ to movies?

    It _____ _____ in 1927.

12. (simple present: *often / make*)

    Movies _____ _____ _____ in Hollywood.

13. (present perfect: *film*)

    How many movies _____ _____ _____ in black and
    white?

The Passive Voice; Participles Used as Adjectives; Get + Participles and Adjectives   **63**

2.3 Passive Voice and Active Voice—Uses

EXAMPLES	EXPLANATION
Compare: **Active:** The man **ate** the fish. **Passive:** The man **was eaten** by the fish.	When the verb is in the active voice, the subject performs the action. When the verb is in the passive voice, the subject receives the action.
A. **Active:** I **see** the Academy Awards ceremony every year. **Passive:** The Academy Awards ceremony **is seen** by millions. **B.** **Active:** **Do** you **know** the winners' names? **Passive:** The winners' names **are not known** until the night of the ceremony. **C.** **Active:** The Academy **presents** awards to the best actors and directors. **Passive:** The awards **are presented** every year.	The active voice focuses on the person who does the action. The passive voice focuses on the receiver or the result of the action. Sometimes the passive voice mentions the agent, the person who does the action (A). Sometimes it is not necessary to mention the agent (B and C).

EXERCISE **3** Write an active sentence and a passive sentence for each subject. Choose an appropriate tense.

EXAMPLE *Active:* The test ___has 12 questions.___

Passive: The test ___will be given in a large auditorium.___

1. *Active:* My textbook _____
   Passive: My textbook _____

2. *Active:* My best friend _____
   Passive: My best friend _____

3. *Active:* Some students _____
   Passive: Some students _____

4. *Active:* I _____
   Passive: I _____

5. *Active:* Actors _____

    Passive: Actors _____

6. *Active:* Movies _____

    Passive: Movies _____

2.4 The Passive Voice Without an Agent

The passive voice is used more frequently without an agent than with an agent.

EXAMPLES	EXPLANATION
The invitations **have been sent** out. The winners' names **are placed** in envelopes.	The passive voice is used when it is not important to mention who performed the action.
A. **Active:** *Someone* **stole** my wallet. **Passive:** My wallet **was stolen** last week. **B.** **Active:** *Someone* **told** me that you like movies. **Passive:** I **was told** that you like movies.	The passive voice is used when we do not know the agent (A) or when we prefer not to mention the agent (B).
a. One person **is chosen** to receive the award. b. Oscar night **has been televised** since 1953.	The passive voice is used when the agent is obvious and doesn't need to be mentioned. a. It is obvious that the Academy chooses the winner. b. It is obvious that TV stations have televised Oscar night.
Compare Active (A) and Passive (P): A: *You* **can rent** DVDs at many stores. P: DVDs **can be rented** at many stores. A: *They* **sell** popcorn in movie theaters. P: Popcorn **is sold** in movie theaters.	In conversation, the active voice is often used with the impersonal subjects *people, you, we,* or *they.* In more formal speech and writing, the passive is used with no agent.

EXERCISE **4**   **Fill in the blanks with the passive voice of the verb in parentheses ( ). Choose an appropriate tense.**

EXAMPLE   Hollywood _____<u>was built</u>_____ in the early 1900s.
                                     (build)

    1. Most American movies _____ in Hollywood.
                                            (make)

    2. Let's get some popcorn. It's fresh. It _____ right now.
                                                   (make)

(continued)

3. Movie listings _____ in the newspaper.
(can/find)

4. Children _____ to see some movies.
(not/allow)

5. Hurry! The winners _____ in ten minutes.
(announce)

6. In 1929, only fifteen Oscars _____.
(present)

7. Before 1941, the winners' names _____ in
(publish)

newspapers the night before the ceremony.

8. A new theater _____ near my house at this time.
(build)

9. We can't get into the movie theater because all the tickets

_____ already.
(sell)

10. Did you see the movie *Harry Potter*? Where _____ it

_____?
(film)

11. I went to the lobby to buy popcorn, and my seat _____.
(take)

12. No one knows why the award _____ "Oscar."
(call)

13. *Slumdog Millionaire* _____ as the best film of 2009.
(choose)

14. In a movie theater, coming attractions[1]_____
(show)

before the feature film begins.

15. Sound _____ to movies in 1927.
(add)

16. The Kodak Theatre, where the awards _____
(present)

each year, _____ in 2001.
(build)

[1]*Coming attractions* are short previews of new movies. Theaters show coming attractions to get your interest in
returning to the theater to see a new movie.

2.5 The Passive Voice with an Agent

Sometimes the passive voice is used with an agent.

ACTIVE	PASSIVE
Active: Steven Spielberg **has made** many movies. **Passive:** Many movies **have been made** by Steven Spielberg. **Active:** Ralph Lauren **designs** many of the actresses' gowns. **Passive:** Many of the actresses' gowns **are designed** by Ralph Lauren.	When the sentence has a strong agent (a specific person: Steven Spielberg, Ralph Lauren), we can use either the active or the passive voice. The active voice puts more emphasis on the person who performs the action. The passive voice puts more emphasis on the action or the result. In general, the active voice is more common than the passive voice when an agent is mentioned.
Active: *The first Oscar ceremony* took place in 1929. **Passive:** *It* **was attended** by 250 people. **Active:** *The Oscar ceremony* is popular all over the world. **Passive:** *It* **is seen** by millions of viewers each year.	Sometimes the passive voice is used to continue with the same subject of the preceding sentence.
Active: Steven Spielberg **directed** *Star Wars*, didn't he? **Passive:** No. *Star Wars* **was directed** by George Lucas.	We can use the passive voice to shift the emphasis to the object of the preceding sentence.
Passive: The dress **was designed** by Vera Wang. **Passive:** The music **was composed** by Bob Dylan. **Passive:** The movie projector **was invented** by Thomas Edison.	We often use the passive voice when the agent *made, discovered, invented, designed, built, wrote, painted,* or *composed* something.
The song **was written** *by Randy Newman*. It **was performed** *by him* too.	When the agent is included, use *by* + noun or object pronoun.

EXERCISE 5 Fill in the blanks with the passive voice of the verb in parentheses ( ). Use the past tense.

1. Mickey Mouse _____ by Walt Disney.
   (create)

2. The movie projector _____ by Thomas Edison.
   (invent)

3. *Romeo and Juliet* _____ by William Shakespeare in 1595.
   (write)

4. Romeo and Juliet _____ into a movie in 1968.
   (make)

5. *My Heart Will Go On* _____ by Celine Dion.
   (sing)

6. *Star Wars* _____ by George Lucas.
   (direct)

EXERCISE 6 Fill in the blanks with the active or passive voice of the verb in parentheses ( ). Use the tense indicated.

EXAMPLES I _____**saw**_____ an old movie on TV last night.
(past: see)

The movie _____**was filmed**_____ in black and white.
(past: film)

It _____**will be shown**_____ again on TV tonight.
(future: show)

1. Many movies _____ in Hollywood.
   (present: make)

2. Steven Spielberg _____ many movies.
   (present perfect: make)

3. We _____ a DVD this weekend.
   (future: rent)

4. Vera Wang _____ beautiful dresses.
   (present: design)

5. The actress _____ a dress that _____
   (past continuous: wear)   (past: design)

   by Ralph Lauren.

6. Who _____ the music for the movie? The music
   (past: write)

   _____ by Randy Newman.
   (past: write)

7. The first Academy Awards presentation _____
   (past: have)

   250 guests.

8. I _____ *Star Wars*.
   (present perfect: never/see)

9. Computer animation _____ in many movies.

(present: use)

10. Movie reviewers _____ predictions weeks before

(present: make)

the Oscar presentation.

11. Oscar winners _____ the people who helped them.

(present: always/thank)

2.6 Verbs with Two Objects

Some verbs have two objects: a direct object (D.O.) and an indirect object (I.O.).

EXAMPLES	EXPLANATION
I.O. **D.O.** **Active:** They gave Spielberg an award. **Passive 1:** Spielberg was given an award. **Passive 2:** An award was given to Spielberg.	When an active sentence has two objects, the passive sentence can begin with either object. Notice that if the direct object *(an award)* becomes the subject of the passive sentence, *to* is used before the indirect object.

Language Note: Some verbs that use two objects are:

bring	lend	pay	serve	teach
give	offer	sell	show	tell
hand	owe	send	take	write

EXERCISE **7**   **Change the following sentences to passive voice in two ways. Omit the agent.**

EXAMPLE   They gave the actress an award.

    The actress was given an award.

    An award was given to the actress.

1. They handed the actress an Oscar.

_____

_____

2. Someone served the guests dinner.

_____

_____

(continued)

3. Someone told the students the answers.

_____

_____

4. Someone will send you an invitation.

_____

_____

5. They have shown us the movie.

_____

_____

6. They will give the winners flowers.

_____

_____

7. Someone has given you the key.

_____

_____

The History of Animation

Before You Read

1. Do you know how cartoons are created?

2. Are cartoons just for children? Do adults enjoy cartoons too?

Gertie the Dinosaur
Created by Winsor McCay

🔊 **Read the following textbook article. Pay special attention to active and passive verbs.**

CD 1, TR 09

Animated movies **have changed** a lot over the last 100 years. Winsor McCay **is considered** the father of animation. In the early 1900s, McCay **animated** his films by himself. He **drew** every picture separately and had them photographed, one at a time. Hundreds of photographs **were needed** to make a one-minute film. Sometimes it would take him more than a year to make a five-minute cartoon.

In 1914, the development of celluloid (a transparent material) made animation easier. Instead of drawing each picture separately, the animator could make a

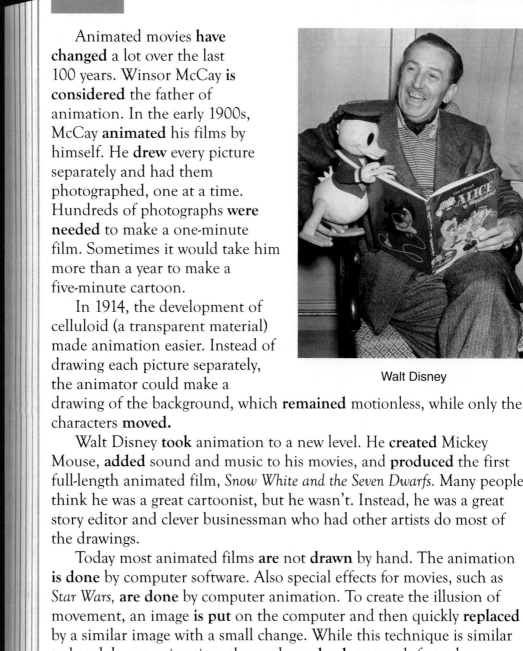

Walt Disney

drawing of the background, which **remained** motionless, while only the characters **moved.**

Walt Disney **took** animation to a new level. He **created** Mickey Mouse, **added** sound and music to his movies, and **produced** the first full-length animated film, *Snow White and the Seven Dwarfs.* Many people think he was a great cartoonist, but he wasn't. Instead, he was a great story editor and clever businessman who had other artists do most of the drawings.

Today most animated films **are** not **drawn** by hand. The animation **is done** by computer software. Also special effects for movies, such as *Star Wars*, **are done** by computer animation. To create the illusion of movement, an image **is put** on the computer and then quickly **replaced** by a similar image with a small change. While this technique is similar to hand-drawn animation, the work **can be done** much faster by computer. In fact, anyone with a home computer and special software **can create** a simple animation.

(continued)

1901 Walt Disney was born.

1914 Winsor McCay **created** the first animation on film, *Gertie the Dinosaur.*

1918 Walt Disney **opened** a cartoon studio in Kansas City, Missouri.

1923 Disney **moved** his studio to Hollywood.

1928 The first Mickey Mouse cartoon **was introduced**. It was the first talking cartoon.

1937 Disney **produced** *Snow White and the Seven Dwarfs*, the first full-length animated cartoon.

1995 *Toy Story* **became** the first full-length film animated entirely on computers.

2009 *WALL-E* **won** the Academy Award for best animated film.

2.7 Transitive and Intransitive Verbs

EXAMPLES	EXPLANATION
Compare: $\overbrace{\text{verb}}$ $\overbrace{\text{object}}$ **Active:** McCay **created** the first animated film. **Passive:** The first animated film **was created** in 1914. $\overbrace{\text{verb}}$ $\overbrace{\text{object}}$ **Active:** Walt Disney **didn't draw** his cartoons. **Passive:** His cartoons **were drawn** by studio artists.	Most active verbs are followed by an object. They can be used in the active and passive voice. These verbs are called *transitive* verbs.
Active Only: Disney **lived** in Hollywood most of his life. He **became** famous when he created Mickey Mouse. He **worked** with many artists. What **happened** to the first Mickey Mouse cartoon? I'd like to see it.	Some verbs have no object. We cannot use the passive voice with these verbs: agree die look seem arrive fall occur sleep be go rain stay become happen recover walk come live remain work These are called *intransitive* verbs.
Compare: a. Disney **left** Kansas City in 1923. b. The DVD **was left** in the DVD player.	*Leave* can be intransitive or transitive, depending on its meaning. In sentence (a), *leave* means "go away from." It is an intransitive verb. It has no passive form. In sentence (b), leave means "not taken." It is a transitive verb. It has a passive form.
Compare: a. Cartoons **have changed** a lot over the years. b. The light bulb **was changed** by the janitor. a. In a cartoon, it looks like the characters **are moving**, but they are not. b. The chairs **were moved** to another room.	*Change* and *move* can be intransitive or transitive. When a change happens through a natural process (a), it is intransitive. When someone specific causes the change (b), it is transitive.
Compare: Walt Disney **was born** in 1901. He **died** in 1966.	Notice that we use *was/were* with *born*, but we don't use the passive voice with *die*. *Born* is not a verb. It is a past participle used as an adjective.

EXERCISE 8 **Which of the following sentences can be changed to passive voice? Change those sentences. If no change is possible, write *no change*.**

EXAMPLES Today they create most animation with computer software.
Today most animation is created with computer software.

Walt Disney moved to Hollywood in 1923.
No change.

1. What happened at the end of the movie?
   _____

2. Someone left a box of popcorn on the seat.
   _____

3. Many movie stars live in California.
   _____

4. Paul Newman was a famous actor. He died in 2008.
   _____

5. I slept during the movie.
   _____

6. You can rent *Finding Nemo* on DVD.
   _____

7. They will show a movie at 9:30 in the auditorium.
   _____

8. They have sold all the tickets.
   _____

EXERCISE 9 **Fill in the blanks with the active or passive form of the verb in parentheses ( ). Use the tense indicated.**

EXAMPLES Walt Disney _____*was*_____ a clever businessman.
                              (past: be)

His cartoons _____*are seen*_____ all over the world.
                         (present: see)

1. Walt Disney _____ famous when he
                        (past: become)

   _____ Mickey Mouse.
         (past: create)

2. Walt Disney _____ most of his cartoon characters.
                        (past: not/draw)

3. Most of his cartoons _____ by studio artists.
                                 (past: draw)

4. Walt Disney _____ 26 Oscars.
   (past: give)

5. Walt Disney _____ his studio to Hollywood.
   (past: move)

6. Walt Disney _____ in Hollywood most of his life.
   (past: live)

7. Disney _____ in 1966.
   (past: die)

8. Today's animations _____ using computers.
   (present: create)

9. Cartoon characters look like they _____.
   (present continuous: move)

10. Even today, Disney's old cartoons _____ beautiful.
    (present: look)

EXERCISE 10

🔊

CD 1, TR 10

Fill in the blanks with the active or passive form of the verb in parentheses ( ). Use the past tense.

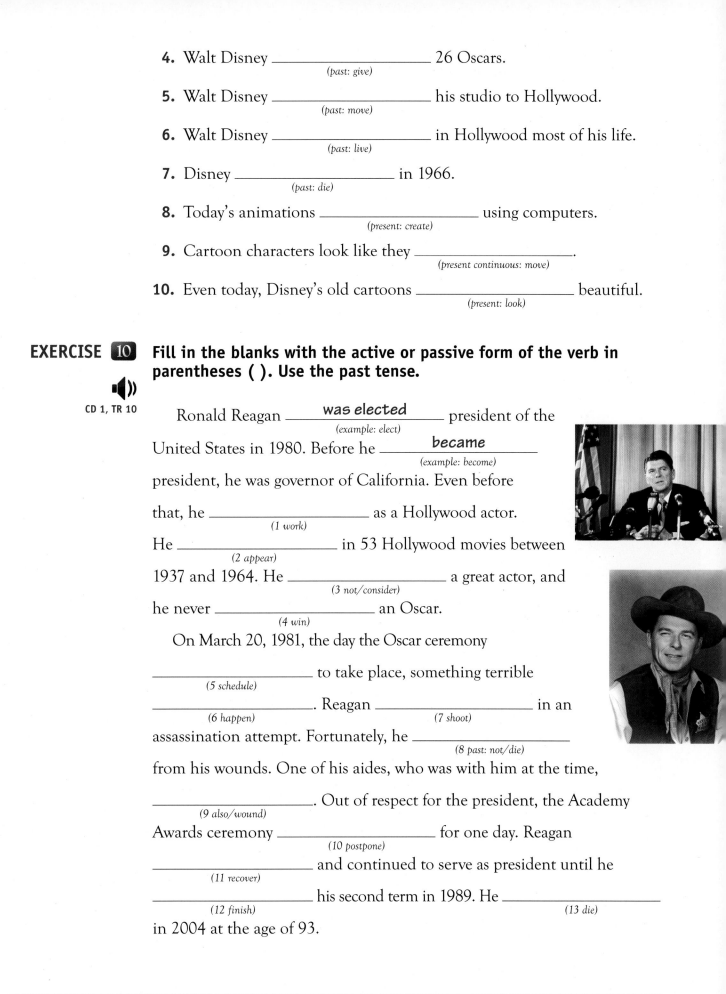

Ronald Reagan ____**was elected**____ president of the
(example: elect)

United States in 1980. Before he ____**became**____
(example: become)

president, he was governor of California. Even before

that, he _____ as a Hollywood actor.
(1 work)

He _____ in 53 Hollywood movies between
(2 appear)

1937 and 1964. He _____ a great actor, and
(3 not/consider)

he never _____ an Oscar.
(4 win)

On March 20, 1981, the day the Oscar ceremony

_____ to take place, something terrible
(5 schedule)

_____. Reagan _____ in an
(6 happen)   *(7 shoot)*

assassination attempt. Fortunately, he _____
(8 past: not/die)

from his wounds. One of his aides, who was with him at the time,

_____. Out of respect for the president, the Academy
(9 also/wound)

Awards ceremony _____ for one day. Reagan
(10 postpone)

_____ and continued to serve as president until he
(11 recover)

_____ his second term in 1989. He _____
(12 finish)   *(13 die)*

in 2004 at the age of 93.

EXERCISE **11** **Find the mistakes with the underlined verbs in the sentences below and correct them. Not every sentence has a mistake. If the sentence is correct, write C.**

EXAMPLES
                                  were
Before the 1950s, most movies <u>filmed</u> in black and white.

I <u>like</u> old movies. *C*

1. We <u>went</u> to see a movie.

2. I don't like scary movies. I <u>can't be slept</u> afterwards.

3. <u>Did</u> the movie <u>directed</u> by Steven Spielberg?

4. People in the audience <u>are eaten</u> popcorn.

5. The popcorn is fresh. It <u>is been popped</u> right now.

6. Popcorn <u>sells</u> in the lobby of the theater.

7. Before the movie, coming attractions <u>are show</u>.

8. At the end of the movie, we <u>were left</u> the theater and went home.

9. A lot of popcorn containers and candy wrappers <u>was left</u> on the floor of the theater.

10. Some movies <u>can be enjoy</u> by the whole family.

11. Tickets <u>can bought</u> online ahead of time.

12. What <u>was happened</u>? I can't find my ticket.

13. The theater is big. Fourteen movies <u>are shown</u> at the same time.

14. The movie is for adults. Children <u>don't permitted</u> to enter.

15. I <u>enjoyed</u> the movie. Did you?

16. Parking is free at the theater, but the parking pass <u>must be validated</u> in the theater.

17. Some movies should not <u>seen</u> by children.

18. Senior citizens <u>can get</u> a discount on tickets.

19. At the Oscar ceremony, the actors <u>are arrived</u> in limousines.

20. The actresses <u>wear</u> beautiful dresses.

PARKING PASS
Boston Parking Authority
Auto Park Garage
6th and Maple Streets
12/15   8:30 pm
Apply date/time stamp here

2.8 The Passive Voice with *Get*

EXAMPLES	EXPLANATION
Hollywood actors **get paid** a lot of money. I don't like violent movies. A lot of people **get shot** and **killed**.	In conversation, we sometimes use *get* instead of *be* with the passive. 　*get paid = be paid* 　*get shot = be shot* 　*get killed = be killed* We usually omit the agent after *get*. Compare: 　He **was shot** by a cowboy. 　He **got shot** three times.
How much **do** actors **get paid** for a movie? She **didn't get paid** last Friday.	When *get* is used with the passive voice, questions and negatives are formed with *do, does, did,* and other auxiliaries. *Be* is not used with *get*. 　*Wrong:* She *wasn't* get paid last Friday.
She **got hired** for the job. He **got laid off** last month.	*Get* is frequently used with: *shot, killed, injured, wounded, paid, hired, fired, laid off, picked, caught, done, sent, stolen.*

EXERCISE 12 **Fill in the blanks with *get* + the past participle of the verb in parentheses ( ). Choose an appropriate tense.**

EXAMPLE   Who _____*got chosen*_____ for the part in the movie?
　　　　　　　　　　　(choose)

1. Reagan _____ on the day of the Oscars.
　　　　　　(shoot)

2. No one _____.
　　　　　　(kill)

3. Did you _____ for the movie role?
　　　　　　(hire)

4. Famous actors _____ millions of dollars for a film.
　　　　　　　　　(pay)

5. His car _____ from in front of his house.
　　　　　(steal)

6. The little boy told a lie, and he _____.
　　　　　　　　　　　　　　　　(punish)

7. Everything will _____ little by little.
　　　　　　　　　(do)

8. The test scores _____ to the wrong person.
　　　　　　　　(send)

9. One student _____ cheating on the exam.
　　　　　　　(catch)

10. If you leave your car there, it might _____.
　　　　　　　　　　　　　　　　　　　(tow)

2.9 Participles Used as Adjectives

A present participle is verb + *-ing*. A past participle is the third form of the verb (usually *-ed* or *-en*). Both present participles and past participles can be used as adjectives.

EXAMPLES	EXPLANATION
We saw an **entertaining** movie. *Star Wars* is an **exciting** movie. *The Matrix* has **amazing** visual effects.	In these examples, a *present participle* is used as an adjective.
What's in the **sealed** envelope? I wasn't **bored** during the movie. Are you **interested** in action movies? Do you like **animated** films?	In these examples, a *past participle* is used as an adjective.

Charlie Chaplin

Before
You Read

1. Have you ever heard of Charlie Chaplin?

2. Have you ever seen a silent movie? Do you think a silent movie can be interesting today?

CD 1, TR 11

Read the following magazine article. Pay special attention to participles used as adjectives.

Charlie Chaplin was one of the greatest actors in the world. His **entertaining** silent movies are still popular today. His **amusing** character "Little Tramp" is well **known** to people throughout the world. Chaplin had an **amazing** life. His idea for this poor character in **worn**-out shoes, round hat, and cane probably came from his childhood experiences.

Born in poverty in London in 1889, Chaplin was abandoned by his father and left in an orphanage by his mother. He became **interested** in acting at the age of five. At ten, he left school to travel with a British acting company. In 1910, he made his first trip to America. He was **talented**, athletic, and **hardworking**, and by 1916 he was earning $10,000

Charlie Chaplin, 1889–1977

a week.[2] He was the highest-**paid** person in the world at that time. He produced, directed, and wrote the movies he starred in.

Even though "talkies" came out in 1927, he didn't make a movie with sound until 1940, when he played a comic version of the **terrifying** dictator, Adolf Hitler.

As Chaplin got older, he faced **declining** popularity as a result of his politics and personal relationships. After he left the U.S. in 1952, Chaplin was not allowed to re-enter because of his political views. He didn't return to the U.S. until 1972, when he was given a special Oscar for his lifetime of **outstanding** work.

2.10 Participles Used as Adjectives to Show Feelings

The participles of a verb can be used as adjectives.

Chaplin's movies <u>interest</u> us.

(verb)

Chaplin's movies are <u>interesting</u>.
(present participle)

We are <u>interested</u> in his movies.
(past participle)

EXAMPLES	EXPLANATION
The movie *bored* us. (*bored* = verb)	In some cases, both the present participle (a) and the past participle (b) of the same verb can be used as adjectives.
a. The movie was **boring**. I left the **boring** movie before it was over.	The present participle (a) gives an active meaning. The movie *actively* caused a feeling of boredom.
b. Some people were **bored**. The **bored** people got up and left.	The past participle (b) gives a passive meaning. It describes the receiver of a feeling. The people were bored by the movie.
Chaplin had an **interesting** life. He was poor and then became very rich. I am **interested** in Chaplin. I would like to know more about him. The main character in *Friday the 13th* is a **frightening** man. I was **frightened** and couldn't sleep after seeing the movie.	A person can cause a feeling in others or he can receive a feeling. Therefore, a person can be both *interesting* and *interested*, *frightening* and *frightened*, etc.
The book is **interesting**. The movie is **entertaining**.	An object (like a book or a movie) doesn't have feelings, so a past participle, such as *interested* or *entertained*, cannot be used to describe an object.

[2]In today's dollars, that amount would be close to $200,000 a week.

(continued)

Language Notes:

1. The following pictures show the difference between (a) a *frightening* man and (b) a *frightened* man.

a. The man is frightening the children. = He's a *frightening man*.

b. The man is frightened by the robber. = He's a *frightened man*.

2. Common paired participles are:

amazing	amazed	exhausting	exhausted
amusing	amused	frightening	frightened
annoying	annoyed	frustrating	frustrated
boring	bored	interesting	interested
confusing	confused	puzzling	puzzled
convincing	convinced	satisfying	satisfied
disappointing	disappointed	surprising	surprised
embarrassing	embarrassed	terrifying	terrified
exciting	excited	tiring	tired

EXERCISE 13 **Use the verb in each sentence to make two new sentences. In one sentence, use the present participle. In the other, use the past participle.**

EXAMPLE   The game entertains the children.

The game is entertaining.

The children are entertained.

1. The movie frightened the children.

_____

_____

2. The book interests the children.

_____

_____

3. The children are amusing the adults.

_____

_____

4. The trip tired the children.

_____

_____

5. The game excited the children.

_____

_____

6. The vacation exhausted the adults.

_____

_____

7. The movie bored the adults.

_____

_____

8. Chaplin interests me.

_____

_____

EXERCISE **14** **Fill in the blanks with the correct participle, present or past, of the verb in parentheses ( ).**

Last night my friend and I went to see a new movie. We thought it was ___boring___. It had a lot of stupid car chases, which
(example: bore)
were not _____ at all. And I didn't like the characters.
(1 excite)
They weren't very _____.
(2 convince)
We were pretty _____ because the reviewers said it was a
(3 disappoint)
good movie. They said it had _____ visual effects. But for
(4 amaze)
me, it wasn't _____ at all. I was _____ that I
(5 interest) (6 annoy)
wasted $10 and a whole evening for such a _____ movie.
(7 disappoint)
The only thing that was _____ was the popcorn.
(8 satisfy)

EXERCISE **15** **ABOUT YOU** **Fill in the blanks and discuss your answers.**

EXAMPLE I'm interested in ___sports___.

1. I'm interested in _____ movies.

2. Now I'm worried about _____.

3. In the past, I was worried about _____.

4. In my opinion, _____ is an amazing (choose one) actor / athlete / politician.

5. I'm not interested in _____.

6. I'm annoyed when people _____.

7. _____ is a boring subject for me.

8. I feel frustrated when _____.

9. I am amazed that _____ in the U.S.

10. It's not surprising that _____ in the U.S.

11. Sometimes I feel embarrassed when I _____

_____.

12. I was very excited when _____.

13. When I came to this school, I was surprised that _____

_____.

2.11 Other Past Participles Used as Adjectives

Some sentences look passive (*be* + past participle), but there is no action in the sentence. The past participles below are used as adjectives.

EXAMPLES	EXPLANATION
	In some cases, we are looking at the result of a previous action. We no longer care about the agent, and the action itself is not important.[3]
a. No one knows the winners' names because the envelope is **sealed**. b. Is this seat **taken**? c. Chaplin was **born** in England.	a. **Previous Action:** Someone *sealed* the envelope. b. **Previous Action:** Someone *took (occupied)* the seat. c. **Previous Action:** His mother *bore* a child.
d. The dress is **made** of silk. e. The door is **locked** now. f. He bought a **used** car.	d. **Previous Action:** The dress *was made* by someone. e. **Previous Action:** The door *was locked* by the janitor. f. **Previous Action:** The car *was used* by another owner.

[3]These forms are sometimes called "stative passives."

EXAMPLES	EXPLANATION
Many people are **involved** in making a movie. Hollywood is **located** in California. Is Geraldine Chaplin **related** to Charlie Chaplin? We are **done** with the video. When you are **finished** with the video, return it to the store. Is the theater **air-conditioned**? The theater was very **crowded**.	In some cases, we use a past participle as an adjective even though there is no previous action. The sentences to the left have no equivalent active form.
a. The glass is **broken**. b. Don't touch the **broken** glass. a. The child is **lost** in the park. b. Let's take the **lost** child to the park office. a. The child seems **tired**. b. Let's put the **tired** child to bed.	Past participles can be used: a. after *be* and other linking verbs (*seem, look, feel, sound,* etc.). OR b. before a noun.
Chaplin was a *well*-**known** actor. He was a *highly* **paid** actor.	To emphasize and further describe the adjectives used as past participles, an adverb can be added.

Language Notes:
1. Some phrases that contain an adverb + past participle are:

a well-liked teacher	a highly skilled worker
a well-educated person	a closely watched experiment
a well-behaved child	a slightly used book
a well-dressed woman	closely related languages
a well-fed dog	an extremely crowded room

2. The following are some common combinations of *be* + past participle:

be air-conditioned	be filled (with)	be married (to)
be accustomed (to)	be finished (with)	be permitted (to)
be allowed (to)	be gone	be pleased (to) (with) (by)
be born	be injured	be prepared (to) (for)
be broken	be insured	be related (to)
be closed	be interested (in)	be taken (*occupied*)
be concerned (about)	be involved (in)	be used
be crowded	be known (for) (as)	be used to
be divorced (from)	be located	be worried (about)
be done	be locked	be wounded
be dressed	be lost	
be educated	be made (of, in)	

EXERCISE **16** Underline the past participle in the following sentences.

EXAMPLE Movie theaters are <u>crowded</u> on Saturday night.

1. The movie theater is closed in the morning.
2. Where is the movie theater located?
3. How many people were involved in making *WALL-E*?
4. Children are not allowed to see some movies.
5. Many movies are made in Hollywood.
6. Ronald Reagan was involved in movies before he became a politician.
7. Chaplin was born in England.
8. He was not an educated man.
9. Chaplin was a well paid actor.
10. He was well known all over the world.
11. Charlie Chaplin was married several times.

EXERCISE **17** Find the mistakes and correct them. Not every sentence has a mistake. If the sentence is correct, write *C*.

EXAMPLES The theater ^is^ located near my house.

Are you interested in action movies? *C*

1. Is Halle Berry marry?

2. I'm concerned about the violence in movies.

3. Almost every seat in the theater is fill.

4. Is this seat taken?

5. How many people are involved in making a movie?

6. Walt Disney born in 1901.

7. When you're finish with the DVD, please return it to the video store.

8. Is the Oscar make of gold?

Being Famous

Before
You Read

1. In the U.S., movie stars get divorced a lot. Is this true in other countries?

2. Do you think being famous would be fun?

CD 1, TR 13

Read the following Web article. Pay special attention to *be* **and** *get* **before past participles and adjectives.**

http://www.hollywood*lives.com

Becoming a Hollywood star is a dream for many. Glamour, money, beauty, and even power make the occupation very attractive. However, the life of a Hollywood star can **be difficult** and **challenging,** both personally and professionally.

Hollywood stars **are known** for their short and frequent marriages—and divorces. Elizabeth Taylor

Elizabeth Taylor and Richard Burton

got married eight times. In fact, she married the same man (Richard Burton) twice—and divorced him twice. Britney Spears **got married** one day and **got divorced** the next day. But, of course, there are exceptions. Paul Newman and Joanne Woodward **were married** for 50 years, until Newman died. And Meryl Streep **has been married** to the same man for over 30 years.

Why is **being famous** so difficult? Some actors **get rich** overnight and don't handle their sudden wealth and fame easily. Life can **be difficult** in the public eye, when reporters record an actor's every moment. Also, Hollywood stars need to look great to stay on top. They do not like to **get old.** Many Hollywood stars use cosmetic surgery to look young. Many work out with a personal trainer because they don't want to **get fat** or out of shape.

(continued)

Some Hollywood actors go into politics when they **get tired** of acting. They use their popularity as actors to win elections. Ronald Reagan and Arnold Schwarzenegger both went from being actors to becoming governor of California. Ronald Reagan went on to become president of the U.S.[4] A famous wrestler, Jessie Ventura, even got to be governor of Minnesota.

Life in the public eye seems wonderful, but it can **be difficult** at times.

Schwarzenegger as actor

Schwarzenegger as governor

2.12 Past Participles and Other Adjectives with *Get*[5]

EXAMPLES	EXPLANATION
a. *Is* Julia Roberts **married**? b. When did she ***get* married**?	a. *Be* + past participle describes the status of a noun over a period of time.
a. The actress *is* **divorced**. b. She ***got* divorced** soon after she ***got* married**.	b. *Get* + past participle means *become*. There is no reference to the continuation of this status.
a. You're yawning. I see you *are* **tired**. b. When Arnold Schwarzenegger ***got* tired** of acting, he went into politics.	
a. Movie stars *are* **rich**. b. A lot of people would like to ***get* rich** quickly.	a. *Be* + adjective describes the status of a noun over a period of time.
a. My grandfather *is* **old**. b. Most stars don't want to ***get* old**. They want to look young forever.	b. *Get* + adjective means *become*.

Usage Note: Notice the difference between *to be married, to marry, to get married.*
Meryl Streep **is married**. She **has been married** to the same man for many years. (*Be married* describes one's status.)
She **married** Don Gummer in 1978. (The verb *marry* is followed by an object.)
Meryl and Don **got married** in 1978. (*Get married* is not followed by an object.)

---

[4]Schwarzenegger can't become president because he was not born in the U.S.
[5]For a list of expressions with *get*, see Appendix C.

Past Participles with *get*		Adjectives with *get*	
get accustomed to	get hurt	get angry	get old
get acquainted	get lost	get dark	get rich
get bored	get married	get fat	get sleepy
get confused	get scared	get hungry	get upset
get divorced	get tired	get nervous	get well
get dressed	get used to		
get worried			

EXERCISE **18** **Circle the correct words to complete this conversation between a young man and a young woman.**

CD 1, TR 14

A: Angelina Jolie is my favorite actress. When she (*was* /(*got*)) married,
(*example*)

I felt so sad. But then she (*was* / *got*) divorced just two years later,
(1)

I was so happy. But then, she started dating Brad Pitt.

B: Happy? Sad? Do you think Angelina (*is* / *gets*)
(2)

interested in you? She doesn't even know you!

A: I keep sending her letters. I would like to (*be* / *get*)
(3)

acquainted with her.

B: She's not going to answer your letters. She

(*is* / *gets*) too rich and famous to pay attention to you.
(4)

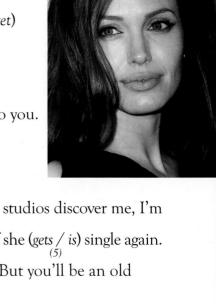

A: Well, I'm an actor too, you know.

B: Mostly you're just a waiter.

A: I'm not always going to be a waiter. When acting studios discover me, I'm

going to be famous, and Angelina will notice me if she (*gets* / *is*) single again.
(5)

B: Well, it's possible that she'll (*get* / *be*) divorced. But you'll be an old
(6)

man when, and if, you are famous.

A: That doesn't matter. Someday it will happen, and I'll meet Angelina.

B: By that time, she will (*be* / *get*) old and you won't be interested in
(7)

her anymore.

A: I'll always (*get* / *be*) interested in her. She's my one true love.
(8)

B: Oh, really? What does your girlfriend have to say about that?

A: I never talk to her about Angelina. One time I told her how much

I like Angelina, and she (*was* / *got*) angry.
(9)

B: I don't think your girlfriend has anything to worry about.

Summary of Lesson 2

1. Passive Voice

Passive Voice = *Be* + Past Participle	Use
With an agent: Mickey Mouse **was created** by Walt Disney. *Star Wars* **was directed** by George Lucas.	The passive voice can be used with an agent, especially if we want to emphasize the result of the action.
Without an agent: a. Hollywood **was built** at the beginning of the twentieth century. b. Children **are** not **allowed** to see some movies. c. The Oscar ceremony **is seen** all over the world. d. I **was told** that you didn't like the movie.	The passive voice is usually used without an agent: a. when it is not important to mention who performed the action b. when the agent is obvious c. when the agent is not a specific person but people in general d. to hide the identity of the agent **Note:** Do not mention the agent if it is not a specific person. *Wrong:* Spanish is spoken *by people* in Mexico.

Reagan **got shot** in 1981.
No one **got killed**. Some people **got wounded**.
	Get can be used instead of *be* in certain conversational expressions. Do not use *get* when the agent is mentioned.
	    Wrong: Reagan got shot *by John Hinckley*.
	    Right: Reagan **was** shot *by John Hinckley*.

2. Participles Used as Adjectives

Examples	Explanation
a. Silent movies are very **interesting**. b. The students are **interested** in the life of Charlie Chaplin.	Use the present participle (a) to show that the noun (silent movies) produced a feeling. Use the past participle (b) to show that the noun (the students) received a feeling.
The movie theater will be **closed** at midnight. Is this seat **taken**?	Use the past participle to show the result of a previous action. **Previous Actions:** Someone *will close* the theater. Someone *took* the seat.
The child is **lost**. The bus is **crowded**. Where is Hollywood **located**?	Some past participles are not related to a previous action.
She **got confused** when the teacher explained participles. I **got lost** on my way to your house. She **got upset** when she couldn't find her keys.	Use *get* with past participles and other adjectives to mean *become*.

Editing Advice

1. Use *be*, not *do / does / did* to make negatives and questions with the passive voice.

   wasn't
   My watch ~~didn't~~ made in Japan.

   was
   When ~~did~~ the movie filmed?

2. Don't use the passive voice with intransitive verbs.

   The accident ~~was~~ happened at 10:30 p.m.

   Her grandfather ~~was~~ died three years ago.

3. Don't confuse the *-ing* form with the past participle.

   eaten
   The popcorn was ~~eating~~ by the child.

4. Don't forget the *-ed* ending for a regular past participle.

   ed
   The floor was wash by the janitor.

   d
   I'm very tire now. I have to go to sleep.

5. Don't forget to use a form of *be* in a passive sentence.

   was
   The movie seen by everyone in my family.

6. Use *by* to show the agent of the action.

   by
   Tom Sawyer was written ~~for~~ Mark Twain.

7. Use an object pronoun after *by*.

   her
   My mother prepared the soup. The salad was prepared by ~~she~~ too.

8. In questions and negatives, use *do, does,* or *did* when you use *get* with the passive voice.

   Did
   ~~Were~~ you get fired from your job?

9. Don't forget to include a verb (usually *be*) before a participle used as an adjective.

           is

My college located on the corner of Broadway and Wilson Avenues.

         was

The movie boring, so we left.

10. Use *be*, not *do*, with past participles used as adjectives.

          isn't

My sister ~~doesn't~~ married.

   Are

~~Do~~ you bored in your math class?

Editing Quiz

Some of the shaded words and phrases have mistakes. Find the mistakes and correct them. If the shaded words are correct, write *C*.

     C

A: Did you ever see the movie *Titanic*? It was the most successful
   (example)

              made

    film ever make.
      (example)

B: I saw part of it. It was shown on my flight to the U.S. But I never
            (1)

    finished watching it because I fell asleep. It was a long and tiring
                             (2)

    flight. I was too exhaust to keep my eyes open.
           (3)

A: You were probably bore because you saw it on a tiny screen. It
              (4)   *(5)*

    should seen on a large screen or at a theater. It's such an interested
     (6)   *(7)*

    movie. It was direct for James Cameron.
        (8)   *(9)*

B: I've never heard of James Cameron. What else was he directed?
                            (10)

A: The *Terminator* movies. And *Avatar* was directed by he too. *Avatar* is
                          (11)   *(12)*

    a 3-D movie.

B: What's that? I've never heard of 3-D.

A: It's a movie with a lot of special effects. Special glasses are worn during
(13)
the movie, which make everything appear three-dimensional.

B: Wow! I'd like to see a movie like that.

A: I saw it in 3-D at a theater. I was eaten popcorn when the movie
(14)
was started and then, suddenly, I couldn't believe what I was seeing.
(15)

B: When did Avatar made?
(16)

A: In 2009.

B: Is it still in the movie theaters?

A: No, but the DVD can rented.
(17)

B: Can it be seeing in 3-D on DVD?
(18)

A: I don't know.

B: So, tell me. What was happened at the end of Titanic? Was the main
(19)   (20)
character died? Or did the man and woman get marry?
(21)   (22)   (23)

A: I'm not going to tell you the ending and spoil it for you. I have the

DVD. I've been watched it three times. Do you want to borrow it?
(24)

B: Thanks. I'd love to.

Lesson 2 Test/Review

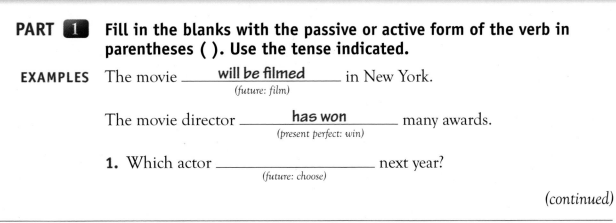

PART 1   **Fill in the blanks with the passive or active form of the verb in parentheses ( ). Use the tense indicated.**

EXAMPLES   The movie _____will be filmed_____ in New York.
(future: film)

The movie director _____has won_____ many awards.
(present perfect: win)

1. Which actor _____ next year?
(future: choose)

(continued)

2. Meryl Streep _____ in many movies.
       (present perfect: see)

3. My sister _____ popcorn during movies.
       (simple present: not/eat)

4. A new movie _____ about World War II.
       (present continuous: make)

5. I _____ the Oscar ceremony last year.
       (past: not/see)

6. The audience _____ the movie.
       (past: enjoy)

7. We _____ our tickets tomorrow.
       (future: buy)

8. Her parents _____ her to watch R-rated movies.
       (present: not/permit)

9. While the movie _____, one of the actors
       (past continuous: make)

_____.
(past: hurt)

10. *Star Wars* is a great movie. It _____ on a large
        (should/see)

screen, not on a TV screen.

11. Today's animation _____ on a computer. It
        (simple present: do)

_____ by hand.
(simple present: not/draw)

12. Charlie Chaplin _____ interested in acting at
        (past: become)

the age of five.

13. Chaplin _____ the U.S. in 1952 and
        (past: leave)

_____ in 1972.
(past: return)

14. President Lincoln _____ while he
        (past: shoot)

_____ a play. He _____ a few
(past continuous: watch)   *(past: die)*

days later. The killer _____.
                       (past: catch)

PART 2 The following sentences would be better in the passive voice. Change to the passive voice using the same tense as the underlined verbs. Do not mention the agent.

EXAMPLE   They <u>considered</u> Charlie Chaplin a great actor.
Charlie Chaplin was considered a great actor.

1. They <u>use</u> subtitles for foreign movies.

   _____

2. They <u>don't permit</u> children to see this movie.

   _____

3. When <u>did</u> they <u>build</u> this theater?

   _____

4. Someone <u>is cleaning</u> the theater now.

   _____

5. Someone <u>has left</u> a popcorn box on the floor.

   _____

6. Someone <u>will make</u> a movie about Chaplin's life.

   _____

7. When <u>is</u> someone <u>going to close</u> the theater?

   _____

PART 3 The following sentences would be better in the active voice. Change to the active voice using the same tense as the underlined verbs.

EXAMPLE   The movie <u>has been seen</u> by my whole family.
My whole family has seen the movie.

1. I <u>will be driven</u> to the theater by my sister.

   _____

2. The movie <u>wasn't seen</u> by me.

   _____

3. The movie <u>is being filmed</u> by George Lucas.

   _____

4. A decision <u>should be made</u> by the director.

   _____

5. A new costume <u>is needed</u> by the actor.

   _____

(continued)

6. <u>Were</u> you <u>met</u> at the theater by your friend?

_____

7. When <u>was</u> the DVD <u>broken</u> by the child?

_____

PART 4 **Fill in the blanks with the present participle or the past participle of the verb in parentheses ( ).**

EXAMPLES   The movie was very good. It wasn't __**boring**__ at all.
(bore)

I liked the ending of the movie. I felt very __**satisfied**__ with the ending.
(satisfy)

1. We read an _____ story about Charlie Chaplin.
(interest)

2. He became _____ in acting when he was a child.
(interest)

3. He was well _____ all over the world.
(know)

4. When he left the U.S. in 1952, he was not _____ to re-enter.
(allow)

5. Chaplin was _____ four times.
(marry)

6. He was an _____ actor.
(entertain)

7. I am never _____ during one of his movies.
(bore)

8. There's an _____ new movie at the Fine Arts Theater.
(excite)

9. Are you _____ in seeing it with me?
(interest)

10. The movie theater is _____ on Saturday night.
(crowd)

11. I was _____ when I saw _Friday the 13th_.
(frighten)

12. It was a very _____ movie.
(frighten)

13. I didn't like the movie I saw last week. I was very _____ in it.
(disappoint)

14. My friend liked the movie. He thought it was a very

_____ movie.
(excite)

Expansion

❶ Tell if these statements are true in your native country. Form a small group and discuss your answers in your group.

1. Popcorn is sold in movie theaters.
2. Movie tickets can be bought on the Internet.
3. Most people have a DVD player and watch movies at home.
4. Musicals are popular.
5. Many movies are shown in the same theater at the same time.
6. Movie tickets are expensive.
7. Senior citizens pay less money to enter a movie theater.
8. Children are not allowed to see some movies.
9. Actors are well-paid.
10. Many famous actors get divorced.
11. Actors are given awards for great performances.
12. Animated films are popular.

❷ Make a list of the movies you've seen recently. Compare your list with another student's list.

Talk
About It

❶ Is it important to give awards to actors and actresses? Why or why not?

❷ Have you ever seen an Academy Awards ceremony? What did you think of it?

❸ How are American films different from films made in other countries?

❹ Who are your favorite actors and actresses?

❺ What American movies have been popular in your native country?

Write
About It

1 Write about an entertainment event that you have recently attended (such as a movie in a theater, a concert, an art fair, or a museum exhibit). Did you enjoy it? Why or why not? Was there anything surprising or unusual about it?

2 Write a short summary of a movie you saw recently.

3 Write about a famous person you admire. Give a short biography of this person and tell why you admire him or her.

EXAMPLE

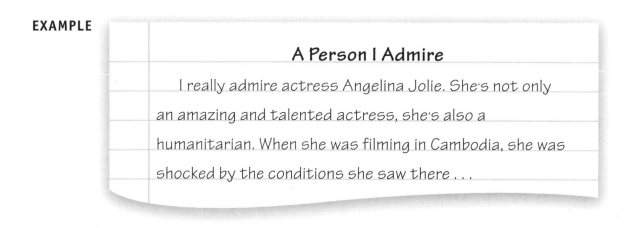

A Person I Admire

I really admire actress Angelina Jolie. She's not only an amazing and talented actress, she's also a humanitarian. When she was filming in Cambodia, she was shocked by the conditions she saw there . . .

For more practice using grammar in context, please visit our Web site.

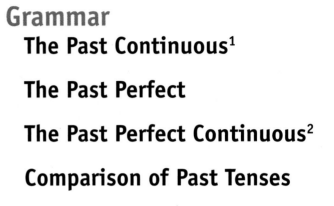

Grammar

The Past Continuous[1]

The Past Perfect

The Past Perfect Continuous[2]

Comparison of Past Tenses

Context

Disasters and Tragedies

[1]The past continuous is sometimes called the *past progressive*.
[2]The past perfect continuous is sometimes called the *past perfect progressive*.

3.1 Overview of Past Tenses

In this lesson, we will be looking at all the past tenses.

TENSE	EXAMPLES
Simple Past Tense	She **drove** to her sister's house last night.
Past Continuous	She **was driving** when the accident happened.
Present Perfect	She **has driven** there many times.
Present Perfect Continuous	She **has been driving** since she was 18 years old.
Past Perfect	She knew the road well because she **had driven** it many times.
Past Perfect Continuous	She **had been driving** for three hours when the accident happened.

The *Columbia* Tragedy

Before
You Read

1. What well-known accidents do you remember from history?

2. Do you remember what you were doing when a famous event occurred?

CD 1, TR 15

Read the following textbook article. Pay special attention to the past continuous and the simple past tense verbs.

Did You Know?

The Columbia was the first reusable space vehicle. Before the Columbia, manned space flight had been limited to rockets, which could only be used once, making the space program much more expensive.

On January 16, 2003, the space shuttle *Columbia* **left** on a science mission orbiting the Earth, with seven crew members aboard. It **stayed** in space for 16 days. On February 1, 2003, it **was traveling** back to Earth after completing its mission. NASA (the National Aeronautics and Space Administration) **received** its last communication from the *Columbia* on February 1, 2003, at 9:00 A.M. While the *Columbia* **was flying** over east Texas just 16 minutes from its landing in Florida, it **disintegrated**.[3] Families who **were** happily **waiting** for the return of their relatives at the Kennedy Space Center in Florida **received** the tragic news. People all over the world **were** shocked and saddened by this tragic loss of lives.

NASA **studied** the causes of this disaster. The investigation **concluded** that a piece of the left wing **fell** off as the *Columbia* **was lifting off**. This **created** a hole in the wing, and super-hot gases **entered** the wing's interior. As the *Columbia* **was approaching** its final destination, its left wing **burned**.

[3]*To disintegrate* means to break into small pieces.

The *Columbia* **was** the United States' second major disaster in space. The first one **was** in January 1986, when the space shuttle *Challenger* **exploded** 73 seconds after liftoff, killing all seven crew members.

NASA **was going to send** another manned rocket into space in March 2003, but this mission **was** postponed. Safety issues **needed** to be studied before another mission could take place. The next manned mission **didn't take place** until 2005.

1957	The USSR[4] puts the first satellite in space to orbit the Earth.
1961	The USSR puts the first man into space.
1966	The USSR lands a spacecraft on the moon.
1969	The first astronauts walk on the moon (Americans).
1970s and 1980s	The USSR and the U.S. explore Venus, Mars, Jupiter, and Saturn in fly-bys.
1986	The USSR launches the space station *Mir*.
1986	The U.S. spacecraft *Challenger* explodes shortly after liftoff. All seven crew members die.
1995	U.S. astronauts meet Russian cosmonauts at space station *Mir*.
2003	Seven U.S. astronauts are killed in the *Columbia* shuttle disaster.
2004	The U.S. lands a spacecraft on Mars.
2005	The U.S. sends seven astronauts into space in the spacecraft *Discovery*.

[4]The USSR no longer exists as a country. In 1991, it broke up into 15 countries, the largest of which is Russia.

3.2 The Past Continuous Tense—Forms

Statements

Subject	Was/Were	Present Participle	Complement	Explanation
I She He It The rocket	**was**	**traveling**	fast.	To form the past continuous tense, use *was* or *were* + present participle (verb + *-ing*).
We You They The astronauts	**were**			

Language Notes:
1. To make the negative, put *not* between *was/were* and the present participle.
   > I **was** *not* **living** in the U.S. in January 2003.
   > Americans **were** *not* **expecting** this tragedy.
2. The contraction for *were not* is *weren't*. The contraction for *was not* is *wasn't*.
3. An adverb can be placed between *was/were* and the present participle.
   > You **were** *probably* **watching** the news.

Questions and Short Answers

Question Word	Was/Wasn't Were/Weren't	Subject	Present Participle	Complement	Short Answer
	Was	the rocket	**traveling**	fast?	Yes, it **was**.
How fast	**was**	it	**traveling**?		
	Weren't	they	**flying**	over Florida?	No, they **weren't**.
Where	**were**	they	**flying**?		
	Were	you	**watching**	it on TV?	No, I **wasn't**.
Why	**weren't**	you	**watching**	it on TV?	
Who	**was**		**watching**	it on TV?	

Passive

Subject	Was/Were	Being	Past Participle	Complement
The landing	**was**	**being**	**filmed**.	
Experiments	**were**	**being**	**done**	in space.

EXERCISE 1 Fill in the blanks with the correct form of the verb in parentheses ( ). Use the past continuous tense.

EXAMPLE The *Columbia* __was approaching__ Florida.
(approach)

1. Family members _____.
   (wait)

2. The *Columbia* _____ over Texas.
   (travel)

3. It _____ over Florida.
   (not/travel)

4. It _____ to Earth after a successful mission.
   (return)

5. The astronauts _____ forward to seeing their families.
   (look)

6. Reporters _____ to interview the astronauts.
   (prepare)

7. How many people _____?
   (wait)

8. Where _____?
   (they/wait)

3.3 The Past Continuous Tense—Uses

EXAMPLES	EXPLANATION
What **were** you **doing** at 9:00 A.M. on February 1, 2003? 　I **was watching** TV. 　My brother **was sleeping**.	The past continuous tense is used to show that an action was in progress at a specific past time. It didn't begin at that time.
The *Columbia* **disintegrated** while it **was traveling** back to the Earth. Family members **were waiting** in Florida when the *Columbia* accident **happened**. The *Columbia* **was approaching** the Earth when it **lost** communication with NASA.	We use the past continuous tense together with the simple past tense to show the relationship of a longer past action to a shorter past action.
While the astronauts **were orbiting** the Earth, they **were doing** scientific studies. While the *Columbia* **was approaching** its Florida destination, family members **were waiting** for the astronauts.	The past continuous can be used in both clauses to show that two past actions were in progress at the same time.

(continued)

EXAMPLES	EXPLANATION
Compare *when* and *while*. a. **While** the *Columbia* **was flying** over Texas, it disintegrated. b. The *Columbia* was flying over Texas **when** it **disintegrated**.	The meaning of sentences (a) and (b) is basically the same. a. *While* is used with a past continuous verb (*was flying*). In conversation, many people use *when* in place of *while*. b. *When* is used with the simple past tense (*disintegrated*).
As the *Columbia* was approaching its final destination, its left wing burned. **While** the *Columbia* was approaching its final destination, its left wing burned.	*As* and *while* have the same meaning.
The astronauts **were going to** return with scientific data. Family members **were going to** celebrate with the astronauts. NASA **was going to** send astronauts into space in March 2003, but this mission was postponed.	*Was/were going to* means that a past plan was not carried out.

Punctuation Note:
If the time clause precedes the main clause, separate the two clauses with a comma.
    The *Columbia* was flying over Texas when it disintegrated. (No comma)
    When the *Columbia* disintegrated, it was flying over Texas. (Comma)

EXERCISE **2**   **ABOUT YOU** **Ask and answer. Ask the student next to you what he or she was doing at this particular time.**

EXAMPLE   at 4 A.M.

    A: What were you doing at 4 A.M.?
    B: I was sleeping, of course.

    1. at ten o'clock last night

    2. at seven o'clock this morning

    3. at two o'clock last night

    4. when the teacher entered the classroom today

    5. at _____ (*your choice of time*)

    6. while the teacher was explaining the past continuous

EXERCISE 3 **Fill in the blanks with the simple past or the past continuous form of the verb in parentheses ( ).**

EXAMPLE We ___**were watching**___ cartoons on TV when we
(watch)

___**heard**___ the bad news.
(hear)

1. While the *Columbia* _____ to Earth, it
(return)

_____.
(disintegrate)

2. My sister _____ when I _____ her
(sleep) (wake)

up to tell her about the accident.

3. When my father _____ about the accident,
(hear)

he _____ to work.
(drive)

4. My brother _____ a TV program when the disaster
(watch)

_____.
(happen)

5. While the *Columbia* _____ to Earth, family
(return)

members _____ in Florida.
(wait)

6. What _____ when the accident
(you/do)

_____?
(happen)

7. The *Challenger* _____ off when it
(lift)

_____ in 1986.
(explode)

8. Many people _____ the *Challenger* liftoff when the
(watch)

accident _____.
(occur)

The Past Continuous; The Past Perfect; The Past Perfect Continuous; Comparison of Past Tenses   103

3.4 The Past Continuous or the Simple Past

EXAMPLES	EXPLANATION

Compare:
a. What **were** you **doing** when you heard the news?
    I **was watching** TV.
b. What **did** you **do** when you heard the news?
    I **called** my sister.
 	
a. She **was driving** to work when she had an accident.
b. She **called** the police when she had an accident.
	a. Use the past continuous to show what was in progress *at* the time a specific action occurred.
	
	b. Use the simple past to show what happened *after* a specific action occurred.

a. On February 1, 2003, relatives **were waiting** in Florida for the astronauts. They **were getting** ready to celebrate. Camera crews **were preparing** to take pictures of the landing. Suddenly, at 9:00 A.M., just minutes before the landing, NASA lost communication with the *Columbia*. b. A NASA official **announced** the tragedy to the public. The president **went** on TV to express his sadness. NASA **began** an investigation of the accident. Investigators **went** to Texas to talk with witnesses.	a. Use the past continuous to show the events *leading up to* the main event of the story (the accident). b. Use the simple past tense to tell what happened *after* the main event of the story (the accident).

EXERCISE **4** **Fill in the blanks to complete these conversations.**

CD 1, TR 16

1. *A reporter is interviewing a family in Texas after the Columbia disaster.*

A: What ___were you doing___ at 9 A.M. on February 1, 2003?
        (example: you/do)

B: I _____. A loud noise _____
      (1 sleep)   *(2 wake)*

me up. I _____ out of bed and
            (3 jump)

_____ outside. I saw my husband outside.
   (4 run)

He _____ our car. We thought it was an earthquake.
       (5 fix)

Then we _____ pieces of metal on our property.
            (6 see)

I _____ to pick up a piece, but my husband told me
   (7 go)

not to. Instead we _____ the police. They told us not
                      (8 call)

to touch anything.

2. *A reporter is interviewing a member of NASA after the Columbia disaster.*

A: How fast _____ when the accident
　　　　　　　　　(9 the Columbia/travel)

_____?
　(10 happen)

B: It _____ at 12,500 m.p.h. We
　　　　(11 travel)

_____ with the *Columbia* when, suddenly,
　(12 communicate)

communication _____.
　　　　　　　　　　(13 stop)

A: What _____ when you _____
　　　　　　(14 you/do)　　　　　　　　　　　　(15 realize)

that the crew members were lost?

B: We _____ the family members and the press.
　　　　(16 notify)

Many of the family members _____ at the Kennedy
　　　　　　　　　　　　　　　　(17 wait)

Space Center in Florida when the accident _____.
　　　　　　　　　　　　　　　　　　　　　　(18 happen)

A: What _____ after that?
　　　　　(19 happen)

B: An investigation _____. We
　　　　　　　　　　　(20 begin)

_____ to look for the pieces of the shuttle and
　(21 start)

_____ to understand the reason for the accident.
　(22 try)

A: _____ all the pieces?
　　(23 you/find)

B: No, of course not. Many of the people of East Texas

_____ to tell us about finding pieces on their land.
　(24 call)

Hunters _____ to tell us that while they
　　　　　(25 call)

_____ in forests, they _____
　(26 hunt)　　　　　　　　　　　　　　　(27 find)

pieces of metal. We _____ enough pieces to come to
　　　　　　　　　　　(28 find)

a conclusion about the cause of the accident.

EXERCISE 5 Fill in the blanks with the simple past or the past continuous tense of the verb in parentheses ( ).

EXAMPLES I ___was walking___ to school when I ___saw___ a car
(walk)   (see)

accident. The police ___came___ and ___gave___
(come)   (give)

a ticket to one of the drivers.

1. I _____ ready for bed when someone
(get)

_____ to my door. I _____ the door
(come)   (open)

and saw my neighbor. He _____ in front of me with a
(stand)

DVD in his hand. He said, "I just rented a movie. Would you like to

watch it with me?" I didn't want to be impolite, so I said yes. While we

_____ the movie, I _____ asleep.
(watch)   (fall)

2. While the baby _____, the babysitter
(sleep)

_____ TV. Suddenly the baby _____
(watch)   (start)

to cry, and the babysitter _____ into the room to see
(run)

what had happened. She _____ up the baby and
(pick)

started to rock her. Then she _____ her back to bed.
(put)

3. When I _____ home, my sister and brothers
(get)

_____ TV. I said, "I'm hungry. Let's eat." But they
(watch)

_____ off the TV. I _____ to cook
(not/turn)   (start)

dinner. They all _____ into the kitchen to see what I
(come)

_____.
(cook)

4. She _____ to the radio while she
(listen)

_____ on the computer. Suddenly she
(work)

_____ the news of a terrible accident. She
(hear)

_____ to the TV to find out more information.
(go)

5. While Sam _____, his cell phone
(drive)

_____. He _____ on his phone
(ring)   (talk)

when he _____ a car accident. He
(have)

_____ a light post. Fortunately, he
(hit)

_____ his seatbelt, so he wasn't hurt.
(wear)

6. When the storm _____ last night, we
(begin)

_____ a scary movie. The lights went out, so we
(watch)

_____ to use candles. While I _____
(have)   (look)

for matches and candles, my little brother suddenly

_____ the room with a flashlight and a scary mask.
(enter)

He really _____ me.
(scare)

7. While I _____ for my gloves in a drawer, I
(look)

_____ an old photograph of myself. In this photo, I
(find)

_____ a silly looking bathing suit. I can't even
(wear)

remember who _____ the picture.
(take)

8. I _____ my composition on the computer when
(type)

suddenly we _____ electrical power. When the power
(lose)

_____ back on, I _____ on the
(come)   (turn)

computer, but all my work was gone. I know how important it is to

save my work. I _____ to save it on my flash drive,
(go)

but I couldn't find it. So I _____ everything and
(lose)

_____ to start all over.
(have)

The Past Continuous; The Past Perfect; The Past Perfect Continuous; Comparison of Past Tenses   **107**

The *Titanic*

Before You Read

1. Have you ever traveled by ship? Where did you go? What was the trip like?

2. Did you see the 1997 movie *Titanic*? If so, did you enjoy it? Why or why not?

CD 1, TR 17

Read the following textbook article. Pay special attention to the past perfect tense.

Did You **Know?**

Only four female passengers in first class died. (These women chose to stay with their husbands.) Almost half of the female passengers in third class died.

The year was 1912. The radio **had** already **been invented** in 1901. The Wright brothers **had** already **made** their first successful flight in 1903. The *Titanic*—the ship of dreams—**had** just **been built** and was ready to make its first voyage from England to America with its 2,200 passengers.

The *Titanic* was the most magnificent ship that **had** ever **been built**. It had luxuries that ships **had** never **had** before: electric light and heat, electric elevators, a swimming pool, a Turkish bath, libraries, and much more. It was built to give its first-class passengers all the comforts of the best hotels.

But rich passengers were not the only ones traveling on the *Titanic*. Most of the passengers in third class were emigrants who **had left** behind a complete way of life and were coming to America with hopes of a better life.

The *Titanic* began to cross the Atlantic Ocean on April 10. The winter of 1912 **had been** unusually mild, and large blocks of ice **had broken** away from the Arctic region. By the fifth day at sea, the captain **had received** several warnings about ice, but he was not very worried; he didn't realize how much danger the ship was in. On April 14, at 11:40 P.M., an iceberg was spotted[5] straight ahead. The captain tried to reverse the direction of his ship, but he couldn't because the *Titanic* was traveling too fast and it was too big. It hit the iceberg and started to sink.

The *Titanic* **had** originally **had** 32 lifeboats, but 12 of them **had been removed** to make the ship look better. While the ship was sinking, rich people were put on lifeboats. Women and children were put on the lifeboats before men. By the time the third-class passengers were allowed to come up from their cabins, most of the lifeboats **had** already **left**.

Several hours later, another ship arrived to help, but the *Titanic* **had** already **gone** down. Only one-third of the passengers survived.

[5]*To spot means to see suddenly.*

3.5 The Past Perfect Tense—Forms

Statements

Subject	*Had*	*Not /* Adverb	Past Participle	Complement	Explanation
The captain	**had**		**received**	several warnings.	To form the past perfect, use *had* + past participle.
He	**had**	not	**paid**	attention.	
The winter	**had**		**been**	unusually mild.	
The ship	**had**	originally	**had**	32 lifeboats.	
Some passengers	**had**	never	**been**	on a ship before.	

Language Notes:
1. The pronouns (except *it*) can be contracted with *had*: *I'd, you'd, she'd, he'd, we'd, they'd.*
   He'd received several warnings.
2. Apostrophe + *d* can be a contraction for both *had* or *would*. The verb form following the contraction will tell you what the contraction means.
   He'd spoken. = He *had* spoken.
   He'd speak. = He *would* speak.
3. For a negative contraction, use *hadn't*.
   He **hadn't** paid attention.
4. For an alphabetical list of irregular past tenses and past participles, see Appendix M.

Questions and Short Answers

Question Word	*Had*	Subject	Past Participle	Complement	Short Answer
	Had	the *Titanic*	**crossed**	the ocean before?	No, it **hadn't**.
How much experience	had	the captain	**had**?		
Who	had		**heard**	of the *Titanic* before?	

(continued)

Passive

Subject	*Had*	Adverb	*Been*	Past Participle
Lifeboats	had		been	removed.
Many passengers	had	never	been	found.
The airplane	had	already	been	invented.

EXERCISE **6** **Fill in the blanks with the past perfect tense of the verb in parentheses ( ) plus any other included words.**

EXAMPLE When we read about the *Titanic*, the story was not new to me because I

_____ had seen _____ the movie.
        (see)

1. The captain of the *Titanic* _____
                                (make)

a serious mistake when he didn't listen to the warnings.

2. When the *Titanic* disaster occurred, how much experience

_____?
                         (the captain/have)

3. I didn't realize that airplanes _____
                             (passive: invent)

by the time of the *Titanic*.

4. In 1912, World War I _____.
                      (not/yet/begin)

5. The story about the *Titanic* was new to me because I

_____ an article about it before.
           (never/read)

6. _____ this story
             (you/already/hear)

before we read about it in class?

7. How many lifeboats _____?
                 (have/the Titanic/originally)

8. Why _____?
           (they/passive: remove)

3.6 The Past Perfect Tense—Use

The past perfect tense is used with the simple past tense to show the relationship of two past events.

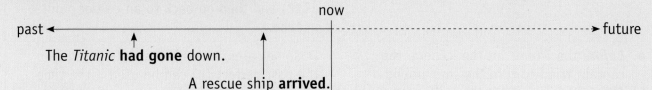

EXAMPLES	EXPLANATION
By the time the rescue ship **arrived**, the *Titanic* **had** already **gone** down. By **1912**, the Wright brothers **had** already **invented** the airplane.	The past perfect is used to show that something happened before a specific date, time, or action.
When people **got** on the lifeboats, the rescue ship **hadn't arrived yet.** **When** the rescue ship **arrived**, many passengers **had already died.**	The past perfect is used to show that something happened or didn't happen before the verb in the *when* clause. *Yet* and *already* help show the time relationship.
There was a lot of ice in the water **because** the previous winter **had been** unusually mild. I knew about the *Titanic* **because** I **had seen** a movie about it.	The past perfect can be used after *because* to show a prior reason.
The captain **didn't realize** how close his ship **had come** to the iceberg. I **didn't know** that you **had seen** a movie about the *Titanic*.	The past perfect can be used in a noun clause[6] when the main verb is past.
The passengers in third class were emigrants **who had left** behind their old way of life. The *Titanic* was the most magnificent ship **that had ever been built.**	The past perfect can be used in a *who/that/which* clause to show a prior action. The past perfect is sometimes used with *ever* after a superlative form.
When they **began** their trip to America, many emigrants on the *Titanic* **had never left** their homelands **before.**	The past perfect can be used with *never . . . before* in relation to a past event (in this case, *they began their trip*).
The ship **had been** at sea **for five days** when it hit an iceberg.	The past perfect can be used with *for* + a time period to show the duration of an earlier past action.

[6]For more about noun clauses, see Lesson 9.

(*continued*)

EXAMPLES	EXPLANATION
The year of the *Titanic* disaster **was** *1912*. The airplane **had** already **been invented**.	The simple past and the past perfect do not have to occur in the same sentence. We can start at some point in time (in this case, 1912) and then go back to an earlier point in time.
a. *Before* the *Titanic* hit the iceberg, the captain **tried** to turn the ship around. b. *Before* the *Titanic* hit the iceberg, the captain **had tried** to turn the ship around. a. The captain *realized* that he **made** a mistake. b. The captain *realized* that he **had made** a mistake.	In some cases, either the simple past (a) or the past perfect (b) can be used if the time relationship is clear. This is especially true with *before, after, because,* and in a noun clause (after *knew, realized, understood,* etc.).

EXERCISE 7 Fill in the blanks with the simple past or the past perfect tense of the verb in parentheses ( ).

EXAMPLE   The *Titanic* had luxuries that ships ___had never had___ before.
(never/have)

1. By 1912, the radio _____.
(passive: already/invent)

2. The *Titanic* was the biggest ship that _____.
(passive: ever/build)

3. The *Titanic* _____ 32 lifeboats.
(originally/have)

4. When the *Titanic* _____ England, many of the
(leave)

lifeboats _____.
(passive: remove)

5. By April 1912, pieces of ice _____ away from
(break)

the Arctic region.

6. The captain of the *Titanic* _____ attention
(not/pay)

to the warnings he _____.
(receive)

7. When the *Titanic* _____ an iceberg, it
(hit)

_____ at sea for five days.
(be)

8. By the time the poor emigrants _____ allowed to come
(be)

up from their cabins, most of the lifeboats _____.
(already/leave)

9. By the time the rescue ship _____ ,
(arrive)

the *Titanic* _____ .
(already/sink)

EXERCISE 8 **ABOUT YOU** Tell if the following had already happened or hadn't happened yet by the time you got to class.

EXAMPLE the teacher / collect the homework
By the time I got to class, the teacher had already collected the homework.

OR

When I got to class, the teacher hadn't collected the homework yet.

1. the teacher / arrive

2. most of the students / arrive

3. the class / begin

4. the teacher / take attendance

5. I / do the homework

6. the teacher / hand back the last homework

7. the teacher / explain the past perfect

EXERCISE 9 Fill in the blanks with the simple past or the past perfect tense of the verb in parentheses ( ).

EXAMPLE By the time the U.S. _____ **sent** _____ a man into space (1962),
(send)

the Russians _____ **had already put** _____ a man in space (1961).
(already/put)

1. When an American astronaut _____ on the moon in
(step)

1969, no person _____ on the moon before.
(ever/walk)

2. By 2003, NASA _____ hundreds of successful
(complete)

space flights.

3. When the *Columbia* mission took off in 2003, NASA

_____ only two serious accidents in its space program.
(have)

4. By the time the 16 days were up, the *Columbia* crew

_____ all its scientific experiments.
(do)

(continued)

The Past Continuous; The Past Perfect; The Past Perfect Continuous; Comparison of Past Tenses   113

5. Until 9 A.M. on February 1, 2003, NASA _____ good
(have)

communication with the *Columbia*.

6. At first, NASA couldn't understand what _____.
(happen)

7. When they lost communication with the *Columbia*, they were

afraid that all of the astronauts _____.
(die)

8. The original date for the *Columbia* mission was July 2002. The date

was postponed until 2003 because cracks in the fuel line

_____.
(passive: find)

9. NASA _____ that the *Columbia*
(know)

_____ a piece of its wing on liftoff, but they didn't
(lose)

think it would be a problem.

10. They _____ that this problem
(not/realize)

_____ a hole in the wing.
(create)

11. By the time the investigation _____ in April 2003,
(end)

NASA _____ 40 percent of the pieces of the *Columbia*.
(collect)

12. By the time the U.S. _____ a mission to Mars, the
(send)

reasons for the *Columbia* accident _____.
(already/passive: discover)

3.7 *When* with the Simple Past or the Past Perfect

Sometimes *when* means *after*. Sometimes *when* means *before*.

EXAMPLES	EXPLANATION
a. **When** the captain saw the iceberg, he **tried** to turn the ship around. b. **When** the captain saw the iceberg, the ship **had been** at sea for five days.	If you use the simple past in the main clause (a), *when* means **after**. If you use the past perfect in the main clause (b), *when*
a. **When** the *Columbia* lifted off, it **lost** a piece of its wing. b. **When** the *Columbia* lifted off in January 2003, it **had had** 27 successful missions.	means **before**.

EXERCISE 10   **Write numbers to show which action happened first.**

                                  1   2

EXAMPLES   When she got home, she took an aspirin.

                                  2   1

When she got home, she had already taken an aspirin.

1. When they came into the room, their son left.

2. When they came into the room, their son had just left.

3. When I got home from school, I did my homework.

4. When I got home from school, I had already done my homework.

5. When she got to my house, she had eaten dinner.

6. When she got to my house, she ate dinner.

7. The teacher gave a test when Linda arrived.

8. The teacher had already given a test when Linda arrived.

EXERCISE 11   **Fill in the blanks with the verb in parentheses ( ). Use the simple past to show that *when* means *after*. Use the past perfect to show that *when* means *before*.**

EXAMPLES   When I saw the movie *Titanic*, I _____**told**_____ my friends about it.
                                                       (tell)

When I saw the movie *Titanic*, I ___**had never heard**___ of this ship before.
                                                (never/hear)

1. When people saw the *Titanic* for the first time, they

           _____ such a magnificent ship before.
               (never/see)

2. When the ship was built, people _____ amazed at how
                                    (be)

    beautiful it was.

3. When the ship left England, 12 lifeboats _____.
                                         (passive: remove)

4. When the Arctic ice started to melt, pieces of ice

           _____ away.
               (break)

5. When the ship hit an iceberg, the captain _____
                                             (receive)

    several warnings.

(continued)

6. When the passengers heard a loud noise, they _____
(run)

to get on the lifeboats.

7. When the *Titanic* sank, a rescue ship _____ to pick
(come)

up the survivors.

8. When the rescue ship arrived, many passengers

_____.
(already/die)

9. When the *Columbia* accident happened, the astronauts

_____ in space for 16 days.
(be)

10. When people in East Texas heard a loud sound, they

_____ it was an earthquake.
(think)

11. When the *Columbia* accident happened, people

_____ shocked.
(be)

12. When relatives of the astronauts heard the news, they

_____ to cry.
(start)

13. When they were in their fields, farmers in East Texas found pieces

of the *Columbia* that _____ on their land.
(fall)

14. When the investigation into the cause of the accident was finished,

NASA _____ to send astronauts into space again.
(begin)

Wildfires in Southern California

Before You Read

1. Do you know about any fires that burned for a long time?

2. Do you know anyone who has lost a home because of a natural disaster?

CD 1, TR 18

Read the following magazine article. Pay special attention to the past perfect and the past perfect continuous tenses.

In October 2003, wildfires in San Diego County burned out of control. Many residents had to leave their homes as they were warned of the approaching fire. They watched and waited as firefighters battled the fire.

One of the fires was started accidentally by a lost hunter in a forest, who **had been trying** to signal his location. Strong winds spread the fire quickly. The San Diego area **had had** very little rain or humidity, and there were millions of dry dead trees that caught fire quickly.

The fire **had been burning** for a week by the time firefighters got it under control. Many residents returned only to find that they **had lost** their homes and all their possessions. "We **had been living** in the same house for the past 26 years when we lost our home," said a San Diego woman, whose family went to stay with relatives nearby. "Now we have nothing, not even a photograph of our former lives."

Many of the firefighters were exhausted because they **had been working** around the clock to get the fire under control. Firefighters from other areas in the U.S. came to help contain the fire. By the time the fire was brought under control, over 2,400 homes and businesses **had been destroyed** and 16 people **had died**.

Did You Know?

California has had many wildfires. Some of the California fires started from natural causes, such as lightning. But it is believed that the 2009 fires, which destroyed 64 homes and killed two firefighters, were started by arson.

3.8 The Past Perfect Continuous Tense—Forms

Statements

Subject	Had	Not / Adverb	Been	Present Participle	Complement	Explanation
We	had		been	living	in the same house.	To form the past perfect continuous tense, use: *had* + *been* + verb *–ing*.
Firefighters	had		been	working	around the clock.	
California	had	not	been	getting	much rain.	
A hunter	had	probably	been	trying	to send a signal.	

Questions and Short Answers

Question Word	Had	Subject	Been	Present Participle	Complement	Short Answer
	Had	it	been	raining?		No, it **hadn't**.
How long	had	the fire	been	burning?		
	Had	you	been	living	in that house?	Yes, we **had**.
Who	had		been	living	in that house?	

EXERCISE **12** **Fill in the blanks with the past perfect continuous tense.**

EXAMPLE   Firefighters ___had been working___ around the clock to control the fire.
(work)

1. The fire _____ for two days by the time firefighters
(burn)

   put it out.

2. We _____ in the same house for 30 years when
(live)

   the fires started.

3. A hunter _____ to send a signal.
(try)

4. The families of the astronauts _____ for several hours
(wait)

   when they heard the news.

5. The *Titanic* _____ for five days when it sank.
(travel)

3.9 The Past Perfect Continuous Tense—Uses

The past perfect continuous tense is used with the simple past tense to show the relationship of two past events.

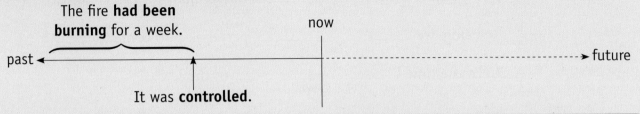

EXAMPLES	EXPLANATION
The fire **had been burning** *for a week* by the time it was controlled. We **had been living** in the same house *for 26 years* when we lost our home.	The past perfect continuous tense is used with a continuous action that was completed before another past action. The duration of the continuous action is expressed with *for*.
a. When the fire started, Southern California **had had** very little rain. b. When residents returned, they found out that their homes **had been destroyed**. c. By the time the fire ended, 16 people **had died**.	We use the past perfect, not the past perfect continuous, with: a. nonaction verbs b. an action of little or no duration c. multiple or repeated actions

EXERCISE **13** **Fill in the blanks with the simple past tense or the past perfect continuous tense of the verb in parentheses ( ).**

EXAMPLE   When I _____came_____ to the U.S., I __had been studying__
                         (come)   (study)

English for three years.

1. I _____ for two years when I _____
        (wait)   (get)

   a chance to leave my country.

2. I _____ in the same house all my life when I
        (live)

   _____ my city.
        (leave)

3. I _____ very sad when I left my job because I
        (feel)

   _____ with the same people for ten years.
        (work)

4. I _____ to be a nurse for six months when a
        (study)

   war _____ in my country.
           (break out)

(continued)

The Past Continuous; The Past Perfect; The Past Perfect Continuous; Comparison of Past Tenses   119

5. When I _____ my country, the war
(leave)

_____ for three years.
(go on)

6. My family _____ in Germany for three months
(wait)

before we _____ permission to come to the U.S.
(get)

7. By the time I _____ to the U.S., I
(get)

_____ for four days.
(travel)

EXERCISE **Fill in the blanks with the past perfect continuous tense for a continuous action. Fill in the blanks with the past perfect tense for a one-time action, multiple or repeated actions, or a nonaction verb.**

CD 1, TR 19

In the year 1800, the population of Chicago was only 5,000. But the

population __**had been growing**__ steadily since the beginning of the
(example: grow)

century. In 1871, Chicago __**had recently passed**__ St. Louis to become
(example: recently/pass)

the fourth largest city in the U.S. Chicago _____ a place
(1 reach)

of importance when the Great Chicago Fire began on October 8, 1871.

That October was especially dry because there _____
(2 be)

very little rain. At the time, most of the streets, sidewalks, bridges, and

buildings were made of wood. On Sunday night, a fire broke out in a barn. The

firefighters were exhausted that night because they _____
(3 fight)

a fire since the day before. Strong winds from the south quickly spread the

fire to the center of the city. When the firefighters finally arrived at the

fire, the fire _____ out of control. It wasn't until two days
        (4 spread)

later, when rain began to fall, that the fire finally died out. By this time,

almost 300 people _____ and more than one hundred
        (5 die)

thousand Chicagoans _____ their homes. Millionaires,
        (6 lose)

who _____ in mansions, as well as poor laborers, found
    (7 live)

themselves homeless. Chicagoans, rich and poor, who

_____ contact with each other, gathered in parks and
(8 have/never)

wondered how they would rebuild their lives.

Because of its great location for industry, Chicago remained strong

after the fire. By 1873, the city _____, this time with brick
                    (9 passive: rebuild)

instead of wood. Chicago continued to grow as a commercial center, and,

by 1890, its population _____ more than one million.
                    (10 reach)

Today Chicago is the third largest city in the U.S.

3.10 The Past Perfect (Continuous) Tense or the Present Perfect (Continuous) Tense

The past perfect (continuous) tense and the present perfect (continuous) tense cannot be used interchangeably.

EXAMPLES	EXPLANATION
Have you ever **seen** a movie about the *Titanic*? I **have** never **been** on a ship. How many disasters **have** we **read** about so far?	The present perfect is used when we look back from the present time. past ◄─────────── | - - - - - - - ► future （? ... now） have never seen
When the *Titanic* was built, people **had** never **seen** such a magnificent ship before. By the time the fires ended in California, many people **had lost** their homes.	The past perfect is used when we look back from a past time. built ... now past ◄─────────── | - - - - - - - ► future had never seen

(continued)

EXAMPLES	EXPLANATION
The U.S **has been exploring** space since the 1950s. Lately, we **have been reading** stories about disasters.	The present perfect continuous is used when we look back from the present time to a continuous action. 1950s now past ←———————→ future has been exploring
When the *Columbia* accident happened, it **had been orbiting** the Earth for sixteen days. When the *Titanic* sank, it **had been traveling** for five days.	The past perfect continuous is used when we look back from a past time to a prior continuous action. 2003 now past ←———————→ future had been orbiting

EXERCISE 15 Fill in the blanks with the present perfect, the present perfect continuous, the past perfect, or the past perfect continuous tense of the verb in parentheses ( ). In some cases, answers may vary.

CD 1, TR 20

A: I'm really interested in space exploration.

B: How long ___have you been___ interested in it?
(example: you/be)

A: Ever since I was a child. By the time I was 10 years old, I

_____ to the space museum in Washington, D.C.
(1 be)

about five times.

B: Who took you?

A: My parents took me most of the time. But one time my fifth grade

class _____ all semester about space, and
(2 study)

our teacher took the class. Since that time, I _____
(3 always/dream)

about becoming an astronaut. I saw a film about the first moon

landing in 1969. It was so exciting to think that no man

_____ on the moon before.
(4 ever/walk)

B: Do you think it's possible for you to become an astronaut?

A: Sure. Why not? I _____ my bachelor's degree in
(5 already/get)

engineering. Lately I _____ a lot about the training that
(6 read)

astronauts go through. I _____ to NASA asking them
(7 already/write)

to send me more information on how to get into the space program.

And next semester I'm going to enter a master's program in physics.

B: Don't you have to be a pilot first?

A: Yes. I _____ 500 hours of flying lessons.
(8 already/take)

B: Aren't you worried about the risks of going into space? NASA

_____ several major disasters so far.
(9 have)

A: Of course there are risks. But the space program needs to continue.

By the time of the *Columbia* disaster, it _____ 27
(10 already/have)

successful missions. And in general, there _____
(11 be)

more successes than failures up to now. Since the *Columbia* tragedy,

NASA _____ ways to improve the safety of its astronauts.
(12 study)

Hurricane Katrina

Before You Read

1. Has your native country ever experienced a natural disaster, such as a hurricane or tornado?

2. How did the country and the people recover from this natural disaster?

Read the following magazine article. Pay special attention to past tense verbs (simple past, past continuous, past perfect, past perfect continuous, present perfect, and present perfect continuous).

New Orleans **has been** a favorite tourist attraction for Americans. It is known for its great music, fun nightlife, interesting food, historic buildings, and pleasant climate. For many years, tourists **have been going** to New Orleans to experience the fun of Mardi Gras[7] in February or March. But all of this **changed** in August 2005.

New Orleans, which is several feet below sea level, **has** always **depended** on levees[8] to protect it from surrounding water. In August 2005, a hurricane **was traveling** over the Gulf of Mexico, causing damage from Florida to Texas. As the hurricane **was approaching** and **gaining** strength, the mayor of New Orleans **ordered** the residents to leave. By the time the storm **hit** land on August 29, most people **had left**. But there **were** many people who **were** too poor or sick to leave. Others **stayed** because they **didn't want** to leave pets behind. Some **believed** that they **had survived** smaller flooding in the past and that they would survive this one too. But the impact of the hurricane **caused** the levees to fail, and within a short time, 80 percent of the city **was** underwater. As the water **was rushing** into their houses, residents **ran** to the roofs of their houses to wait for rescue teams. Some **had been waiting** for three days by the time they **were rescued**.

Little by little, families **were evacuated** from the roofs of their houses. By the time the rescue effort **was** over, at least 1,800 people **had died** by drowning or from lack of food, water, and medical attention. Many of the rescued **were taken** to shelters. When they **were** finally able to return to their homes, they **realized** that they **had lost** everything.

To this day, New Orleans **has** not **been** able to recover from the devastation of Katrina. Since the disaster **struck**, the city **has been rebuilding**, hoping to bring New Orleans back to its place as one of the most interesting cities in the U.S. And the survivors of this disaster **have been trying** to rebuild their lives too. Some **have started** lives in new locations, too sad or afraid to go back to the places where they **had experienced** so much loss. Many **have had** to replace everything they **had lost** in the disaster.

Hurricane Katrina **has been** the worst natural disaster in U.S. history to date.

---

[7]*Mardi Gras* is a carnival. It occurs the last day before Lent begins. Lent, which ends with Easter, is a serious period for Christians.
[8]A *levee* is a wall built to hold back water.

3.11 Comparison of Past Tenses

EXAMPLES	EXPLANATION
a. The mayor **ordered** the residents to leave. b. My grandmother **lived** in New Orleans for 30 years. c. The hurricane **hit** land on August 29, 2005. d. We **visited** New Orleans five times.	The **simple past tense** shows an action that started and ended in the past. It does not show the relationship to another past action. It can be used for a short action (a) or a long action (b). It can be used for a single action (c) or a repeated action (d).
On August 29, the hurricane **was approaching** quickly. As the water **was rushing** into the houses, residents ran to the roofs.	The **past continuous tense** shows that something was in progress at a specific time in the past.
a. When the storm **hit**, most people **had left**. b. By the time the rescue effort **was over**, 1,800 people **had died**.	The **past perfect tense** shows the relationship of an earlier past action to a later past action. a. earlier = *had left*; later = *hit* b. earlier = *had died*; later = *was over*
Some people **had been waiting** *for three days* by the time they **were rescued**. The *Titanic* **had been traveling** *for five days* when it **sank**.	The **past perfect continuous tense** is used with a continuous action of duration that happened before another past action. *For* is used to show the duration of the previous action.
New Orleans **has** always **been** a tourist attraction. California **has had** many fires.	The **present perfect tense** uses the present time as the starting point and looks back.
Since 2005, New Orleans residents **have been trying** to put their lives back together. NASA **has been exploring** space since the 1950s.	The **present perfect continuous tense** uses the present time as the starting point and looks back at a continuous action that is still happening.
a. ***When*** the hurricane **hit**, people went to the roofs of their houses. b. ***When*** the hurricane **hit**, some people **were sleeping**. c. ***When*** the hurricane **hit**, many people **had** already **left** their homes.	Be especially careful with *when*. In sentence (a), they went to the roofs *after* the hurricane hit. In sentence (b), they were sleeping *at the same time* the hurricane hit. In sentence (c), they left their homes *before* the hurricane hit.

Language Notes:
1. Sometimes the past continuous and the past perfect continuous can be used in the same case. The past perfect continuous is more common with a *for* phrase.
   People **were waiting** on their roofs when they were rescued.
   People **had been waiting** on their roofs *for three days* when they were rescued.
2. Sometimes the simple past or the past perfect can be used in the same case.
   Some people **had taken** a few things before they left.
   Some people **took** a few things before they left.

EXERCISE 16 Fill in the blanks with the correct past tense. Use the passive voice where indicated. In some cases, more than one answer is possible.

EXAMPLE Hurricane Katrina _____**struck**_____ New Orleans on August 29, 2005.
(strike)

1. Many hurricanes _____ New Orleans over the years.
(strike)

2. _____ New Orleans?
(you/ever/visit)

3. By the time rescuers came, many people _____.
(already/die)

4. When I came to the U.S., I _____ of New Orleans
(never/hear)
before.

5. How many disaster stories _____ so far?
(we/read)

6. What _____ when you _____ the
(you/do)   (hear)
news about Katrina?

7. I _____ TV when I _____ the news.
(watch)   (hear)

8. I have a friend who left his home in New Orleans in 2005. He

_____ in Chicago since 2005. He has never returned
(live)
to New Orleans.

9. The *Titanic* _____ in Ireland.
(passive: build)

10. The *Titanic* _____ fast when it
(travel)

_____ an iceberg.
(hit)

11. Many people _____ when they
(sleep)

_____ a loud noise.
(hear)

12. When third-class passengers _____ to the top deck,
(go)

most of the lifeboats _____.
(already/leave)

13. A few hours later, another ship _____, but the *Titanic*
(arrive)

_____.
(already/sink)

14. In 1985, the ship _____ in the North Atlantic.
    (passive: find)

15. In 1912, the sinking of the *Titanic* was the worst tragedy that

_____.
    (ever/occur)

16. People are still interested in the *Titanic*. People _____
    (be)

interested in it for almost a hundred years.

EXERCISE 17 A teacher and a student are talking about heroes in the Hurricane Katrina disaster. Fill in the blanks with the correct past tense to complete this conversation. In some cases, more than one answer is possible.

CD 1, TR 22

S: Yesterday we _____**read**_____ the story about
    (example: read)

Hurricane Katrina. _____ New Orleans?
    (1 you/ever/visit)

T: I _____ New Orleans many times. It's one of my
    (2 visit)

favorite cities in the U.S. I think I'll go back someday because

I love the food and the music there. Even though the city

_____ completely, tourists _____
    (3 not/be/rebuild)   *(4 start)*

to go back. _____ in the U.S. in August 2005,
    (5 you/live)

at the time of Hurricane Katrina?

S: No, I _____. I _____ in Mexico
    (6)   *(7 live)*

at that time. But we _____ about the hurricane on
    (8 hear)

the news. We heard many interesting rescue stories.

T: I'm always interested in rescue stories. Which one interested you the most?

S: In 2005, I _____ an interesting program about the
    (9 see)

heroes of Hurricane Katrina, and one of them was a six-year-old boy.

T: What _____?
    (10 he/do)

(continued)

The Past Continuous; The Past Perfect; The Past Perfect Continuous; Comparison of Past Tenses   **127**

S: After the hurricane, volunteer workers _____ (11 find) a six-year old boy with six other small children. He was the oldest in the group, and he _____ (12 carry) a five-month-old baby. There were five other small children with him. By the time rescue workers found them, they _____ (13 walk) around the streets for several hours. The oldest boy, Deamonte Love, told the volunteers that a helicopter _____ (14 take) them from their parents and that his mother _____ (15 cry) when they _____ (16 leave).

T: What _____ (17 happen) next? _____ (18 they/find) his mother?

S: Yes. A few days later, his mother _____ (19 passive: find) in a shelter.

T: How did she get separated from her children?

S: While the family and neighbors _____ (20 wait) to be rescued, their building filled with water. They went to the roof and waited. A helicopter _____ (21 arrive) and picked up the kids. They said that they would come back in 25 minutes for the adults. But the helicopter _____ (22 not/come) back. By the time the adults were rescued a few days later, they _____ (23 live) without electricity or food for four days.

T: I didn't realize that so many children _____ (24 become) separated from their parents. Were all the children brothers and sisters?

S: No. The baby was Deamonte's brother and the others were cousins and neighbors.

T: Deamonte _____ (25 be) a real hero.

Summary of Lesson 3

1. Showing the relationship between two past actions:

The Past Perfect

The reference point is past.	Another action preceded it.
When the rescue ship **arrived**,	many people **had died**.
In **1912**,	the airplane **had** already **been invented**.

The Past Perfect Continuous

The reference point is past.	A continuous action preceded it.
The captain **couldn't turn** the ship around	because it **had been traveling** so fast.
When the family **was rescued**,	they **had been waiting** on the roof for three days.

The Past Continuous

An action was in progress . . .	. . . at a specific time or when a shorter action occurred.
They **were sleeping**	at 11:40 P.M.
We **were watching** TV	when we heard about the *Columbia* accident.

2. Relating the past to the present:

The Present Perfect	The Present Perfect Continuous
Have you ever **seen** the movie *Titanic*? I **have** never **seen** it, but I'd like to. I **have seen** two movies so far this month. I**'ve** always **been** interested in space exploration.	She is watching the movie now. She **has been watching** it for 45 minutes. I**'ve been reading** a book about space exploration.

3. Describing the past without relating it to another past time:

The Simple Past Tense
The mayor **ordered** the residents of New Orleans to leave.   The hurricane **struck** on August 29, 2005.   Some people **stayed**. They **didn't want** to leave their pets.   Some families **lost** everything.

Editing Advice

1. The simple past tense does not use an auxiliary.

   came
   He ~~was come~~ home at six o'clock last night.

2. Don't forget *be* in a past continuous sentence.

   was
   I ∧ walking on the icy sidewalk when I fell and broke my arm.

3. Do not use a present tense for an action that began in the past. Use the present perfect (continuous) tense.

   have been
   I ~~am~~ married for ten years.

   has been
   She ~~is~~ working at her present job for seven months.

4. Don't forget *have* with perfect tenses.

   have
   I ∧ been living in the U.S. for six months.

5. Don't confuse the present perfect and the past perfect tenses. The past perfect tense relates to a past event. The present perfect tense relates to the present.

   had
   When I started college, I ~~have~~ never owned a laptop before.

   has
   She's a teacher now. She ~~had~~ been a teacher for 15 years.

6. Use the simple past tense with *ago*.

   came
   He ~~was coming~~ to the U.S. four years ago.

7. Use *when*, not *while*, for an action that has no continuation.

   when
   I was washing the dishes ~~while~~ I dropped a plate.

8. Use the simple past tense, not the present perfect tense, in a *since* clause.

   came
   She has had her car ever since she ~~has come~~ to the U.S.

9. Don't use the continuous form for a repeated action.

   drunk
   By the time I got to work, I had ~~been drinking~~ four cups of coffee.

10. Don't confuse the *-ing* form with the past participle.

seen
When he moved to Chicago, he had never ~~seeing~~ a skyscraper before.

11. Be careful to choose the correct past tense in a sentence with *when*.

came
When I left my hometown, I ~~had come~~ to New York.

had begun
When I arrived in class, the test ~~began~~ already.

12. Don't confuse active and passive.

found
In 1985, the *Titanic* was ~~finding~~.

Editing Quiz

Some of the shaded words and phrases have mistakes. Find the mistakes and correct them. If the shaded words are correct, write *C*.

saw
Last night I ~~seen~~ a program on TV about the survivors of the *Titanic*.
(example)

C
Even though I had already seen the movie *Titanic*, I was still interested in
(example)

this program because it told the stories of real people.

The last American survivor, Lillian Asplund, was died in 2006. She was
                                                (1)

just five years old when she traveling on the ship with her parents and
                                    (2)

brothers. They were returning to the U.S. from Sweden, where they have spent
                        (3)   (4)

several years.

She and her mother got on a lifeboat with one of her brothers, but her
                        (5)

father and other three brothers have waited. Her father promised that he
                                        (6)   (7)

would get on the next lifeboat. When Lillian and her mother saw him for

the last time, her father was smile. She never saw her father and brothers
                            (8)   (9)

again. Her mother lived until the age of 91, but she had never gotten over
                    (10)   (11)

the tragedy of losing her husband and three sons.   *(continued)*

The last survivor was an English woman, Millvina Dean. At two months old, she has been (12) the youngest passenger on the *Titanic*. She and her family were immigrate (13) to the U.S. from England when the tragedy occurred (14). She and her mother and brother were rescuing (15), but her father went down with the ship. With her husband gone, Millvina's mother decided (16) to take the children back to England. Because Millvina was just a baby at the time, she had no memories of the tragedy and didn't even know that she had being (17) on the *Titanic* until she was eight years old. At that time, her mother told (18) her the story of what had happened (19). Until 1997, she has lived (20) quietly in England when, suddenly, journalists became (21) interested in her. She was invited (22) to travel by ship to the U.S. and she accepted (23). This was the second time in her life that she traveled by ship.

Ms. Dean died (24) in 2009 at the age of 97. Her brother died on April 14, 1992, the anniversary of the *Titanic* disaster! He was 80 years old.

It's amazing that people are still fascinated with the story of the *Titanic*. People are (25) interested in this story for 100 years! And I am (26) interested since I saw the movie *Titanic*.

Lesson 3 Test/Review

PART 1 Read a survivor's account of the night of the *Titanic* disaster.[9] Fill in the blanks with the simple past, the past perfect, or the past continuous tense of the verb in parentheses. In some cases, more than one answer is possible.

We ___**had just fallen**___ asleep when my wife

(example: just/fall)

_____ a noise. She _____ me up and

(1 hear)   (2 wake)

_____ that something _____ to the

(3 say)   (4 happen)

ship. We _____ up on deck and everything

(5 go)

_____ normal at first. The orchestra

(6 seem)

_____.

(7 still/play)

At first the officers _____ that the *Titanic* could not

(8 insist)

sink in less than ten hours. We were told that the *Titanic*

_____ with other nearby ships and that help would reach

(9 communicate)

us in an hour or two.

The crew _____ to lower the lifeboats. They

(10 start)

_____ us that there _____ no danger,

(11 assure)   (12 be)

that they were just taking precautions.

After about six or seven lifeboats were lowered, people

_____ to realize that they _____ in great

(13 start)   (14 be)

danger. I saw an officer shoot two passengers who _____

(15 fight)

to get on a lifeboat.

The thirteenth boat _____ with about 25 children

(16 passive: *fill*)

and a few women. While the boat _____, all of them

(17 passive: *lower*)

_____.

(18 scream)

I _____ one of the officers on the *Titanic* because

(19 know)

I _____ with him before on another ship. He

(20 travel)

_____ me into the thirteenth boat and

(21 push)

_____ me to take care of the children.

(22 order)

[9]This account is adapted from *The Bulletin*, San Francisco, April 19, 1912.

(continued)

As our boat _____ (23 leave) , we _____ (24 hear) the orchestra playing a religious song.

I will never forget the terrible scene as our boat _____ (25 move) away. Husbands and fathers _____ (26 wave) and _____ (27 throw) kisses to their wives and children.

The ship _____ (28 sink) only three hours after it _____ (29 hit) the iceberg.

PART 2 **Fill in the blanks with one of the past tenses: simple past, past continuous, present perfect (continuous), or past perfect (continuous). In some cases, more than one answer is possible.**

A: What _____ **happened** _____ to your car?
(happen)

B: I _____ (1 have) an accident yesterday.

A: How _____ (2 it/happen) ?

B: I _____ (3 drive) to work when a dog _____ (4 run) in front of my car. I _____ (5 stop) my car suddenly, and the car behind me _____ (6 hit) my car because the driver _____ (7 follow) me too closely.

A: _____ (8 you/get) a ticket?

B: No, but the driver who hit me did.

A: Who will pay to have your car fixed?

B: The other driver. When he _____ (9 hit) me, he _____ (10 get) out of his car and _____ (11 give) me his insurance card. He's a new driver. He _____ (12 only/have) his driver's license for two months.

A: You're a new driver too, aren't you?

B: Oh, no. I _____ (13 drive) for 20 years.

A: I thought you _____ (14 get) your driver's license a few months ago.

B: In this state, I have a new license. But I _____ (15 have) a driver's license for many years before I _____ (16 move) here.

A: _____ you ever _____ (17 get) a ticket?

B: One time. I _____ (18 drive) about 65 miles an hour on the highway when a police officer _____ (19 stop) me. She said that the speed limit was only 55. She _____ (20 give) me a ticket for speeding. She also gave me a ticket because I _____ (21 not/wear) my seat belt.

Expansion

Classroom
Activities

❶ **In a small group or with the entire class, turn to the person next to you and say a year. The person next to you has to tell a short story about his/her life at or before that time.**

EXAMPLES

2005
I had just graduated from high school. I was living with my parents.
I hadn't thought about coming to the U.S. at that time.

1983
I hadn't been born yet.

2004
I had just had my second child. We were living with my wife's parents.

❷ **On an index card, write the following sentence, filling in the blank to make a true statement about yourself. The teacher will collect the cards and read the sentences. Try to guess who wrote the sentences.**

When I came to this school, I had never _____ before.

EXAMPLE

When I came to this school, I had never called a teacher by his first name before.

❸ **On an index card, write the following sentence, filling in the blank to make a true statement about yourself. The teacher will collect the cards and read the sentences. Try to guess who wrote the sentences.**

I've never _____, but I'd like to.

EXAMPLE

I have never gone fishing, but I'd like to.

Talk

About It

1 Why do you think that women and children were put on lifeboats before men?

2 Do you think the space program should continue?

Write

About It

1 Choose one of the following topics and write a short composition.

- an accident or unusual experience that happened to you
- an important event in the history of your native country
- a famous person who died in an accident, assassination, or another unusual way

2 Write about a tragedy in recent history. Tell what you *were doing* when you heard the news. Tell what you *did* when you heard the news.

EXAMPLE

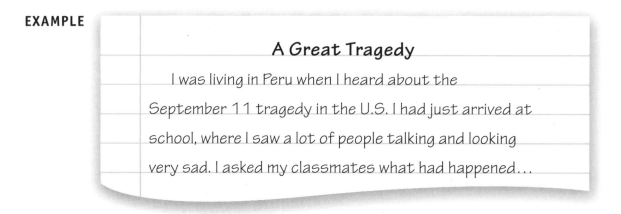

A Great Tragedy

I was living in Peru when I heard about the September 11 tragedy in the U.S. I had just arrived at school, where I saw a lot of people talking and looking very sad. I asked my classmates what had happened...

 For more practice using grammar in context, please visit our Web site.

Grammar
Modals—Present and Future

Related Expressions

Context
Consumer Warnings

4.1 Overview of Modals and Related Expressions

The modal verbs are *can, could, shall, should, will, would, may, might,* and *must.*

EXAMPLES	EXPLANATION
She **should** leave. (advice) She **must** leave. (necessity) She **might** leave. (possibility)	Modals add meaning to the verbs that follow them.

He **can help** you.
They **should eat** now.
You **must pay** your rent.
	The base form follows a modal.
	    Wrong: He can *helps* you.
	    Wrong: They should *eating* now.
	    Wrong: You must *to* pay your rent.
	The modal never has an *-s* ending.
	    Wrong: He *cans* help you.

You **should not** leave now. He **cannot** speak English.	To form the negative, put *not* after the modal. *Cannot* is written as one word.
A pen **should be used** for the test. The movie **can be seen** next week.	A modal can be used in passive voice: modal + *be* + past participle
He **must** go to court. = He **has to** go to court. You **must not** park your car there. = You **are not supposed to** park your car there. He **can** speak English well. = He **is able to** speak English well.	The following expressions are like modals in meaning: *have to, have got to, be able to, be supposed to, be allowed to, be permitted to, had better*.
British: We **shall** study modals. **American:** We **will** study modals.	For the future tense, *shall* is more common in British English than in American English. Americans sometimes use *shall* in a question to make a suggestion or invitation. *Shall* we dance?

Language Note: Observe statements and questions with modals:
    Affirmative: He *can* speak German.
    Negative: He *can't* speak French.
    ***Yes/No* Question:** *Can* he speak English?
    Short Answers: Yes, he *can.*/No, he *can't.*
    ***Wh-* Question:** What languages *can* he speak?
    Negative Question: Why *can't* he speak French?
    Subject Question: Who *can* speak French?

Sweepstakes or Scam?

1. Do you get a lot of junk mail?

2. What do you do with these pieces of mail?

CD 2, TR 01

Read the following magazine article. Pay special attention to modals.

Did you ever get a letter with your name printed on it telling you that you have won a prize or a large amount of money? Most people in the U.S. get these letters.

We often get mail from sweepstakes companies. A sweepstakes is like a lottery. To enter a sweepstakes, you usually **have to** mail a postcard. Even though the chances of winning are very small, many people enter because they have nothing to lose and **might** even win something.

Are these offers of prizes real? Some of them are. Why would someone give you a prize for doing nothing? A sweepstakes is a chance for a company to promote its products, such as magazines. But some of these offers **might** be deceptive,[1] and you **should** read the offer carefully. The government estimates that Americans lose more than one billion dollars every year through "scams," or tricks to take your money. You **should** be careful of letters, e-mails, and phone calls that tell you:

- You **must** act now or the offer will expire.
- You **may** already be a winner. To claim your gift, you only **have to** pay postage and handling.
- You've won! You **must** call a 900 number to claim your prize.
- You've won a free vacation. All you **have to** do is pay a service fee.

You **shouldn't** give out your credit card number or Social Security number if you are not sure who is contacting you about the sweepstakes.

Senior citizens **should** be especially careful of scams. Eighty percent of the victims of scams are 65 or older. They often think that they **have to** buy something in order to win a prize and often spend thousands of dollars on useless items. Or they think that their chances of winning **might** increase if they buy the company's product. But in a legitimate sweepstakes, you **don't have to** buy anything or send any money. The law states that "no purchase necessary" **must** appear in big letters. In addition, the company **is supposed to** tell you your chances of winning.

How **can** you avoid becoming the victim of a scam? If you receive a letter saying you are a guaranteed winner, you **ought to** read it carefully. Most people just throw this mail in the garbage.

[1]Something that is *deceptive* tries to make you believe something that is not true.

4.2 Possibilities—*May, Might, Could*

EXAMPLES	EXPLANATION
You **may** already be a winner. You **might** win a prize. This **could** be your lucky day!	Use *may, might, could* to show possibilities about the present or future.
She **may not** know that she is a winner. Some people **might not** understand the conditions of a sweepstakes.	For negative possibility, use *may not* or *might not*. Don't use *could not*. It means *was/were not able to*. Do not make a contraction with *may not* or *might not*.
Do you think I might win? **Do you think I could** get lucky?	To make questions about possibility with *may, might, could,* say, "Do you think . . . *may, might, could* . . .?" The clause after *Do you think* uses statement word order.
Compare: a. **Maybe** you are right. b. You **may be** right. a. **Maybe** he is a winner. b. He **may be** a winner.	*Maybe*, written as one word (a), is an adverb. It is usually put before the subject. *May be*, written as two words (b), is a modal + verb. The meaning of (a) and (b) are the same, but notice that the word order is different. *Wrong:* He *maybe* is a winner.

EXERCISE **1** **Fill in the blanks with appropriate verbs to complete this conversation. Answers may vary.**

CD 2, TR 02

A: What are you going to do this summer?

B: I haven't decided yet. I might _____*go*_____ back to Peru, or I may
(example)

_____ here and look for a summer job. What about you?
(1)

A: I'm not sure either. My brother might _____ here. If he
(2)

does, we might _____ some interesting places in the U.S. I
(3)

received a letter a few days ago telling me that if I mail in a postcard,

I could _____ a trip for two to Hawaii.
(4)

B: I don't believe those letters. When I get those kinds of letters, I just

throw them away.

A: How can you just throw them away? You could _____ a winner.
(5)

B: Who's going to give us a free trip to Hawaii for doing nothing?

A: Well, I suppose you're right. But someone has to win those prizes. It could _____ me. And if I buy a lot of magazines from this
(6)
company, my chances of winning might _____.
(7)

B: That's not true. Those letters always say, "No Purchase Necessary."

A: I really want to go to Hawaii with my brother.

B: Then I suggest you work hard and save your money.

A: I might _____ 90 years old by the time I have enough money.
(8)

EXERCISE 2 **Answer these questions by using the word in parentheses ( ).**

EXAMPLE Is the company legitimate? (*might*)
It might be legitimate.

1. Does the company give out prizes? (*may*)
2. Are the prizes cheap? (*could*)
3. Will I be chosen as a winner? (*might*)
4. Will this company take my money and give me nothing? (*might*)
5. Will I win a trip? (*could*)

EXERCISE 3 **ABOUT YOU** **Fill in the blanks with possible results for the following situations.**

EXAMPLE If I pass this course, __I might take a computer course next semester.__

1. If I work hard, _____
2. If I save a lot of money, _____
3. If I drink a lot of coffee tonight, _____
4. If I eat a lot of sugar, _____
5. If I don't get enough sleep, _____
6. If I exercise regularly, _____
7. If I increase my computer skills, _____
8. If I win a lot of money, _____
9. If I come late to class, _____
10. If I don't do my homework, _____

4.3 Necessity and Urgency with *Must, Have To, Have Got To*

MODAL	EXPLANATION
Individuals and companies **must** (or **have to**) obey the law. Sweepstakes companies **must** (or **have to**) tell you the truth. "No Purchase Necessary" **must** (or **has to**) appear in big letters.	For legal obligation, use *must* and *have to*. *Must* has a very official tone. It is often used in court, in legal contracts (such as rental agreements), and in rule books (such as a book of driving rules and laws).

You **must** act now! Don't wait or you will lose this fabulous offer!
 	
You**'ve got to** act now!
 	
You **have to** act now!
	Must, have to, and *have got to* express a sense of urgency. All three sentences to the left have the same meaning.
	
	Have got to is usually contracted:
	    I have got to = I've got to
	    He has got to = He's got to

I**'ve got to** help my sister on Saturday. She **has to** move.	Avoid using *must* for personal obligations. It sounds very official or urgent and is too strong for most situations. Use *have to* or *have got to*.

Pronunciation Note: In relaxed, informal speech,
- *have to* is often pronounced "hafta."
- *has to* is pronounced "hasta."
- *have got to* is often pronounced "gotta." (*Have* is often not pronounced before "gotta.")

EXERCISE 4   **Fill in the blanks with an appropriate verb to talk about sweepstakes rules. Answers may vary.**

EXAMPLE   Sweepstakes companies must ___*obey*___ the law.

1. Sweepstakes companies must _____ "No Purchase Necessary" in big letters in the information they send to you.

2. Sweepstakes companies sometimes tell people that they must _____ a 900 number to win a prize.

3. Sweepstakes companies often tell people, "You must _____ now. Don't wait."

4. Companies must _____ the truth about the conditions of the contest.

5. If a sweepstakes company tells you that you must _____ something, it is not a legitimate sweepstakes.

EXERCISE 5 Fill in the blanks with an appropriate verb (phrase) to talk about driving rules. Answers may vary.

EXAMPLE Drivers must ___*stop*___ at a red light.

1. A driver must _____ a license.
2. In a car, you must _____ a baby in a special car seat.
3. You must _____ when you hear a fire truck siren.
4. In many cities, drivers must _____ a parking sticker on their windshields.
5. A car must _____ a license plate.
6. In some cities, you must not _____ a cell phone while driving.

EXERCISE 6 **ABOUT YOU** Fill in the blanks with words that describe personal obligations.

EXAMPLE I have to ___*call my parents*___ once a week.

1. After class, I've got to _____.
2. This weekend, I have to _____.
3. Before the next class, we've got to _____.
4. Every day I have to _____.
5. Once a month, I've got to _____.
6. When I'm not sure of the spelling of a word, I have to _____
   _____.
7. Before I go to sleep at night, I have to _____.
8. A few times a year, I've got to _____.
9. My English isn't perfect. I have to _____.
10. Before I take a test, I've got to _____.

EXERCISE 7 **ABOUT YOU** Make a list of personal obligations you have to do on the weekends.

EXAMPLE *On Saturdays, I have to take my sister to ballet lessons.*

_____
_____
_____

EXERCISE 8 **ABOUT YOU** Make a list of obligations you have at your job, at your school, or in your house.

EXAMPLE   At work, I've got to answer the phone and fill out orders.

_____

_____

_____

_____

_____

_____

4.4 Obligation with *Must* or *Be Supposed To*

EXAMPLES	EXPLANATION
"No Purchase Necessary" **must** appear in big letters. This is the law. The sweepstakes company **must** tell you your chances of winning. People who win money **must** pay taxes on their winnings.	*Must* has an official tone.
Compare: a. Police officer to driver: "You **must** wear your seat belt." b. Driver to passenger: "You**'re supposed to** wear your seat belt." a. Teacher to student: "You **must** write your composition with a pen." b. Student to student: "You**'re supposed to** write your composition with a pen."	a. A person in a position of authority (such as a police officer, parent, or teacher) can use *must*. The tone is very official. b. Avoid using *must* if you are not in a position of authority. Use *be supposed to* to remind someone of a rule.
Companies **are supposed to** follow the law, but some of them don't. Drivers **are supposed to** use a seat belt, but they sometimes don't. Students **are supposed to** be quiet in the library, but some talk.	*Be supposed to*, not *must*, is used when reporting on a law or rule that has been broken.

Pronunciation Note:
The *d* in *supposed to* is not usually pronounced.

EXERCISE 9 A teenager is talking about rules his parents gave him and his sister. Fill in the blanks with *be supposed to* + an appropriate verb. Answers may vary.

EXAMPLE I _'m supposed to babysit_ for my little sister when my parents aren't home.

1. I _____ my homework before I watch TV.
2. I (not) _____ on the phone with my friends for more than 30 minutes.
3. I _____ my room once a week. My mother gets mad when I leave it dirty.
4. If I go to a friend's house, I _____ my parents where I am so they won't worry.
5. I have a part-time job. I _____ some of my money in the bank. I (not) _____ my money on foolish things.
6. I _____ my parents with jobs around the house. For example, I _____ the dishes once a week. I _____ the garbage every day.
7. My sister _____ her toys away when she's finished playing.
8. She (not) _____ the stove.
9. She (not) _____ TV after 8 P.M.
10. She _____ to bed at 8:30 P.M.
11. We _____ our homework before dinner.

EXERCISE 10 **ABOUT YOU** Report some rules in one of the following places: in your apartment, in court, in traffic, in a library, in class, on an airplane, or in the airport.

EXAMPLES In my apartment, the landlord is supposed to provide heat in the winter.

On an airplane, we're not supposed to use a cell phone.

_____

_____

_____

_____

_____

_____

EXERCISE **11**   **ABOUT YOU** Tell about an obligation you or a member of your family has that is often not done.

EXAMPLES   My sister is supposed to finish her homework before watching TV,

but she usually watches TV as soon as she gets home from school.

I'm supposed to wash the dishes in my house, but I often leave them

in the sink for the next day.

_____

_____

_____

_____

_____

_____

_____

4.5 Advice with *Should, Ought To,* and *Had Better*

EXAMPLES	EXPLANATION
Senior citizens **should** be careful of scams. You **should** read the offer carefully to see what the conditions are. You **shouldn't** give your credit card number to people you don't know. You **shouldn't** believe every offer that comes in the mail.	*Should* shows advisability. It is used to say that something is a good idea. *Shouldn't* means that something is a bad idea. The action is not advisable.
If you receive a letter saying you are a winner, you **ought to** throw it away. You **ought to** work hard and save your money. Don't expect to get rich from a sweepstakes. You **ought to** be careful when someone offers you something for nothing.	*Ought to* has the same meaning as *should*. **Note:** *Ought* is the only modal followed by *to*. We don't usually use *ought to* for negatives and questions. Use *should*. *Ought to* is pronounced /ɔtə/.
I'm expecting an important phone call. **I'd better** leave my cell phone on so I won't miss it. You**'d better not** give your credit card number to strange callers, or they might use it to make purchases in your name.	*Had better (not)* is used in conversation to show caution or give a warning. A negative consequence may result. Use *'d* to contract *had* with a pronoun. In some fast speech, *'d* is omitted completely.
Compare: a. Companies and individuals **must** obey the law. b. You **should** read the letter carefully.	a. Use *must* for rules, laws, and urgent situations. b. Use *should* for advice.

EXERCISE **12** **Give advice to people who are saying the following. Answers will vary.**

EXAMPLES   I'm lonely. I don't have any friends.
You should get a dog or a cat for companionship.

I'm so tired. I've been working hard all day.
You ought to get some rest.

1. I've had a headache all day.

2. The teacher wrote something on my paper, but I can't read it.

3. Every time I write a composition and the teacher finds mistakes, I have to write it all over again.

4. I got a letter telling me that I won a million dollars.

5. My old TV doesn't work well anymore. It's too expensive to repair.

6. I received an offer for a new job. It pays double what I get now.

7. My car is making a strange noise. I wonder what it is.

8. I sit at a desk all day. I don't get enough exercise. I'm gaining weight.

9. Whenever I tell my personal problems to my coworker, he tells other people.

10. I have to write a résumé, but I don't have any experience with this.

EXERCISE 13 **ABOUT YOU** Give advice about what people should do or say in the following social situations in your native culture. Share your answers with the class.

EXAMPLE   If you are invited to someone's house for dinner, _you should bring a_ _small gift._

1. If you invite a friend to eat in a restaurant, _____

   _____

2. If you bump into someone, _____

   _____

3. If you don't hear or understand what someone says, _____

   _____

4. If someone asks, "How are you?" _____

   _____

5. If you want to leave the dinner table while others are still eating, _____

   _____

6. If a woman with a small child gets on a crowded bus, _____

   _____

7. If you're invited to someone's house for dinner, _____

   _____

8. If you meet someone for the first time, _____

   _____

EXERCISE 14 Give a warning by using *you'd better (not)* in the following conversations. Answers may vary.

EXAMPLE   **A:** Someone's at the door. I'll go and open it.

B: You _'d better not open it_ if you don't know who it is.

1. **A:** The caller wants my Social Security number.

   B: Do you know who the caller is?

   A: No.

   B: You _____ him your Social Security number then.

2. A: I got a letter about a sweepstakes. Do you think I should enter?

B: You've probably got nothing to lose. But you _____ the letter carefully to make sure that it's legitimate.

3. A: This offer says the deadline for applying is Friday.

B: You _____. You don't have much time.

4. (*phone conversation*)

A: Hello?

B: Hello. I'd like to speak with Mrs. Green.

A: Speaking.

B: You are a winner! You _____ or you might lose this offer. You don't have much time.

A: You keep calling me and telling me the same thing. You _____, or I'll report you.

5. A: You are the only person in the office who wears jeans.

B: What's wrong with that?

A: You _____ appropriately, or you might lose your job.

6. A: I don't like my supervisor's attitude. I'm going to tell her about it.

B: You _____. She might not like it.

7. A: I typed my composition on the computer, but I forgot to bring a flash drive to save it. I'll just print it.

B: Here. Use my flash drive. You _____ in case you have to revise it.

8. (*a driver and a passenger in a car*)

A: I'm getting sleepy. Can you drive for a while?

B: I can't. I don't have my driver's license yet. You _____ for a while.

Telemarketing

1. Do you ever get calls from people who are trying to sell you something? How do you respond to these calls?

2. Do you have Caller ID on your home phone?

CD 2, TR 03

Read the following Web article. Pay special attention to *may, can, be permitted to, be allowed to,* **and other modals.**

http://www.telemarketing*info.com

You have just sat down to dinner when suddenly the phone rings. Someone is trying to sell you a magazine, a phone service, or a vacation. Has this ever happened to you?

Millions of these calls are placed each year. Consumers became so annoyed with "robocalls" (calls with recorded messages) that the government passed a law in 2009 prohibiting companies from using them without your written permission. Companies that continue to use robocalls **may** face a penalty of $16,000 per call. But calls made by humans continue. If you find these calls annoying, as most people do, there is something you can do to take action.

In 2003, the U.S. government[2] created a "Do Not Call" registry. You **can** register your phone number online or by phone. If you do so, most telemarketers **are not permitted to** call you. However, some telemarketers **can** still call you: political organizations and charities. Also, companies with which you do business, such as your bank, **may** call you to offer you a new product or service. However, when they call, you **can** ask them not to call you again. If you make this request, they **are not allowed to** call you again.

It **may take** up to 31 days for your registration to take effect, and it lasts for as long as you keep your phone. You **can** register all of your phone numbers. In the meantime, here are some suggestions for dealing with telemarketers:

- You **could** get Caller ID to see who is calling.
- You **could** ask your phone company if they have a "privacy manager," a service that screens unidentified phone calls. The phone will not even ring in your house unless the caller identifies himself.

Did You Know?

Many telemarketing calls you receive come from call centers in India, Mexico, and other countries, where callers are paid much less than in the U.S.

[2]The Federal Trade Commission (FTC) is the government department that created this registry.

- If you are not interested in the offer, you **can** try to end the phone call quickly. But you **shouldn't** get angry at the caller. He or she is just trying to make a living.
- If you do decide to buy a product or service, remember, you **should** never give out your credit card number if you are not sure who the caller is.

4.6 Permission and Prohibition

EXAMPLES	EXPLANATION
Political organizations **may** call you. (They **are permitted to** call you.) Charities **can** call you. (They **are allowed to** call you.)	Use *may* or *can* to show that something is permitted. Alternate forms are *be allowed to* and *be permitted to*.
If you put your phone number on a "Do Not Call" registry, companies **may not** call you. If you ask a company to stop calling you, this company **cannot** call you again.	Use *may not* or *cannot (can't)* to show that something is prohibited. *May not* has no contracted form.
You **can** wear jeans to class. **Can** you call your teacher by her first name?	In addition to legal permission, *can* also has the meaning of social acceptability.

Language Note: The meaning of *cannot* or *may not* (not permitted) is very similar to the meaning of *must not* (prohibited).

Compare:
a. You *can't* talk during a test.
b. You *may not* talk during a test.
c. You *must not* talk during a test.

a. You *can't* bring food into the computer lab.
b. You *may not* bring food into the computer lab.
c. You *must not* bring food into the computer lab.

EXERCISE **15** **Fill in the blanks to talk about what is and isn't permitted. Answers will vary.**

EXAMPLE We can _____talk_____ in the hall, but we can't

_____talk_____ in the library.

1. If you put your name on a "Do Not Call" registry, companies may

not _____.

2. In the library, you may not _____.

3. During a test, we can _____ but we cannot

_____.

4. Books, CDs, and DVDs are protected by law. We are not permitted

to _____.

5. In this building, we may not _____.

EXERCISE **16** **ABOUT YOU** **Fill in the blanks with an appropriate permission word to talk about what is or isn't permitted in your native country.**

EXAMPLES High school students ___are permitted to___ leave the school building for lunch.

Students _____can't_____ use a cell phone in class.

1. Teenagers _____ drive.

2. People under 18 _____ get married.

3. Children _____ work.

4. Children _____ see any movie they want.

5. A married woman _____ get a passport without her husband's permission.

6. Teachers _____ talk about religion in public schools.

7. Drivers _____ talk on a cell phone while driving.

8. Students _____ write in their textbooks.

9. People _____ travel freely.

10. People _____ live anywhere they want.

EXERCISE **17** Write about what is or isn't permitted in these places. Use *can, may, be allowed to,* or *be permitted to.*

EXAMPLES In the U.S., ___teenagers can get a job.___

In a theater, ___you can't yell "fire."___

1. In the U.S., _____
2. In the computer lab, _____
3. In this classroom, _____
4. In a courtroom, _____
5. In my house/apartment building, _____
6. In an airplane, _____
7. In an airport, _____
8. In this city, _____

EXERCISE **18** **ABOUT YOU** Tell if these things are socially acceptable in your country or native culture.

EXAMPLE Students can call their teachers by their first names.
In my country, students can't call their teachers by their first names. It's very impolite.

1. Parents can take small children to a party for adults.
2. If you are invited to a party, you can invite your friends.
3. Students can wear jeans to class.
4. Students can use a cell phone in class.
5. Students can remain seated when the teacher enters the room.
6. Students can call their teachers by their first names.
7. Students can talk to each other during a test.
8. Students can argue with a teacher about a grade.
9. Teenagers can date.
10. Men and women can hold hands in public.

Identity Theft

1. What do you do with your important mail, such as bills or bank statements?

2. Do you have a password for different things, such as e-mail or an ATM? Do you memorize all your passwords?

CD 2, TR 04

Read the following conversation. Pay special attention to negative modals and related expressions.

A: I hate to have so much paper. Every time I get a credit card or bank statement, I just throw it in the garbage.

B: You **shouldn't** do that. Someone can steal your identity.

A: What do you mean?

B: There are identity thieves who go through the garbage looking for personal information, like bank account numbers or Social Security numbers. I read an article that said that about 9 million Americans have their identities stolen each year.

A: What do the thieves do with these numbers? They **can't** use my number without my credit card.

B: They can and they do. They can make a purchase by phone and charge it to your credit card. You **may not** realize that your identity has been stolen until you review your statement a month later.

A: So what should I do?

B: You **shouldn't** just throw away papers with personal information. You should shred them. I bought a shredder at an office supply store and shred all papers with my personal information. I've also started to do my banking online. That way I don't get so much paper in the mail.

A: How does that work?

B: For most of my bills, like electricity and telephone, the money goes directly to these companies from my checking account. I **don't** even **have to** write checks. And I **don't have to** pay for a stamp. And I **don't have to** worry about identity theft.

A: Can you help me sign up for online banking?

B: Sure. Let's go to your computer and find your bank's Web site. Now you have to choose a password.

A: I think I'll use my birth date.

B: You **shouldn't** use your birth date or any other obvious number.

A: OK. I chose another password, but it's rejected. I used my mother's maiden name.

B: You **can't** use all letters. Your bank says you have to choose a combination of letters and numbers.

A: OK. I've got one now. I'm going to write down the password in my checkbook.

B: You'd **better not**. What if someone steals your checkbook? You'd better memorize your password.

A: Now they're asking me all these questions: "What's your pet's name? Who was your favorite teacher? What's the name of your elementary school?" Why are they asking me all these questions?

B: Those are security questions. Only you know the answers to those questions. The bank wants to make sure it's you and not someone else going into your account.

A: Thanks for telling me about this.

4.7 Comparing Negative Modals

EXAMPLES	EXPLANATION
Students **must not** talk during the test. You **must not** park at a bus stop.	*Must not* shows that something is prohibited. There is no choice in the matter. *Must not* has an official tone.
Sweepstakes companies **are not supposed to** ask you for your Social Security number. I told the telemarketers not to call me anymore, but they did. They**'re not supposed to** do that.	*Be supposed to* is used as a reminder of a rule. It has an unofficial tone. Often the rule has already been broken.
You **can't** use all letters for your password. Telemarketers **may not** call you if you ask them to take you off their list.	*Cannot* and *may not* show that something is not permitted. The meaning is similar to *must not* but is less formal.
You **shouldn't** use your birth date as your password. You **shouldn't** give strange callers your credit card number.	*Should not* shows that something is a bad idea.
A: I'm going to write my password in my checkbook. **B:** You**'d better not**. What if someone steals your checkbook? **A:** I'm going to throw my credit card statement in the garbage. **B:** You**'d better not** do that. Someone might steal your identity.	*Had better not* gives a warning. A negative consequence is stated or implied.
The advantages of banking online are: • You **don't have to** use a stamp. • You **don't have to** remember to pay your bills. They are paid automatically. • There are no paper statements, so you **don't have to** worry so much about identity theft.	*Not have to* shows that something is not necessary or required.

Language Notes:
1. Even though *must* and *have to* are similar in meaning in affirmative statements, they are completely different in meaning in negative statements.
   > Companies *must* obey the law. = Companies *have to* obey the law.
   > You *must not* talk during the test. = This is prohibited.
   > You *don't have to* use a pen for the test. = It is not necessary. You have a choice. You can use a pencil.
2. Don't confuse *should not* and *don't have to*.
   > You *shouldn't* put important papers in the garbage. (It's not a good idea.)
   > To enter a sweepstakes, you *don't have to* buy anything. (It's not necessary to buy anything.)

EXERCISE 19 **ABOUT YOU** Tell if students at this school or another school you have attended have to or don't have to do the following.

EXAMPLES   wear a uniform
Students in my country don't have to wear a uniform.

take final exams
Students at this school have to take final exams.

    1. stand up to answer a question

    2. go to the board to answer a question

    3. call the teacher by his or her title (for example, "Professor")

    4. buy their own textbooks

    5. pay tuition

    6. attend classes every day

    7. have a written excuse for an absence

    8. get permission to leave the classroom

    9. study a foreign language

    10. attend graduation

EXERCISE 20 **ABOUT YOU** Tell if you have to or don't have to do the following.

EXAMPLES   work on Saturdays
I have to work on Saturdays.

dress formally for school
I don't have to dress formally for school.

    1. throw out the garbage every day

    2. study English

    3. get up early on Sundays

    4. cook every day

    5. come to school on Saturdays

EXERCISE 21 Fill in the blanks with *don't have to* or *must not*.

EXAMPLE   If you receive a sweepstakes postcard, you _____don't have to_____ send it back.

    1. You _____ buy anything to win. No purchase is necessary.

    2. Sweepstakes companies _____ break the law.

    3. In a legitimate sweepstakes, you _____ call a 900 number to win a prize.

(continued)

4. I use automatic bill payment. I save money because I

_____ use a stamp to pay my bills.

5. You _____ steal. It's against the law.

6. If you register on the "Do Not Call" list, telemarketers

_____ call you.

7. You _____ register with the "Do Not Call" list. It's

your choice.

EXERCISE 22 **Fill in the blanks with _don't have to_ or _should not_ to describe situations in a public library.**

EXAMPLES   You _____*shouldn't*_____ make noise in the library.

You ____*don't have to*____ know the name of the author to find a book.
You can find the book by the title.

1. You _____ wait until the due date to return a book.
You can return it earlier.

2. You _____ take out more books than you need. Other
people might want them.

3. You _____ disturb other people.

4. You _____ return your books to the circulation desk.
You can leave them in the book drop.

5. You _____ study in the library. You can study at home.

6. You _____ return books late if you don't want to pay
a fine.

EXERCISE 23 **ABOUT YOU** **Work with a partner. Use _be (not) supposed to_ to write a list of rules the teacher has for this class. Use affirmative and negative statements.**

EXAMPLES   We're not supposed to use our books during a test.

We're supposed to write five compositions this semester.

_____

_____

_____

_____

_____

EXERCISE 24 Write a list of driving rules. Use *must not* or *can't*. (Use *you* in the impersonal sense.)

EXAMPLE You must not pass a car when you're going up a hill.

_____

_____

_____

_____

_____

EXERCISE 25 Circle the correct words to complete these sentences.

EXAMPLES We (shouldn't / don't have to) talk loudly in the library.

We (shouldn't / don't have to) bring our dictionaries to class.

1. The teacher says we (can't / don't have to) use our books during a test.

2. The teacher says we (shouldn't / don't have to) sit in a specific seat in class. We can sit wherever we want.

3. We (can't / don't have to) talk to each other during a test. It's not permitted.

4. We (must not / don't have to) type our compositions. We can write them by hand.

5. We (shouldn't / can't) speak our native language in class. It's not a good idea.

6. We (don't have to / aren't supposed to) come back after the final exam, but we can in order to pick up our tests.

7. Parents often tell children, "You (shouldn't / don't have to) talk to strangers."

8. Parents (aren't supposed to / don't have to) send their kids to public schools. They can send them to private schools.

9. Teachers (aren't supposed to / don't have to) teach summer school if they don't want to.

10. English teachers (shouldn't / don't have to) talk fast to foreign students.

11. A driver who is involved in an accident must report it to the police. He (must not / doesn't have to) leave the scene of the accident.

(continued)

12. I'm warning you. You (*don't have to / 'd better not*) spend so much time watching TV. You won't have time to study.

13. Drivers (*don't have to / must not*) go through red lights.

14. You (*shouldn't / don't have to*) make noise and disturb your neighbors.

15. Most American students (*don't have to / had better not*) study a foreign language in college. They have a choice.

16. I have a test tomorrow morning. I (*'d better not / must not*) stay out late tonight, or I won't be alert in the morning.

17. Some students (*shouldn't / don't have to*) pay tuition because they have a scholarship.

18. You (*may not / don't have to*) bring food into the computer lab. It's against the rules.

19. You (*shouldn't / may not*) eat while driving. Even though it's permitted, it's not a good idea.

20. You (*don't have to / shouldn't*) leave your cell phone on in class. It might disturb the class.

21. Those students are talking in the library. They should be quiet. They (*must not / are not supposed to*) talk in the library.

EXERCISE 26 **Fill in the blanks to make true statements.**

EXAMPLE I don't have to ___*make an appointment to see the teacher*___.

1. In this class, we aren't supposed to _____.

2. In this class, we don't have to _____.

3. The teacher doesn't have to _____, but he/she does it anyway.

4. In this building, we must not _____.

5. You'd better not _____, or the teacher will get angry.

6. We're going to have a test next week, so you'd better not _____ the night before.

7. When another student doesn't know the answer, you shouldn't _____. You should let him try to find it himself.

8. You can't _____ in the computer lab. It's not permitted.

9. Teachers should be patient. They shouldn't _____ when students don't understand.

10. You don't have to _____ to win a sweepstakes prize.

EXERCISE **27** **In your opinion, what laws should be changed? What new laws should be created? Fill in the blanks to complete these statements, using *must/must not, have to/don't have to, can/can't, should/shouldn't*. You may work with a partner or in small groups.**

EXAMPLE There ought to be a law that says *that people who want to have a baby must take a course in parenting.*

1. There ought to be a law that says _____

_____

2. There ought to be a law that says _____

_____

3. There ought to be a law that says _____

_____

4.8 Making Suggestions

EXAMPLES	EXPLANATION
How **can** I protect myself from identity theft? You **could** shred all your important papers. You **can** get your bank statements online rather than by mail.	*Can* and *could* are used to offer suggestions. More than one choice is acceptable. *Can* and *could* have the same meaning in offering suggestions. *Could* does not have a past meaning in offering suggestions.

Compare *can/could* and *should*:
a. I'm having a problem with annoying telemarketing calls.
  You **could** get Caller ID. Or you **can** just hang up. Or you **can** put your phone number on a "Do Not Call" registry.
b. A caller asked for my credit card number.
  You **should** be careful. You **shouldn't** give out your credit card number to strangers.
	a. Use *could* or *can* to offer one or more of several possibilities.
	
	b. Use *should* or *shouldn't* when you feel that there is only one right way.

EXERCISE 28 **Offer at least two suggestions to a person who says each of the following statements. You may work with a partner.**

EXAMPLE I need to find a book about American history.

You could go to a bookstore. You can get one at the public library.

You could try an online bookstore.

1. I'm leaving for vacation tomorrow, and I need to find out about the weather in the city where I'm going.

_____

_____

2. I type very slowly. I need to learn to type faster.

_____

_____

3. My landlord is raising my rent by $50, and I can't afford the increase.

_____

_____

4. I'd like to learn English faster.

_____

_____

5. I want to know the price of an airline ticket to my country.

_____

_____

6. I need to buy a new computer, and I want to compare prices.

_____

_____

7. I'm going to a party. The hostess asked each guest to bring something to eat.

_____

_____

8. I need to lose ten pounds.

_____

_____

Infomercials

Before You Read

1. Do you think TV commercials are interesting?

2. Do you believe what you see in commercials?

CD 2, TR 05

Read the following magazine article. Pay special attention to *be supposed to*.

We sometimes see "programs" on TV for products that **are supposed to** make our lives better. These look like real, informative TV shows, but they are not. They are called "infomercials" (*information* + *commercial*).

You**'re supposed to** think that you are watching an informative TV show and getting advice or information from experts and celebrities. These "shows" usually last 30 minutes, like regular TV shows. And they have commercial breaks, like regular TV shows, to

make you believe they are real shows. These "shows" tell you that their products **are supposed to** make you thin, young, rich, or beautiful. For example, you may see smiling people with great bodies using exercise equipment. You**'re supposed to** believe that it's easy and fun to lose weight if you buy this equipment. But weight loss takes hard work and a lot of time.

Be careful when buying products from infomercials, because the results may not be what you see on TV.

4.9 Expectations with *Be Supposed To*

Be supposed to is used to show that we have an expectation about something based on information we received.

EXAMPLES	EXPLANATION
This diet pill **is supposed to** make you thinner in 30 days. This cream **is supposed to** grow hair in 30 days. Let's rent *The Matrix* this weekend. It**'s supposed to** be a good movie. Let's go to Mabel's Restaurant. The food there **is supposed to** be very good. I was just listening to the radio. It**'s supposed to** rain this weekend, but tomorrow **is supposed to** be a nice day.	In the examples on the left, we have an expectation about something because we received information from a friend, TV, radio, a newspaper, the Internet, etc. The information we receive is not necessarily correct.
The movie **is supposed to** begin at 8 P.M. The plane **is supposed to** arrive at 7:25.	In these examples, we have an expectation because of a schedule.

Be supposed to is used to show that something is expected of the subject of the sentence because of a rule, requirement, custom, or commitment (promise).

EXAMPLES	EXPLANATION
Sweepstakes companies **are supposed to** tell you your chances of winning. Drivers **are supposed to** wear seat belts. We**'re not supposed to** talk during the test. You**'re not supposed to** talk in the library, but some students do anyway.	A person is expected to do something because of a law or rule. (See section 4.4.)
I**'m supposed to** write a paper for my class. I**'m supposed to** write about my favorite TV commercial.	A person is expected to meet a requirement (in these cases, by the teacher).
In many cultures, you**'re supposed to** take off your shoes before you enter a house. In the U.S., you**'re supposed to** leave a 15% to 20% tip in a restaurant if you're happy with the service.	A person is expected to behave in a certain way because of a custom.
I can't come to class tomorrow. I**'m supposed to** take my mom to the doctor. My friends are moving on Saturday. I**'m supposed to** help them.	A person is expected to do something because he or she has made a promise or commitment.

EXERCISE 29 **Write a sentence telling what this new product is supposed to do.**

EXAMPLE
Are you starting to look old? Try Youth Cream.
It's supposed to make you look younger.

1. Are you bald? Use Hair Today, a new cream.
   _____

2. Do you look weak? Use Muscle Power, a new cream.
   _____

3. Do you forget things? Try Memory Builder, a new pill.
   _____

4. Is English hard for you? Try *QuickEnglish*, a new video.
   _____

5. Do you have stained teeth? Try WhiteBright toothpaste.
   _____

6. Do you want to make money in 30 days? Buy *Fast Money*, a new book.
   _____

7. Are you overweight? Try SlimTrim, a new diet drink.
   _____

8. Do you want to make your work in the kitchen easier? Buy Quick-Chop,
   a new device for chopping vegetables.
   _____

EXERCISE 30 **Fill in the blanks with the correct form of *be* + *supposed to* and an appropriate verb in this conversation between a wife (W) and a husband (H).**

CD 2, TR 06

W: What's that tube of cream I saw in the bathroom?

H: It's HairFast. It **'s supposed to grow** a lot of hair on my head quickly.
   _____(example)_____

W: How often _____ it?
   _(1)_

H: I _____ it three times a day.
   _(2)_

W: How much does it cost?

H: It's about $20 for each tube.

W: Twenty dollars? How long does a tube last?

H: One tube _____ for a week.
   _(3)_

(continued)

W: Just a week? How long will it take you to grow hair?

H: It _____ about six months before I start to see results.
(4)

W: Do you know how much money that's going to cost us?

H: I know it's expensive, but just imagine how much better I'll look with hair.

W: You know we want to buy a new house. We _____
(5)
our extra money into our house fund. But you're wasting it on a

product that may—or may not—bring results.

H: What about all the money you spend on skin products? All those silly

creams that _____ you look younger?
(6)

W: Well, I want to look young and beautiful.

H: Do you really think those products work?

W: This expensive cream I bought _____
(7)
the wrinkles around my eyes.

H: You'll always be
beautiful to me. I have
an idea. Why don't you
forget about the creams
and I'll forget about the
hair product. We can
save our money, buy a
house, and just get old
together—in our new
home.

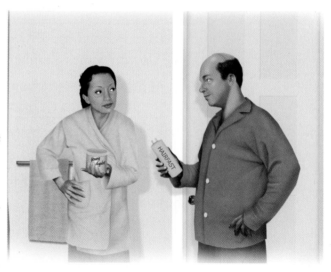

EXERCISE **31** **ABOUT YOU** **Work with a partner. Write a list of three things the teacher or this school expects from the students. Begin with _we_.**

EXAMPLE <u>We're supposed to come to class every day.</u>

1. _____

2. _____

3. _____

EXERCISE 32   **ABOUT YOU** Work with a partner. Write a list of three things that you expect from the teacher in this class. Begin with *he* or *she*.

EXAMPLE   *She's supposed to correct us when we make a mistake.*

1. _____

2. _____

3. _____

My Elderly Neighbor

Before
You Read

1. Why do you think elderly people enter so many sweepstakes?

2. Do you think elderly people are lonelier than younger people?

CD 2, TR 07

Read the following conversation. Pay special attention to *must*.

A: I'm worried about my elderly neighbor.

B: How old is she?

A: She **must be** about 80.

B: Why are you worried? Is her health bad?

A: No, she's fine. But she's all alone. Her children live far away. They don't call her very often.

B: She **must be** lonely.

A: I think she is. She enters sweepstakes and buys useless things all the time. She **must think** that if she buys things, she'll increase her chances of winning. I was in her garage yesterday, and she **must have** more than 50 boxes of things she doesn't use.

B: Doesn't she read the offers that are sent to her? Can't she see that her chances of winning are very small and that she doesn't have to buy anything to win?

(continued)

A: She **must not read** those letters very carefully. In addition to these letters, she told me she gets about five or six calls from telemarketers every day. Her name **must be** on hundreds of lists.

B: Our family **must get** a lot of those calls too, but we're at work all day so we don't even know about them. Telemarketers don't usually leave a message.

A: Do you think I should warn my neighbor? I read an article that says that these companies take advantage of elderly people.

B: Why don't you talk to her about it? You can tell her to use Caller ID to see who's calling, or to put her name on a "Do Not Call" list.

A: I think I should.

4.10 Logical Conclusions

Must has two completely different uses. In Sections 4.3 and 4.4, we studied *must* as an expression of necessity. In the preceding reading and in the examples below, *must* shows a conclusion.

EXAMPLES	EXPLANATION
My elderly neighbor lives alone. Her children are far away. She **must be** lonely. She **must think** that if she buys things, her chances of winning will increase.	We make a conclusion based on information we have or observations we make.
How old is she? She **must be** about 80. How many boxes does she have? She **must have** more than 50 boxes.	We can use *must* to make an estimate.
She **must not read** the letters carefully. She **must not understand** the conditions of the contest.	For a negative conclusion, use *must not*. Do not use a contraction.
Language Note: *Must*, in the above cases, talks about the present only, not the future.	

EXERCISE 33 In each of the conversations below, fill in the blanks with an appropriate verb to make a logical conclusion.

EXAMPLE **A:** Have you ever visited Japan?

B: I lived there when I was a child.

A: Then you must <u>know how to speak</u> Japanese.

B: I used to, but I've forgotten it.

1. *This is a conversation between two female students.*

A: Would you introduce me to Lee?

B: Who's Lee?

A: You must _____ who I'm talking about. He's in your speech class. He sits next to you.

B: You mean Mr. Song?

A: Yes, Lee Song. The tall, handsome guy with glasses. He doesn't wear a wedding ring. He must _____ single.

B: I'm not so sure about that. Not all married men wear a wedding ring.

2. *This is a conversation between a married woman (M) and a single woman (S).*

M: My husband spends all his free time with our children.

S: He must _____ kids very much.

M: He does.

S: How many kids do you have?

M: We have four.

S: Raising kids must _____ the hardest job in the world.

M: It is, but it's also the most rewarding.

(continued)

3. *This is a conversation between a teacher (T) and a student (S).*

T: Take out the paper I gave you last Monday.

S: I don't have it. Could you give me one, please?

T: Were you in class last Monday?

S: Yes, I was.

T: Then you must _____ it.

S: Oh, yes. You're right. Here it is.

4. *This is a conversation between an American (A) and an immigrant (I).*

A: It must _____ hard to start your life in a new country.

I: Yes, it is.

A: You must _____ lonely at times.

I: Yes. You must _____ how it feels. You went to live in Japan for a few years, didn't you?

A: Yes, I did. It took me a long time to get used to it.

5. *This is a conversation between two friends.*

A: I saw some experts on TV talking about a cure for baldness. They must _____ what they're talking about because they're experts.

B: You must _____ that if you see it on TV it's true. But don't believe everything you see.

6. *This is a conversation between two friends.*

A: I saw your uncle yesterday at the gym. How old is he?

B: I'm not sure. My mother is 69 and he's her older brother. So he must _____ in his seventies. He goes to the gym four days a week to work out.

A: He must _____ in great health.

B: He is.

7. *This is a conversation between two students in the school cafeteria.*

A: I see you're not eating your apple. In fact, you never eat fruit. You

must not _____ fruit very much.

B: You're right. I don't like fruit. Do you want my apple?

A: Thanks. You're always eating potato chips. They're so fattening.

They must _____ a million calories in them.

B: Probably, but I never think about it.

A: You should.

B: You're always talking about calories. You must

_____ about getting fat.

A: I don't worry about it. I just try to eat well.

8. *This is a conversation between two co-workers.*

A: Do you want to see a picture of my new baby?

B: Yes.

A: Here she is. She's about two months old now.

B: She's so beautiful. You and your wife must _____

very happy.

A: We are. But we don't get much sleep these days. You have a small

baby. You must _____ what I'm talking about.

B: I sure do.

9. *This is a conversation between a young couple.*

A: Do you see that beautiful ring in the window? I really love it.

Don't you?

B: Yes, it's very beautiful. (*Thinking to himself:* This is an expensive

jewelry shop. The ring must _____ over $5,000.

She must _____ that I'm rich.)

(continued)

10. *This is a conversation between two strangers on the street.*

A: I see you're looking at a map. You must _____ a

tourist. Are you lost?

B: Please repeat.

A: Are you lost?

B: Speak slowly, please.

A: ARE YOU LOST? (*To herself:* He must not _____

any English.)

B: (*To himself:* I asked her to speak more slowly and she's shouting

instead. She must _____ that I'm deaf.)

4.11 Possibility vs. Probability in the Present

May/might and *must* can show degrees of certainty.

DEGREES OF CERTAINTY	EXPLANATION
Who's calling? a. I have Caller ID. I see it's my sister. b. I don't know. I don't have Caller ID. It **might be** my sister. Or it **may be** my mother or it **could be** a telemarketer. c. It **must be** my mother. It's 3:00 P.M. and she calls me every day at three o'clock.	In sentences (a), we are certain that the information is true. In sentences (b), we have little or no evidence or information. There are many possibilities. In sentences (c), we conclude that something is probable based on information we have or an estimate we make.
a. My neighbor **has** a box near her door. b. She **might have** more boxes inside. I really don't know. c. I've seen her garage. She **must have** at least 50 boxes in there.	

EXERCISE **34** **Decide if the situation is probable or possible. Fill in the blanks with *must* for probability or *may/might/could* for possibility.**

EXAMPLES **A:** Where is Linda Ramirez from?

B: Ramirez is a Spanish name. She ___might___ be from Mexico. She ___may___ be from Colombia. There are so many countries where Spanish is spoken that it's hard to know for sure.

A: She ___could___ be from the Philippines. Filipinos have Spanish names too.

B: Where is Tran Nguyen from?

A: I know that's a Vietnamese name. He ___must___ be from Vietnam.

1. **A:** What time is it?

   B: I don't have a watch. The sun is directly overhead, so it _____ be about noon.

2. **A:** Where's the teacher today?

   B: No one knows. She _____ be sick.

3. **A:** Does Yoko speak Japanese?

   B: She _____ speak Japanese. She's from Japan.

4. **A:** Where's Washington Avenue?

   B: I don't know. We're lost. There's a woman over there. Let's ask her. She _____ know.

5. **A:** Why is that student sneezing so much?

   B: I don't know. She _____ have a cold, or it _____ be an allergy.

6. **A:** Is Susan married?

   B: She _____ be married. She's wearing a wedding ring.

7. **A:** Why didn't Joe come to the party?

   B: Who knows? He _____ not like parties.

8. **A:** I need to make some copies, but don't have change for the copy machine.

   B: I _____ have some change. Let me look in my pocket.

9. **A:** I've never lived far from my parents before.

   B: You _____ miss them very much.

   A: I do.

10. **A:** Look at that young couple. They're always holding hands, smiling at each other, and kissing.

    B: They _____ be in love.

(continued)

11. A: Linda never answers any questions in class.

    B: She _____ be shy or she _____ not know the answers to the questions.

12. A: I have a question about grammar.

    B: Let's ask the teacher. She _____ know the answer.

13. A: I have a question about American history.

    B: Why don't you ask our grammar teacher? He _____ know the answer.

4.12 Modals with Continuous Verbs

EXAMPLES	EXPLANATION
A: What's that noise? **B:** That's my husband using the shredder. He **must be shredding** our important papers. **A:** What are you watching on TV? **B:** It's a program about how to get muscles. **A:** You**'re supposed to be doing** your homework now. **A:** My friend isn't answering his cell phone. I know he always has it with him. **B:** He **might be taking** a shower now. I'm sure he doesn't take his phone into the shower!	Use modal + *be* + verb *–ing* for a present continuous meaning.

EXERCISE 35   **Fill in the blanks to complete each statement.**

EXAMPLE   I know I should _____ *be studying* _____ for my test and not watching TV now. But there's a great program on now.

1. My sister said she might go to a movie today. She's not answering her cell phone. She must _____ watching a movie now.

2. Why are you reading now? It's midnight. You're supposed _____ sleeping.

3. It's late. Everyone is yawning. They _____ be getting tired.

4. You're sitting too close to the TV. Move back. You shouldn't be _____ so close to the TV.

5. My daughter's been using the Internet all day. She

_____ be _____ her homework or

she _____ chatting with her friends.

6. Please be quiet. This is a library. You're not supposed to be

_____ so loudly.

7. There's so much noise coming from my neighbor's apartment. She

might _____ a party.

8. You _____ be _____ on your cell

phone while driving. It could be dangerous.

EXERCISE **36** **Read this conversation. Choose the correct words in parentheses ( ) to complete the conversation. Sometimes both choices have the same meaning, so both answers are correct.**

CD 2, TR 08

A: I received a letter about a sweepstakes. I think I (may / am supposed to)
(example)

buy magazines in order to enter the contest.

B: You're wrong. You (must not / don't have to) buy anything.
(example)

A: But if I buy something, that (might / may)
(1)

increase my chances of winning.

B: That's not true. I've read several articles

on the Internet about sweepstakes and

scams recently.

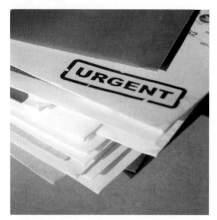

A: Then you (must / could) know a lot
(2)

about this topic.

B: I think I do. But you (shouldn't / don't have to) believe everything you
(3)

read on the Internet either.

A: How do I know what to believe?

B: You (may / should) use common sense. If an ad tells you that you are
(4)

already a winner, you (shouldn't / must not) believe it.
(5)

A: But if a letter tells me I've won a million dollars, I'd be crazy not to

look into it further.

B: You'd be crazy if you did. Do you think someone is going to give you

a million dollars for nothing?

(continued)

A: No, but . . .

B: If you want to get rich, you (*might / should*) work hard and save your
(6)
money.

A: But it (*could / might*) take years to get rich that way.
(7)

B: That's the only way. Yes, you (*could / can*) enter sweepstakes,
(8)
but you probably won't win.

A: I get offers by e-mail too. There are offers for products that
(*must / are supposed to*) make me lose weight. I'm a bit overweight
(9)
and I (*have to / have got to*) lose 20 pounds.
(10)

B: If you want to lose weight, you (*might / ought to*) eat a healthy diet
(11)
and exercise every day.

A: But that takes time. It (*could / might*) take months before I see a
(12)
difference.

B: That's right. But it's the only way. All those ads tell you that problems
(*can / must*) be fixed with easy solutions. But life isn't like that.
(13)

A: You (*must / should*) think I'm stupid for believing all these things I
(14)
see and hear.

B: I don't think you're stupid. Some companies are very clever about
getting your interest. For example, infomercials often have celebrities
talking about a product. You (*are expected to / are supposed to*)
(15)
trust the celebrity and believe what he or she says is true.

A: The government (*should / might*) do something to stop these
(16)
ads from appearing in our e-mail, in our postal mailboxes, and on TV.

B: I agree. There are already laws telling companies what they
(*are allowed to / are permitted to*) do or not. But some companies don't
(17)
do what they (*are supposed to / could*) do. It's up to you to be
(18)
informed, use your common sense, and protect yourself.

A: Well, thanks for your advice.

Summary of Lesson 4

EXAMPLES	EXPLANATION
You **must** take a test to get a driver's license. You **must not** drive without a license.	Law or rule (official tone) Negative: Prohibition
You**'re supposed to** wear your seat belt. He's **not supposed to** park here, but he did.	Law or rule (unofficial tone) Negative: Prohibition, rule often broken
I **have to** mail a letter. I**'ve got to** mail a letter. I **don't have to** go to the post office. I can put it in the mailbox.	Personal obligation Negative: Lack of necessity, other options possible
You**'d better** study tonight, or you might fail the test. You**'d better not** stay up late tonight, or you won't be alert in the morning.	Warning; negative consequences stated or implied
You **should** exercise every day. You **ought to** exercise every day. You **shouldn't** eat so much ice cream.	Advice Negative: It's not advisable.
You **may/can** write the test with a pencil. You **cannot/may not** talk during a test.	Permission Negative: Prohibition, less formal than *must* not
Students in the U.S. **can** wear jeans to class.	Social acceptability
I get annoying telemarketing calls. What **can** I do? You **could** listen politely, or you **can** say you're not interested and hang up.	Suggestions
You **may** win a prize if you enter the contest. You **might** win a prize if you enter the contest. You **could** win a prize if you enter the contest.	Possibility about the future
It**'s supposed to** rain tomorrow. This face cream **is supposed to** make you look younger. My brother **is supposed to** call me this weekend. We**'re supposed to** write five compositions. You**'re supposed to** take your hat off in church. The movie **is supposed to** begin at 8 P.M.	Expectation because of information we receive or because of a promise, requirement, custom, or schedule
She won a lot of money. She **must** be happy. She's eating very little. She **must not** be very hungry.	Deduction or logical conclusion about the present
I can't find my keys. They **might be** in your pocket. Did you look there? They **could be** on the table. Or they **may be** in your car. She looks confused. She **may not** know the answer. She **might not** understand the question.	Possibility about the present

Editing Advice

1. Don't use *to* after a modal. (Exception: *ought to*)

   You should ~~to~~ buy a new car.

2. Use the base form after a modal.

   go
   She can't ~~goes~~ with you.

   study
   You should ~~studying~~ every day.

3. Don't forget **d** in *supposed to*, *permitted to*, and *allowed to*.

   d
   He's not suppose‿to drive. He's too young.

   ed
   You're not allow‿to talk during the test.

4. Don't forget **'d** to express *had better*.

   'd
   You‿better take the bus to work. Your car isn't working well.

5. Use *have/has* before *got to* in writing.

   've
   We‿got to leave now.

6. Don't put two modals together.

   be able to
   You must ~~can~~ drive well before you can get your license.

7. Don't forget *be* or *to* in these expressions: *be supposed to*, *be able to*, *be permitted to*, *be allowed to*.

   are
   They‿supposed to leave at 6 A.M.

   to
   I'm able‿work on Saturday.

8. Use the correct word order in a question with a modal.

   should I
   What ~~I should~~ do?

Editing Quiz

Some of the shaded words and phrases **have mistakes. Find the mistakes and correct them. If the shaded words are correct, write C. *Do not change the modal itself. Only look for mistakes in grammar.***

must I   C

A: I'm going to enter a sweepstakes. What ~~I must~~ do to enter? Can you help
(example)   *(example)*

me?

B: You're suppose to mail in this postcard.
(1)

A: Must I buy something too?
(2)

B: That's not necessary. You can to enter the sweepstakes without buying
(3)

anything.

A: I think that if I buy something, I'll be able to increase my chances of
(4)

winning.

B: You ought to read this information carefully. It says here "No Purchase
(5)

Necessary."

A: Oh, I see.

B: I always throw those things away.

A: But you might winning a lot of money. Anyway, what you can lose?
(6)   *(7)*

It's so simple. You got to put a stamp on the postcard and fill in some
(8)

information. That's all. You should do it too. You might be able win a
(9)   *(10)*

million dollars.

B: I think entering a sweepstakes is a waste of time. Anyway, I'm not allowed
(11)

enter that sweepstakes.

A: Why not?

B: Because I work for that company. Employees not permitted to
(12)

participate. It says so right here. You better read the small print so you
(13)

can understand this better.
(14)

PART **1** Look at the job application. On the following pages, circle the best words to complete each sentence. The numbers on the application refer to each one of the sentences on pages 181–182.

① Fill out the following form. Print in black ink. Mail or fax the application to:

Ms. Judy Lipton
P.O. Box 32X
Chicago, IL 60640
FAX number: 312-555-4321

Applications must be submitted by November 15.

② Name _____ _____ _____
  (last) (first) (middle initial)

Address _____
  City _____ State _____ Zip code _____
③ Telephone (   ) _____
④ E-mail address (optional) _____ Sex _____ ⑤
⑥ Date of birth _____ _____ _____ (You must be at least 18.) ⑦
  (month) (day) (year)
⑧ Social Security number _____-_____-_____

⑨ Educational background:

	Date graduated	Degree or major
High School	_____	_____	_____
College	_____	_____	_____
Graduate School	_____	_____	_____

⑩ Employment history (Please start with your present or last job.)

Company	Position	Dates	Supervisor	Reason for leaving
_____	_____	_____	_____	_____
_____	_____	_____	_____	_____
_____	_____	_____	_____	_____
_____	_____	_____	_____	_____
_____	_____	_____	_____	_____

Do not write in the shaded box. For office use only.

⑪
Rec'd. by _____
Amer. cit. _____
Doc. checked _____
Transcripts received _____

⑫ The Immigration Act of 1986 requires all successful applicants to present documents to prove U.S. citizenship or permanent residence with permission to work in the U.S.

⑬ This company is an Equal Opportunity Employer. Race, religion, nationality, marital status, and physical disability will not influence our decision to hire.

⑭ I certify that these answers are true.

⑮ Signature: _____ Date: _____

EXAMPLE You (*aren't supposed to* / *couldn't*) use a red pen to fill out the application.

1. You (*have to* / *might*) submit the application to Ms. Lipton. Ms. Lipton (*must* / *should*) be the person in charge of hiring. She wants the application by November 15. Today is November 14. You (*'d better not* / *mustn't*) send it by regular mail. If you use regular mail, it (*must not* / *might not*) arrive on time. You (*could* / *are supposed to*) send it by overnight express mail, or you (*might* / *can*) fax it to Ms. Lipton's office.

2. You (*could* / *are supposed to*) write your last name before your first name.

3. You (*are supposed to* / *could*) include your phone number.

4. You (*shouldn't* / *don't have to*) include your e-mail address.

5. For sex, you (*might* / *are supposed to*) write M for male or F for female.

6. To write the date of your birth in the U.S., you (*should* / *can*) write the month before the day. You have several choices in writing the date. You (*must* / *could*) write June 7 or 6/7 or 6–7. If you put the day before the month, an American (*might* / *should*) think you mean July 6 instead of June 7.

7. To apply for the job, you (*might* / *must*) be over 18.

8. People who work in the U.S. (*may* / *must*) have a Social Security number.

9. You (*may* / *are supposed to*) include the schools you attended.

10. In the employment history section, you are asked why you left your last job. The employer (*might* / *should*) want to know if you were fired or if you left on your own.

11. You (*can't* / *aren't supposed to*) write in the shaded box. "Amer. cit." (*must* / *should*) mean American citizen.

12. You (*must not* / *don't have to*) be an American citizen to apply for the job. You can be a permanent resident. You (*have to* / *should*) prove your citizenship or residency. If you don't have permission to work in the U.S., you (*might not* / *cannot*) apply for this job.

(continued)

13. The company (*might not / may not*) choose a worker based on race, religion, or nationality.

14. You (*don't have to / must not*) lie on the application form.

15. You (*may / must*) sign the application and include the date.

PART **2** **Read the pairs of sentences. If the sentences have the same meaning, write *S*. If the sentences have a different meaning, write *D*.**

EXAMPLES   You <u>have</u> to wear your seat belt. / You <u>must</u> wear your seat belt.   S

You <u>must</u> open the window. / You <u>should</u> open the window.   D

1. She <u>can</u> drive a car. / She <u>is able to</u> drive a car.

2. He <u>can't</u> speak Korean. / He <u>might not</u> speak Korean.

3. I'<u>m supposed to</u> help my sister on Friday. / I <u>might</u> help my sister on Friday.

4. You <u>don't have to</u> drive to work. / You <u>shouldn't</u> drive to work.

5. You'<u>re not supposed to</u> write the answer. / You <u>don't have to</u> write the answer.

6. You'<u>re not allowed to</u> use a pencil for the test. / You <u>may not</u> use a pencil for the test.

7. We <u>should</u> visit our mother. / We <u>ought to</u> visit our mother.

8. You <u>should</u> make a right turn here. / You <u>must</u> make a right turn here.

9. If you need more help, you <u>could</u> go to a tutor. / If you need more help, you <u>can</u> go to a tutor.

10. You <u>shouldn't</u> wear jeans. / You <u>must not</u> wear jeans.

11. You <u>must not</u> come back after the final exam. / You <u>don't have to</u> come back after the final exam.

12. I <u>have to</u> work tomorrow. / I'<u>ve got to</u> work tomorrow.

13. You <u>can't</u> eat in the computer lab. / You <u>are not allowed to</u> eat in the computer lab.

14. I <u>may</u> go to New York next week. / I <u>might</u> go to New York next week.

15. I <u>could</u> be wrong. / I <u>might</u> be wrong.

16. You <u>don't have to</u> drive. / <u>It is not necessary to</u> drive.

17. You <u>don't have to</u> fill out the application with a red pen. / You <u>aren't supposed to</u> fill out the application with a red pen.

18. You<u>'d better</u> wake up early tomorrow morning. / You <u>could</u> wake up early tomorrow morning.

Expansion

Classroom Activities

❶ Form a small group. Take something from your purse or pocket that says something about you. Show it to your group. Your group will make deductions about you.

EXAMPLE   car keys
You must have a car.

❷ On the left are some American customs. On the right, tell if there is a comparable custom in your native culture or country. Write what that custom is.

In the U.S.	In my native culture or country
When someone sneezes, you're supposed to say, "Bless you."	
If you're invited to a party, in most cases you're not supposed to take your children.	
Americans sometimes have potluck parties. Guests are supposed to bring food to the party.	
There are some foods you can eat with your hands. Fried chicken and pizza are examples.	
Students are not supposed to talk to each other during an exam.	
When you're too sick to go to work, you're supposed to call your employer and say you're not coming in that day.	

❸ Bring in two copies of an application. It can be an application for a job, driver's license, license plate, apartment rental, address change, check cashing card, rebate, etc. Work with a partner. One person will give instructions. The other person will fill the application out. Use modals to help the other person fill it out correctly.

EXAMPLE   You're not supposed to write below this line.

❹ Find a partner and write some sentences to give advice for each of the following problems.

a. I got permission to come to the U.S. I have a dog. I've had this dog for six years, since she was a puppy, but I can't take her with me. What should I do?

b. I got a D in my biology class. I think I deserve a C. What should I do?

c. I need a new car, but I don't have enough money right now. What should I do?

d. I found an envelope with $100 in it in front of my apartment building. There is no name on it. What should I do?

e. My uncle came to live with us. He never cooks, cleans, or washes the dishes. I have to do everything. I'm very unhappy with the situation. What should I do?

Talk
About It

❶ Why do you think the elderly are often the victims of scams?

❷ Have you ever seen a TV infomercial? For what kind of products? Do you believe the claims about the product?

❸ How do you respond to telemarketing calls?

❹ What do you think of TV commercials?

❺ Did you ever win a prize in a contest, sweepstakes, or raffle? What did you win?

❻ Did you ever buy a product that claims to do something but doesn't do it?

Write About It

1 Write about a TV commercial that annoys you. Describe the commercial and tell why it annoys you.

2 Write about a time someone tricked you into buying something or paying money for something you didn't get.

3 What is your experience with telemarketing calls? Write one paragraph telling how you respond to them. Write another paragraph giving advice to someone who gets these calls.

EXAMPLE

Telemarketing Calls

It seems whenever I sit down with my family to eat dinner, the phone rings. I probably shouldn't answer the phone but I do. Companies are always telling me that I should get a new service or buy a new product that I don't need...

 For more practice using grammar in context, please visit our Web site.

Richard M. Nixon, president 1969–1974

Grammar
Modals in the Past

Context
American Presidents

Abraham Lincoln, president 1861–1865

John F. Kennedy, president 1961–1963

Slavery, Lincoln, and the Civil War

Before
You Read

1. What do you know about President Lincoln?

2. Has your country ever had a civil war?

CD 2, TR 09

Read the following textbook article. Pay special attention to *should have*, *must have*, *may have*, and *could have*.

> From the time of the first English colonies in America, Africans were brought to America as slaves. Most of them were taken to the South, where they worked on farms in the production of sugar, cotton, and other crops. The prosperity of the white farmers in the South **couldn't have happened** without slaves. But many northerners were against slavery. One of those was Abraham Lincoln, the president who finally brought the end of slavery in the U.S.
>
> Today many people consider Abraham Lincoln to be one of the greatest presidents of the United States. But during his time, many had their doubts about his ability to lead the country during the growing conflict between the North and the South. Before he became president, other politicians did not take him seriously. Lincoln's parents were poor and uneducated, and Lincoln had only 18 months of schooling. But he loved to read, and he educated himself. Lincoln dressed in poorly fitting clothes and didn't look like the polished politicians of the East. One newspaper had called Lincoln "a fourth-rate lecturer, who cannot speak good grammar." Because Lincoln had so little schooling, journalists **must have thought** he was not very smart.
>
> Much to his opponents' surprise, Lincoln won the election for president in 1860. At that time, the Southern slave owners wanted to continue slavery, but Lincoln wanted to stop the spread of slavery. What followed was the worst internal crisis in American history: the Civil War. More than half a million soldiers died on both sides of the conflict, the most of any war that the U.S. fought in. One especially terrible battle took place at Gettysburg, Pennsylvania. On November 19, 1863, President Lincoln was invited to say a few words at the battleground. Edward Everett, the main speaker, gave a speech that lasted two hours in front of a crowd of almost 20,000 people. Lincoln followed Everett with a two-minute speech. When he was finished, the audience was silent. The audience **may have been surprised** by the brevity[1] of the speech. Some people thought he **must not have been** finished. Seeing the reaction of the crowd, Lincoln

Did You Know?

In 1860, the population of the U.S. was 31 million; almost 4 million of these people were slaves.

---

[1]*Brevity* is the noun form for the adjective "brief."

turned to Everett and said he was afraid his speech had been a failure. He said he **should have prepared** it more carefully. Everett did not agree. He said the speech was perfect. He said the president had said more in two minutes than he, Everett, had said in two hours. This speech, known as the Gettysburg Address, is considered one of the greatest speeches in American history. In his speech, Lincoln said that the country was dedicated to freedom and that "government of the people, by the people, for the people" had to continue.

The Civil War continued until April 9, 1865, when the North finally won. Less than three weeks later, on April 26, Lincoln was assassinated.

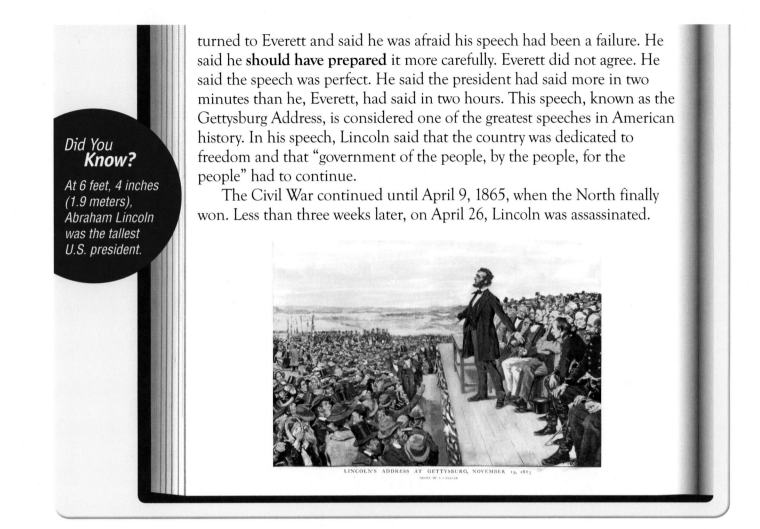

LINCOLN'S ADDRESS AT GETTYSBURG, NOVEMBER 19, 1863
DRAWN BY A. I. KELLER

5.1 Modals in the Past

To form the past of a modal, use modal + *have* + past participle.

Active					
Subject	**Modal**	*Not*	*Have*	**Past Participle**	**Complement**
I	**should**		**have**	**prepared**	the speech more carefully.
People	**may**	**not**	**have**	**realized**	that his speech was finished.
Southern farmers	**could**	**not**	**have**	**become**	rich without slaves.
Some people	**must**		**have**	**thought**	(that) Lincoln was not very smart.
Pronunciation Note: In informal speech, *have* is often pronounced like *of* or /ə/.					

(continued)

To form the passive of a past modal, use modal + *have* + *been* + past participle.

Passive					
Subject	**Modal**	*Not*	*Have Been*	**Past Participle**	**Complement**
The people	**might**		**have been**	**surprised**	by the speech.
Lincoln	**could**		**have been**	**elected**	again.
Slavery	**should**	**not**	**have been**	**permitted**	in the U.S.

EXERCISE 1 Fill in the blanks to complete the sentences.

A: Did you read the story about Lincoln before class?

B: No. I didn't have time.

A: You should ____have____ read it. Our lesson depends on it. It's
        (example)

about Lincoln.

B: Who's Lincoln?

A: What do you mean, "Who's Lincoln?" Abraham Lincoln. You must

have _____ of him. He was one of the most well-known
            (1)

presidents of the U.S.

B: Oh. Abraham Lincoln. Of course I've heard of him. I thought you

said "Leeko."

A: Oh. I must _____ pronounced his name wrong. Sorry. Anyway,
                    (2)

he gave one of the greatest speeches of any American president. But

after the speech, he said, "I should have _____ it more carefully."
                                            (3)

B: He must have _____ it very fast.
                    (4)

A: No. I don't think he wrote it fast. I think he chose his words very

carefully. The people in the audience might _____ expected a
                                              (5)

longer speech. But it was a perfect speech, and he was a great president.

B: If he was such a good president, he must _____ well-liked.
                                                (6)

A: He was well-liked by many in the North, but most Southerners didn't

like him because they wanted slavery to continue.

5.2 Past Possibility and Probability

EXAMPLES	EXPLANATION
Lincoln thought, "I **might have bored** the audience." Why didn't the audience react after Lincoln's speech? They **could have been** surprised. They **may have expected** him to say more.	To express possibility about the past, use *may have*, *might have*, or *could have* + past participle. The sentences on the left express "maybe" about the past. *I might have bored the audience. = Maybe I bored the audience.* *They could have been surprised. = Maybe they were surprised.* *They may have expected him to say more. = Maybe they expected him to say more.*
Lincoln thought, "I **may not have given** a very good speech." Lincoln thought, "I **might not have prepared** well enough."	To show negative possibility, use *may not have* and *might not have*. Don't use *could not have* because it has a different meaning. (See Section 5.8)
Because Lincoln had so little schooling, some journalists **must have thought** he was not very smart. When Lincoln finished his speech after two minutes, some people thought that he **must not have been finished.** Lincoln thought, "They **must not have liked** my speech."	We use *must have* + past participle to make a statement of logical conclusion or deduction about a past event based on observations we make or information we have. We are saying that something is probably true. *They must have thought he wasn't smart. = They probably thought he wasn't smart.* *He must not have been finished. = He probably wasn't finished.* *They must not have liked my speech. = They probably didn't like my speech.*

EXERCISE **2** Change these *maybe* statements to statements with *may have, might have,* or *could have.* Situation: A student dropped out of a course after the first few weeks. These are some guesses about why he did it.

EXAMPLE Maybe he registered for the wrong section. (may)
He may have registered for the wrong section.

1. Maybe he preferred an earlier class. (could)
2. Maybe he wanted to be in his friend's class. (might)
3. Maybe the class was too hard for him. (may)
4. Maybe he got sick. (could)
5. Maybe he didn't like the teacher. (may)
6. Maybe he found a full-time job. (might)
7. Maybe he had a lot of problems at home. (could)
8. Maybe he left town. (might)

EXERCISE **3** Fill in the blanks with an appropriate verb for past possibility. Answers may vary.

1. **A:** I was trying to call your house last night, but you didn't answer.

   B: What time did you call?

   A: After 8 P.M.

   B: Let's see. Where was I? I might _____have been_____ at the
   (example)
   library at that time.

   A: But I tried calling your cell phone too.

   B: I may _____ it off. I usually turn it off when
   I'm at the library. Why didn't you leave a message?

   A: I did leave a message.

   B: Oh. I might _____ it by mistake.

   A: You deleted my message?

   B: Sorry.

2. **A:** Have you seen my keys?

   B: You're always losing your keys. You may _____
   them in your pocket.

   A: No, they're not there. I already looked.

B: Well, you could _____ them as you were getting out of the car.

A: When I drop keys, I can hear them hit the ground, so I'm sure that's not it.

B: Well, you might _____ them in the door when you came in last night.

A: Oh, you're right! They're in the door. Thanks.

3. **A:** I'm so upset. I left my dictionary in class yesterday. Now I'll have to buy a new one.

   B: Why don't you ask the teacher? She might _____

   _____.

   A: I already did. She didn't pick it up.

   B: Why don't you go to the "lost and found"? Somebody may

   _____ it and returned it there.

   A: Where's the "lost and found"?

   B: In front of the cafeteria.

4. **A:** I applied for a job three weeks ago, but so far I haven't heard anything. I probably didn't do well on the interview.

   B: You don't know that. They might _____ hundreds of candidates for the job. Anyway, why don't you call and tell the company you're still interested?

   A: But they could _____ someone else already.

   B: You won't know if they hired someone else unless you ask.

5. **A:** I asked my boss for a raise last week, and she said she'd get back to me. But so far she hasn't mentioned anything.

   B: She might _____ about it. I'm sure she has a lot on her mind and can easily forget something. Why don't you ask her again?

(continued)

6. A: I sent an e-mail to an old friend and I got a message saying it was

undeliverable.

B: You might _____ the address wrong.

A: No. I checked. I wrote it correctly.

B: Your friend may _____ his old account and

opened a new one.

CD 2, TR 10

EXERCISE **4** **Fill in the blanks with an appropriate verb for past probability. Answers may vary.**

1. A: Kennedy's death was such a tragedy.

B: Who's Kennedy?

A: You don't know who Kennedy was? He was so famous. You must

_____**have heard**_____ of him. There's a picture of him in this book.
(example)

B: No, I've never heard of him. Wow. He was so handsome. He must

_____ a movie star.

A: No. He was an American president. He was assassinated in 1963

when he was only 46 years old.

B: That's terrible. It must _____ a hard time for

Americans.

A: Yes, it was. I remember my parents telling me about it. They were in

high school when it happened. They must _____

about 15 or 16 years old.

2. A: I followed your directions to go downtown yesterday. I took the

number 60 bus, but it didn't take me downtown.

B: You must _____ me. I said, "16," not "60."

A: Yes. I misunderstood you. I thought you said, "60."

B: It's hard to hear the difference between 16 and 60. Even

native speakers misunderstand each other. Anyway, you must

_____ a terrible day.

A: Yes, I had an awful day. When I got off the bus, I was totally lost, so I took a taxi downtown.

B: A taxi must _____ you over $20!

A: In fact, it cost me $30. So I wasted a lot of time and money yesterday.

3. **A:** I called you yesterday, but you didn't answer the phone.

B: You must _____ a wrong number. I always keep my cell phone on. What time did you call?

A: About 8 P.M.

B: Oh. I must _____ in the shower. Why did you call?

A: I forgot already.

B: Then it must not _____ very important.

4. **A:** How did you like the party last Saturday, Terri?

B: I wasn't there.

A: What do you mean you weren't there? We talked for a few hours.

B: You must _____ with my twin sister, Sherri. We look alike.

A: She must _____ that I was crazy. I kept calling her Terri.

B: I'm sure she didn't think anything of it. She's used to it.

5. **A:** How did you do on the last test?

B: I didn't know about the test, so I didn't study. I failed it.

A: The teacher announced it last Thursday.

B: I must _____ absent that day.

A: I think Rona must _____ it too. When she got her paper, she started to cry.

B: Did you see Paula? She was so excited when she saw her exam. She must _____ an A.

(continued)

6. A: Maria's relatives just went back to Mexico. They were here for

a month.

B: She must _____ a wonderful time with them.

A: Yes, but she must _____ sad when she took them

to the airport. She didn't want them to leave. She took them

everywhere—to museums, to restaurants, to concerts.

B: She must _____ a lot of money.

A: She knew she was going to spend a lot of money, so she saved a lot

before they came.

7. A: I thought I was driving east, but now I think I'm driving north.

B: You must _____ a wrong turn somewhere. Let's

take a look at the map. (*After looking in the glove compartment*)

I can't find the map.

A: I must _____ it on the kitchen table. I was looking

at it before we got in the car.

B: No problem. Let's just call our friends. They'll tell us how to get to

their house. Let me use your cell phone.

A: Oh, no. The battery is dead. I must _____ to

recharge it.

B: Not again. You always forget to recharge it. Why don't we just stop

at a gas station and get directions?

A: You know I don't like to ask for directions.

8. A: I said, "How are you?" to one of my classmates, and she answered,

"I'm 58 years old." What was she thinking?

B: She must _____ that you said, "How *old* are you?"

A: She gave me a strange look. She must _____ that

I was impolite asking about her age.

B: That's nothing. When I didn't speak much English, I went to a restaurant and asked the waitress for "soap" instead of "soup."

A: So did she bring you soap or soup?

B: Soup, of course.

A: Then she must _____ you in spite of your mistake.

9. **A:** I haven't seen Peter this semester. Have you?

B: He must _____.

A: Why would he drop out? He was close to getting his degree.

B: He said that he wouldn't come back if he didn't get financial aid. He must not _____ financial aid this semester.

A: That's too bad.

10. **A:** You look tan. You must _____ out in the sun.

B: I was. I was in Florida for vacation.

A: That must _____ wonderful.

B: Actually, it was terrible. First, we lost our money and credit cards.

A: What did you do?

B: The credit card company canceled our card and gave us a new one. We used the credit card to get cash.

A: So then the rest of your trip was fine, wasn't it?

B: Not really. We rented a car and it kept breaking down.

A: But it must _____ nice to get away from winter here and be in the sun.

B: We were there for two weeks. It must _____ for all but the last few days. Finally when the rain stopped, I got some sun.

The Cuban Missile Crisis

Before You Read

1. Has your native country ever been at war with another country?

2. Do you think a nuclear war is possible today?

CD 2, TR 11

Read the following textbook article. Pay special attention to *could have* **+ past participle.**

In October 1962, the United States and the Soviet Union[2] came close to war. The U.S. discovered that the Soviet Union was beginning to send nuclear missiles to Cuba, which is only about 90 miles from Florida. President John Kennedy saw this as a direct threat to national security; these weapons **could have been** used to destroy cities and military bases in the U.S. On October 22, President Kennedy announced on TV that any attack from Cuba would be considered an attack from the Soviet Union, and he would respond with a full attack on the Soviets. He sent out the U.S. Navy to block Soviet ships from delivering weapons to Cuba. For 13 days, the world was at the edge of a major war. Finally, the Soviets agreed to send their missiles back and promised to stop building military bases in Cuba. In exchange, the U.S. promised to remove its missiles from Turkey.

In October 2002, there was a reunion of many of the surviving players in this crisis. Cuban president Fidel Castro met with former Secretary of Defense Robert McNamara and other Americans, Cubans, and Russians involved in the decisions made 40 years earlier. Remembering their experiences, they all agreed that this was indeed a major crisis that **could have changed** the world as we know it. Discussing the viewpoints and experiences of the Americans, McNamara explained that a nuclear attack on a U.S. ship **could** easily **have grown** into a full nuclear war between the U.S. and the Soviet Union. A former CIA[3] analyst who studied spy photos told the group that at least 16 intermediate-range missiles in Cuba **could have reached** any point in the continental United States[4] except the northwest corner. He said at the conference, "October 27 is a day I'll never forget. The planet **could have been destroyed**." A former Kennedy aide added, "It **could have been** the end of the world, but here we are, 40 years later."

Fortunately, diplomacy[5] won over war. What **could have been** a tragic event is now only a chapter in history.

---

[2]In 1991, the country then called the *Soviet Union*, broke up into 15 different countries, the largest of which is Russia.
[3]The *CIA* is the Central Intelligence Agency. It gathers information about other countries' secrets.
[4]The *continental* United States refers to all states except Hawaii and Alaska, which are not part of the U.S. mainland.
[5]*Diplomacy* is skillful negotiation between countries to try to work out problems without fighting.

5.3 Past Direction Not Taken

We use *could have* + past participle to show that something did not happen.

EXAMPLES	EXPLANATION
The Cuban Missile Crisis **could have been** the end of the world. An attack on a U.S. ship **could have grown** into a full nuclear war. Missiles **could have reached** almost any place in the U.S.	Use *could have* + past participle to show that something came close to happening, but didn't.
Kennedy and his advisors looked at several possibilities. They **could have attacked** immediately. They **could have invaded** Cuba. But they decided to give the Soviets a chance to remove the missiles and turn the ships around.	Use *could have* + past participle to show that a past opportunity was not taken. Several options were possible; all but one were rejected.
I heard you moved last weekend. Why didn't you tell me? I **could have helped** you.	Use *could have* + past participle to show missed opportunities.
I was so hungry (that) I **could have eaten** the whole pie by myself. I was so tired (that) I **could have slept** all day. I was so happy when I got an A on the test (that) I **could have kissed** the teacher. When the missiles were removed, we **could have jumped** for joy.	Use *could have* + past participle to show an exaggeration of a result.
Driver to pedestrian: Watch out, you idiot! I **could have killed** you. Father to son: Don't play baseball so close to the house. Your ball came within inches of the window. You **could have broken** the window.	Use *could have* + past participle to show that something almost happened.

EXERCISE 5 Fill in the blanks with the correct form of the verb in parentheses ( ) to exaggerate the result.

EXAMPLE   The party was so wonderful that I could ___**have stayed**___ all night.
(stay)

1. I was so tired that I could _____ for 12 hours yesterday.
(sleep)

2. I was so embarrassed when I made a mistake in my speech that I could

_____ of shame.
(die)

3. She was so happy when she fell in love she could _____
(walk)

on air.

4. I was so happy when my counselor told me about my scholarship that

I could _____ him.
(kiss)

5. The movie was so good I could _____ it again
(watch)

and again.

6. Your cookies were so good that I could _____ all of them.
(eat)

7. I enjoyed dancing so much last night that I could _____
(dance)

all night.

8. It was so hot yesterday that we could _____ an egg
(fry)

on the street.

EXERCISE 6 Fill in the blanks with an appropriate verb for past direction not taken. Answers may vary.

EXAMPLE   **A:** Did you read about the Cuban Missile Crisis?
B: Yes. The U.S. almost went to war with the Soviet Union.
A: Those two superpowers could ___**have destroyed**___ the whole world!

1. A: I heard you bought a condo.

B: We did.

A: Why didn't you buy a house? Was it too expensive?

B: We could _____ a house, but we don't have enough time to take care of things. So we thought a condo would be better. There's someone to take care of the grass in the summer and the snow in the winter.

2. **A:** What do you do for a living?

B: I'm a waiter, but I could _____ a famous actor. Everyone says I've got a lot of talent. And my wife could _____ a career in modeling. She's so beautiful.

A: It's not too late to follow your dream.

B: We have small kids to support. So I think my acting dreams and her modeling dreams are over.

3. **A:** Do you want to see our new apartment? We moved last Saturday.

B: Why did you move? You had a lovely apartment. I'm surprised you didn't stay there.

A: We could _____ there. The rent wasn't too bad and the landlord was nice. But it was too far from school and work.

B: Who helped you move?

A: We did it all ourselves.

B: Why didn't you let me know? I could _____ you.

A: We didn't want to bother our friends.

B: What are friends for?

A: Anyway, you have a small car. We needed to rent a van.

B: I could _____ my sister's van. She always lets me borrow it if I have to move stuff.

A: We appreciate your kindness, but everything worked out fine.

(continued)

4. A: I can't believe you tried to fix the ceiling light without shutting off the electricity first. You could _____ yourself.

B: But I didn't. I'm still alive and the light is fixed.

A: You shouldn't take chances. And you got up on that tall ladder when you were home alone. You could _____, and no one would have been here to help you.

B: But I didn't fall. You worry too much. Everything's okay. The light is fixed, and I didn't break a leg.

5. A: I bought stocks and sold them a few months later. Now they're worth four times as much as what I sold them for. I could _____ a lot of money.

B: You never know with the stock market. You could _____ a lot of money too.

6. A: Sorry I'm so late.

B: What happened?

A: I had to take three buses to get to a job interview in the suburbs. It took me almost two hours to get there.

B: Why didn't you tell me? I could _____ you there in my car.

A: I didn't want to bother you.

B: You wasted a whole day today. You could _____ home hours ago.

A: That's not a problem. I'm home now. And I did my homework while I was on the bus on the way there. On the way home, I slept most of the way. It's a good thing the person sitting next to me woke me up. I could _____ my bus stop.

EXERCISE **7** **ABOUT YOU** Fill in the blanks to tell about a missed opportunity in your life. Share your answers in a small group or with the entire class.

EXAMPLE *I could have gone to Germany instead of coming to the U.S., but it's*

easier to find a job in my profession in the U.S.

I could have _____ instead of

_____, but

_____.

Election 2000: Bush vs. Gore

Before You Read

1. What do you know about the election process in the U.S.?

2. Do you think it's important for every citizen to vote?

CD 2, TR 12

Read the following conversation. Pay special attention to *should have* **+ past participle.**

A: Did you vote in the last election?

B: I couldn't. I'm not a citizen. You're a citizen. Did you vote?

A: No. I was busy that day. Besides, one person's vote is not important.

B: That's not true. You **should have voted**. Didn't you hear about the presidential election in 2000?

A: No. I wasn't in the U.S. at that time. What happened?

B: George W. Bush was running against Al Gore.

A: So? George Bush won, didn't he?

B: Yes. But a lot of people thought Al Gore **should have won**.

A: Why?

B: The election was very close. Al Gore had more of the popular vote, but he lost.

(continued)

A: How could that happen? He **shouldn't have lost** if he had the people's vote.

B: The U.S. has a strange way of picking a president. It's very complicated, but each state has a certain number of electoral votes based on population. It's possible to win the popular vote and lose the electoral vote.

A: I don't understand.

B: It's really hard to understand. But anyway, Florida had 25 electoral votes, which is a lot. The candidate who would win Florida in 2000 would win the election.

A: So how did Florida vote?

B: At first the news reported that Gore had won. A few hours later, they said that Bush had won.

A: The news reporters **should have waited** until all the votes were counted.

B: I agree. Usually the result of an election is known the same night or early the next morning. But Gore asked that the votes be counted again, just to make sure. The Florida Supreme Court decided that Bush won the state by about 500 votes.

A: Wow! That's a close election.

B: You see? That's why you **should have voted**. Every vote counts.

5.4 Past Mistakes

EXAMPLES	EXPLANATION
You **should have voted** in the last election. The news reporters **shouldn't have announced** the winner so soon. Who **should have won** the election of 2000?	We use *should have* + past participle to comment on a mistake in the past. We are not really giving advice because it is impossible to change the past.
You **ought to have voted**.	Less frequently, we use *ought to have* + past participle. *Ought to* is not usually used for negatives.

Usage Note: When a person receives an unexpected gift, he may be a little embarrassed. This person might say, *"You shouldn't have."* This means, "You shouldn't have gone to so much trouble or expense." or "You shouldn't have given me a gift. I don't deserve it." Saying this is considered polite, and an appropriate response might be, *"But it's my pleasure."*

EXERCISE 8 Fill in the blanks with an appropriate verb for past mistakes.

EXAMPLES A: I didn't study for the last test, and I failed it.

B: You should _____have studied_____.

A: I know, but there was a great party the night before, and I went with my friends.

B: You shouldn't _____have gone_____ to a party the night before a test.

1. A: I'm so hungry. I didn't have time to eat breakfast this morning.

   B: You should _____ something before class.

   A: I know, but I was late.

   B: What time did you get up?

   A: About 45 minutes before class.

   B: You should _____ earlier. By the way, what topic did you use for your composition?

   A: Oh, my gosh! I forgot about the composition.

   B: You should _____ down the assignment.

   A: You're right. I'll get a calendar, and from now on, I'll write down all my assignments.

2. (*cell phone conversation*)

   A: Hi. I'm at the supermarket now. Did you ask me to buy cereal?

   B: Yes. Don't you remember? You should _____ the list.

   A: I know, but I thought I'd remember everything, so I didn't take the list.

   B: This is what we need: a gallon of milk, a bag of dog food, and a watermelon.

   A: Those things are heavy. How do you expect me to carry all of those things home?

   B: In the car, of course.

   A: Oh. I came here by bike. I should _____.

   B: Yes, you should have.

(*continued*)

3. A: How was your trip during spring break?

B: It was great. You should _____ with us.

A: I wanted to go with you, but I didn't have enough money.

B: You should _____ your money instead of spending it eating out in restaurants all the time.

A: You're right. And I shouldn't _____ so many CDs.

B: Did you get my postcard?

A: No. When did you send it?

B: Over two weeks ago. I should _____ it to the post office instead of putting it in the hotel mailbox.

4. (*husband and wife*)

H: I washed my blue pants with my new white shirt and now my shirt looks blue.

W: You should _____ the clothes by color before putting them in the washing machine. I always separate mine.

H: I should _____ my clothes to you to wash.

W: I may be your wife, but I'm not your maid. So don't give me your dirty clothes.

5. (*wife and husband*)

W: This is a terrible trip. Why did you suggest going to the mountains? We should _____ to the coast. It's too cold here. I don't like cold weather.

H: You should _____ me that before we left.

W: I *did* tell you that, but you didn't pay attention. We didn't take jackets. We should _____ our jackets.

H: We can go and buy some.

W: I don't want to spend money on jackets when we've got perfectly good ones at home.

H: Maybe we should _____ home instead of taking a trip.

6. (*student and teacher*)

S: Can you tell me my midterm grade?

T: Didn't you receive it by mail?

S: No. I moved right after the semester began.

T: You should _____ a change of address in the school office when you moved.

S: I'll report it today. So can you tell me my grade?

T: It's a C.

S: Why a C? I got Bs and As on the tests.

T: But you didn't do all your homework. You should _____ all your homework.

S: But I had to work full-time.

T: You should _____ about that before you registered for four courses.

S: You're right. I didn't think much about homework when I registered.

7. A: I took a young woman from class out for dinner last week, but I didn't have enough money.

B: You should _____ enough money with you.

A: I took about $30 with me. I thought we were going to go to a fast-food place, but she chose a fancy restaurant.

B: You should _____ the restaurant.

(continued)

A: I realized that later. She ordered appetizers, then dinner, then dessert and coffee. I thought she would pay for part of the dinner. But when the bill came, she just sat there.

B: You should _____ her that you wanted to split the bill.

A: I couldn't tell her that. I was trying to impress her.

B: So what did you do?

A: I went to the bathroom and called my brother on my cell phone. He rushed over to the restaurant and brought me some money. He pretended that our meeting there was an accident.

B: You should _____ her the truth. Lying to her is no way to start a relationship.

A: I don't think I'm going to go out with her again.

8. **A:** What happened to your car?

B: I had an accident. Someone hit me from behind.

A: What did the police say?

B: We didn't call the police. The other driver gave me his phone number and told me he would pay for the damage. But when I called, it was a disconnected number.

A: You should _____ the police.

B: And I should _____ information from his driver's license.

A: You mean you didn't even take information from his driver's license?

B: No. He looked honest.

A: You should _____ information about his insurance too.

B: I know. It's too late to get it now.

5.5 *Be Supposed To* in the Past

EXAMPLES	EXPLANATION
We **were supposed to** get the results of the election on election night, but we didn't.	*Was/were supposed to* is used for rules or promises that have been broken or expectations that have not been met.
The teacher **was supposed to** explain the election process to us, but she didn't have time.	
We **were supposed to** have a test today, but the teacher was absent.	
I **was supposed to** call my parents last night, but I forgot.	

EXERCISE 9 **Fill in the blanks with a verb. Answers may vary.**

EXAMPLE She was supposed to ___finish___ the report by Friday, but she didn't have enough time.

1. I was supposed to _____ my homework, but my printer wasn't working. So I wrote it by hand.

2. You were supposed to _____ me this morning. I waited all morning for your call.

3. Our plane was supposed to _____ at 9:45, but it was late. We had to wait in the airport for two more hours to start our trip.

4. The teacher was supposed to _____ our compositions yesterday, but he was sick and didn't do it.

5. It was supposed to _____ last weekend, so we canceled our picnic. But it never rained.

6. I got a parking ticket yesterday. I wasn't supposed to _____ on the east side of the street, but I didn't see the signs.

7. I couldn't get into the building. I was supposed to _____ my student ID, but I left it at home.

8. The kids weren't supposed to _____ the cookies before they ate dinner, but they did.

9. The play was supposed to _____ at 8 P.M., but it didn't begin until 8:10.

10. You were supposed to _____ out the application with a black pen, but you used a red pen.

The Media and Presidential Elections

Before
You Read

1. Have you ever voted in an election?

2. Do you think we learn a lot about candidates from TV?

CD 2, TR 13

Read the following textbook article. Pay special attention to _must have_ + past participle and _had to_ + base form. Also pay attention to _couldn't have_ + past participle and _couldn't_ + base form.

Harry S. Truman, president 1945–1953

The media—newspapers, magazines, radio, television, and now the Internet—play an important part in getting out information and often shaping public opinion. The media even played a historical role in two notable presidential elections.

When President Franklin Roosevelt died in 1945, Vice President Harry S. Truman became president. But in 1948, Truman **had to campaign** for re-election. He ran against Thomas Dewey. At that time, television was still new and most people did not own one. So candidates **had to travel** from city to city by train to meet the people. Truman traveled tirelessly, but Dewey was considered the stronger candidate.

Polls[6] were so sure of a Dewey victory that they stopped asking for public opinion a week before the election. The media, especially newspapers and the radio, thought that Truman **couldn't win**. When Truman went to bed the night of the election, he thought that he would lose.

The election results were coming in slowly and newspapers **had to prepare** the news of the election. On the basis of early opinion polls, the media concluded that Dewey **must have won** the election, and many newspapers showed Dewey's victory. However, they were wrong. Truman won by 2 million votes. When the votes were all counted, the newspapers **had to admit** their mistake.

[6]A _poll_ is an analysis of public opinion on different matters compiled by special agencies. Statistics are made based on the answers to questions.

Another example of how the media can influence results took place in the 1960 presidential race between John Kennedy and Richard Nixon. For the first time in history, the two candidates debated[7] each other on TV. They **had to** answer difficult

Kennedy and Nixon debate

questions. Many people who heard the Nixon-Kennedy debate on the radio thought that Nixon was the stronger candidate. But people who saw the debate on TV thought that the young, handsome Kennedy was the stronger candidate. Also, Nixon was sweating under the hot lights, and people thought that he **must have been** nervous and uncomfortable with the questions. It was a close election, but Kennedy won. Many people think Kennedy **couldn't have won** without TV.

In the 2008 presidential election, John McCain lost to Barack Obama. Obama reached out to the Internet generation; McCain didn't even know how to use a computer. He **had to** depend on his wife to read and send e-mail. Although it may not be important for a president to be an Internet user (after all, he has staff who can do it for him), McCain wasn't in touch with the social, cultural, and economic realities of the Internet.

It is clear that political hopefuls now need the media to get their images and messages across.

5.6 *Must Have* vs. *Had To*

Must have + past participle and *had to* + base form have completely different meanings.

EXAMPLES	EXPLANATION
Truman became president in 1945 when Franklin Roosevelt died. But he **had to** campaign for re-election in 1948. Truman **had to** travel by train to meet the people. During the debate, the candidates **had to** answer difficult questions. John McCain **had to** depend on his wife to do e-mail.	To show necessity (personal or legal) in the past, we use *had to* + base form. We cannot use *must* in the past with this meaning.
Based on opinion polls, the newspapers concluded that Dewey **must have won.** Truman **must have been** surprised when he found out that he had won. TV viewers thought that Nixon **must have been** nervous and uncomfortable during the debate.	When *must* shows a conclusion or deduction in the past, use *must have* + past participle.

[7]In a *debate*, the candidates have to answer questions (on TV or radio) so that the public can judge who is the better candidate.

EXERCISE 10   **Below is a conversation between two American citizens about the 2000 presidential election. Write *had to* + base form for a past necessity. Write *must have* + past participle for a past deduction or conclusion.**

CD 2, TR 14

A: The 2000 election between Al Gore, the Democratic candidate, and George W. Bush, the Republican candidate, was so strange.

B: It was?

A: Don't you remember? The election was close and they ___**had to count**___ the votes again to see who won. It took them
(example: count)
five weeks to figure out who won the election.

B: Bush and Gore ___**must have been**___ nervous the whole time,
(example: be)
waiting to find out the results.

A: Yes, they probably were. And there were so many problems with the election that they _____ to the Supreme
(1 go)
Court to decide who won.

B: Did you vote in that election?

A: Of course.

B: You always vote for a Democrat, so you _____
(2 vote)
for Gore.

A: Yes, I did.

B: You _____ very disappointed when they finally
(3 be)
announced that Gore lost.

A: Yes, I was. What about you? Who did you vote for?

B: I _____ overtime that day so I didn't vote.
(4 work)

A: That's no excuse for not voting. Besides, your boss is required to give you time off to vote.

B: One person's vote doesn't matter much anyway.

A: It did in 2000. Every vote counted. The election was on November 7 and we _____ until December 13 to find out who
(5 wait)
won the election because it was such a close race.

5.7 Could + Base Form vs. Could Have + Past Participle

There are several ways to express *can* in the past, depending on the meaning you want to convey.

EXAMPLES	EXPLANATION
Now I can speak English well. A few years ago, I **could speak** only a few words of English. I **was able to communicate** in very simple English.	In affirmative statements, *could* + base form means *used to be able to*. The person had this ability over a period of time. *Was/were able to* can also be used for ability over a past period of time.
President Kennedy **was able to prevent** a war. He **was able to convince** the Soviets to send back their missiles. I looked on the Internet and **was able to find** Lincoln's Gettysburg Address.	Use *was/were able to* for success in doing a single action. Do not use *could* for a single action.
I **couldn't vote** in the last election because I wasn't a citizen. I **wasn't able to vote** in the last election because I wasn't a citizen. The newspapers **weren't able to predict** the outcome of the 1948 election. The newspapers **couldn't predict** the outcome of the 1948 election.	In negative statements, *couldn't* and *wasn't/ weren't able to* are used interchangeably.
Al Gore **could have run** for president again, but he decided to stay out of politics. The Cuban Missile Crisis **could have destroyed** the world.	Use *could have* + past participle for an action that didn't happen.
Some people thought that Kennedy **couldn't have won** the election without TV. Farmers in the South **couldn't have become** rich without slaves.	Use *couldn't have* + past participle to show that something was impossible in the past.

EXERCISE 11 **ABOUT YOU** Fill in the blanks and discuss your answers.

EXAMPLE When I didn't know much English, I couldn't <u>talk to people on the phone</u>.

1. When I was young, I could always count on _____.
2. When I was younger, I could _____ better than I can now.

(continued)

3. When I was younger, I couldn't _____ as well as
I can now.

4. One of my goals was to _____.
I was/wasn't able (*choose one*) to achieve my goal.

5. I could never understand why _____.

6. When I didn't know much English, I couldn't _____.

7. I couldn't _____ a few years ago
because _____.

8. When I first came to the U.S., I was/wasn't (*choose one*) able to

_____.

EXERCISE **12**   **Fill in the blanks with *have* + a past participle.**

EXAMPLE   I could ____**have driven**____ to work, but I decided to ride
my bike instead.

   1. When Lincoln gave the Gettysburg Address, he could
   _____ a long speech, but he decided to give a very
   short speech.

   2. My sister is a citizen and she could _____ in the last
   election, but she was sick that day.

   3. We could _____ the election results on TV, but we
   decided to listen to the news on the radio instead.

   4. She could _____ English in her country, but she
   decided to study French instead.

   5. I could _____ my mom, but I sent her a text message
   instead to tell her I'd be home late.

   6. You could _____ your homework on the computer,
   but I see you did it by hand.

   7. Why didn't you tell me you were moving last Saturday? I'm sure you
   needed help. I could _____ you.

   8. I could _____ the bus today, but the weather was
   nice so I decided to walk.

   9. I could _____ a quick e-mail to my grandmother but
   I decided to write her a long letter by hand.

   10. We could _____ in a restaurant last weekend, but we
   saved money and ate at home.

5.8 More on *Couldn't Have*

EXAMPLES	EXPLANATION
A: My parents voted for Kennedy in 1964. B: What? They **couldn't have voted** for him in 1964. He died in 1963. A: I think I saw your brother at the library yesterday. B: It **couldn't have been** him. He's in Europe on vacation.	*Couldn't have* + past participle is used to show disbelief or to show that someone's statement is absolutely impossible. We are saying that we can't believe this information because it is illogical.
Thanks so much for helping me paint my house. I **couldn't have done** it without you.	When we want to show gratitude or appreciation for someone's help, we often say, "*I couldn't have done it without you.*"
Compare: a. I **couldn't vote** in the last election because I was out of town. b. You say you voted in the last election? You **couldn't have voted** because you weren't a citizen at that time. a. I **couldn't move** the refrigerator myself, so my brother helped me. b. You say you moved the piano by yourself? You **couldn't have moved** it by yourself. It's too heavy for one person.	In sentences (a), you know that something didn't happen in the past. In sentences (b), you are responding in disbelief to someone's statement about the past.

EXERCISE 13   **Fill in the blanks to make statements of disbelief.**

EXAMPLE   A: When I was a child, I saw President Kennedy.

B: You ___couldn't have seen him___. He died before you were born.

1. A: U.S. athletes won ten gold medals at the 1980 Olympics.

   B: They _____.

   The U.S. didn't participate in the 1980 Olympics.

2. A: We had an English test on December 25.

   B: You _____.

   The school was closed on Christmas Day.

3. A: President Kennedy ran for re-election in 1964.

   B: He _____.

   He died in 1963.

(continued)

4. **A:** George W. Bush ran for re-election in 2008.

   B: You're wrong. He _____ because he had

   already been president for two terms, and that's the limit.

5. **A:** Look at the big fish I caught yesterday.

   B: You _____ that fish. It has a price tag on it. You

   must have bought it at the store.

6. **A:** I got an A on my math test.

   B: That's impossible. The teacher said that the highest grade was a B+.

   You _____ an A.

7. **A:** One student gave the teacher a perfect composition with no mistakes.

   B: The teacher thinks that the student _____ it

   by himself. She thinks somebody must have helped him.

8. **A:** Somebody called me last night at midnight and didn't leave a

   message. Was it you?

   B: It _____ me. I was sleeping at midnight.

9. **Teacher:** You failed the test.

   Student: What? I _____ the test. I studied for hours!

10. **A:** I can't find my house keys.

    B: Maybe you left them at work.

    A: I _____ them at work. I used them to open the

    door and get into the house a few minutes ago.

11. **A:** Thanks for helping me move last Saturday.

    B: My pleasure.

    A: I _____ without your help.

12. **A:** Hi. Don't you remember me?

    B: No, I'm sorry.

    A: We met in a math class last year.

    B: We _____ last year. I just started school two

    weeks ago.

5.9 Continuous Forms of Past Modals

We use continuous modals in the past to talk about a specific time in the past.

Subject	Modal	*Not*	*Have Been*	Present Participle	Complement
They	**must**		**have been**	**waiting**	at 8:30 P.M.
He	**might**		**have been**	**sleeping**	at 10:30 P.M.
You	**could**		**have been**	**doing**	your homework this morning.
I	**should**	**not**	**have been**	**driving**	so fast.

EXERCISE 14 Fill in the blanks with the continuous form of the modal.

EXAMPLE   **A:** I was injured in a car accident. I wasn't wearing a seat belt.

B: You should __*have been wearing*__ your seat belt.

1. **A:** Why didn't you finish your homework?

   B: I was watching a movie on TV last night.

   A: You should _____ your homework instead.

2. **A:** I wasted so much time when I was young. I didn't take my studies seriously.

   B: But you had a good education.

   A: I know. But I could _____ English instead of playing soccer every day after school.

3. **A:** I tried to call you a few hours ago but there was no answer.

   B: I was home. I must _____ a shower when you called.

4. **A:** What do you think of last night's rainstorm?

   B: I didn't hear it. I must _____.

   A: How could you sleep through so much thunder?

   B: I'm a heavy sleeper.

(continued)

5. A: I went to your house last Saturday, but you didn't answer the door. I thought you were going to be home.

B: I often work on my car on Saturdays. I might _____ on my car when you arrived. Did you look in the garage?

A: No. I didn't think of it.

6. (*teacher to student*)

T: Peter, can you answer question number six?

S: I'm sorry. I wasn't listening. I was thinking of something else. What was the question?

T: You should _____.

Summary of Lesson 5

Modals

Must

Meaning	Present/Future	Past
Legal obligation	I **must go** to court next week.	I **had to go** to court last week.
Urgency	I **must talk** to the doctor right now!	
Strong necessity	I **must study** for the test next week.	I **had to study** for the test last month.
Prohibition	You **must not tell** a lie in court.	
Deduction; conclusion	He's wearing a coat inside. He **must be** cold.	I can't find my keys. There's a hole in my pocket. I **must have lost** them.

Should

Meaning	Present/Future	Past
Advice	You **should buy** a new car next year.	You **should have bought** a new car last year.
Mistakes (in past)	You **shouldn't eat** fatty foods.	I **shouldn't have eaten** so many potato chips last night.

Can/Could

Meaning	Present/Future	Past
Ability	I **can speak** English now.	I **could speak** German when I was a child.
Acceptability	You **can wear** jeans to class every day.	You **could have worn** jeans to the party last night.
Permission/ prohibition	We **can use** a dictionary to write a composition. We **can't use** our books during a test.	We **could use** a dictionary to write the last composition. We **couldn't use** a dictionary during the last test.
Suggestion	To learn about computers, you **can take** a course, or you **could buy** a book and teach yourself.	
Possibility	Mary isn't here today. She **could be** sick.	Mary wasn't here yesterday. She **could have been** sick.
Direction not taken		I **could have gone** to Canada, but I decided to come to the U.S.
Impossibility; disbelief		**A:** I voted for President Obama in 2008. **B:** You **couldn't have voted** for Obama. You weren't a citizen in 2008.

May/Might

Meaning	Present/Future	Past
Permission	You **may use** a dictionary during the test.	
Possibility	I **may have** a job interview next week. I'm still not sure. The teacher isn't here. She **might be** sick.	Simon is wearing a suit to class. He **may have had** a job interview this morning. The teacher wasn't here yesterday. She **might have been** sick.

Ought To

Meaning	Present/Future	Past
Advice	She **ought to buy** a new car soon.	She **ought to have bought** a new car last year. (*rare*)

Related Expressions

Have To

Meaning	Present/Future	Past
Necessity (personal or legal)	I **have to study** now. I **have to go** to court next week.	I **had to study** yesterday. I **had to go** to court last week.
Lack of necessity	My job is close to my home. I **don't have to drive**. I can walk.	My last job was close to my home. I **didn't have to drive**. I could walk.

Have Got To

Meaning	Present/Future	Past
Necessity	I**'ve got to go** to court next week.	

Be Able To

Meaning	Present/Future	Past
Ability	She **is able to play** chess now.	She **was able to play** chess when she was a child.

Be Allowed To / Be Permitted To

Meaning	Present/Future	Past
Permission	We **are not allowed to talk** during a test. You **are not permitted to park** at a bus stop.	We **were not allowed to talk** during the last test. You **were not permitted to park** on this street yesterday because the city was cleaning the streets.

Be Supposed To

Meaning	Present/Future	Past
Expectation	My brother **is supposed to arrive** at 10 P.M. The weatherman said it **is supposed to rain** tomorrow. I**'m supposed to help** my brother move on Saturday. You **are supposed to wear** your seat belt.	My brother **was supposed to arrive** at 10 P.M., but his plane was delayed. The weatherman said it **was supposed to rain** yesterday, but it didn't. I **was supposed to help** my brother move last Saturday, but I got sick. He **was supposed to wear** his seat belt, but he didn't.

Had Better

Meaning	Present/Future	Past
Warning	You'**d better take** an umbrella, or you'll get wet.	

Editing Advice

1. After a modal, always use a base form.

   have
   He could ~~has~~ gone to the party.

2. To form the past of a modal, use *have* + past participle.

   have eaten
   I shouldn't ~~ate~~ so much before I went to bed last night.

3. Don't use *of* after a modal to express past. Use *have*.

   have
   You should ~~of~~ gone to bed earlier last night.

4. Don't confuse *couldn't have* + past participle and *couldn't* + base form.

   find
   Last night when I got home, I couldn't ~~have found~~ a parking space.

5. Use the correct form for the past participle.

   gone
   He should have ~~went~~ to the doctor when he felt the pain in his chest.

6. Don't forget the *d* in *supposed to*. Don't forget the verb *be*.

   d
   You were suppose‸to meet me after class yesterday.

   was
   I‸supposed to work last Saturday, but I got sick.

7. *Can* is never used for the past.

   couldn't drive
   He ~~can't drove~~ his car this morning because the battery was dead.

Editing Quiz

Some of the shaded words and phrases have mistakes. Find the mistakes and correct them. If the shaded words are correct, write C.

                                                     C

I had a terrible day yesterday. I was supposed to be at work early, but I
(example)

couldn't start

~~can't started~~ my car in the morning. The battery was dead. I
(example)

must had forgotten to turn off the lights the night before. I saw a neighbor
(1)

of mine and asked him to help, but he can't stopped because he was in a
(2)

hurry. He had to attend an important meeting. I stopped another neighbor
(3)

and asked for help, but she couldn't have helped me because she was
(4)

taking her kids to school. I stopped a third neighbor and said, "Do you

remember when I helped you push your car last winter?" He answered,

"It couldn't have been me. I just moved here last month. It must of been
(5)   *(6)*

someone else." He must thought I was crazy.
(7)

   I was suppose to arrive at work at 8 A.M. but I didn't arrive until
(8)

10:30. I should have took the subway to work. It might have been a
(9)   *(10)*

lot easier.

Lesson 5 Test/Review

PART 1   **A husband (H) and wife (W) are driving to a party and are lost. They are arguing in the car. Fill in the blanks to complete this conversation.**

W: We're lost. And we don't even have a map. You should

_____**have taken**_____ a map.
       (example)

H: I didn't think we were going to need one. I must _____
                                                        (1)

a wrong turn.

W: I think you were supposed to make a right turn at the last intersection, but you turned left. We should _____ for directions (2) the last time we stopped for gas.

H: You know I don't like to ask for directions.

W: Let's use the cell phone and call the Allens and ask them how to get to their house.

H: Let's see. I thought I had the cell phone in my pocket. I can't find it. I must _____ it at home. (3)

W: No, you didn't leave it at home. I've got the phone here in my purse. Oh, no. You forgot to recharge the battery. You should _____ it last night. (4)

H: Why is it my fault? You could _____ it too. (5)

W: Well, we'll just have to look for a pay phone. Do you have any change?

H: I only have dollar bills.

W: You should _____ some change with you. (6)

H: Again, it's my fault.

W: Watch out! You could _____ that other car! (7)

H: I wasn't going to hit that car. I didn't come anywhere close to it.

W: I don't know why we're going in our car anyway. The Petersons offered us a ride. We could _____ with them. (8)

H: You should _____ with the Petersons and I should (9) _____ home. I could _____ (10) (11) the football game today instead of listening to you complain!

PART **2** **Look at the job application. Complete each sentence on the next page.**

Fill out the following form. Print in black ink. Mail or fax the application to:

Ms. Judy Lipton
P.O. Box 32X
Chicago, IL 60640
FAX number: 312-555-4321

Applications must be submitted by November 15.

Name ___Wilson___ ___Jack___ ___N___
(last) (first) (middle initial)

Address ___5040 N. Albany Ave.___

City ___Chicago___ State ___IL___ Zip code _____

Telephone ( ) ___539-2756___

E-mail address (optional) ___jnwilson00@e*mail.com___ Sex ___M___

Date of birth ___18___ ___2___ ___69___ (You must be at least 18.)
(month) (day) (year)

Social Security number ___549___ . ___62___ . ___71XX___

Educational background:

		Date graduated	Degree or major
High School	Roosevelt	1897	
College			
Graduate School			

Employment history (Please start with your present or last job.)

Company	Position	Dates	Supervisor	Reason for leaving
Apex	stock boy	5/88–3/94	R. Wilinot	personal
Smith, Inc.	warehouse	5/94–12/01	M. Smith	pay
Olson Co.	loading dock	1/02-present	B. Adams	

Do not write in the shaded box. For office use only.

Rec'd. by ___J.W.___
Amer. cit. ___yes___
Doc. checked ___?___
Transcripts received ___yes___

The Immigration Act of 1986 requires all successful applicants to present documents to prove U.S. citizenship or permanent residence with permission to work in the U.S.

This company is an Equal Opportunity Employer. Race, religion, nationality, marital status, and physical disability will not influence our decision to hire. ___Catholic___

I certify that these answers are true.

Signature: ___Jack N. Wilson___ Date: ___November 13___

EXAMPLE   He didn't read the instructions carefully. He should
_____**have read**_____ them more carefully.

   1. He wrote his application with a pencil. He was supposed to

_____.

   2. He didn't write his zip code. He should _____ his

zip code.

   3. He forgot to include his area code. He should _____ it.

   4. He included his e-mail address. He didn't have to

_____ it.

   5. He wrote the day (18) before the month (2). He should

_____.

   6. He wrote that he graduated from high school in 1897. He couldn't

_____ in 1897. That's more than 100 years ago! He

must _____ 1987.

   7. He didn't fill in any college attended. He might not

_____ college.

   8. He said that he left his first job for personal reasons. He might

_____ because he didn't like his boss.

   9. He didn't fill in his reason for leaving his last job. He should

_____.

 10. He wrote his first job first. He was supposed to _____.

 11. He wrote in the shaded box. He wasn't supposed to

_____. He must not _____ the

directions very carefully.

 12. He included his religion. He wasn't supposed to _____

it. He must not _____ the sentence about religion.

 13. He printed his name on the bottom line. He was supposed to

_____.

 14. He mailed the application, but he could _____

instead.

 15. For today's date, he wrote only the month and day. He should

_____ the year too.

PART **3** **Fill in the blanks with the past of the modal or expression in parentheses ( ).**

After Alan (A) has waited for two hours for his friend Bill (B) to arrive for dinner, Bill finally arrives.

A: Why are you so late? You _____ **were supposed to** _____ be here two hours ago.

(example: be supposed to)

B: I'm sorry. I got lost and I _____ your house.

(1 can't/find)

A: You _____ a road map.

(2 should/take)

B: I did, but I _____ it while I was driving.

(3 can/not/read)

I _____ a wrong turn.

(4 must/make)

A: Where did you get off the highway?

B: At Madison Street.

A: That's impossible. You _____ off at Madison Street.

(5 can/not/get)

There's no exit there.

B: Oh. It _____ Adams Street, then.

(6 must/be)

A: But Adams Street is not so far from here.

B: I know. But I had a flat tire after I got off the highway.

A: Did you call for a tow truck?

B: I _____ for a tow truck because I'm a member of a

(7 can/call)

motor club. But I thought it would take too long. So I changed the

tire myself.

A: But you're over two hours late. How long did it take you to change

the tire?

B: It _____ about 15 minutes, but then

(8 might/take)

I _____ home, take a shower, and change clothes.

(9 have to/go)

I was so dirty.

A: You _____ me.

(10 should/call)

B: I wanted to, but I _____ the paper where I had your

(11 can/not/find)

phone number. I _____ it while I was changing the tire.

(12 must/lose)

A: Well, thank goodness you're here now. But you'll have to eat dinner

alone. I got hungry and _____ for you.

(13 can/not/wait)

Expansion

❶ A student will read one of the following problems out loud to the class. The student will pretend that this is his or her problem. Other students will ask for more information and give advice about the problem. Try to use past and present modals.

Problem A My mother-in-law came to the U.S. last May. She stayed with us for three months. I told my husband that he had to find another apartment for her. He didn't want to. I finally said to my husband, "Tell her to leave, or I'm leaving." So he helped her move into her own apartment. Now my husband is mad at me. Do you think I did the right thing?

Problem B My wife gave me a beautiful watch last Christmas. While I was on a business trip in New York last month, I left my watch in my hotel room. A few days later, I called the hotel, but they said that no one reported finding a watch. So far, I haven't told my wife that I lost the watch. What should I do?

Problem C A very nice American family invited me to dinner last night. The wife worked very hard to make a beautiful dinner. I'm not used to eating American food and thought it tasted awful. But I ate it so I wouldn't hurt their feelings. They invited me to dinner again next week. What can I do about the food?

Problem D *Write your own problem, real or imaginary.*

❷ Fill out the application on page 180 of Lesson Four. Make some mistakes on purpose. Find a partner and exchange books with him or her. Tell each other about the mistakes using modals.

EXAMPLE   For "sex" you wrote M. You're a woman, so you should have written *F*.

❶ The following excerpt from a poem by John Greenleaf Whittier is about regret. Discuss the meaning of the poem.

> For all sad words of tongue or pen,
> The saddest are these: "It might have been!"

❷ Talk about the election process in your native country. How is the leader chosen?

❸ Talk about how the media influences our decisions in voting or buying.

Write

❶ Write about a mistake you once made. Tell about what you should have done to avoid the problem.

❷ Write a short composition about another direction your life could have taken. What made you decide not to go in that direction?

❸ The assassinations of Abraham Lincoln and John F. Kennedy were great American tragedies. Write about the tragic death of a famous person.

❹ Write about how a tragedy occurred and what was done (or not done) to solve this problem.

EXAMPLE

Hurricane Katrina

In our English class, we read an article about Hurricane Katrina in New Orleans. The mayor told residents to leave before the hurricane struck. Everyone should have left immediately, but many people stayed . . .

For more practice using grammar in context, please visit our Web site.

Grammar
Adjective Clauses

Descriptive Phrases

Context
The Internet

An adjective clause is a group of words that describes or identifies the noun before it.

EXAMPLES	EXPLANATION
I have a friend **who is a computer programmer**.	In the sentence on the left, the adjective clause tells you about the friend.
You should buy a computer **that has a lot of memory**.	In the sentence on the left, the adjective clause tells you about the computer.
a. I have a friend **who plays computer games all day**. b. Web sites **that have a lot of ads** annoy me.	The adjective clause can describe any noun in the sentence. In sentence (a), the adjective clause describes the object (*friend*). In sentence (b), the adjective clause describes the subject (*Web sites*).

Spam

Before
You Read

1. Do you get unwanted e-mail asking you to buy products or order services?

2. What do you do with e-mail after you read it?

🔊 **Read the following magazine article. Pay special attention to adjective clauses.**

Do you ever get e-mail **that promises to make you rich or thin?** Do you get e-mail **that tries to sell you a mortgage or a vacation package?** Do you ever receive an offer **that will give you a college diploma in a year?** This kind of advertising through e-mail is called "spam." Spam is commercial e-mail **that you haven't asked for.** It is the electronic equivalent of junk mail or telemarketing calls. Approximately 94 percent of the e-mail sent today is spam. In 2002, 260 billion spam e-mails were sent. Now there are about 14.5 billion spam messages sent a day! Bill Gates, the founder of Microsoft, calls spam "pollution of the e-mail ecosystem."

How do spammers get your e-mail address? They use several methods. When you buy something online, you are often asked for an e-mail address when you place an order. Spammers buy addresses from online companies. In addition, spammers search chat rooms, bulletin boards, and newsgroups for e-mail addresses. Spammers regularly sell lists of e-mail addresses to other spammers.

Where does spam come from? It comes from companies **that want your money.** Many of these companies try to take your money by making false claims ("Lose 50 pounds in 10 days!"). Most people delete this kind of e-mail without even reading it. So why do spammers send e-mail **that nobody wants to read?** The answer is simple: Some people *do* read this mail and a very small percentage even buy the product or order the service **that is offered.** And a small percentage of trillions of e-mails means money. One spammer **who lives in Florida** made so much money that he sold his business for $135 million dollars and retired at the age of 37.

What can you do to eliminate spam?

- You could simply delete it.
- You could get anti-spam software. (Some software is free, offered by the Internet service provider **you use.**)
- You can get a separate e-mail address to give to retailers **who require an e-mail address**, and use your primary e-mail address just for people **you know.**
- On a Web site, when you see a box **that asks you if you want more information**, make sure to uncheck the box.

Many people **who are unhappy with the amount of spam they receive** are asking their lawmakers to enact laws **that would stop spam.**

6.2 Relative Pronoun as Subject

The relative pronouns *who*, *that*, and *which* can be the subject of an adjective clause.

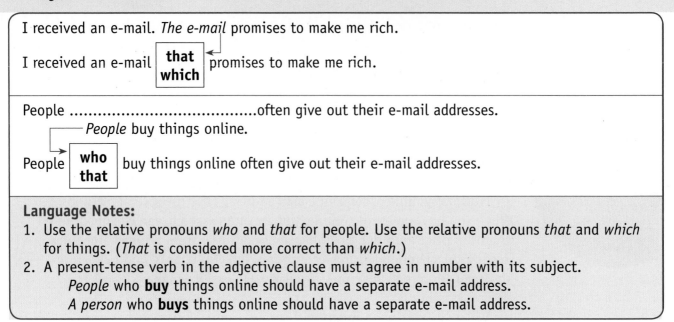

I received an e-mail. *The e-mail* promises to make me rich.

I received an e-mail | **that** / **which** | promises to make me rich.

People ....often give out their e-mail addresses.
—*People* buy things online.

People | **who** / **that** | buy things online often give out their e-mail addresses.

Language Notes:
1. Use the relative pronouns *who* and *that* for people. Use the relative pronouns *that* and *which* for things. (*That* is considered more correct than *which*.)
2. A present-tense verb in the adjective clause must agree in number with its subject.
   People who **buy** things online should have a separate e-mail address.
   A person who **buys** things online should have a separate e-mail address.

EXERCISE **1** **Fill in the blanks with *who*, *that*, or *which* + the correct form of the verb in parentheses ( ) to complete the adjective clause.**

EXAMPLE   Spam comes from companies _____*that want*_____ to sell you something.
                                                              (want)

1. Companies _____ you spam want your money.
                         (send)

2. People _____ spam are often annoyed.
                    (receive)

3. People_____ products and services online give
                    (buy)

   out their e-mail addresses.

4. Sometimes you see a box _____ a check in it already.
                                          (have)

   Don't forget to uncheck the box if you don't want more information.

5. I know a student _____ all her books online.
                              (buy)

   She never goes to the bookstore anymore.

6. A spammer _____ in Florida became very rich and
                       (live)

   retired young.

7. You shouldn't believe an offer _____ that you will
(promise)

lose 50 pounds in a week.

EXERCISE 2 **Write a complete sentence, using the phrases below as the subject or object of your sentence.**

EXAMPLES   a computer that has little memory
A computer that has little memory is not very useful today.

a company that promises to make me rich in three weeks
I wouldn't want to do business with a company that promises
to make me rich in three weeks.

1. e-mail that comes from friends and relatives

_____

2. companies that send spam

_____

3. students who don't have a computer

_____

4. children who spend all their time playing computer games

_____

5. e-mail that comes from an unknown sender

_____

6. Web sites that offer music downloads

_____

7. Web sites that offer a college diploma in six months

_____

8. people who don't know anything about computers

_____

EXERCISE 3   **ABOUT YOU** **Fill in the blanks with an adjective clause. Discuss your answers.**

EXAMPLE   I don't like people ____ *who say one thing but do something else.*

1. I don't like apartments _____

2. I like movies _____

3. I like teachers _____

4. I like to have neighbors _____

(continued)

Adjective Clauses; Descriptive Phrases   **233**

5. I like to read books _____

6. I've never met a person _____

7. I can't understand people _____

8. I like classes _____

9. I don't like to be around people _____

10. A good friend is a person _____

EXERCISE **4** **Write a sentence with each of the words given to give your opinion about the ideal situation for learning. You may use singular or plural. You may work with a partner.**

EXAMPLES   class   *Classes that have fewer than 20 students are better*
than large classes.

teacher   *I prefer to have a teacher who doesn't explain things*
in my language.

1. teacher _____

_____

2. college/school _____

_____

3. textbook _____

_____

4. class _____

_____

5. classroom _____

_____

6. computer _____

_____

7. school library _____

_____

8. classmate _____

_____

9. dictionary _____

_____

6.3 Relative Pronoun as Object

The relative pronouns *who(m)*, *that*, and *which* can be the object of an adjective clause.

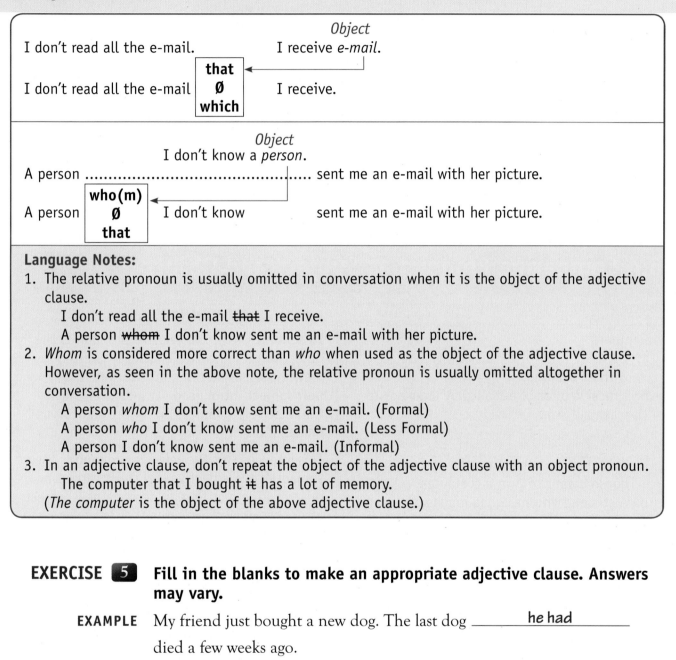

Language Notes:
1. The relative pronoun is usually omitted in conversation when it is the object of the adjective clause.

    I don't read all the e-mail ~~that~~ I receive.

    A person ~~whom~~ I don't know sent me an e-mail with her picture.
2. *Whom* is considered more correct than *who* when used as the object of the adjective clause. However, as seen in the above note, the relative pronoun is usually omitted altogether in conversation.

    A person *whom* I don't know sent me an e-mail. (Formal)

    A person *who* I don't know sent me an e-mail. (Less Formal)

    A person I don't know sent me an e-mail. (Informal)
3. In an adjective clause, don't repeat the object of the adjective clause with an object pronoun.

    The computer that I bought ~~it~~ has a lot of memory.

    (*The computer* is the object of the above adjective clause.)

EXERCISE 5 **Fill in the blanks to make an appropriate adjective clause. Answers may vary.**

EXAMPLE My friend just bought a new dog. The last dog _____he had_____ died a few weeks ago.

1. I have a hard teacher this semester. The teacher _____ last semester was much easier.
2. I studied British English in my native country. The English _____ now is American English.
3. The teacher gave a test last week. Almost everyone failed the test _____.

(continued)

4. When I read English, there are many new words for me. I use my dictionary to look up the words I _____.

5. I had a big apartment last year. The apartment _____ now is very small.

6. Did you contact the owner of the wallet _____ on the street?

7. I write poetry. One of the poems _____ won a prize.

8. The last book _____ was very sad. It made me cry.

9. She has met a lot of people at school, but she hasn't made any friends. The people _____ are all too busy to spend time with her.

6.4 Comparing Pronoun as Subject and Object

EXAMPLES	EXPLANATION
Compare: a. I receive a lot of e-mail **(that)** I delete without reading. b. I receive a lot of e-mail **that** promises to make me rich.	In sentences (a), the relative pronoun is the object of the adjective clause. It is often omitted, especially in conversation. The new subject introduced (*I*) indicates that the relative pronoun is an object and can be omitted.
a. A student **(whom)** I met in my math class doesn't want to own a computer. b. A student **who** has good grades can get a scholarship.	In sentences (b), the relative pronoun is the subject of the adjective clause. It cannot be omitted. The fact that there is no new subject after *that* or *who* indicates that the relative pronoun is the subject. *Wrong:* A student has good grades can get a scholarship.

EXERCISE **6** **Fill in the blanks with an adjective clause. Answers may vary.**

CD 2, TR 16

A: I'm so tired of all the spam ____I get____.
  (example)

B: Do you get a lot?

A: Of course, I do. Doesn't everyone?

B: I don't.

A: How is that possible?

B: I have an e-mail address _____ just (1)

for shopping online. I don't use it for anything else.

The e-mail address _____ to my (2)

friends is private. I don't give it to anyone else.

A: I never thought about having different e-mail

addresses for different things. Don't you have to pay for each e-mail account?

B: There are a lot of e-mail providers _____ for free. (3)

For example, you can use Hotmail™ or Yahoo!™ for free. But they

have limited space and aren't good for everything. I like to send a lot

of photos. The photos _____ are often too big for (4)

my free Hotmail account, but it's perfect for the shopping

_____ online. (5)

A: Do you do a lot of shopping online?

B: Yes. For example, I buy a lot of books online. The books

_____ online can be sent directly to my house. (6)

A: How can I get one of these free accounts?

B: You just go to their Web site and sign up. Choose a username and

password. If the username _____ has already been (7)

chosen by someone else, you can choose another one or simply add

some numbers to it. For example, I chose SlyFox, but it was already

taken, so I added the year of my birth, 1986. So I'm SlyFox1986.

A: Why did you choose that name?

B: That's the name _____ when I was a child. My older (8)

brother was always giving people nicknames. After you choose a

username, choose a password. Make sure it's a number or word

_____ easily. If you forget your password, you won't be (9)

able to use your account. The password _____ should (10)

never be obvious. Never, for example, use your address, phone number,

or Social Security number.

(continued)

A: What password did you choose?

B: The password _____ is a secret. I'll never tell it to
　　　　　　　　　　　　　(11)
anyone.

6.5 Relative Pronoun as Object of Preposition

The relative pronouns can be the object of a preposition (*to, about, with, of, for,* etc.).

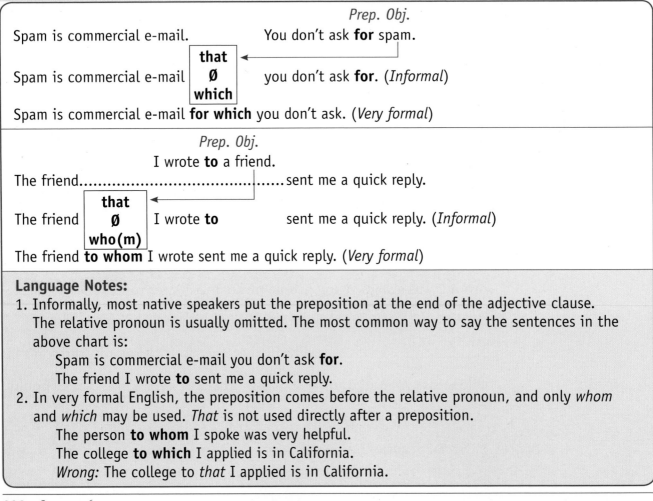

	Prep. Obj.
Spam is commercial e-mail.	You don't ask **for** spam.

Spam is commercial e-mail **that / Ø / which** you don't ask **for.** (*Informal*)

Spam is commercial e-mail **for which** you don't ask. (*Very formal*)

	Prep. Obj.
The friend..sent me a quick reply.	I wrote **to** a friend.

The friend **that / Ø / who(m)** I wrote **to** sent me a quick reply. (*Informal*)

The friend **to whom** I wrote sent me a quick reply. (*Very formal*)

Language Notes:

1. Informally, most native speakers put the preposition at the end of the adjective clause. The relative pronoun is usually omitted. The most common way to say the sentences in the above chart is:

   Spam is commercial e-mail you don't ask **for.**

   The friend I wrote **to** sent me a quick reply.

2. In very formal English, the preposition comes before the relative pronoun, and only *whom* and *which* may be used. *That* is not used directly after a preposition.

   The person **to whom** I spoke was very helpful.

   The college **to which** I applied is in California.

   Wrong: The college to *that* I applied is in California.

EXERCISE 7 **ABOUT YOU** **Complete each statement.**

EXAMPLE   The class I was in last semester _____ was very crowded. _____

1. The city I come from _____
2. The school I graduated from _____
3. The house/apartment I used to live in _____
4. The elementary school I went to _____
5. The teacher I studied beginning grammar with _____
    _____
6. Most of the people I went to elementary school with _____
    _____
7. _____ is a subject I'm very interested in.
8. _____ is a topic I don't like to talk about.

EXERCISE 8 **Make these sentences more informal by taking out the relative pronoun and putting the preposition at the end of the adjective clause.**

EXAMPLE   He visited several Web sites in which he was interested.
    He visited several Web sites he was interested in.

1. There is a new Web site about which everyone is talking.
    _____
2. The link on which you click will take you to that Web site.
    _____
3. The information for which you are looking can be found on the Web.
    _____
4. There are several Web sites on which I depend frequently.
    _____
5. The job for which I am responsible is to maintain a company's Web site.
    _____
6. This is a job to which I am accustomed.
    _____

This is a conversation between two friends. One just came back from an island vacation where he had a terrible time. Fill in each blank with an adjective clause. Answers may vary.

A: How was your trip?

B: Terrible.

A: What happened? Didn't your travel agent give you good advice?

B: I didn't use a travel agent. I asked some friends for cheap ways to take a

vacation. One friend I _____**talked to**_____ told me to look for
(example)

vacations online. So I did. There was a choice of hotels. The name of

the hotel _____ was "Ocean View," so I thought I
_(1)_

would see the ocean from my window. The view _____
_(2)_

from my window was of a brick wall. I didn't see any water at all. The

only water _____ was in the bathroom sink.
_(3)_

A: What kind of food did they serve?

B: The food _____ made me sick.
_(4)_

A: Did you meet any interesting travelers?

B: I didn't like the other travelers _____. They were
_(5)_

unfriendly.

A: Did you travel with an interesting companion?

B: The person _____ was boring. We weren't interested
_(6)_

in the same things. The things _____ were different
_(7)_

from the things _____.
_(8)_

A: Did you take pictures?

B: The pictures _____ didn't come out.
_(9)_

A: Did you find any interesting souvenirs?

B: The souvenirs _____ were cheaply made. I didn't
_(10)_

buy any.

A: Could you communicate with the people on the island? Do they speak

English?

B: No. I don't understand the language _____.
_(11)_

A: Did you spend a lot of money?

B: Yes, but the money _____ was wasted.
(12)

A: Why didn't you change your ticket and come home early?

B: The ticket _____ couldn't be changed.
(13)

A: Are you going to have another vacation soon?

B: The next vacation _____ will be in December. I think
(14)
I'll just stay home.

eBay

**Before
You Read**

1. What do you do with old things of yours that you no longer
   want? Do you sell them or throw them away?

2. Do you collect anything (coins, stamps, dolls, etc.)? Where can you buy
   your collectibles?

CD 2, TR 18

Read the following Web article. Pay special attention to _when_ and _where_.

http://www.buy*sell*on*web.com

Did you ever want to sell an ugly lamp that your aunt gave you for your
birthday? Or an old toy that is taking up space in your closet? Or are you
trying to buy another train for your toy train collection? In the old days,
buyers and sellers were limited to newspapers, garage sales, and flea
markets[1] in their area to buy and sell unusual things. But since 1995,
eBay has provided an online global community **where** people buy and
sell almost anything. People are no longer limited to finding buyers and
sellers in the local area **where** they live.

The creator of eBay, Pierre Omidyar, graduated from Tufts University
in 1988 with a degree in computer science. He got his idea of an online
trading community in 1995, **when** his wife, a collector of plastic candy
dispensers, was trying to buy a piece for her unusual collection. From
his California home, Omidyar developed an online trading site, and,
within a short period of time, his wife was able to find what she was
looking for, and Omidyar made a little money on the trade.

**Did You
Know?**

Pierre Omidyar's
wealth was
estimated to be
$3.6 billion
in 2009.

[1]A _flea market_ is a large area where individuals rent a space to sell used goods. It is often outdoors.

(continued)

Pierre Omidyar

Using this idea, Omidyar created eBay, a Web site **where** people can put a photo of the object they want to sell, and give a starting price for an auction. In an auction, the person who makes the highest offer within a certain period of time gets to buy the item. Not everything on eBay is sold by auction. Some items have fixed prices too. eBay makes its money by charging the seller a small percentage of the final price.

By 1998, eBay had become so big that Omidyar and his partner could no longer handle the business without expert help. They brought in Meg Whitman, whose knowledge of business helped make eBay the success it is today. She changed eBay from a company that sold several categories of used things to a large marketplace of 78 million items in 50,000 categories of both new and used merchandise. Every second, more than $1,900 worth of goods is traded on the site. In the year 2007 alone, over $60 billion worth of merchandise changed hands on eBay, including cars, jewelry, toys, computers—and anything else you can imagine.

Not only can you buy and sell on eBay, but you can also meet people whose interests you share. For example, doll collectors all over the world can "meet" each other and exchange information on bulletin boards and in chat rooms. Friendships are formed on eBay among people who share an interest in the same collectibles.

eBay is now among the most visited Web sites on the Internet.

6.6 *Where* and *When* in Adjective Clauses

EXAMPLES	EXPLANATION
eBay is a Web site *where* people can buy and sell things. eBay is a community *where* you can meet people who share your hobby.	*Where* means "in that place." *Where* cannot be omitted.
There was a time (*when*) collectors were limited to their local areas. There was a time (*when*) people didn't have personal computers.	*When* means "at that time." *When* can be omitted.

EXERCISE 10 Use an adjective clause with *where* to tell what information you can find on certain Web sites. If you're not sure, go to the Web site. Or you can take a guess and check it out later.

EXAMPLE WhiteHouse.gov is a Web site __where you can read about__
__the White House and the president.__

1. Weather.com is a Web site _____

2. Mapquest.com is a Web site _____

3. CNN.com is a Web site _____

4. USPS.com is a Web site _____

5. Hotmail.com is a Web site _____

6. Travelocity.com is a Web site _____

7. Newsweek.com is a Web site _____

8. IRS.gov is a Web site _____

9. Redcross.org is a Web site _____

10. Harvard.edu is a Web site _____

EXERCISE 11 Fill in the blanks.

EXAMPLE I like to use the computer lab at a time when __it isn't crowded.__

1. The teacher shouldn't give a test on a day when _____
_____

2. I like to study at a time when _____

3. Saturday is the day when _____

4. _____ is the season when _____
_____

(continued)

5. Between 7 and 9 A.M. is the time when _____

_____

6. _____ was the year when _____

_____

EXERCISE **12** **ABOUT YOU** **Fill in the blanks to tell about yourself.**

EXAMPLE _____ June _____ is the month when I was born.

1. _____ is a place where I can relax.

2. _____ is a place where I can have fun.

3. _____ is a place where I can be alone and think.

4. _____ is a place where I can meet my friends.

5. _____ is a place where I can study undisturbed.

6. _____ is a time when I can relax.

7. _____ is a time when I like to watch TV.

8. _____ is a day when I have almost no free time.

9. _____ is a time when I like to use the Internet.

6.7 *Where, When, That,* or *Which* in Adjective Clauses

EXAMPLES	EXPLANATION
a. In 2002, Pierre gave the graduation speech at the college *where* **he had gotten his degree**. b. In 2002, Pierre gave the graduation speech at the college *from which* **he had gotten his degree**. c. In 2002, Pierre gave the graduation speech at the college (*that*) **he had gotten his degree** *from*.	Sentence (a) uses *where* to introduce the adjective clause. Sentence (b) uses preposition + *which* to express the same idea. Sentence (c) uses (*that*) + clause + preposition to express the same idea.
a. 1995 is the year *when* **eBay got its start**. b. 1995 is the year *in which* **eBay got its start**. c. 1995 is the year (*that*) **eBay got started** *in*.	Sentence (a) uses *when* to introduce the adjective clause. Sentence (b) uses preposition + *which* to express the same idea. Sentence (c) uses (*that*) + clause + preposition to express the same idea.

EXAMPLES	EXPLANATION
Compare: a. She lives in a home **where** people use the computer a lot. b. She lives in a home **that** has three computers.	In sentence (a), *where* means *there* or *in that place.* People use the computer a lot *there.* In sentence (b), *that* means *home.* The *home* has three computers.
a. February is the month **when** I was born. b. February is the month **that** has only 28 days.	In sentence (a), *when* means *then* or *in that month.* I was born *then.* In sentence (b), *that* means *the month.* The *month* has only 28 days.

EXERCISE 13   **Fill in the blanks with *where, that,* or *which.***

EXAMPLE   The home __*where*__ I grew up had a beautiful fireplace.

1. The store _____ I bought my computer is having a sale now.

2. Do you bookmark the Web sites _____ you visit often?

3. The box at the top of your browser is the place in _____ you type the Web address.

4. There are Web sites _____ you can compare prices of electronics.

5. The city _____ I was born has a lot of parks.

6. I don't like cities _____ have a lot of factories.

7. I like to shop at stores _____ have products from my country.

8. I like to shop at stores _____ I can find products from my country.

9. A department store is a store in _____ you can find all kinds of goods—clothing, furniture, toys, etc.

10. I have a photograph of the home _____ I grew up.

11. The office _____ you can get your transcripts is closed now.

12. She wants to rent the apartment _____ she saw last Sunday.

13. I would like to visit the city _____ I grew up.

14. The town in _____ she grew up was destroyed by the war.

EXERCISE 14   **Fill in the blanks with *when, that,* or Ø. Ø means no word is necessary.**

EXAMPLE   January 1, 2000, was a time __*when*__ people celebrated the beginning of the new century.

1. Six o'clock is the time _____ the auction stops.

2. Do you remember the year _____ Meg Whitman started to work for eBay?

(continued)

3. 2008 was a year _____ had 366 days.

4. New Year's Eve is a time _____ I love.

5. February is the only month _____ has fewer than 30 days.

6. My birthday is a day _____ I think about my past.

7. December is a time _____ a lot of Americans buy gifts.

8. My parents' anniversary is a date _____ has a lot of meaning for them.

9. Do you give yourself the time _____ you need to write a good composition?

10. She wrote about a time _____ she couldn't speak English well.

11. Our vacation to Paris was the best time _____ we had ever had.

Freecycle

Before You Read

1. What do you do with things that you don't need or use anymore?

2. Do you think that Americans throw too many things in the garbage?

CD 2, TR 19

Read the following magazine article. Pay special attention to adjective clauses beginning with _whose_.

Do you have an old computer that you don't need anymore?
Or are you trying to find a radio but don't want to spend money? Then Freecycle is for you. The name combines the word "free" and the word "recycle." Freecycle.org is an online community **whose members** help each other get what they need—for free! It is also a geographical community. You join in the area where you live.

Americans generate almost five pounds of garbage per person per day. And 55 percent of this garbage is buried in what is called "landfill." Buried garbage can cause environmental problems. This garbage often contains useful items.

Freecycle was created in 2003 by Deron Beal, **whose idea** was to protect the environment by keeping usable goods out of landfills. He also wanted to encourage neighbors to help each other. As of 2009, there were about 8 million members in close to 4,800 Freecycle communities around the world. The Freecycle Network reports that its members are keeping 55 tons of goods out of landfills each day! Typical postings on Freecycle might look like this:

Did You Know?

People in the U.S. keep 64 million tons of garbage out of landfills every year through recycling.

OFFER: girls' size 10 clothes. Good condition. My daughter has outgrown them.

WANTED: clock radio. Mine broke. Need another one.

TAKEN: collection of hip-hop CDs. Sorry. They've been taken.

How do the members deliver or receive the item? The person **whose offer** you respond to will suggest a way for you to get it. Very often, the item will be left in front of the giver's house for the receiver. Or sometimes the giver and receiver will meet. It may not be safe to let a stranger into your house.

It's always important to be polite. You should always send a thank-you e-mail to the person **whose item** you received.

6.8 *Whose* + Noun in an Adjective Clause

Whose is the possessive form of who. It stands for his, her, its, their, or the possessive form of the noun.

Whose + noun can be the subject of the adjective clause.

                 Subject

Freecycle is an online community. ***Its* members** help each other.

Freecycle is an online community ***whose* members help each other**.

                 Subject

People can offer their kids' old clothes. ***Their* children** are growing.

People ***whose* children are growing** can offer their kids' old clothes.

Whose + noun can be the object of the adjective clause.

                       Object

You should always thank the person. You received ***her* item**.

You should always thank the person ***whose* item you received**.

        Object

You respond to ***a person's* offer**. The person will suggest a way for you to get it.

The person ***whose* offer you respond to** will suggest a way for you to get it.

EXERCISE 15 **Underline the adjective clause in each sentence.**

EXAMPLE I received toys on Freecycle from a member <u>whose children are too old to use them</u>.

1. The person whose furniture I received is moving to another city.
2. I got a bike from a man whose son just got a bigger bike.
3. Spammers send e-mail to all the people whose names are on their lists.
4. On eBay you can meet people whose interests you share.
5. I sent an e-mail to all the people whose e-mail addresses are in my address book.
6. I only open attachments from senders whose names I recognize.
7. A company whose Web site I visit often sends me coupons by e-mail.
8. Companies whose computers are infected with a virus can lose all their data.
9. I have to talk to the coworker whose laptop I borrowed.
10. Companies whose sites you visit may sell your e-mail address to spammers.

EXERCISE 16 **Use the sentence in parentheses to form an adjective clause.**

EXAMPLE eBay is a company <u>whose customers buy and sell thousands of items a day</u>. (Its customers buy and sell thousands of items a day.)

1. Pierre Omidyar is a creative person _____
   _____
   (His idea for eBay made him a very wealthy man.)
2. My friend has a sister _____
   _____
   (Her daughter is studying to be a computer programmer.)
3. The teacher _____
   uses a computer in the classroom. (I'm taking his class.)
4. Freecycle is an online community _____
   _____
   (Its members help each other to get the things they need.)
5. Freecycle is an organization _____
   _____
   (Its goal is to protect the environment from unnecessary landfill.)

6. The person _____
just bought a new flat-screen TV. (I received her old TV.)

7. I give my son's clothes to a woman _____

_____

(Her son is smaller than my son.)

6.9 Adjective Clauses After Indefinite Pronouns

An adjective clause can follow an indefinite pronoun: *someone, something, everyone, everything, no one, nothing, anything.*

EXAMPLES	EXPLANATION
IP RP Everyone **who received my e-mail** knows about the party. IP RP I don't know anyone **who has never used e-mail.**	The relative pronoun (RP) after an indefinite pronoun (IP) can be the subject of the adjective clause. The relative pronoun cannot be omitted.
IP RP Something **(that) he wrote** made me angry. IP RP I didn't understand anything **(that) you said.**	The relative pronoun (RP) after an indefinite pronoun (IP) can be the object of the adjective clause. In this case, it is often omitted.

Language Notes:
1. An indefinite pronoun takes the -s form for present tense.
   Everyone who **uses** e-mail has an e-mail address.
   I don't know anyone who **doesn't** have a computer.
2. An adjective clause does not usually follow a personal pronoun, except in very formal language and in some proverbs.
   He who laughs last laughs best.
   He who hesitates is lost.

EXERCISE **17** **Fill in the blanks with an adjective clause. Use information from nearby sentences to help you. Answers may vary.**

🔊
CD 2, TR 20

A woman (W) is trying to break up with a man (M).

M: I heard you want to talk to me.

W: Yes. There's something ___I want to tell you___.
                                      (example)

M: What do you want to tell me?

W: I want to break up.

M: Are you angry at me? What did I say?

W: Nothing _____ made me angry.
                               (1)

(continued)

M: Did I do something wrong?

W: Nothing _____ (2) made me mad.

M: Then what's the problem?

W: I just don't love you anymore.

M: But I can buy you anything _____ (3).

W: I don't want anything from you. In fact, I'm going to return everything

_____ (4).

M: But I can take you anywhere _____ (5).

W: I don't want to go anywhere with you.

M: What about all the love letters I sent you by e-mail?

W: I deleted everything _____ (6).

M: Didn't you believe anything _____ (7)?

W: I found out that you wrote the same thing to three other women.

M: That's not true. Everything _____ (8)

was sincere.

W: How can it be sincere? You wrote the same thing to my cousin's best

friend, my neighbor, and my classmate. The only thing you changed

was the name after "Dear." Everything else _____ (9)

was the same. So good-bye!

EXERCISE 18 **Fill in the blanks with an adjective clause. Answers may vary.**

EXAMPLE I don't send e-mail to everyone _____ I know _____.

1. You should read everything _____
   in an e-mail before sending it.

2. When sending an e-mail, you shouldn't write anything _____

_____

3. I received 20 e-mails today. Nothing _____
   was important. It was all spam.

4. Some people delete everything _____ after they read it.

5. If you have a buddy list, you can send an instant message to

   someone _____.

6. People you don't know may send you attachments. You shouldn't open an attachment from anyone _____. It may contain a virus.

EXERCISE 19   **ABOUT YOU**   **Fill in the blanks with an adjective clause.**

EXAMPLE   I know someone ___who can speak four languages_____.

1. I don't know anyone _____.
2. I know someone _____.
3. I'd like to get something _____.
4. I can't imagine anyone _____.
5. Everything _____ is useful to me.

EXERCISE 20   **Circle the correct words in parentheses ( ) to complete the sentences. Ø means no word is necessary.**

EXAMPLE   What is a computer virus? A virus is a computer code (*what /* (*that*) */ who / whose*) attaches itself to other programs and causes harm to programs, data, or hardware.

1. Viruses are written by people (*they / who / whom / whose*) enjoy causing problems for the rest of us.
2. What is spam? Spam is commercial e-mail (*who / where / what / Ø*) you haven't asked for.
3. Who is Bill Gates? Bill Gates is the man (*who / whom / which / what*) created Microsoft.
4. Bill Gates was born at a time (*when / that / which / then*) personal computers were not even in people's imaginations.
5. Who is Meg Whitman? She is the woman (*to who / whom / to whom / to which*) Pierre Omidyar turned over the operation of eBay in 1998.
6. Omidyar needed to bring in someone (*who / whose / who's / who his*) knowledge of business was greater than his own.
7. A computer is a tool (*Ø / whom / about which / whose*) most of us use today for fast access to information.
8. The Internet is a tool (*that / what / when / Ø*) has been around since the 1970s.

(continued)

9. What is eBay? eBay is a Web site (that / *where* / *there* / *which*) you can buy and sell items.

10. My parents were born at a time (*where* / *when* / *that* / *which*) the Internet didn't yet exist.

11. The people (Ø / *which* / *whose* / *where*) you meet in chat rooms are sometimes very rude.

12. I have all the e-mails (*that* / *what* / *where* / *whose*) my friends have sent to me.

13. The computer lab is never open at a time (*which* / *then* / *where* / *when*) I need it.

14. I always delete the spam (*who* / *that* / *when* / *whose*) I receive.

15. On eBay, you can meet people (*who* / *whom* / *who they* / *they*) have the same interests as you do.

16. You can create an address book (*when* / *that* / *where* / *whose*) you can keep the e-mail addresses of all your friends.

17. You can create an address book (*which* / *in which* / *there* / *in that*) you can keep the e-mail addresses of all your friends.

18. There are chat rooms (*there* / *where* / *which* / *that*) people with the same interests can meet each other.

19. A virus writer is a person (*his* / *whose* / *who* / *whom*) enjoyment comes from creating problems for computer users.

20. Do you know anyone (Ø / *who* / *whom* / *which*) doesn't own a computer?

21. A man (*who* / *whom* / *whose* / *who's*) in my math class doesn't own a computer.

22. Don't believe everything (*what* / *who* / *whom* / Ø) you read on the Internet.

EXERCISE 21 Fill in the blanks with an adjective clause by using the sentences in parentheses or the context to give you clues.

A: How was your move last month?

B: It was terrible.

A: Didn't you use the moving company ___I recommended___?
(example)

(*I recommended a company.*)

B: The company _____ was not available
(1)

on the day _____. (*I had to move on this day.*)
(2)

I used a company _____. (*I found*

the name on the Internet.)

A: What happened?

B: First of all, it was raining on the day _____.
(4)

That made the move take longer, so it was more expensive than I

thought it would be.

A: It's not the company's fault that it rained.

B: I know. But there are many other things _____.
(5)

(*Things were their fault.*) The movers broke the mirror

_____. (*I had just*
(6)

bought the mirror.) And they left muddy footprints on the carpet

_____. (*I had just cleaned the carpet.*) I thought I was
(7)

getting professional movers. But the men _____
(8)

(*They sent these men to my home.*) were college students. They didn't

have much experience moving. Because the move took them so long,

they charged me much more than I expected to pay. The information

_____ (*They have information.*) on their Web site says
(9)

$100 an hour. But they charged me $800 for six hours of work.

A: You should talk to the owner of the company.

B: I called the company several times. The woman _____
(10)

(*I talked to a woman.*) said that the owner would call me back, but he

never has.

A: You should keep trying. Make a list of everything

_____. (*They broke or ruined things.*)
(11)

Their insurance will probably pay for these things.

B: I don't know if they have insurance.

A: You should never use a company _____.
(12)

B: Everyone _____ (*I've talked to people.*)
(13)

tells me the same thing.

(*continued*)

A: Don't feel so bad. Everyone makes mistakes. We learn from the

mistakes _____ . Why didn't you ask
                    (14)

your friends to help you move?

B: Everyone _____ (*I know people.*) is so busy.
                         (15)

I didn't want to bother anyone.

A: By the way, why did you move? You had a lovely apartment.

B: It wasn't mine. The person _____
                                            (16)

(*I was renting her apartment.*) spent a year in China, but when she came

back last month, I had to leave.

A: How do you like your new place?

B: It's fine. It's across the street from the building _____ .
                                                                      (17)

(*My sister lives in that building.*) So now we get to see each other more

often. Why don't you come over sometime and see my new place?

A: I'd love to. How about Saturday after 4 P.M.? That's the only time

_____ . (*I don't have too much to do*
              (18)

at that time.)

B: Saturday would be great.

Creating The World Wide Web

**Before
You Read**

1. Besides computers, what other inventions have changed the way people communicate with each other?

2. When you think about computers and the Internet, what famous names come to mind?

Read the following article. Notice that some adjective clauses are separated from the main clause with a comma.

http://www.berners*lee.com

Most people have never heard of Tim Berners-Lee. He is not rich or famous like Bill Gates.

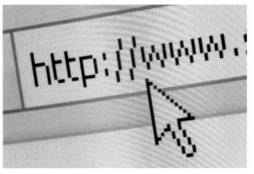

Berners-Lee, **who works at the Massachusetts Institute of Technology,** is the creator of the World Wide Web. The creation of the Web is so important that some people compare Berners-Lee to Johann Gutenberg, **who invented printing by moveable type in the fifteenth century.**

Berners-Lee was born in England in 1955. His parents, **who helped design the world's first commercially available computer,** gave him a great love of mathematics and learning.

In 1980, Berners-Lee went to work at CERN, a physics laboratory in Geneva, Switzerland, **where he had a lot of material to learn quickly.** He had a poor memory for facts and wanted to find a way to keep track of things he couldn't remember. He devised a software program that allowed him to create a document that had links to other documents. He continued to develop his idea throughout the 1980s. He wanted to find a way to connect the knowledge and creativity of people all over the world.

Tim Berners-Lee

In 1991, his project became known as the World Wide Web. The number of Internet users started to grow quickly. Today the Internet has more than 1.5 billion users. However, Berners-Lee is not completely happy with the way the Web is used today. He thinks it has become a passive tool for so many people, not the tool for creativity that he had imagined.

In 1999, Berners-Lee published a book called *Weaving the Web,* in which he answers questions he is often asked: "What were you thinking when you invented the Web?" "What do you think of it now?" "Where is the Web going to take us in the future?"

Did You Know?

What is the difference between the Web and the Internet? The Internet started in the 1970s, but it wasn't until Berners-Lee created his system of hyperlinks that the Internet became easy for everyone to use. A hyperlink is a word or picture that you can click on to quickly go to another Web page. This system of hyperlinks is what is known as the (World Wide) Web.

6.10 Nonessential Adjective Clauses

EXAMPLES	EXPLANATION
Berners-Lee, **who was born in England**, now lives in the U.S.	Some adjective clauses are not essential to the meaning of the sentence. A nonessential adjective clause adds extra information. The sentence is complete without it.
Berners-Lee's parents, **who helped design the first computer**, gave their son a love of learning.	
Berners-Lee went to work at CERN, **which is a physics laboratory in Geneva**.	A nonessential adjective clause is separated by commas from the main part of the sentence.
Berners-Lee was born in 1955, **when personal computers were beyond people's imagination**.	A nonessential adjective clause begins with *who, whom, which, where, when,* or *whose. That* is not used in a nonessential adjective clause.
Pierre Omidyar, **who created eBay**, was born in France.	
Pierre Omidyar, **whose wife is a collector**, got his idea for eBay in 1995.	
Omidyar brought in Meg Whitman, **whose knowledge of business helped make eBay the success it is today**.	

EXERCISE 22 Put commas in the following sentences to separate the adjective clause from the main part of the sentence.

EXAMPLE The abacus, which is a wooden rack with beads, was probably the first computer.

1. The abacus which was created about 2,000 years ago helped people solve arithmetic problems.
2. The first modern computer which was called ENIAC took up a lot of space (1,800 square feet).
3. ENIAC was created in 1942 when the U.S. was involved in World War II.
4. ENIAC which helped the government store important data was built at the University of Pennsylvania.
5. Personal computers which were introduced in the 1970s are much smaller and faster than previous computers.
6. The Internet which has been around since the 1970s was not available to most people until the Web was created.

7. Berners-Lee whose name is not widely recognized made a great contribution to the world.

8. Bill Gates went to Harvard University where he developed the programming language BASIC.

9. Bill Gates dropped out of Harvard to work with Paul Allen who was his old high school friend.

10. Together Gates and Allen founded Microsoft which has made both of them very rich.

11. In 1984, Apple produced the first Macintosh computer which was easier to use than earlier computers.

12. In 1985, Bill Gates introduced Windows which was Microsoft's version of the popular Macintosh operating system.

Bill Gates

6.11 Essential vs. Nonessential Adjective Clauses[2]

EXAMPLES	EXPLANATION
Bill Gates, **who created Microsoft**, never finished college. Berners-Lee, **whose parents helped design the first computer**, loved mathematics. Berners-Lee works at MIT, **where he is a professor of engineering.** eBay was in Omidyar's hands until 1998, **when he turned over the operation of the company to Meg Whitman.**	In the examples to the left, the adjective clause is **nonessential** because without it, we can still identify the noun in the main clause. Try reading the sentences without the adjective clause. The sentences are complete. The adjective clause adds extra information to the sentence. A nonessential adjective clause is set off from the rest of the sentence by commas.
The people **who built the first computers** worked in the engineering department of the University of Pennsylvania. There are many people **whose only online activity is sending and receiving e-mail.**	In the examples to the left, the adjective clause is **essential** because without it, we can't identify the noun. Try reading the sentences without the adjective clause. If we take it out, the noun isn't properly identified and the idea isn't complete.
Compare: a. The computer, **which was invented in the 1940s**, has become part of our everyday lives. (Nonessential) b. The computer **(that** or **which) I bought two years ago** is slow compared to today's computers. (Essential)	Example (a) refers to the whole class of computers as an invention. Example (b) refers to only one computer, which is identified by the adjective clause.
Compare: a. A person **who invents something** is very creative and intelligent. (Essential) b. Berners-Lee, **who invented the Web**, is not famous. (Nonessential)	In sentence (a), the adjective clause is essential in order to explain which person is creative and intelligent. In sentence (b), the adjective clause is nonessential because it provides extra information. Berners-Lee is unique and does not need to be identified.
Compare: a. The computer **(*which* or *that*) she just bought** has a lot of memory. (Essential) b. Microsoft, ***which* Bill Gates helped create**, is a billion-dollar company. (Nonessential)	In an essential adjective clause (a), the relative pronouns *which* or *that* can be used or omitted. In a nonessential adjective clause (b), only the relative pronoun *which* can be used. It cannot be omitted.

[2]Nonessential adjective clauses are often called nonrestrictive adjective clauses.

> **Language Note:** Here are some questions to help you decide if the adjective clause needs commas. If the answer to any of these questions is *yes*, then the adjective clause is set off by commas.
> - Can I put the adjective clause in parentheses?
>   Bill Gates **(who created Microsoft)** never finished college.
> - Can I write the adjective clause as a separate sentence?
>   Bill Gates created Microsoft. **He never finished college.**
> - If the adjective clause is deleted, does the sentence still make sense?
>   Bill Gates never finished college.
> - Is the noun a unique person or place?
>   **Berners-Lee**, who works at MIT, invented the Web.
> - If the noun is plural, am I including all members of a group (all my cousins, all my friends, all Americans, all computers)?
>   **My friends**, who are wonderful people, always help me. (All my friends are wonderful people.)
>
> **Compare:**
>   I e-mailed some photos to my friends **who have an Internet connection.**
>   (Not all of my friends have an Internet connection.)

EXERCISE 23 **Decide which of the following sentences contains a nonessential adjective clause. Put commas in those sentences. If the sentence doesn't need commas, write NC.**

EXAMPLES   People who send e-mail often use abbreviations.   NC

My father, who sent me an e-mail yesterday, is sick.

1. Kids who spend a lot of time on the computer don't get much exercise.

2. My grammar teacher who has been teaching here for 20 years knows a lot about computers.

3. Freecycle which was created in 2003 helps keep things out of landfills.

4. People who get spam every day can get very annoyed.

5. My best friend who gets at least 30 pieces of spam a day wrote a letter to his senator to complain.

6. Berners-Lee whose parents were very educated loves learning new things.

7. Meg Whitman who ran eBay for ten years decided to run for governor of California.

8. Berners-Lee worked in Switzerland where the CERN physics laboratory is located.

9. The Windows operating system which was developed by Microsoft came out in 1985.

(continued)

10. Did you like the story that we read about Berners-Lee?

11. The computer you bought three years ago doesn't have enough memory.

12. The computer which is one of the most important inventions of the twentieth century has changed the way people process information.

13. Bill Gates who created Microsoft with his friend became a billionaire.

14. My best friend whose name is on my buddy list contacts me every day through an instant message.

EXERCISE 24 **Combine the two sentences into one. The sentence in parentheses ( ) is not essential to the main idea of the sentence. It is extra information.**

EXAMPLE   eBay is now a large corporation. (It was started in Pierre Omidyar's house.)
eBay, which was started in Pierre Omidyar's house, is now

a large corporation.

1. Freecycle.org was created by Deron Beal. (His idea was to protect the environment.)

_____

_____

2. The World Wide Web is used by billions of people around the world. (It was created by Tim Berners-Lee.)

_____

_____

3. Tim Berners-Lee was born in England. (We saw his picture on page 255.)

_____

_____

4. The book *Weaving the Web* answers a lot of questions about the creation of the Web. (It was written by Berners-Lee in 1999.)

_____

_____

5. Berners-Lee knew about computers from an early age. (His parents helped design one of the first computers.)

_____

_____

6. Tim Berners-Lee works at MIT. (He does research on artificial intelligence there.)

   _____

   _____

7. Pierre Omidyar got his idea for eBay in 1995. (His wife couldn't find one of her favorite collectibles at that time.)

   _____

   _____

8. eBay hired Meg Whitman in 1998. (More expert business knowledge was needed at that time to run the company.)

   _____

   _____

9. E-mail did not become popular until the 1990s. (It was first created in 1972.)

   _____

   _____

10. Bill Gates often gets spam asking him if he wants to become rich. (He's the richest person in the U.S.)

   _____

   _____

11. Pierre Omidyar came to the U.S. when he was a child. (His father was a professor of medicine.)

   _____

   _____

12. Freecycle helps people get things for free. (Its members live in the same community.)

   _____

   _____

6.12 Descriptive Phrases

Some adjective clauses can be shortened to descriptive phrases. We can shorten an adjective clause in which the relative pronoun is followed by the verb *be*.

EXAMPLES	EXPLANATION
Compare: a. People **who are unhappy with the amount of spam they receive** should write to their lawmakers. b. People **unhappy with the amount of spam they receive** should write to their lawmakers. a. Pierre Omidyar, **who is the founder of eBay**, is one of the richest men in the world. b. Pierre Omidyar, **the founder of eBay**, is one of the richest men in the world.	Sentences (a) have an adjective clause. Sentences (b) have a descriptive phrase.
a. One-half of all of the e-mail **that is sent today** is spam. b. One-half of all the e-mail *sent* today is spam. a. There are about 78 million items **that are listed on eBay**. b. There are about 78 million items *listed* on eBay.	A descriptive phrase can begin with a **past participle**. Compare sentences (a) with an adjective clause to sentences (b) with a descriptive phrase.
a. A man **who is living in Florida** retired at the age of 37 after making millions in the spam business. b. A man *living* in Florida retired at the age of 37 after making millions in the spam business. a. Shoppers **who are using eBay** can locate a hard-to-find item. b. Shoppers *using* eBay can locate a hard-to-find item.	A descriptive phrase can begin with a **present participle** (verb *-ing*). Compare sentences (a) with an adjective clause to sentences (b) with a descriptive phrase.
a. Spam, **which is unwanted commercial e-mail**, is an annoying problem. b. Spam, **unwanted commercial e-mail**, is an annoying problem. a. eBay, **which is an auction Web site**, is very popular. b. eBay, **an auction Web site**, is very popular.	A descriptive phrase can give a definition or more information about the noun it follows. This kind of descriptive phrase is called an **appositive**. Compare sentences (a) with an adjective clause to sentences (b) with an appositive.
a. A man **who is in Florida** retired at the age of 37. b. A man *in* Florida retired at the age of 37. a. Pierre, **who is from France**, created eBay. b. Pierre, *from* France, created eBay.	A descriptive phrase can begin with a preposition (*with, in, from, of,* etc.). Compare sentences (a) with an adjective clause to sentences (b) with a prepositional phrase.

Language Notes:
1. A descriptive phrase can be essential or nonessential. A nonessential phrase is set off by commas.

   People **unhappy** with the amount of spam they receive should write to their lawmakers. (*Essential*)

   Pierre Omidyar, **the founder of eBay**, is one of the richest people in the world. (*Nonessential*)
2. An appositive is always nonessential.

   Amazon.com, **an online store**, is a very popular Web site.

EXERCISE 25 Shorten the adjective clauses to a descriptive phrase by crossing out the unnecessary words.

EXAMPLE   On eBay, people ~~who are~~ living in California can sell to people ~~who are~~ living in New York.

1. Google, which is a popular search engine, is used by millions of people.
2. Bill Gates, who is one of the richest people in the world, gets spam asking him if he wants to become rich.
3. There are a lot of dishonest companies which are trying to take your money.
4. eBay takes a percentage of each sale that is made on its Web site.
5. A virus is a harmful program which is passed from computer to computer.
6. Tim Berners-Lee, who was born in England, now works at MIT.
7. MIT, which is located in Cambridge, Massachusetts, is an excellent university.
8. Berners-Lee developed the idea for the Web when he was working at CERN, which is a physics lab in Switzerland.
9. Berners-Lee's parents worked on the first computer that was sold commercially.
10. People who are using the Web can shop from their homes.
11. People who are interested in reading newspapers from other cities can find them on the Web.
12. The World Wide Web, which is abbreviated WWW, was first introduced on the Internet in 1991.

(continued)

13. Computers which are sold today have much more memory and speed than computers which were sold ten years ago.

14. Freecycle.org, which is an online community, helps people get things they need for free.

15. Deron Beal, who is from Arizona, created Freecycle.org.

EXERCISE 26 **Combine the two sentences. Use a phrase for the sentence in parentheses ( ).**

EXAMPLE   Microsoft Windows made personal computers easy to use. (Windows was created by Bill Gates.)
Microsoft Windows, created by Bill Gates, made personal computers
easy to use.

1. Google is very easy to use. (It is a popular search engine.)
   _____

   _____

2. Have you ever used Mapquest? (It is a Web site that gives maps and driving directions.)
   _____

   _____

3. Tim Berners-Lee works at MIT. (This is a university in Massachusetts.)
   _____

   _____

4. Tim Berners-Lee was born in 1955. (This is the same year Bill Gates was born.)
   _____

   _____

5. Freecycle.org helps the environment. (It was created in 2003.)
   _____

   _____

EXERCISE 27   **Combine these short sentences into longer sentences using adjective clauses or descriptive phrases.**

EXAMPLE   Pierre Omidyar came to the U.S. when he was a child. His father was a professor of medicine.

Pierre Omidyar, whose father was a professor of medicine, came to the U.S. when he was a child.

1. Pierre Omidyar was born in France. He wrote his first computer program at age 14.

   _____

   _____

2. *BusinessWeek* named Meg Whitman among the 25 most powerful business managers. *BusinessWeek* is a popular business magazine.

   _____

   _____

3. Bill Gates was born in 1955. His father was a lawyer.

   _____

   _____

4. Bill Gates wrote his first computer program in 1967. He was only 12 years old at that time.

   _____

   _____

5. Bill Gates has three children. His wife was a marketing executive at Microsoft.

   _____

   _____

6. Paul Allen helped create Microsoft. Bill Gates met Paul Allen in high school.

   _____

   _____

7. Bill Gates started Microsoft at the age of 19. He dropped out of Harvard during his second year.

   _____

   _____

(continued)

8. Freecycle.org is an online network. Its members can receive goods for free.

_____

_____

9. Michael Dell created Dell computers. He dropped out of college after his first year.

_____

_____

10. Dell's parents were worried about Michael. His grades were dropping.

_____

_____

11. Dell's business started to perform well at the end of his first year of college. At that time, his business was making over $50,000 a month.

_____

_____

12. Dell Computers was one of the first companies to sell computers online. It was selling about $18 million of computers a day by the late 1990s.

_____

_____

13. In 2000, _Forbes_ named Dell Computers the third most admired company in the U.S. _Forbes_ is a business magazine.

_____

_____

14. In 2008, Meg Whitman resigned from eBay. She worked at eBay for ten years.

_____

_____

Summary of Lesson 6

	ESSENTIAL	NONESSENTIAL
Pronoun as subject	People **who** (or **that**) **use Freecycle.org** can get a lot of things for free. I just bought a computer **that** (or **which**) **has a lot of memory.**	Deron Beal, **who created Freecycle.org**, wants to help the environment. eBay was created in San Jose, **which is a city near San Francisco.**
Pronoun as object	The first computer (**that** or **which**) **I bought** didn't have very much memory. The people (**who, whom, that**) **you meet in chat rooms** are sometimes very silly.	My first computer, **which I bought in 2004**, is much slower than my new computer. My father, **whom you met at the party**, is a programmer.
Pronoun as object of preposition	The person **to whom I sent an e-mail** never answered me. (Formal) The person (**whom, who, that**) **I sent an e-mail to** never answered me. (Informal)	Berners-Lee, **about whom we read**, is an interesting person. (Formal) Berners-Lee, **who(m) we read about**, is an interesting person. (Informal)
Where	The store **where I bought my computer** has good prices.	Berners-Lee works at the Massachusetts Institute of Technology, **where he does research.**
When	I'll never forget the day (**when**) **I saw a personal computer for the first time.**	The Web was created in 1991, **when most people did not have home computers.**
Whose + noun as subject	Children **whose parents are wealthy** often have the best technology in the home.	Berners-Lee, **whose parents worked on computers**, learned a lot in his home.
Whose + noun as object	I sent a thank-you e-mail to the person **whose bicycle I received** through Freecycle.	My neighbor, **whose computer I bought**, just bought a new laptop.
Adjective clause after indefinite compound	I don't know anyone **who doesn't have a computer.** Everything (**that**) **I learned about computers** is useful.	
Descriptive phrase	Home computers **made 20 years ago** didn't have a lot of memory.	Bill Gates, **the founder of Microsoft**, became a billionaire.

Editing Advice

1. Never use *what* as a relative pronoun.

   who
   She married a man ~~what~~ has a lot of money.

   that
   Everything ~~what~~ you did was unnecessary.

2. You can't omit a relative pronoun that is the subject of the adjective clause.

   who
   I know a man ˄ speaks five languages.

3. If the relative pronoun is the object of the adjective clause, don't put an object after the verb.

   The car that I bought ~~it~~ has a stick shift.

4. Make sure you use subject-verb agreement.

   I know several English teachers who speak~~s~~ Spanish.

   has
   A car that ~~have~~ a big engine is not economical.

5. Put a noun before an adjective clause.

   The student w
   ~~W~~ho wants to leave early should sit in the back.

6. Don't confuse *whose* with *who's*.

   whose
   A student ~~who's~~ grades are good may get a scholarship.

7. Put the subject before the verb in an adjective clause.

   my cousin bought
   The house that ~~bought my cousin~~ is very beautiful.

8. Use *whose*, not *his*, *her*, or *their*, to show possession in an adjective clause.

   whose
   I have a friend ~~who his~~ knowledge of computers is very great.

Editing Quiz

Some of the shaded words and phrases have mistakes. Find the mistakes and correct them. If the shaded words are correct, write C.

Last semester I took a photo editing *class that* has helped me a lot.

C

(example)

The teacher *what* taught the class is an expert in photo editing.

who

(example)

This teacher, whose name is Mark Ryan, is patient, helpful, and fun.

(1)

A lot of the photos I took were too dark. I learned how to lighten the

(2)

parts what needed lightening without lightening the whole photo. I also

(3)

learned to cut out parts I don't want them. For example, I have a family

(4)

picture, but it has one person who's not in the family. It's a woman

(5)

who live next door to us. She came right at the time when

(6)

was taking the picture my friend and she wanted to be in it. It's a great

(7)

photo, except for her. I tried scanning it and editing it at home, but I

didn't do a good job. My teacher, who his scanner is much better than

(8)

mine, scanned the photo and showed me how to cut the neighbor out. I

learned many things in this class. Everything what I learned is very helpful.

(9)

I started to take another photo class this semester. The teacher

whose class I'm taking now is not as good as last semester's teacher. Who

(10)   *(11)*

wants to learn a lot about photo editing should take Mark Ryan's class.

Lesson 6 Test/Review

PART **1** **Fill in the blanks to complete the adjective clause. Answers may vary.**

EXAMPLE **A:** Do you like your new roommate?

B: Not really. The roommate ___I had last year___ was much

nicer.

EXAMPLE **A:** Are there any teachers at this school ___who speak Spanish___?

B: Yes. Ms. Lopez speaks Spanish.

1. **A:** I heard you had a car accident. You hit another car.

   B: Yes. The woman whose _____ wants me to pay

   her $700.

2. **A:** I bought a laptop for $1,500.

   B: That's a lot of money. The laptop _____ only

   cost $1,000.

3. **A:** Did you buy your textbooks at Berk's Bookstore?

   B: No. The store _____ is about ten blocks from

   school. Books are cheaper there.

4. **A:** My husband's mother always interferes in our married life.

   B: That's terrible. I wouldn't want to be married to a man whose

   _____.

5. **A:** What did the teacher say about registration?

   B: I don't know. She spoke very fast. I didn't understand everything

   _____.

6. **A:** Do you remember your first day in the U.S.?

   B: Of course. I'll always remember the day _____

   in my new country.

7. A: The teacher is talking about a very famous American, but I didn't hear his name.

B: The man _____ is John Kennedy.

8. A: Did you buy the dictionary I recommended to you?

B: No, but the dictionary _____ is just as good as the one you recommended.

9. A: Do you remember the names of all the students?

B: No. There are some students _____.

PART **2** **Combine each pair of sentences into one sentence. Use the words in parentheses ( ) to add a nonessential adjective clause to the first sentence.**

EXAMPLE Pierre Omidyar got the idea for eBay in 1995. (His wife is a collector.)
Pierre Omidyar, whose wife is a collector, got the idea for eBay in 1995.

1. Berners-Lee was born in 1955. (Most people knew nothing about computers in 1955.)

_____

2. The Internet changed the way people get their information. (It became popular in the 1990s.)

_____

3. Berners-Lee studied physics in college. (His parents were programmers.)

_____

4. Berners-Lee is not a well-known person. (We read about him in this lesson.)

_____

5. Berners-Lee works at MIT. (He is an engineering professor there.)

_____

PART **3** Some of these adjective clauses can be shortened to descriptive phrases. Shorten them by crossing out unnecessary words. Some of the adjective clauses cannot be shortened. Do not change them. Write "no change" (*NC*).

EXAMPLES   Thanksgiving, ~~which is~~ an American holiday, is in November.

Everyone who came to dinner enjoyed the food.   **NC**

1. The English that is spoken in the U.S. is different from British English.
2. A lot of people like to shop on eBay, which is an auction Web site.
3. Do not disturb the students who are studying in the library.
4. In the U.S. there are many immigrants who are from Mexico.
5. The computer you bought has a lot of memory.
6. Freecycle, which was created in 2003, is good for the environment.
7. Everyone who is in my computer class has a laptop.
8. Everyone I met at the party was very interesting.
9. The children who are using the computer are not getting enough exercise.
10. Bill Gates, who is one of the richest people in the world, donates a lot of money to help others.
11. The teacher with whom I studied beginning grammar comes from Canada.
12. The Web, which was introduced in 1991, has changed the way many companies do business.

PART **4** Some of the following sentences need commas. Put them in. If the sentence doesn't need commas, write "no commas."

EXAMPLES   The last article we read was about the Internet. *no commas*
MIT, which is a well-known university, has a good engineering department.

1. Ms. Thomson who was my English teacher last semester will retire next year.
2. I don't like teachers who give a lot of homework.
3. I studied engineering at the University of Michigan which is located in Ann Arbor, Michigan.
4. The computer I bought last month has a lot of memory.
5. The computer which is one of the most important inventions of the twentieth century can be found in most American homes.
6. eBay is a Web site where people can buy and sell items.

7. My mother who lives in Miami has a degree in engineering.

8. I have two sisters. My sister who lives in New Jersey has three children.

9. Our parents who live with us now are beginning to study English.

10. I often use Freecycle.org which has communities in most big cities.

11. The city where I was born has beautiful museums.

12. St. Petersburg where I was born has beautiful museums.

Expansion

Classroom Activities

❶ Make a sentence with each of the following phrases. Discuss your answers in a small group.

a. children who use the Internet a lot

b. people who don't have a computer

c. Web sites that have a lot of ads

d. the spam I get in my mailbox

e. people who work with computers all day

f. schools that don't have modern computer equipment

❷ Fill in the blanks and discuss your answers:

a. _____ is one of my favorite Web sites.

b. One thing I really like about the Web is _____

_____.

c. One thing I don't like about the Web is _____

_____.

Talk About It

❶ In what ways does the computer make life better? In what ways does it make life worse?

❷ One way to get rid of things you don't need is by using Freecycle. What do you do with things you have no more use for?

Write

❶ Write a paragraph telling the different ways you use your computer.

❷ Write about an important person you know of who did something great but isn't well-known (like Tim Berners-Lee).

❸ Write about some type of technology that you use today that you didn't use ten years ago.

EXAMPLE

Using Facebook

A few years ago I started using Facebook, and I love it. I can see what my friends are doing. Also I can make new friends by seeing whom my friends have included as their friends. Any of my friends who want to know what I'm doing can see my page ...

For more practice using grammar in context, please visit our Web site.

Grammar
Infinitives

Gerunds

Context
Helping Others

7.1 Infinitives—An Overview

An infinitive is *to* + the base form: *to go, to be, to see*.

EXAMPLES	EXPLANATION
I *want* **to help.**	An infinitive is used after certain verbs.
I want *him* **to help.**	An object can be added before an infinitive.
I'm *happy* **to help.**	An infinitive can follow certain adjectives.
It's important **to help** others.	An infinitive follows certain expressions with *it*.
Do you volunteer your time *in order* **to help** others?	An infinitive is used to show purpose.
He's old *enough* **to help.** She's *too* young **to help.**	An infinitive is used after expressions with *too* and *enough*.

Andrew Carnegie, Philanthropist[1]

Before You Read

1. Who are some of the richest people today?

2. Should rich people help others?

CD 3, TR 01

Read the following textbook article. Pay special attention to infinitives.

Andrew Carnegie, 1835–1919

[1]A *philanthropist* is a person who gives away money to help other people.

Andrew Carnegie was one of the world's richest men. He made a fortune[2] in the oil and steel industries but spent most of his life giving his money away.

Carnegie was born in Scotland in 1835. When he was 13 years old, his family immigrated to the United States. A year later, he started **to work** for $1.20 a week. He was intelligent and hardworking, and it didn't take him long **to become** rich. But he always remembered the day he wanted **to use** a library in Pittsburgh but was not permitted **to enter**. He was disappointed **to learn** that the library was for members only.

Carnegie Library of Pittsburgh

As Carnegie's fortunes grew, he started **to give** his money away. One of his biggest desires was **to build** free public libraries. He wanted everyone **to have** access to libraries and education. He believed that education was the key to a successful life. In 1881, there were only a few public libraries. Carnegie started to build free libraries for the people. Over the doors of the Carnegie Library of Pittsburgh, carved in stone, are his own words, "Free to the People." By the time Carnegie died, there were more than 2,500 public libraries in the English-speaking world.

But building libraries was not his only contribution. In his book *The Gospel of Wealth*, he tried **to persuade** other wealthy people **to give** away their money. These are some of the ideas he wrote about in his book:

- **To give** away money is the best thing rich people can do.
- It is the moral obligation of the wealthy **to help** others.
- It is important for a rich person **to set** an example for others.
- It is not good **to have** money if your spirit is poor.
- It is the mind that makes the body rich.
- It is a disgrace[3] **to die** rich.

By the time he died in 1919, Carnegie had given away more than $350 million.

---

[2]A *fortune* is a very large quantity of money.

[3]A *disgrace* is something that brings shame or dishonor.

7.2 Verbs Followed by an Infinitive

EXAMPLES	EXPLANATION
Carnegie *wanted* **to build** libraries. He *started* **to work** when he was 14. He *decided* **to give** away money. Everyone *deserves* **to have** an education.	Some verbs are followed by an infinitive.
I want **to make** money *and* **help** others.	In a sentence with two infinitives connected by *and*, the second *to* is usually omitted.
Everyone wants **to be given** an opportunity to succeed.	To make an infinitive passive, use *to be* + past participle.

Language Note:
The verbs below can be followed by an infinitive.

agree	continue*	intend	offer	seem
appear	decide	know how	plan	start*
attempt	deserve	learn	prefer*	try*
begin*	expect	like*	prepare	want
can('t) afford	forget	love*	pretend	wish
can't stand*	hate*	manage	promise	would like
choose	hope	need	refuse	

*These verbs can also be followed by a gerund with little or no change in meaning. See Section 7.14.

EXERCISE **1** **Fill in the blanks with an infinitive based on the article you just read. Answers may vary.**

EXAMPLE   Andrew Carnegie started _____ *to work* _____ when he was very young.

1. He tried _____ a library when he was young, but he wasn't allowed inside.

2. He wanted _____ free public libraries.

3. He thought it was important for rich people _____ poor people.

4. He thought it was better _____ a rich spirit than a big bank account.

5. He thought that rich people needed _____ an example for others.

6. He decided _____ a lot of money to help others.

7. He thought it was a terrible thing _____ rich.

EXERCISE 2 **ABOUT YOU** Fill in the blanks with an infinitive. Share your answers with the class.

EXAMPLE I like _____ to eat Chinese food _____.

1. I don't like _____, but I have to do it anyway.
2. I can't afford _____.
3. I've decided _____.
4. I want _____, but I don't have enough time.
5. I don't want _____.
6. I sometimes forget _____.
7. I love _____.
8. I need _____ and _____ every day.
9. I don't know how _____, but I'd like to learn.
10. I would like _____.

EXERCISE 3 **ABOUT YOU** Answer these questions. You may discuss your answers.

EXAMPLE Why did you decide to come to this city?
I decided to come here because I wanted to go to this school.

1. Why did you decide to come to this school?
2. What did you need to do to register at this school?
3. When did you start to study English?
4. What do you expect to have five years from now (that you don't have now)?
5. What do you hope to accomplish in your lifetime?
6. Do you want to learn any other languages? Which ones? Why?
7. Do you plan to get a college degree? In what field?
8. Do you plan to transfer to a different school?
9. What do you plan to do after you graduate?

EXERCISE 4 Fill in the blanks with the passive form of the verb in parentheses ( ).

EXAMPLE Children like _____ to be given _____ attention.
                                    (give)

1. Children have _____ about giving, not just taking.
                        (teach)

(continued)

2. My elderly neighbor needs _____ to the hospital
(drive)

because he can't drive. I'm going to offer to drive him.

3. Some people who make donations don't want their names

_____.
(know)

4. Money for a charity needs _____.
(collect)

5. There are many ways to help. Parks need _____.
(clean)

6. There are many ways of helping children. Children need

_____ and _____.
(love)   (respect)

7. Carnegie thought that libraries needed _____ for
(build)

the public.

8. Everyone wants _____ a chance to succeed in life.
(give)

7.3 Object Before Infinitive

After the verb, we can use an object + an infinitive.

EXAMPLE	EXPLANATION
a. Carnegie wanted **poor people to have** the same opportunities as rich people. b. He encouraged **rich people to help** others. c. He wanted **them to donate** money. d. Our parents want **us to help** others.	The object can be a noun (a and b) or a pronoun (c and d).
Carnegie encouraged rich people **not to be** selfish. He reminded them **not to forget** about the poor.	Put *not* before an infinitive to make a negative.

Language Note: The verbs below can be followed by a noun or object pronoun + an infinitive.

advise	expect	persuade
allow	forbid	remind
appoint	force	teach*
ask	invite	tell
beg	need	urge
convince	order	want
encourage	permit	would like

*After *teach, how* is sometimes used: He taught me *how to ski.*

EXERCISE 5　**ABOUT YOU**　**Tell if you want or don't want the teacher to do the following.**

EXAMPLES　speak fast
I don't want the teacher to speak fast.

answer my questions
I want him to answer my questions.

1. explain the grammar
2. review modals
3. give us a lot of homework
4. give us a test on gerunds and infinitives
5. give a lot of examples
6. speak slowly
7. correct my pronunciation
8. teach us idioms

EXERCISE 6　**ABOUT YOU**　**Tell if the teacher expects or doesn't expect you to do the following.**

EXAMPLES　come on time
The teacher expects us to come on time.

wear a uniform to class
The teacher doesn't expect us to wear a uniform to class.

1. write perfect compositions
2. learn English in six months
3. do the homework
4. stand up to answer a question
5. raise our hands to answer
   a question
6. ask questions
7. study on the weekend
8. practice English every day
9. speak English without an accent
10. use the Internet

EXERCISE 7　**Change the following imperative statements to statements with an object pronoun plus an infinitive.**

EXAMPLE　A woman says to her husband, "Teach the children good values."
She wants him to teach the children good values.

1. My parents always said to me, "Help others."
   They expected _____

2. A mother says to her children, "Be kind to others."
   She wants _____

3. The father said to his children, "Give to charity."
   He advised _____

4. Parents say to their children, "Be good."
   They want _____

5. I said to you, "Work hard."

I would like _____

6. My parents said to us, "Give money to the poor."

They reminded _____

7. A father says to his daughter, "Be generous."

He wants _____

8. My parents said to me, "Don't be selfish."

They encouraged _____

9. Parents say to their children, "Be polite."

They expect _____

EXERCISE 8 **ABOUT YOU** Use the words given to tell what your family wanted from you when you were growing up.

EXAMPLES want / watch TV
My father didn't want me to watch TV.

expect / be polite
My parents expected me to be polite.

1. expect / respect older people
2. allow / stay out late at night
3. want / help them
4. expect / get good grades in school
5. encourage / have a lot of friends
6. want / be obedient
7. want / be independent
8. permit / choose my own friends
9. expect / do chores
10. encourage / read
11. advise / be honest
12. encourage / get an education

Charity and Volunteering

Before You Read

1. Do you ever receive address labels in the mail with your name and address printed on them?

2. Do you ever watch a TV channel that asks you to send money to support it?

Read the following magazine article. Pay special attention to verbs followed by infinitives and base forms.

There are more than 600,000 charities in the U.S. that you can give to.

In addition, there are thousands of volunteer organizations. But it isn't always easy to **get** people **to give** willingly.

One way charities **get** people **to contribute** is by offering a payroll deduction at work. An employee can have a certain amount of each paycheck deducted, so the money goes to charity before the employee even sees it. If you are asked to give at your job, keep in mind that it is voluntary; no one can **make** you **give**.

Another way to **get** you **to give** is to send you something free in the mail, such as address labels with your name and address printed on them. Some people feel guilty about accepting the gift without giving something. Also, some charities **have** volunteers **stand** at intersections with a can or box, asking passing drivers for donations. Often they give you something, such as candy, for your donation.

Public TV and radio stations have fundraisers. Several days out of the year, they ask for your money to support the programs you like. The station **has** volunteers **answer** phones to take your credit card number.

Besides giving money, people can volunteer their time. Some volunteers **help** kids **learn** to read; others **help feed** the homeless; others **help** elderly people **get** meals.

Helping others **makes** us **feel** good. To encourage us **to give**, the government **lets** us **deduct** our contribution, which lowers our taxes.

7.4 Causative Verbs

Some verbs are called *causative* verbs because one person causes, enables, or allows another to do something.

EXAMPLES	EXPLANATION
Carnegie *persuaded* wealthy people **to give** away their money.	*Get*, *persuade*, and *convince* are followed by an object + infinitive.
You *convinced* me **to help** the poor.	*Get*, in the example on the left, means persuade.
They *got* us **to contribute** to charity.	
Carnegie **helped** people **to get** an education. Some volunteers **help** kids **learn** to read.	After *help* + object, either the infinitive or the base form can be used. The base form is more common.
The government **lets** you **deduct** your contribution to charity. The teacher doesn't **let** us **talk** during a test.	*Let* means permit. *Let* is followed by an object + base form. (*Permit* and *allow* are followed by an infinitive.) **Compare:** The teacher doesn't **let** us **talk**. The teacher doesn't **permit** us **to talk**.
a. No one can **make** you **give** to charity. b. Volunteering my time **makes** me **feel** good.	*Make* is followed by an object + base form. In sentence (a), *make* means force. In sentences (b), *make* means to cause something to happen.
Public TV stations **have** volunteers **answer** the phones and take donations. The teacher **had** us **write** a composition about charity.	*Have* means to give a job or task to someone. *Have*, in this case, is followed by an object + base form.

EXERCISE 9 Fill in the blanks with the base form or the infinitive of the verb in parentheses ( ).

🔊
CD 3, TR 03

I volunteer for my local public radio station. Several times a year, the

station tries to persuade listeners _____to give_____ money to the
                                    (example: give)

station. Without listener support, the radio station could not exist. The

station managers have us _____ the phones when listeners
                          (1 answer)

call to contribute. We let callers _____ by check or credit
                                    (2 pay)

card. To get listeners _____, the station offers some prizes.
                        (3 contribute)

For example, for a $60 contribution, you can get a coffee mug. For a $100

contribution, you can get a book. Everyone can listen to public radio for free. No one makes you _____ for it. But listeners should pay for
(*4 pay*)
this service, if they can. They should help the station _____
(*5 pay*)
for its excellent programming.

EXERCISE 10 **ABOUT YOU** **Fill in the blanks with the base form of a verb and finish the sentence.**

EXAMPLE   The teacher lets us __*talk in groups when we work on a problem.*__

1. When I was a child, my parents didn't let me _____

   _____

2. When I was a child, my parents made me _____

   _____

3. During a test, the teacher doesn't let us _____

   _____

4. The teacher often has us _____

5. My parents helped me _____

7.5 Adjective Plus Infinitive

Certain adjectives can be followed by an infinitive.

EXAMPLES	EXPLANATION
Some people are *happy* **to help** others. Are you *willing* **to donate** your time? I am *proud* **to be** a volunteer. I am *sad* **to see** so many needy people in the world. We are *pleased* **to help**.	Certain adjectives can be followed by an infinitive. Many of these adjectives describe a person's emotional or mental state.

Language Note: The following adjectives can be followed by an infinitive.

afraid	eager	pleased*	sad
ashamed*	glad	prepared*	sorry
delighted*	happy	proud	surprised*
disappointed*	lucky	ready	willing

*Note: Many *-ed* words are adjectives.

EXERCISE  **A college student has volunteered her time with an agency that delivers food to needy families. She is discussing her duties with the volunteer coordinator. Fill in the blanks with an appropriate infinitive. Answers may vary.**

A: Are you willing _____*to donate*_____ your time on the weekends?
(example)

B: Yes. I'm eager _____ people who need my help. I'm
_(1)_

ready _____ whatever you need me to do.
_(2)_

A: You're going to deliver meals to people in this neighborhood who don't

have enough food.

B: I'm surprised _____ that some people don't have
_(3)_

enough to eat. This seems like a middle-class neighborhood.

A: It is. But the economy is bad. Most people are lucky

_____ a job. But many people have lost their jobs.
_(4)_

Some people are ashamed _____ for help.
_(5)_

B: I can understand that. But don't worry. I'm willing

_____ anyone who needs my help.
_(6)_

A: Don't be afraid _____ into a stranger's home.
_(7)_

Someone will always go with you.

B: I'm happy _____ food to people who need it.
_(8)_

A: I'm glad _____ you work with us. Your parents must
_(9)_

be proud _____ such a wonderful daughter.
_(10)_

EXERCISE **12** **ABOUT YOU** **Fill in the blanks with an infinitive (phrase).**

EXAMPLE Before I came here, I was afraid ____*to speak English.*____

1. When I started this course, I was eager _____

_____

2. When I started to attend this school, I was surprised (to see, learn, find

out) _____

3. When I was a child, I was afraid _____

_____

4. Now I'm afraid _____

5. I'm happy _____

6. I'm lucky _____

7. When I left my hometown, I was sorry _____

_____

8. When I was _____ years old, I was ready _____

_____

CD 3, TR 04

EXERCISE **13**   **Fill in the blanks with an infinitive or a base form in this conversation between an uncle (U) and his nephew (N). Answers may vary.**

U: What do you plan ___*to do*___ this summer?
            (example)

N: I wanted _____ a summer job, but I couldn't
                  (1)

find one. It's going to be boring. I'm ready _____,
                                                (2)

but no one wants _____ me. And my parents
                      (3)

expect me _____ a job. My mom won't let
               (4)

me _____ home all day and watch TV or hang
       (5)

out with my friends at the swimming pool.

U: Are you trying _____ money for your college education?
                        (6)

N: Not really. I haven't even thought about saving for college yet. I want a

job because I'm planning _____ a car.
                              (7)

U: You need _____ about college too. You're going to graduate
                   (8)

next year.

N: I'm planning _____ to a community college, so it won't be so
                       (9)

expensive. And my parents are willing _____ for my college
                                            (10)

tuition.

U: Have you thought about volunteering your time this summer?

N: Not really. I just want _____ money.
                                 (11)

U: Don't just think about money. Try _____ about how you can help
                                            (12)

other people. You can help little kids _____ to read. Or you can
                                            (13)

help _____ the parks by picking up garbage.
        (14)

N: I keep telling you. I just want _____ money. What will I get if I do
                                         (15)

those things? I won't get my car.

(continued)

U: You'll get satisfaction. Helping others will make you _____ (16) good. And you will learn _____ (17) responsible. After you finish community college and go to a four-year college, it will look good on your application if you say you volunteered. It will help you _____ (18) into a good college.

N: Why are you trying so hard to get me _____ (19) a volunteer?

U: I volunteered when I was your age, and I found that it was more valuable than money.

N: OK. I'll volunteer if you're willing _____ (20) me the money for the car.

One Step at a Time

Before You Read

1. Have you ever done volunteer work? What did you do?

2. Do you know anyone who has started a volunteer project?

CD 3, TR 05

Read the following article. Pay special attention to *in order to* and *to*.

Joyce Koenig loves to help people. She's also an artist. She wanted to combine her love of art and her desire to help others. About ten years ago, Joyce heard about One Step at a Time, an organization that helps children with cancer to go to a special camp and just have fun. **In order to send** these kids to camp, though, the organization needs to raise money. Joyce had an idea: She started making and selling beautiful cards **to raise** money for these kids. Because these cards are all handmade, it was taking a long time for her to make a lot of cards. So Joyce had another idea. She started inviting friends to her house **to help** her make the cards. Often she has a card-making party; the guests go into her studio **in order to make** the cards together. At first her friends were hesitant. Many said that they were not artistic and didn't know how to make cards. But once they saw the beautiful materials that she had in her studio, her friends felt more comfortable designing, cutting, and pasting **in order to make** an original card.

To make money without spending money, Joyce asks for and gets donations of paper, glue, scissors, ribbon, and other supplies from many sources. She sells her cards for $2 each at various art fairs during the year. Since she started her project, she has raised more than $30,000—two dollars at a time.

7.6 Using the Infinitive to Show Purpose

EXAMPLES	EXPLANATION
Joyce sells cards **in order to raise** money. The organization needs money **in order to help send** kids to camp.	*In order to* shows purpose. It answers the question "Why?" or "What for?"
Joyce sells cards **to raise** money. The organization needs money **to help send** kids to camp.	*In order to* can be shortened. We can simply use *to*.
a. **In order to raise** money, Joyce sells cards. a. **To economize**, Joyce asks for donations. b. Joyce sells cards **in order to raise** money. b. Joyce asks for donations **to economize**.	a. The purpose phrase can precede the main clause. Use a comma after the purpose phrase. b. The purpose phrase can follow the main clause. Don't use a comma.

EXERCISE 14 **Fill in the blanks to complete the sentences. Answers may vary.**

EXAMPLE   In order to _____*learn more about volunteering*_____, you can use the Internet. You can find lots of information there.

1. Carnegie donated his money to _____ libraries.

2. You can volunteer in order to _____ job experience. But in order to _____ money, you need a paying job.

3. To _____ a job, you need experience. To _____ experience, you need a job.

4. You can volunteer your time in order to _____ people. There are many people who need help.

5. Joyce started making and selling cards in order to _____ _____.

6. The organization One Step at a Time needs money in order to _____.

EXERCISE 15 **ABOUT YOU** Complete each sentence.

EXAMPLE I _____*try to speak with Americans as much as possible*_____ to improve my English.

1. I want to learn English in order to _____.
2. I came to this school to _____.
3. I use my dictionary to _____.
4. I _____ in order to relax.
5. I _____ to learn new words.

EXERCISE 16 Complete each sentence. Answers may vary.

EXAMPLE Many students have jobs in order _____*to pay for their education*_____.

1. We're studying this lesson to _____.
2. Many people use spell-check in order to _____.
3. Many people use Caller ID to _____.
4. You should register early to _____.
5. Many students apply for financial aid to _____.
6. If you aren't satisfied with your score on the TOEFL test, you can take it a second time in order to _____ your score.
7. If you're absent, you can call a classmate to _____.
8. You need a password in order to _____.
9. You can use the Web site Weather.com to _____.
10. Some shoppers use coupons to _____.

7.7 Infinitive as Subject

EXAMPLES	EXPLANATION
It's good **to help** other people. **It** was Carnegie's dream **to build** libraries. **It**'s fun **to make** cards.	An infinitive phrase can be the subject of a sentence. We usually begin the sentence with *it* and put the infinitive phrase at the end of the sentence.
It is important **for rich people to set** an example. It is necessary **for Joyce to get** donations of supplies.	*For* + an object can give the infinitive a specific subject.
It costs a lot of money **to build** a library. **It takes** time and effort **to raise** money.	An infinitive is often used after *cost* + money and *take* + time.

EXAMPLES	EXPLANATION
Carnegie was a poor immigrant, but it didn't **take** him long **to become** rich. How much did it **cost** him **to build** a library?	An indirect object can follow *take* and *cost*.
To build libraries was Carnegie's dream. **To give** money away is the best thing rich people can do. **To help** others gives a person satisfaction.	Sometimes we begin a sentence with an infinitive phrase. A sentence that begins with an infinitive is very formal.

EXERCISE 17 Complete each statement with an infinitive phrase.

EXAMPLE It isn't polite _____ to interrupt a conversation. _____

1. It's dangerous _____
2. It isn't healthy _____
3. It's wonderful _____
4. It's illegal _____
5. It's a good idea _____
6. It's the teacher's responsibility _____
7. It costs a lot of money _____
8. It's important for me _____
9. It's boring for the students _____
10. It's fun for children _____
11. It's easy for Americans _____
12. It took me a long time _____
13. It cost me a lot of money _____
14. It will probably take me a long time _____

EXERCISE 18 Make sentences with the words given.

EXAMPLE dangerous / children
It's dangerous for children to play with matches.

1. fun / children

   _____

2. necessary / children

   _____

3. important / a family

   _____

(continued)

4. difficult / a large family

_____

5. necessary / working parents

_____

6. difficult / most people

_____

7. hard / single parents

_____

8. difficult / the teacher

_____

EXERCISE 19 **Complete each statement. Begin with an _it-_ phrase.**

EXAMPLES   _____ It's impossible _____ to be perfect.

_____ It cost me $ 2.49 _____ to mail a package to my hometown.

     1. _____ to work hard.

     2. _____ to fall in love.

     3. _____ to get married.

     4. _____ to make a mistake in English.

     5. _____ to be lonely.

     6. _____ to help other people.

     7. _____ to take a taxi from this school to my house.

     8. _____ to eat lunch in a restaurant.

     9. _____ to go to college.

   10. _____ to buy my textbooks.

   11. _____ to learn English.

   12. _____ to give away money.

   13. _____ to have a lot of friends.

   14. _____ to travel.

EXERCISE 20 **Change these statements to make them less formal by starting them with _it_.**

EXAMPLE   To raise money for charity is a good thing.

It's a good thing to raise money for charity. _____

     1. To raise $30,000 is not easy.

_____

2. To fight disease takes a lot of money.

_____

3. To give away money is the responsibility of the rich.

_____

4. To produce high-quality public radio takes a lot of money.

_____

5. To build libraries was Carnegie's dream.

_____

6. To raise money for children with cancer is Joyce's goal.

_____

7.8 Infinitive with _Too_ and _Enough_

Too shows that the adjective or adverb is excessive for a specific purpose. _Enough_ shows that an adjective, adverb, or noun is sufficient for a specific purpose.

EXAMPLES	EXPLANATION
Young Carnegie was **too poor to enter** the library. You drive **too slowly to drive** on the highway. She's **too old to cook** for herself. A volunteer delivers her meals.	Word order: _too_ + adjective/adverb + infinitive
I have **too much work to do**, so I have no time to volunteer. There are **too many problems** in the world **to solve** in one day.	Word order: _too much_ + noncount noun + infinitive _too many_ + plural count noun + infinitive
Am I **talented enough to design** a card? Joyce sells cards **easily enough to raise** money for her charity.	Word order: Adjective/adverb + _enough_ + infinitive
Carnegie had **enough money to build** libraries. I have **enough time to volunteer** this summer.	Word order: _enough_ + noun + infinitive
There is enough volunteer work **for everyone to do.** Making cards is not hard **for me to do.**	The infinitive phrase can be preceded by _for_ + object.
a. I can't volunteer this summer because I'm **too busy**. b. Carnegie could build libraries because he had **enough money**.	Sometimes the infinitive phrase can be omitted. It is understood from the context: a. too busy to volunteer b. enough money to build libraries

EXERCISE 21 Fill in the blanks with the words in parentheses. Put the words in the correct order. Add *to* where necessary.

A: I heard about your card project, and I'd like to help you. But I don't have

_____enough talent_____. I'm _____ something new.
     (example: enough/talent)   (1 old/too/learn)

B: But it's so _____ cards. Anyone can do it.
                  (2 easy/make)

A: But I think it takes _____ a card. I don't have
                          (3 too/long/make)

_____.
     (4 time/enough)

B: It only takes about 15 minutes _____ a card.
                                       (5 make)

A: I'd really like to help but I'm _____ you at this time.
                                      (6 busy/too/help)

I have _____ at this time.
       (7 work/too much/do)

B: That's not a problem. When people have _____, they
                                              (8 time/enough/help)

help. If not, that's okay too.

A: But I'd really like to help. Is there anything else I can do?

B: You can make a donation.

A: I'm not sure I have _____ a donation.
                          (9 enough/money/make)

B: You can buy just one card for $2.

A: Really? They're so inexpensive. I have _____ five
                                             (10 enough/money/buy)

cards now.

B: Great! Every dollar helps. Choose the cards you like. Each one is original.

A: They're all so beautiful. It's _____ only five.
                                    (11 hard/too/choose)

EXERCISE 22 Fill in the blanks with *too, too much, too many,* or *enough* and any other words necessary to fill in the blanks. Answers may vary.

A: I heard about a volunteer project at the park. We can go and pick up

garbage.

B: Why would you want to do that? I don't have _____enough time_____ to
                                                    (example)

do that. I have _____ things to do today.
                (1)

A: You always say you want to volunteer. About 50 volunteers are coming. It

won't take _____ to finish the job.
            (2)

B: But it's _____ to spend the whole day in the sun. It's
(3)
almost 90 degrees today.

A: We can go swimming afterwards. The park has a big swimming pool.

B: The water is deep there, and I don't swim _____ to
(4)
swim in deep water.

A: Don't worry. There's a shallow end and a deep end. You can stay in the
shallow end.

B: The shallow end has a lot of kids. And the kids make

_____ noise. They're always yelling.
(5)

A: I guess you're just not interested in helping today.

7.9 Gerunds—An Overview

To form a gerund, put an *-ing* ending on a verb. A gerund is used as a noun (subject or object).

EXAMPLES	EXPLANATION
Subject **Charity** is a good thing. **Helping others** is a good thing. *Object* I enjoy **summer**. I enjoy **helping people.**	You can use a gerund (phrase) in the same place you use any subject or object.
Contributing money is one way to help. **Volunteering your time** is another way to help.	A gerund (phrase) can be used as the subject of a sentence.
I enjoy **volunteering my time.** Joyce appreciates **getting help** from volunteers.	A gerund (phrase) can be used as the object of a sentence.
I'm excited *about* **making cards.** Let's volunteer this summer instead *of* **wasting our time at the beach.**	A gerund (phrase) can be used as the object of a preposition.
Carnegie accused some rich people of ***not* helping** others. ***Not* being** able to enter a library made Carnegie feel bad.	To make a gerund negative, put *not* before the gerund.
I appreciate **being told** about volunteer opportunities. Sick children enjoy **being given** the opportunity to go to camp.	A gerund can be passive: *being* + past participle.

Helping Others Get an Education

1. Do you think that all rich people like to live in luxury?

2. Do you know anyone who is very generous?

CD 3, TR 06

Read the following magazine article. Pay special attention to gerunds.

When we think of philanthropists, we usually think of the very rich and famous, like Andrew Carnegie or Bill Gates.

However, Matel Dawson, who was a forklift driver in Michigan, was an ordinary man who did extraordinary things.

Matel Dawson, 1921–2002

Dawson started **working** at Ford Motor Company in 1940 for $1.15 an hour. By **working** hard, **saving** carefully, and **investing** his money wisely, he became rich. But he didn't care about **owning** expensive cars or **taking** fancy vacations. Instead of **spending** his money on himself, he enjoyed **giving** it away. Since 1995, he donated more than $1 million for college scholarships to help poor students who want to get an education.

Why did Dawson insist on **giving** his money away to college students? One reason was that he did not have the opportunity to finish school. He had to drop out of school after the seventh grade to help support his poor family. He realized the importance of **having** an education and regretted not **having** the opportunity. Also, he learned about **giving** from his parents. He watched them work hard, save their money, and help others less fortunate. His mother made Dawson promise to always give something back. He was grateful to his parents for **teaching** him the importance of **helping** others.

When he became rich, he didn't change his lifestyle. He continued **driving** his old car and **living** in a one-bedroom apartment. And he didn't stop **working** until shortly before he died at the age of 81. When asked why he worked long past the time when most people retire, he replied, "It keeps me **going, knowing** I'm helping somebody."

7.10 Gerund as Subject

EXAMPLES	EXPLANATION
Working gave Dawson satisfaction. **Giving away money** made Dawson feel good.	A gerund or a gerund phrase can be the subject of the sentence.
Helping others *gives* a person pleasure.	A gerund subject takes a singular verb.
Not **finishing** school can affect your whole life.	To make a gerund negative, put *not* before the gerund.

EXERCISE 23 **Fill in the blanks with a gerund. Answers may vary.**

EXAMPLE ___Helping___ others made Dawson feel good.

1. _____ in a factory was not an easy job.

2. Not _____ an education always bothered Dawson.

3. _____ an education is expensive in the U.S.

4. _____ money didn't give Dawson satisfaction.

5. _____ an old car was not a problem for Dawson.

6. _____ a vacation wasn't important for Dawson.

7. _____ that he was helping people was very important for Dawson.

EXERCISE 24 **Complete each statement. Answers will vary.**

EXAMPLE Owning a lot of things ___doesn't give people much satisfaction.___

1. Having a lot of money _____

2. Helping less fortunate people _____

3. Volunteering your time _____

4. Getting an education _____

5. Working hard _____

EXERCISE 25 **ABOUT YOU** **Complete each statement with a gerund (phrase) as the subject.**

EXAMPLE ___Taking a warm bath___ relaxes me at the end of the day.

1. _____ is difficult for me.

2. _____ was an important decision in my life.

3. _____ makes me feel good.

4. _____ makes me feel bad.

(continued)

5. _____ makes me feel proud.

6. _____ has always been easy for me.

7.11 Gerund after Prepositions and Nouns

EXAMPLES	EXPLANATION
Dawson **didn't care about owning** fancy things. He **believed in helping** others.	Verb + preposition + gerund
Carnegie was **famous for building** libraries. Dawson was **concerned about helping** poor college students. Joyce is **successful at raising** money for children with cancer.	Adjective + preposition + gerund
Dawson **thanked his parents for teaching** him to save money.	Verb + object + preposition + gerund
Dawson didn't **spend money going** on vacations or **eating** in expensive restaurants. He didn't **have a hard time saving** money.	A gerund is used directly after the noun in the following expressions: *have a difficult time, have difficulty, have experience, have fun, have a good time, have a hard time, have a problem, have trouble, spend time, spend money.*

EXERCISE 26   **ABOUT YOU** Complete the questions with a gerund (phrase). Then ask another student these questions.

EXAMPLE   Are you lazy about _____ *writing compositions?* _____

1. Are you worried about _____

2. Are you interested in _____

3. Do you ever think about _____

4. Were you excited about _____

5. Do you ever dream about _____

EXERCISE 27   **ABOUT YOU** Fill in the blanks with a gerund phrase.

EXAMPLE   I had problems _____ *getting a student loan.* _____

1. I had a hard time _____

2. I have a lot of experience _____

3. I don't have much experience _____

4. I spent a lot of money _____

5. I don't like to spend my time _____

6. I have a lot of fun _____

7. I don't have a good time _____

8. I don't have a problem _____

7.12 Using the Correct Preposition

It is important to choose the correct preposition after a verb, adjective, or noun.

PREPOSITION COMBINATIONS		COMMON PHRASES	EXAMPLES
Verb + Preposition	verb + *about*	care about complain about dream about forget about talk about think about worry about	I **care about helping** people. Carnegie **dreamed about opening** public libraries.
	verb + *to*	adjust to look forward to object to	I **am looking forward to volunteering**.
	verb + *on*	depend on insist on plan on	I **insist on helping** my grandmother.
	verb + *in*	believe in succeed in	Does he **believe in giving** to those in need?
Verb + Object + Preposition	verb + object + *of*	accuse . . . of suspect . . . of	He **accused me of leaving** work early.
	verb + object + *for*	apologize to . . . for blame . . . for forgive . . . for thank . . . for	They **thanked me for taking** care of their children.
	verb + object + *from*	keep . . . from prevent . . . from prohibit . . . from stop . . . from	He **kept me from finishing** my work on time.
	verb + object + *about*	warn . . . about	The librarian **warned the students about talking** in the library.

(continued)

PREPOSITION COMBINATIONS		COMMON PHRASES	EXAMPLES
Adjective + Preposition	adjective + *of*	afraid of capable of guilty of proud of tired of	I'm **afraid of going** out at night.
	adjective + *about*	concerned about excited about upset about worried about	The students are **worried about passing** the exam.
	adjective + *for*	responsible for famous for grateful to . . . for	The children are **grateful to** the volunteers **for helping** them.
	adjective + *at*	good at successful at	Joyce is very **good at making** cards.
	adjective + *to*	accustomed to used to	I'm not **accustomed to wearing** glasses.
	adjective + *in*	interested in	Are you **interested in getting** a volunteer job?
Noun + Preposition	noun + *of*	in danger of in favor of the purpose of	The students are all **in favor of having** class outside.
	noun + *for*	a need for a reason for an excuse for technique for	What is your **reason for going** home early?

Language Notes:

1. *Plan, afraid,* and *proud* can be followed by an infinitive too.

    I **plan on volunteering** on weekends. / I **plan to volunteer** on weekends.

    I'm **afraid of going** out at night. / I'm **afraid to go** out at night.

    He's **proud of being** a volunteer. / He's **proud to be** a volunteer.

2. Notice that in some expressions, *to* is a preposition followed by a gerund, not part of an infinitive.

Compare:

    I need **to wear** glasses. (infinitive)

    I'm not accustomed **to wearing** glasses. (*to* + gerund)

EXERCISE 28 **Fill in the blanks with a preposition and the gerund of the verb in parentheses ( ). If no preposition is necessary, write Ø.**

CD 3, TR 07

A: My father's going to retire next month. He's

worried ___about having___ nothing to do.
   (example: have)

B: I don't blame him _____
   (1 be)

worried. For a lot of people, their self-worth

depends _____, and when
   (2 work)

they retire, they feel worthless.

A: My mother is afraid that he'll spend all his

time _____ TV. Besides, she's
   (3 watch)

not accustomed _____ him home all day.
   (4 have)

B: Doesn't he have any interests?

A: Well, he's interested _____, but he lives in an apartment
   (5 garden)

now so he doesn't have a garden. When he had a house, he was always

proud _____ the nicest garden on the block.
   (6 have)

B: Has he thought _____ at the Botanical Gardens?
   (7 volunteer)

A: Do they use volunteers?

B: I think so. He would have a great time _____ there.
   (8 work)

A: You're right. He would be good _____ tours because
   (9 give)

he knows so much about flowers. This would give him a reason

_____ up in the morning. I'm grateful to you
   (10 get)

_____ me this idea. I can't wait to tell him.
   (11 give)

B: I'm sure your mother will be grateful too.

EXERCISE 29 **ABOUT YOU** Ask a question with the words given. Use the correct preposition (if necessary) and a gerund. Another student will answer.

EXAMPLES   fond / read
A: Are you fond of reading?
B: Yes, I am.

care / get a good grade
A: Do you care about getting a good grade?
B: Of course I do.

1. have trouble / understand spoken English

2. lazy / do the homework

3. have a technique / learn new words

4. afraid / fail this course

5. good / spell English words

6. interested / study computer programming

7. have experience / work with computers

8. think / buy a house some day

7.13 Verbs Followed by Gerunds

EXAMPLES	EXPLANATION
Dawson enjoyed **giving** money away. He couldn't imagine not **helping** others. Students appreciate **receiving** financial aid.	Many verbs are followed by a gerund.

The following verbs take a gerund.

admit	delay	finish	permit	recommend
advise	deny	imagine	postpone	resent
appreciate	discuss	keep (on)	practice	risk
avoid	dislike	mind[2]	put off[3]	stop
can't help[1]	enjoy	miss	quit	suggest
consider				

Language Notes:
[1]*Can't help* means to have no control: When I see a sad movie, I *can't help* crying.
[2]I *mind* means that something bothers me. I *don't mind* means that something is OK with me; it doesn't bother me: Do you *mind* living with your parents? No, I don't *mind*.
[3]*Put off* means postpone: I can't *put off* buying a car. I need one now.

EXAMPLES	EXPLANATION
Do you **go shopping** every day? Do you like to **go fishing**?	*Go* + gerund is used in many idiomatic expressions of sport and recreation.

Below are expressions with *go* + gerund.

go boating	go fishing	go sailing	go skiing
go bowling	go hiking	go shopping	go swimming
go camping	go hunting	go sightseeing	
go dancing	go jogging	go skating	

EXERCISE 30 **Fill in the blanks with a gerund (phrase) to complete these statements about the reading on Matel Dawson. Answers may vary.**

EXAMPLE Matel Dawson liked ___helping students___.

1. He regretted not _____.

2. Students appreciated _____ from Dawson.

3. He didn't mind _____ an old car.

4. He couldn't imagine not _____, so he didn't retire.

5. He didn't mind _____ in a small apartment.

6. He kept on _____ until shortly before he died at the age of 81.

EXERCISE 31 **ABOUT YOU Complete the sentences with a gerund (phrase).**

EXAMPLE I avoid ___walking alone at night.___

1. I don't mind _____

2. I've considered _____

3. I enjoy _____

4. I don't enjoy _____

5. I can't imagine _____

6. I don't like to go _____

7. I avoid _____

8. I appreciate _____

9. I often put off _____

7.14 Verbs Followed by Gerund or Infinitive

EXAMPLES	EXPLANATION
Dawson liked **giving** money away. He liked **to give** money away. He started **working** in 1940. He started **to work** in 1940.	Some verbs can be followed by either a gerund or an infinitive with no difference in meaning.

Language Note: The verbs below can be followed by either a gerund or an infinitive with no difference in meaning.

begin	continue	like	prefer
can't stand*	hate	love	start

*Can't stand means can't tolerate: I *can't stand* living in a cold climate.

EXERCISE 32 In the following sentences, change gerunds to infinitives and infinitives to gerunds.

EXAMPLE Dawson's parents loved to help others.
Dawson's parents loved helping others.

They hated seeing people suffer.
They hated to see people suffer.

1. Dawson began working when he was 19 years old.
2. He liked giving away money.
3. He continued to work until he was 80 years old.
4. He preferred to live in a small apartment.
5. He loved to help students get an education.

EXERCISE 33 This is a conversation between a teenager and her older brother. Fill in the blanks with an appropriate gerund or infinitive. It doesn't matter which one you use. Answers may vary.

CD 3, TR 08

A: I want to work this summer, but I can't decide what to do.

B: How about volunteering in a museum?

A: I can't stand _____**being**_____ indoors all day. I prefer
                 (example)
_____ outdoors.
       (1)

B: You're a great swimmer. Why don't you volunteer to teach kids how to swim?

A: I hate _____ with kids. It's hard work.
            (2)

B: Well, what do you like?

A: I love _____ at the beach.
(3)

B: Maybe you should get a job as a lifeguard.

A: Great idea! I'll start _____ for a job tomorrow.
(4)

B: That's what you said yesterday.

A: I guess I'm lazy. I just don't like _____.
(5)

7.15 Infinitive and Gerund as Subject

EXAMPLES	EXPLANATION
It is expensive **to go** to college. **It** is important **to have** a college education. **It** makes me feel good **to give** money to poor people.	An infinitive phrase can be the subject of a sentence. We usually begin the sentence with *it* and put the infinitive phrase at the end of the sentence or clause.
Going to college is expensive. **Having a college education** is important. **Giving money to poor people** makes me feel good.	A gerund phrase can be used as the subject.
To pay for college is difficult for most families. **To build** libraries was Carnegie's dream. **To give** money away is the best thing rich people can do, according to Carnegie.	Sometimes we begin a sentence with an infinitive phrase. A sentence that begins with an infinitive is very formal.

EXERCISE 34 Change these statements. Change the subject to a gerund form.

EXAMPLE It is wonderful to help others.
Helping others is wonderful.

1. It costs a lot of money to go to college.

   _____

2. It is hard to work and study at the same time.

   _____

3. It is important to invest your money wisely.

   _____

4. It is difficult to work in a factory.

   _____

(continued)

5. It can be boring to do the same thing every day.

_____

6. It is satisfying to help others.

_____

7. It is a wonderful thing to help sick kids.

_____

8. It is necessary to ask viewers to contribute to public TV.

_____

7.16 Gerund or Infinitive after a Verb: Differences in Meaning

After _stop_, _remember_, and _try_, the meaning of the sentence depends on whether you follow the verb with a gerund or an infinitive.

EXAMPLES	EXPLANATION
a. Dawson loved to work. He didn't **stop working** until he was 80. b. Dawson wanted to finish school, but he **stopped to get** a job.	a. _Stop_ + gerund = quit or discontinue an activity b. _Stop_ + infinitive = quit one activity in order to start another activity
a. Do you **remember reading** about Carnegie? b. Dawson's mother said, "Always **remember to help** other people."	a. _Remember_ + gerund = remember that something happened earlier b. _Remember_ + infinitive = remember something and then do it
a. Dawson always had a simple lifestyle. When he became rich, he **tried living** a fancier lifestyle, but it didn't bring him satisfaction. a. I always write my compositions by hand. I **tried writing** them on a computer, but I don't type fast enough. b. Carnegie **tried to enter** a library when he was young, but he was told it was for members only. b. Joyce always **tries to help** sick kids.	a. _Try_ + gerund = experiment with something new. You do something one way, and then, if that doesn't work, you try a different method. b. _Try_ + infinitive = make an effort or an attempt
Language Note: There is a big difference between _stop/remember_ + gerund and _stop/remember_ + infinitive. For _try_, the difference is not as clear.	

EXERCISE 35 **Read the following conversation between a son (S) and his mother (M). Fill in the blanks with the gerund or infinitive of the word in parentheses ( ).**

CD 3, TR 09

S: Hi, Mom. I'm calling to say good-bye. I'm leaving tomorrow.

M: Where are you going?

S: To California.

M: You didn't tell me.

S: Of course I did. I remember ___**telling**___ you about it when I was at
(example: tell)
your house for dinner last week.

M: Oh, yes. Now I remember _____ you say something about it.
(1 hear)
Why are you going?

S: I have a good friend there, and we've decided to do some volunteer
work in a forest during our summer vacation.

M: Have I met your friend?

S: He was here last year at my birthday party. You met him then.

M: I don't remember _____ him. Anyway, how are you
(2 meet)
getting to California?

S: I'm driving.

M: Alone?

S: Yes.

M: If you get tired, you should stop _____ at a rest area.
(3 rest)
And you can stop _____ a cup of coffee every few hours.
(4 get)

S: I will.

M: Don't stop _____ strangers. It could be dangerous.
(5 pick up)

S: Of course I won't.

M: And remember _____ your cell phone on in case I want to call
(6 leave)
you. Last night I wanted to talk to you and I couldn't reach you. First
I tried _____ your cell phone. Then I tried _____ your home
(7 call)   (8 call)
phone. But all I got was your voice mail.

(continued)

S: Did you leave a message?

M: I tried _____ a message but your mailbox was full.
(9 leave)

S: Don't worry. I'll leave my phone on.

M: You'll be outdoors all day. Remember _____ sunscreen. You don't
(10 use)
want to get a sunburn.

S: Mom, stop _____ so much. And stop _____ me so much
(11 worry)   (12 give)
advice. I'm 24 years old!

M: Try _____. I'm your mother. Of course I worry.
(13 understand)

Mimi's Bike Ride

Before
You Read

1. After reading the articles in this lesson, can you think of ways you'd like
   to volunteer to help others?

2. What do you think motivates people to volunteer?

Read the following journal entry by Mimi, a woman who helped raise money for AIDS research. Pay special attention to *used to*, *be used to*, and *get used to*.

In 1994, a Californian named Dan Pallotta had an idea to raise money for AIDS research. He organized a bike ride from Los Angeles to San Francisco. There were 471 riders who rode 525 miles. Each rider asked friends and relatives to give donations to support the ride. Since then, hundreds of thousands of people have taken part in the rides and more than $50 million has been raised for AIDS research. I decided to do my part to help too.

Before I went on my first AIDS ride, I **used to think** that one person's contribution is not very important. But I was wrong. In 1998, I went on my first AIDS ride, from San Francisco to Los Angeles.

Even though I bike to and from work every day (20 miles round trip), I **wasn't used to riding** long distances. Also, I live in Chicago, where the land is flat, so I **wasn't used to riding** in hills and mountains. I trained for about six months before the ride, riding at least 150 miles a week.

I **used to own** a 10-speed road bike, but I realized that I would need something better for the long, hilly ride. I bought a new 24-speed mountain bike. This new bicycle helped me a lot in the California trip. It was so satisfying to complete the ride. I raised almost $5,000 for AIDS research. I felt so good about it that I started looking for more rides to do.

In 2001, I did the Alaska ride, which was especially difficult. It was much colder than expected. Some of the riders couldn't **get used to** the cold and had to quit. But I'm proud to say that I finished it and went on to do four more AIDS rides.

7.17 Used To / Be Used To / Get Used To

Used to + the base form and *be used to* + a gerund have completely different meanings.

EXAMPLES	EXPLANATION
Mimi **used to own** a 10-speed bike. Now she owns a 24-speed bike. She **used to think** that one person couldn't make a difference. Now she knows that every person's contribution counts. I didn't **use to speak** English at all. Now I **speak** it fairly well.	*Used to* + the base form shows that an activity was repeated or habitual in the past. This activity has been discontinued. For the negative, use *didn't use to*. **Note:** Omit the *d* in the negative.
Mimi **is used to riding** her bike in Chicago, which is flat. She **is used to riding** in nice weather. She **isn't used to the cold wind** in Alaska.	*Be used to* + gerund or noun means "be accustomed to." The sentences to the left describe a person's habits. They show what is normal and comfortable. For the negative, use *be + not + used to*.
Some of the riders **couldn't get used to** the **cold wind** and had to quit. Chicago is flat. Mimi had to **get used to riding** her bike in the mountains.	*Get used to* + gerund or noun means "become accustomed to." Often we use *can, can't, could,* or *couldn't* before *get used to*. For the negative, use *can't* or *couldn't get used to*. **Note:** Do not omit the *d* in the negative.

Pronunciation Note: The *d* in *used to* is not pronounced.

EXERCISE 36 **Finish these statements. Answers may vary.**

EXAMPLE   I used to __exercise once a week__, but now I exercise every day.

1. I used to _____ to work. Now I ride my bike. It's good exercise and I save money.

2. I used to _____ a 10-speed bike. Now I have a 24-speed bike.

3. I used to _____ that one person can't make a difference. Now I know that everyone can make a difference.

4. I used to _____ my bike only in the summer. But now I do it all year round.

5. I used to _____ only money. Now I donate time and money to help others.

6. I used to _____ my extra money, but now I donate it to charity.

EXERCISE 37 **ABOUT YOU** Write sentences comparing the way you used to live with the way you live now.

EXAMPLES

I used to live with my whole family. Now I live alone.

I used to work in a restaurant. Now I'm a full-time student.

I didn't use to speak English at all. Now I speak English pretty well.

Ideas for sentences:

school	job	hobbies	fashions
apartment/house	family life	friends	music

1. _____

2. _____

3. _____

4. _____

5. _____

EXERCISE 38 A student wrote about things that are new for her in the U.S. Fill in the blanks with a gerund or a noun. Answers may vary.

EXAMPLE   I'm not used to _shopping in large supermarkets_. In my native country, I shopped in small stores.

1. I'm not used to _____ a small apartment. In my native country, we lived in a big house.

2. I'm not used to _____. In my hometown, it's warm all year round.

3. I'm not used to _____ a student. I'm 35 years old, and I've been out of school for 15 years.

4. I'm not used to _____. I studied British English in my native country.

5. I'm not used to _____ on Sundays. In my native country, Sunday is a day when people rest, not shop and do laundry.

6. I'm not used to _____ in class. In my native country, the teacher talks and the students only listen and write.

7. I'm not used to _____ on the right side of the road. In my country, India, we drive on the left side of the road.

EXERCISE 39 **ABOUT YOU** Write three different sentences beginning with "I'm not used to . . ."

EXAMPLE   I'm not used to wearing a coat in the winter.

1. _____
2. _____
3. _____

EXERCISE 40 **ABOUT YOU** Fill in the blanks with three different answers.

EXAMPLES   When I came to this city, it was hard for me to get used to:

living in a small apartment.

American pronunciation.

1. _____
2. _____
3. _____

EXERCISE 41 **Here is a story of a San Francisco man who did the Alaska AIDS ride. Circle the correct words in parentheses ( ) to complete the story.**

CD 3, TR 11

In 2000 I went on the AIDS bike ride in Alaska. My friends told me about it and asked me to join them. At first I was afraid. My friends are good bikers. They (*used to / are used to*) (*ride / riding*) long distances
(1)   (2)
because they do it all the time. They persuaded me to try it because it was for such a good cause.

To get ready for the ride, I had to make some lifestyle changes. (*I'm / I*) used to be a little overweight, so I had to slim down and get in
(3)
shape. First, I went on a diet. (*I / I'm*) used to a lot of meat, but now
(4)
I try to eat mostly vegetables and fish. Also, I decided to get more exercise. I used to (*take / taking*) the bus to work every day, but
(5)
I decided to start riding my bike to work. I work ten miles from home, so it was hard for me at first. But little by little, I (*got used to / used to*) it.
(6)

On the weekends, I started to take longer rides. Eventually I got used to (*ride / riding*) about 45–50 miles a day.
(7)

When the time came for the AIDS ride, I thought I was prepared. I live in San Francisco, which is hilly, so I was used to (*ride / riding*) up (8) and down hills. But it's not cold in San Francisco. On some days the temperature in Alaska was only 25 degrees Fahrenheit with strong winds. At first I (*wasn't / couldn't*) get used to the cold. It was especially hard (9) to (*used / get used*) to the strong winds. But little by little, I got (*use / used*) to it. (10) (11)

I am proud to say I was one of the 1,600 riders who finished the ride. I didn't (*use / used*) to think that one person could make a difference, (12) but I raised close to $4,000. As a group we raised $4 million. And I've become a much healthier person because of this experience.

Global Volunteers

Before You Read

1. Is there a place you would like to go to work as a volunteer?
2. How can we help poor people in other countries?

Michele Gran and Bud Philbrook, founders of Global Volunteers

Read the following magazine article. Pay special attention to base forms and -ing forms after sense-perception verbs (see, listen, hear, etc.).

When Michele Gran and Bud Philbrook were planning to get married in 1979, they were thinking about taking a relaxing honeymoon cruise. But whenever Michele turned on the world news, she **saw** people **living** in poverty. She **saw** children **go** without proper nutrition and education. Instead of their planned honeymoon, Michele suggested that they spend a week helping poor people in Guatemala.

When their friends and relatives **listened** to them **tell** about their unusual honeymoon, they became interested in how they could also help. In 1984, Bud and Michele established Global Volunteers, an organization that helps people throughout the world. Since then, they have sent almost 22,000 volunteers to 30 countries. Volunteers work together with the local people on projects, such as building schools in Ghana or taking care of orphans in Romania.

Bud used to practice law and Michele used to work in state government, but in the early '90s, they quit their jobs to spend all their time with Global Volunteers.

7.18 Sense-Perception Verbs

After sense-perception verbs (*hear, listen to, feel, smell, see, watch, observe*), we can use either the *-ing* form or the base form with only a slight difference in meaning.

EXAMPLES	EXPLANATION
a. Their friends **listened to** them **tell** about their unusual honeymoon. b. Matel Dawson **saw** his mother **work** hard.	The base form shows that a person sensed (*saw*, *heard*, etc.) something from start to finish. a. They listened to Bud and Michele tell the whole story. b. All his life, Dawson saw his mother's work habits.
a. Michele **saw** people **living** in poverty. b. When I entered the classroom, I **heard** the teacher **talking** about volunteer programs.	The *-ing* form shows that something is sensed while it is in progress. a. In Guatemala, Michele saw people who were living in poverty. b. I heard the teacher while she was talking about volunteer programs.

EXERCISE 42 Fill in the blanks with the base form or *-ing* form of the verb in parentheses ( ). In many cases, both forms are possible.

By their example, my parents always taught me to help others. One time when I was a child going to a birthday party with my father, we saw a small boy __walking__ alone on the street. As we approached him, we heard him _____. My father went up to him and asked him what was wrong.
(example: walk)

(1 cry)

The boy said that he was lost. I saw my father _____ his hand and
(2 take)

heard him _____ the boy that he would help him find his parents.
(3 tell)

My father called the police on his cell phone. Even though we were in a hurry to go to the party, my father insisted on staying with the boy until the police arrived. I really wanted to go to the party and started to cry.

I felt my father _____ my hand and talk to me softly. He said, "We
(4 take)

can't enjoy the party while this little boy is alone and helpless." Before the police arrived, I saw a woman _____ frantically in our direction. It
(5 run)

was the boy's mother. She was so grateful to my father for helping her son that she offered to give him money. I heard my father _____ her,
(6 tell)

"I can't take money from you. I'm happy to be of help to your son."

Another time we saw new neighbors _____ into the house next
(7 move)

door. We saw them _____ to move a piano into the apartment. We
(8 struggle)

had planned a picnic that day, but my parents suggested that we help them. I heard my mother _____ my father, "We can have a picnic
(9 tell)

another day. But these people need to move in today. Let's offer them a hand." There are many other cases where I saw my parents _____
(10 sacrifice)

their own pleasure to help others.

I hear so many children today _____, "I want" or "Buy me" or
(11 say)

"Give me." I think it's important to teach children to think of others before they think of themselves. If they see their parents _____
(12 help)

others, they will probably grow up to be charitable people.

EXERCISE **43** **Read the true story of a young woman, Charity Bell, who became a foster mother (a person who gives temporary care to a child in her home). Fill in the blanks with the correct form of the verb in parentheses ( ) and add prepositions, if necessary, to complete the story.**

CD 3, TR 13

It's difficult _____ *for* _____ a college student _____ *to have* _____
        (example)   (example: have)
time for anything else but studying. But when Charity Bell was a student at

Harvard, she made time in her busy schedule _____
                                                        (1 help)
babies in need. Bell, a single woman at the time, became a foster mother.

Bell became interested in _____ needy babies when she
                                    (2 help)
was 23 years old. At that time, she volunteered at a hospital for very sick

children. The volunteer organization wanted her _____ to
                                                           (3 read)
the kids and _____ games with them. The parents of
                   (4 play)
these very sick children were there too, but they were often too tired

_____ or _____ with their kids. They
       (5 read)   (6 play)
were grateful to her _____ them. One day she went to
                              (7 help)
the hospital and heard a baby _____ loudly in the next
                                       (8 cry)
room. She went into that room and picked up the baby; the baby

immediately stopped _____. She stayed with the baby for
                              (9 cry)
a few hours. When she began _____, the baby started
                                     (10 leave)
_____ again. Bell asked the nurse about this baby, and
       (11 cry)
the nurse told her that the baby was taken away from her parents and they

couldn't find a temporary home for her.

The next day, Bell made some phone calls and started

_____ about how to be a foster parent. She made herself
       (12 learn)
available to help on nights and weekends. Her phone started

_____ immediately. She got used to
       (13 ring)
_____ up the phone in the middle of the night. She
       (14 pick)

became accustomed _____ (15 take) in children that no one else

wanted. Before she started taking care of babies, she used

_____ (16 sleep) seven or eight hours a night. Now she sometimes

gets as little as three or four hours of sleep a night.

By the time she was 28 years old and in graduate school, Bell had

been foster mother to 50 children. _____ (17) order

_____ (18) complete her studies, she had

_____ (19) take "her" babies to class with her. Her professors

let her _____ (20 do) this. They understood that it was

necessary _____ (21) her _____ (22 study) and

_____ (23 take) care of the babies at the same time. And her

classmates didn't complain about _____ (24 have) a baby crying in

the back of the class. Everyone understood how important it was

_____ (25) her _____ (26 help) these babies.

Usually, she takes in babies for a few days, but one time she had a baby

for six months. Even though she is sometimes tired, she is never too tired

_____ (27 take) in a child that needs her. Incredibly, she gets very

little money for _____ (28 take) care of these children. However,

she gets great satisfaction watching a baby _____ (29 grow). Bell has

had as many as eight children at a time. It is hard _____ (30)

her _____ (31 see) "her" babies _____ (32 leave), but there

are more babies waiting for her. _____ (33 bring) love to an

unwanted child is her greatest joy.

Summary of Lesson 7

Infinitives and Base Forms

EXAMPLES	EXPLANATION
Matel Dawson *wanted* **to help** others.	An infinitive is used after certain verbs.
His mother wanted *him* **to help** others.	An object can be added before an infinitive.
He was *happy* **to give** away his money.	An infinitive can follow certain adjectives.
Joyce makes cards **in order to raise** money for sick children. Dawson donated his money **to help** students get an education.	An infinitive is used to show purpose.
It's important **to help** others. **To help** others is our moral obligation.	Informal: *It* can introduce an infinitive subject. Formal: The infinitive can be in the subject position.
It's important *for* **rich people to help** others. It's fun *for* **me to volunteer**.	*For* + noun or object pronoun is used to give the infinitive a subject.
Carnegie had *enough* money **to build** libraries. Dawson was *too* poor **to finish** school.	An infinitive can be used after *too* and *enough*.
Dawson *heard* his mother **talk** about helping others.	After sense perception verbs, a base form is used. The *-ing* form can also be used in some cases: I hear the baby **crying**.
It is important **to be loved**.	An infinitive can be used in the passive voice.
She *let* me **work**. She *made* me **work**. She *had* me **work**.	After causative verbs *let, make,* and *have*, use the base form.
She *got* me **to work**. She *convinced* me **to work**. She *persuaded* me **to work**.	After causative verbs *get, convince,* and *persuade*, use the infinitive.
Dawson *helped* students **to get** an education. He *helped* them **pay** their tuition.	After *help*, either the infinitive or the base form can be used.

Gerunds

EXAMPLES	EXPLANATION
Going to college is expensive in the U.S.	A gerund can be the subject of the sentence.
Dawson *enjoyed* **giving** money away.	A gerund follows certain verbs.
Dawson learned *about* **giving** from his parents.	A gerund is used after a preposition.
He had a hard *time* **supporting** his family.	A gerund is used after certain nouns.
He doesn't like to **go shopping**.	A gerund is used in many idiomatic expressions with *go*.
I dislike **being told** a lie.	A gerund can be used in the passive voice.

Gerund or Infinitive—Differences in Meaning

EXAMPLES	EXPLANATION
I **used to take** the bus to work. Now I ride my bike. I **used to be** overweight. Now I'm in great shape.	Discontinued past habit or situation
She has six children. She **is used to being** around kids. I walk five miles a day. I **am used to walking** in all kinds of weather.	Present custom
I have never lived alone before and it's hard for me. I can't **get used to living** alone.	Change of custom
I met a friend at the library, and I **stopped to talk** to her.	Stop one activity in order to do something else
I had a fight with my neighbor, and we **stopped talking** to each other.	Stop something completely
I **try to give** a little money to charity each year. Mimi **tries to ride** her bike to work a few times a week.	*Try* = make an attempt or effort
I put a dollar in the vending machine and nothing came out. I **tried hitting** the machine, but still nothing happened.	*Try* = experiment with a different method
You must **remember to turn off** the stove before you leave the house.	Remember and then do
My grandmother repeats herself a lot. She didn't **remember telling** the story, so she told it again.	Remember something about the past

For a list of words followed by gerunds or infinitives, see Appendix D.

Editing Advice

1. Don't forget *to* when introducing an infinitive.

   He needs ^{to} leave.

   It's necessary ^{to} have a job.

2. Don't omit *it* when introducing an infinitive after an impersonal expression.

   It's
   ~~Is~~ important to know a second language.

3. After *want, need,* and *expect,* use the object pronoun, not the subject pronoun, before the infinitive.

   me to
   She wants ~~that I~~ speak English all the time.

4. Don't use *to* between *cost* or *take* and the indirect object.

   It cost ~~to~~ me $500 to fly to Puerto Rico.

   It took ~~to~~ him three months to find a job.

5. Use *for,* not *to,* when you give a subject to the infinitive.

   for
   It is easy ~~to~~ me to speak Spanish.

6. Use *to* + base form, not *for,* to show purpose.

   to
   He exercises every day ~~for~~ improve his health.

7. Use a gerund or an infinitive, not a base form, as a subject.

   ing
   Find a good job takes time. OR *It takes time to find a good job.*

8. Don't confuse *used to* and *be used to.*

   My brother ~~is~~ used to live in New York. Now he lives in Boston.

   'm   living
   I've lived in Alaska all my life and I love it. I used to ~~live~~ in Alaska.

9. Be careful to use the correct form after *stop.*

   ing
   Stop ~~to~~ watch TV and go to bed.

10. Use a gerund, not an infinitive, after a preposition.

ing
I thought about ~~to~~ return to my hometown.
                       ^

11. Make sure to choose a gerund after certain verbs and an infinitive after others.

ing
I enjoy ~~to~~ walk in the park.
                 ^

to buy
He decided ~~buying~~ a new laptop.

12. Use a base form or an *-ing* form after a sense-perception verb.

I saw the accident ~~to~~ happen.

ing
I can smell the soup ~~to~~ cook.
                          ^

13. Use the base form, not the infinitive, after causative verbs *let*, *make*, and *have*.

He let me ~~to~~ borrow his car.

The teacher made me ~~to~~ rewrite my composition.

Editing Quiz

Some of the shaded words and phrases have mistakes. Find the mistakes and correct them. If the shaded words are correct, write C.

C   to
It's important for everyone do something for others. I often thought
(example)   (example)

about to help other people. My parents wanted I help in their business,
(1)   (2)

but I saw my parents to work hard. However, they had very little satisfaction
(3)

or time for our family. I decided become a nurse instead. It took to me three
(4)   (5)

years to complete the nursing program, and I'm happy I did it. First, find a job
(6)   (7)

was easy because nurses are always in demand. Second, I enjoy working
(8)

with sick people and make them to feel better. Some of my friends think
(9)   (10)

(continued)

is depressing to work with sick people all day, but it's easy for me to do it
(11)   (12)   (13)   (14)

because I love helping people.
                (15)

There's one thing I don't like about my job: I have to work nights,
                                                             (16)

from 11 P.M. to 7 A.M. At first, I couldn't get used to sleep in the
                                                      (17)

day. My kids are home on Saturday and Sunday, and when I was trying

sleeping, they sometimes wouldn't stop to make noise. When they were
(18)   (19)

younger, they're used to make a lot of noise, but now that they're older,
            (20)

they understand. My wife made them understand that their dad needed
                                          (21)

his sleep and she needed them be quiet in the morning. My daughter is
                            (22)

now thinking about become a nurse too.
                        (23)

People work for make money, but it's important for everyone
              (24)   (25)

finding a job that gives them satisfaction. Working as a nurse gives me a
(26)   (27)

lot of satisfaction.

Lesson 7 Test/Review

PART **1** **Fill in the blanks with the gerund, the infinitive, or the base form of the verb in parentheses ( ). In some cases, more than one answer is possible.**

EXAMPLE <u>Answering</u> the phone during dinner really bothers me.
          (answer)

1. I started _____ dinner last night and the phone rang.
                  (eat)

2. Someone was trying _____ me something.
                          (sell)

3. I don't enjoy _____ during dinner.
                    (passive: interrupt)

4. Sometimes they want you _____ money to charity, but I don't
                              (donate)

like _____ my credit card number to strangers on
      (give)

the phone. Usually they just want _____ you something.
                                  (sell)

5. I tell them I'm not interested in _____ their product.
(buy)

6. _____ them you're not interested doesn't stop them.
(tell)

They don't let you _____ their sales pitch.
(interrupt)

7. I used to _____ to the caller politely, but I don't do it anymore.
(listen)

8. I've told them politely that I don't want to _____,
(passive: bother)

but they don't listen.

9. I keep _____ these phone calls.
(get)

10. I've thought about _____ my phone number, but I heard that
(change)

they'll get my new number.

11. _____ my phone number is not the answer to the problem.
(change)

12. It's impossible _____ them from _____ you.
(stop)   *(call)*

13. I finally decided _____ Caller ID.
(get)

14. It's better _____ who's calling before you pick up the phone.
(see)

15. Now I have the choice of _____ up or _____ up the phone
(pick)   *(not pick)*

when it rings.

PART 2   **Fill in the blanks with the correct preposition.**

EXAMPLE   We must concentrate _____*on*_____ learning English.

    1. What is the reason _____ doing this exercise?

    2. Your grade in this course depends _____ passing the tests and doing the homework.

    3. I dreamed _____ climbing a mountain.

    4. The teacher insists _____ giving tests.

    5. Andrew Carnegie was famous _____ building free libraries.

    6. I hope I succeed _____ passing this course.

    7. Most students care _____ getting good grades.

    8. I'm not accustomed _____ wearing jeans to school.

    9. Students are interested _____ improving their pronunciation.

(continued)

10. Are you afraid _____ getting a bad grade?

11. Are you worried _____ getting a bad grade?

12. I'm not used _____ speaking English all the time.

PART 3 **Tell if these pairs of sentences mean about the same thing or have completely different meanings. Write *same* or *different*.**

EXAMPLES
It's important to spell correctly.
To spell correctly is important. _____same_____

I used to live in New York.
I'm used to living in New York. ____different____

1. I can't remember to brush my teeth.
I can't remember brushing my teeth. _____

2. I like to cook.
I like cooking. _____

3. Going to college is expensive.
It's expensive to go to college. _____

4. I plan to buy a computer.
I plan on buying a computer. _____

5. I stopped watching TV.
I stopped to watch TV. _____

6. She started to lose weight.
She started losing weight. _____

7. I'm used to playing soccer.
I used to play soccer. _____

8. To help poor people is a wonderful thing.
Helping poor people is a wonderful thing. _____

Expansion

❶ Tell about teachers and students in your school. What do students expect from teachers? What do teachers expect from students? Find a partner, and compare your lists.

Teachers (don't) expect students to:
Teachers expect students to come to class on time.

Students (don't) expect teachers to:
Students don't expect teachers to be friendly.

---

❷ Fill in the blanks. Discuss your answers in a small group.

   a. I used to worry about _____.

   b. Now I worry about _____.

   c. I used to have difficulty _____.

   d. Now I have difficulty _____.

   e. People in my family are not used to _____.

   f. Americans are not used to _____.

   g. I'm used to _____ because I've done it all my life.

   h. I'm not used to _____

      because _____.

   i. I often used to _____, but I don't do it anymore.
     (OR I rarely do it.)

Talk

About It

❶ These words are written on Andrew Carnegie's tombstone: "Here lies a man who was able to surround himself with men far cleverer than himself." What do you think this means?

❷ In your native culture, do rich people help poor people?

❸ Do you ever give money to people on the street who collect money for charity? Why or why not?

❹ If a homeless person asks you for money, do you help this person? Why or why not?

Write

About It

❶ Write a paragraph telling if you agree or disagree with the following statements by Andrew Carnegie:

- It is not good to have money if your spirit is poor.
- It is the mind that makes the body rich.
- It is a disgrace to die rich.

❷ Write about an expectation that your parents had for you that you did not meet. Explain why you did not do what they expected.

❸ Would you like to volunteer your time to help a cause? What would you like to do?

EXAMPLE

> #### Volunteering
>
> I have often thought about volunteering to help children. I enjoy being with kids and watching them learn new things. I thought it would be a good idea to volunteer at a library near my house in an after-school reading program…

 For more practice using grammar in context, please visit our Web site.

Grammar

Adverbial Clauses and Phrases

Sentence Connectors

So/Such . . . That

Context

Coming to America

8.1 Adverbial Clauses—An Overview

An adverbial clause gives more information about the main clause. It is also called a *dependent clause*.

Main clause	Adverbial clause
I like living in the U.S.	**even though I miss my country.**

EXAMPLES	TYPE OF CLAUSE
She went to Canada **before she came to the U.S.**	Time clause
She went to Canada first **because she couldn't get a visa for the U.S.**	Reason clause
She came to the U.S. **so that she could be with her relatives.**	Purpose clause
She came to the U.S. **even though she didn't know English.**	Contrast clause
She will go back to her country **if she saves enough money.**	Condition clause

Language Notes:
1. An adverbial clause is dependent on the main clause for its meaning. It must be attached to the main clause.
   Wrong: She went to Mexico. Because she wanted to study Spanish.
   Right: She went to Mexico because she wanted to study Spanish.
2. The dependent clause can come before or after the main clause. If it comes before, it is usually separated from the main clause with a comma.

Compare:
   I went to Canada before I came to the United States. (No comma)
   Before I came to the United States, I went to Canada. (Comma)

A Nation of Immigrants

Before
   You Read

1. Why do many people leave one country and move to another?

2. What do immigrants have to give up? What do they gain?

Read the following textbook article. Pay special attention to different ways of giving reasons.

The United States is unique in that it is a nation of immigrants, old and new. The U.S. takes in more immigrants than the rest of the world combined, more than one million a year. In 2007, 37 million people, or 12.5 percent of the population, was foreign-born. Why have so many people from other countries left family and friends, jobs, and traditions to start life in a new country? The answer to that question is as diverse as the people who have come to the U.S.

Between 1820 and 1840, many Germans came **because of** political unrest and economic problems. Between 1840 and 1860, many Irish people came **because of** famine.[1] The potato crop, which they depended on, had failed. Between 1850 and 1882, many Chinese people also came to America **because of** famine.

The early groups of immigrants came from Northern and Western Europe. In 1881, large groups started arriving from Eastern and Southern Europe. Jews from Eastern Europe came **to** escape religious persecution; Italians came **for** work. Most came **to** find freedom and a better life. The number of immigrants grew; between 1881 and 1920, more than 23.4 million immigrants came. In 1910, 15 percent of the population was foreign-born.

In 1924, Congress passed a law restricting the number of immigrants, and immigration slowed. In 1965, Congress opened the doors again and immigration started to rise. In the 1960s and 1970s, Cubans and Vietnamese people came **to** escape communism. In the 1980s, Jews from the former Soviet Union came **because of** anti-Semitism,[2] and in the 1990s, Bosnians came **because of** war. Many people came **so that** they could be reunited with their families who had come before.

In addition to legal immigration, about 300,000 come to the U.S. each year illegally. **Since** the U.S. Census cannot count these people, this number is only an estimate.

[1] *Famine* means extreme hunger because of a shortage of food.
[2] *Anti-Semitism* means prejudice or discrimination against Jews.

8.2 Reason and Purpose

There are several ways to show reason and purpose.

EXAMPLES	EXPLANATION
We came to the U.S. *because* **our relatives came here.** *Because* **he couldn't find a job in his country,** he came to the U.S.	*Because* introduces a clause of reason.
Many Irish immigrants came to the U.S. *because of* **hunger.** *Because of* **war in their country,** many people left Bosnia.	*Because of* introduces a noun or noun phrase.
Since **the U.S. Census cannot count illegal immigrants,** their number is only an estimate. *Since* **the U.S. limits the number of immigrants it will accept,** many people cannot get an immigrant visa.	*Since* means *because*. It is used to introduce a fact. The main clause is the result of this fact.
In order to **make money,** my family came to the U.S. Many people come to the U.S. *to* **escape economic hardship.**	*In order to* shows purpose. The short form is *to*. We follow *to* with the base form of the verb.
Many people come to the U.S. *so (that)* **they** *can* **be reunited with family members.** *So (that)* **I** *would* **learn English,** I came to the U.S.	*So that* shows purpose. The short form is *so*. The purpose clause usually contains a modal: *can, will,* or *may* for future; *could, would,* or *might* for past.
People come to the U.S. *for* **freedom.** Some people come to the U.S. *for* **better jobs.**	*For* + noun or noun phrase shows purpose.
Compare: a. She came here *to* **be with her family.** b. They came here *for* **a better life.**	a. Use *to* before a verb. b. Use *for* before a noun.
Compare: a. He came to the U.S. *because* **he wanted to be** reunited with his brother. b. He came to the U.S. *so that* **he could be** reunited with his brother.	a. *Because* can be followed with *want*. b. Do not follow *so that* with *want*. *Wrong:* He came to the U.S. *so that he wanted to be* reunited with his brother.

Language Notes:
1. Remember: *Since* can also be used to show time.
   He has been in the U.S. *since* 2003.
   The context tells you the meaning of *since*.
2. *So* is also used to show result.

Compare:
   Purpose: I came to the U.S. alone **so** I could get an education.
   Result: I came to the U.S. alone, **so** I miss my family.
   Notice that in the above sentences, a comma is used for result but not for purpose.

EXERCISE 1 Fill in the blanks with *because, because of, since, for, (in order) to,* or *so (that)*.

EXAMPLE Many immigrants came to the U.S. _____*to*_____ escape famine.

1. Many immigrants came _____ they didn't have enough to eat.

2. Many immigrants came _____ they could feed their families.

3. Many immigrants came _____ they could escape religious persecution.

4. Many immigrants came _____ the political situation was unstable in their countries.

5. Many immigrants came _____ the poor economy in their countries.

6. Many immigrants came _____ be reunited with their relatives.

7. _____ war destroyed many of their homes and towns, many people had to leave their countries.

8. Many immigrants came _____ escape poverty.

9. Many immigrants came _____ freedom.

10. Often immigrants come _____ they can make more money.

11. Often immigrants come _____ make more money.

12. Often immigrants come _____ they see a better future for their children in the U.S.

13. Most immigrants come to the U.S. _____ a better life.

EXERCISE 2 **ABOUT YOU** Fill in the blanks with a reason or purpose.

EXAMPLE I'm studying English because __I'm an immigrant in the U.S. and English__ __is spoken here.__

1. I chose to live in this city because _____

2. I chose to study at this school because _____

3. I come to this school for _____

4. I use my dictionary to _____

5. I'm saving my money because _____

(continued)

6. I'm saving my money so that _____

7. I'm saving my money for _____

8. I'm saving my money in order to _____

9. People from my country often come to the U.S. because _____

_____

EXERCISE **3** **Fill in the blanks with *because, because of, since, so (that)*, or (*in order*) *to*. Answers may vary.**

CD 3, TR 15

Two women are talking.

A: I heard you moved.

B: Yes. We moved last month. We bought a big house

_____ **so that** _____ we would have room for my parents. They're
　　　(example)

coming to the U.S. next month _____ they want to be
　　　　　　　　　　　　　　　(1)

near their children and grandchildren.

A: Don't you mind having your parents live with you?

B: Not at all. It'll be good for them and good for us. _____
　　　　　　　　　　　　　　　　　　　　　　　　　　(2)

our jobs, we don't get home until after 6 P.M.

A: Aren't your parents going to work?

B: No. They're not coming here _____ jobs. They're in
　　　　　　　　　　　　　　　(3)

their late 60s and are both retired. They just want to be grandparents.

A: It's great for kids to be near their grandparents.

B: I agree. Grandparents are the best babysitters. We want the kids

to stay with their grandparents _____ they won't
　　　　　　　　　　　　　　　(4)

forget our language. Also, we want them to learn about our native

culture _____ they have never been to our country.
　　　　　(5)

Our son, who's five, is already starting to speak more English than

Spanish. He prefers English _____ all his friends in
　　　　　　　　　　　　　　(6)

kindergarten speak English.

A: That's how kids are in America. They don't want to speak their

native language _____ they want to be just like
　　　　　　　　　　　(7)

their friends. Do your parents speak English?

B: Just a little. What about your parents? Where do they live?

A: They live a few blocks away from me.

B: That's great! You can see them any time.

A: Yes, but we almost never see each other _____ we
   _(8)_
   don't have time. _____ they work in the
   _(9)_
   day and I work in the evening, it's hard for us to get together.

The Lost Boys of Sudan

Before
You Read

1. What are some things a new immigrant has to adjust to in the U.S.?

2. Is adjustment to American life harder for some immigrants than for others?

CD 3, TR 16

Read the following magazine article. Pay special attention to time words: *when, while, until, during, for, as, since,* **and** *whenever.*

Besides immigrants, the United States takes in thousands of refugees a year. A refugee is a person who was forced from his or her homeland and crossed the border into another country for safety. The Lost Boys of Sudan, as one group is called, had a long and difficult journey to the U.S.

Three Lost Boys living in Chicago:
David, John, and Peter

The Lost Boys were just children, living in southern Sudan in the late 1980s, when their long journey to the United States began. **While** these young boys were in the field taking care of their cattle, their villages were bombed. These boys, mostly between the ages of 4 and 12, ran for their lives. **For** three months, they walked hundreds of miles **until** they reached Ethiopia. They survived by eating leaves, roots, and wild fruit. **During** that time, many died of starvation and disease or were eaten by lions. They finally reached Ethiopia, where they stayed in refugee camps **until** 1991, **when** a war started in Ethiopia and the camps were closed. They ran again, back to Sudan and then to Kenya, where they stayed in a refugee camp **for** almost ten

(continued)

years. Of the approximately 27,000 boys who fled Sudan, only 11,000 of them survived.

During their time in the refugee camp, they got some schooling and learned basic English. In 1999, the United Nations and the U.S. government agreed to resettle 3,800 Lost Boys in the U.S. **As** they were coming to America, they were thinking about the new and uncertain life ahead. Things in the U.S. would certainly be different.

When they arrived in the U.S., they had to learn a completely new way of life. They had to learn about city life, strange foods, new technologies, and much more. They had not even seen a refrigerator or stove or telephone **until** they came to America. In addition to their home surroundings, their world around them was completely different. **When** they saw an American supermarket for the first time, they were amazed by the amount of food. One boy asked if the supermarket was the palace of the king.

Agencies helped them with money for food and rent for a short time **until** they found jobs. Most of them have been studying English and working full-time **since** they arrived. Some have graduated from college and have started projects to help their villages back home. Peter Magai of Chicago is helping his village build a school.

Although their future in the U.S. looks bright, **whenever** they think about their homeland, they are sad because so many of their family members and friends have died.

8.3 Time Expressions

EXAMPLES	EXPLANATION
When their villages were bombed, the Lost Boys ran. Some Sudanese young men think they will go home **when** their country is at peace.	*When* means "at that time" or "immediately after that time." In a future sentence, use the present tense in the time clause.
Whenever they think about their country, they are sad. **Whenever** they tell their story, Americans are amazed.	*Whenever* means "any time" or "every time."
They walked **until** they reached Ethiopia. They received money for a short time **until** they got jobs.	*Until* means "up to that time."
Some of them have had no news of their families **since** they left Sudan. They have been studying English **ever since** they came to the U.S.	*Since* or *ever since* means "from that time in the past to the present." Use the present perfect or present perfect continuous in the main clause.

EXAMPLES	EXPLANATION
They walked **for** three months. They stayed in a refugee camp **for** many years.	Use *for* with the amount of time.
During the day, they walked. **During** their time in the refugee camp, they studied English.	Use *during* with a time such as *day*, *night*, or *summer*, a specific time period (*the time they were in Ethiopia, the month of August, the week of March 2*), or an event (*the class, the trip, the movie, the meeting*).
While they were taking care of their cattle, their villages were bombed. **As** they were coming to the U.S., they were thinking about their new life ahead.	Use *while* or *as* with a continuous action.
Compare: a. They walked **for** three months. a. Some of them have been in the U.S. **for** over ten years. b. They walked **during** the day. b. They lived in refugee camps **during** their childhood.	a. Use *for* with the amount of time. b. Use *during* with a named period of time (such as *the day, their childhood, the month of May*).
Compare: a. They were taking care of their cattle **when** their villages were bombed. b. **While** they were taking care of their cattle, their villages were bombed.	a. Use *when* with a simple past action. b. Use *while* with a continuous action.

EXERCISE 4 Fill in the blanks with *since, until, while, when, as, during, for,* or *whenever.* In some cases, more than one answer is possible.

EXAMPLE The Lost Boys were very young ___when___ they left Sudan.

1. The Lost Boys walked _____ many months.

2. _____ their march to Ethiopia, many of them died.

3. They lived in Ethiopia _____ about four years.

4. They crossed the river _____ the rainy season.

5. Some died _____ they were marching to Ethiopia.

6. They studied English _____ they were living in Kenya.

7. They had very little to eat _____ they came to the U.S.

8. _____ they were traveling to the U.S., they were wondering about their future.

9. They had never seen a gas stove _____ they came to the U.S.

10. _____ they came to the U.S., they saw modern appliances for the first time.

11. Some of them have not heard anything about their families _____ they left Sudan.

12. _____ they came to the U.S., they have been studying English.

13. In the U.S. many of them work _____ they are going to school.

14. _____ they think about their families and their homeland, they feel sad.

EXERCISE 5

CD 3, TR 17

Fill in the blanks with an appropriate time word. In some cases, more than one answer is possible.

____**When**____ I was a child, I heard many stories about life in America.
(example)

_____ I saw American movies, I imagined that one day I would be in
(1)

a place like the one I saw. My uncle had lived in the U.S. _____ many
(2)

years, and he often came back to visit. _____ he came back, he used
(3)

to tell me stories and show me pictures of the U.S. _____ I was a
(4)

teenager, I asked my mother if she would let me visit my uncle _____
(5)

my summer vacation, but she said I was too young and the trip was too

expensive. _____ I was 20, I finally decided to come to the U.S.
(6)

_____ I was traveling to the U.S., I thought about all the stories my
(7)

uncle had told me. But I really knew nothing about the U.S. _____
(8)

I came here.

_____ I came to the U.S., I've been working hard and
(9)

trying to learn English. I haven't had time to meet Americans or have

much fun _____ I started my job. I've been here _____ five
(10) ... *(11)*

months now, and I just work and go to school. _____ I'm at school,
(12)

I talk to my classmates _____ our break, but on the weekends I'm
(13)

alone most of the time. I won't be able to make American friends _____
(14)

I learn more English.

The American movies I had seen showed me beautiful places, but I

never imagined how much I would miss my family and friends.

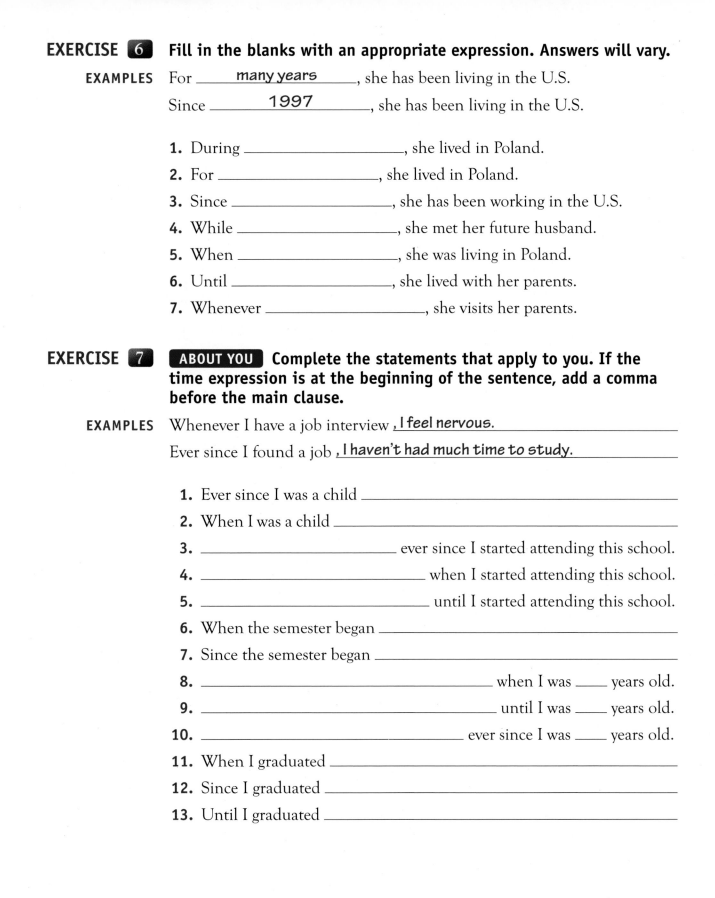

EXERCISE 6   **Fill in the blanks with an appropriate expression. Answers will vary.**

EXAMPLES   For _____many years_____, she has been living in the U.S.

Since _____1997_____, she has been living in the U.S.

1. During _____, she lived in Poland.
2. For _____, she lived in Poland.
3. Since _____, she has been working in the U.S.
4. While _____, she met her future husband.
5. When _____, she was living in Poland.
6. Until _____, she lived with her parents.
7. Whenever _____, she visits her parents.

EXERCISE 7   **ABOUT YOU**   **Complete the statements that apply to you. If the time expression is at the beginning of the sentence, add a comma before the main clause.**

EXAMPLES   Whenever I have a job interview ,I feel nervous. _____

Ever since I found a job ,I haven't had much time to study. _____

1. Ever since I was a child _____
2. When I was a child _____
3. _____ ever since I started attending this school.
4. _____ when I started attending this school.
5. _____ until I started attending this school.
6. When the semester began _____
7. Since the semester began _____
8. _____ when I was ____ years old.
9. _____ until I was ____ years old.
10. _____ ever since I was ____ years old.
11. When I graduated _____
12. Since I graduated _____
13. Until I graduated _____

(continued)

14. _____ when I found a job.

15. _____ since I found a job.

16. _____ until I found a job.

17. When my family came to the U.S. _____

18. Until my family came to the U.S. _____

19. Since my family came to the U.S. _____

20. Whenever I think about my future _____

8.4 Using the -*ing* Form after Time Words

If the subject of a time clause and the subject of the main clause are the same, the time clause can be changed to a participial phrase. The subject is omitted, and the present participle (-*ing* form) is used.

EXAMPLES
Subject   *Subject* a. The Lost Boys went to Ethiopia after **they left** Sudan. b. The Lost Boys went to Ethiopia after **leaving** Sudan.   *Subject*   *Subject* a. While **they were crossing** a river, some of the Lost Boys drowned. b. While **crossing** a river, some of the Lost Boys drowned.

EXPLANATION
In sentences (a), the subject of the main clause and the subject of the time clause are the same. In sentences (b), we delete the subject after the time word (*after, while*) and use a present participle (-*ing*).

EXERCISE **8**   **Change the time clause to a participial phrase.**

EXAMPLE While they were running from their homes, they saw many dangerous animals.

<u>While running from their homes, they saw many dangerous animals.</u>

1. The Lost Boys went to Kenya before they came to the U.S.

_____

2. While they were living in Kenya, they studied English.

_____

3. Before they came to the U.S., the Lost Boys had never used electricity.

_____

4. John Bul learned how to use a computer after he came to the U.S.

_____

5. Until he found a job, John got help from the U.S. government.

_____

6. John wants to go back to Sudan after he graduates from college.

_____

Slavery—An American Paradox[3]

Before You Read

1. What do you know about the history of slavery in the U.S.?

2. Do you think everyone is equal in the U.S. today?

CD 3, TR 18

Read the following textbook article. Pay special attention to _even though_, _although_, and _in spite of_ (_the fact that_).

> **Did You Know?**
>
> African-Americans make up about 13.5 percent of the U.S. population today.

For the first three centuries after Columbus came to America in 1492, the largest group of immigrants arrived in America—unwillingly. Ten to twelve million Africans were brought to work as slaves in the agricultural South.

In 1776, when America declared its independence from England, Thomas Jefferson, one of the founding fathers of the United States, wrote, "All men are created equal" and that every person has a right to "life, liberty, and the pursuit of happiness." **In spite of** these great words, Jefferson owned 200 slaves at that time.

Even though the importation of slaves finally ended in 1808, the slave population continued to grow as children were born to slave mothers. The country became divided over the issue of slavery, and the Civil War between the North and the South was fought from 1861 to 1865. **In spite of the fact that** that the North won and African-Americans were freed, it took another 100 years for Congress to pass a law prohibiting discrimination because of race, color, religion, sex, or national origin.

Although many new arrivals see the U.S. as the land of equality, it is important to remember this dark period of American history.

[3]A _paradox_ is a situation that has contradictory aspects.

8.5 Contrast

EXAMPLES	EXPLANATION
Even though slavery ended, African-Americans did not get equality.	For an unexpected result or contrast of ideas, use a clause* beginning with *even though*, *although*, or *in spite of the fact that*.
Although the U.S. means freedom to many people, it is important to remember the dark days of slavery.	
In spite of the fact that Jefferson wrote about equality for everyone, he owned 200 slaves.	*A clause is a group of words that has a subject and a verb.
In spite of Jefferson's declaration of liberty for all, he owned slaves.	Use *in spite of* + noun or noun phrase to show contrast. A clause doesn't follow *in spite of*.
In spite of the slaves' freedom, discrimination continued for many years.	
Even though the Lost Boys are happy in the U.S., they **still** miss their families in Sudan.	*Still* and *anyway* can be used in the main clause to emphasize the contrast.
Even though it's hard for Peter to work and go to school, he has to do it **anyway**.	

Language Note: In conversation, people often use *though* at the end of a statement to show contrast with the preceding statement.
   I don't like to work and go to school. I have to do it, **though**.

EXERCISE **9** **Choose the correct phrase to complete each sentence.**

When I was 16 years old, I wanted to come to the U.S. (*Even* / *Even though*)
                                                                    (example)
I was very young, my parents gave me permission to leave home and live

with my uncle in New Jersey. (*In spite of the fact that* / *In spite of*) I was only
                                                        (1)
in high school, I worked part-time and saved money for college.

(*Although* / *In spite of*) it was hard, I managed to finish high school and
            (2)
start college.

My uncle always encouraged me to go to college (*in spite of* / *even though*)
                                                                    (3)
he is not an educated man. A lot of my friends from high school didn't go

to college (*even though* / *in spite of*) the opportunities they had. I decided
                            (4)
to become an English teacher (*even though* / *even*) I still have a bit of an
                                            (5)
accent.

EXERCISE **10** **Fill in the blanks with *in spite of* or *in spite of the fact that*.**

EXAMPLES _In spite of the fact that_ the law says everyone has equal rights, some people are still suffering.

In spite of Thomas Jefferson's declaration of equality for all, he owned slaves.

1. _____ slavery ended in 1865, African-Americans did not receive equal treatment under the law.

2. The slave population continued to grow _____ Americans stopped importing slaves from Africa.

3. Many immigrants come to America _____ the difficulty of starting a new life.

4. The Lost Boys of Sudan have not lost their hopes for a bright future _____ the difficulties they face.

5. _____ their busy work schedules, the Lost Boys of Sudan go to school.

6. _____ everything in America is new for them, the Lost Boys of Sudan are adapting to American life.

7. _____ life is not perfect in the U.S., many immigrants want to come here.

EXERCISE **11** **ABOUT YOU Complete each statement in different ways. You can write about your job, a class, your apartment, this city, and so on.**

EXAMPLES I like _my math teacher_ even though _she gives a lot of_ homework.

I like _to watch TV a lot_ in spite of _the fact that it's usually a_ waste of time.

1. I like _____ in spite of _____
_____

2. I like _____ even though _____
_____

3. I have to _____ even though _____
_____

4. In spite of _____ I often _____
_____

EXERCISE 12 **Complete each statement by making a contrast. Answers will vary.**

EXAMPLE Even though many students have jobs, _they manage to come to class_
and _do their homework._

1. Even though the U.S. is a rich country, _____
_____

2. Even though I don't speak English perfectly, _____
_____

3. In spite of the fact that my teacher doesn't speak my native language, _____
_____

4. Even though students don't like taking tests, _____
_____

5. In spite of my accent, _____
_____

The Changing Face of America

Before
   You Read

1. What do you think is the largest ethnic minority in the U.S.?
2. Do you ever see signs in public places in Spanish or any other language?

Read the following magazine article. Pay special attention to condition clauses beginning with *if* and *unless*.

The U.S. population is over 300 million.

This number is expected to rise to more than 400 million by 2050. **Unless** there are changes in immigration patterns, nearly one in five people will be an immigrant in 2050.

For most of the nineteenth and twentieth centuries, the majority of immigrants to the U.S. were Europeans. However, since 1970, this trend has changed dramatically. Today most immigrants are Hispanics.[4] In 2003, Hispanics passed African-Americans as the largest minority. The Hispanic population increased more than 50 percent between 1990 and 2000. **If** current patterns of immigration continue and **if** the birth rate remains the same, Hispanics, who are now almost 15 percent of the total population,

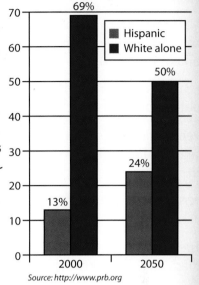

Estimated and Projected U.S. Population, White and Hispanic Origin, 2000 and 2050.

Source: http://www.prb.org

will be 24 percent of the population by 2050. Hispanics are already about 36 percent of the population of California and Texas. More than 50 percent of the people who have arrived since 1970 are Spanish speakers. The largest group of Hispanic immigrants comes from Mexico.

Because of their large numbers, Hispanic voters are gaining political power. **If** they vote as a group, they will have a great influence on the choice of our nation's leaders.

There are many questions about the future of America. One thing is certain: the face of America is changing and will continue to change.

Linda Sanchez and Loretta Sanchez

---

[4] A *Hispanic* is an American whose origin is a Spanish-speaking country, such as Mexico or Cuba.

8.6 Condition

If, even if, and **unless** are used to show that a condition is needed for something to happen.

EXAMPLES	EXPLANATION
If current immigration patterns and birth rates **remain** the same, Hispanics **will be** 24 percent of the population by 2050. **If** Hispanics **vote** together, they **will have** a lot of political power.	Use *if* to show that the condition affects the result. In a future sentence, use the simple present tense in the condition clause.
Even if the immigration of Hispanics **slows** down, their number **will increase** because of their present birth rate. **Even if** the economy of my country **improves**, I **won't go** back.	Use *even if* to show that the condition doesn't affect the result.
Unless immigration laws **change**, nearly one in five Americans **will be** an immigrant in 2050. My brother **won't come** to the U.S. *unless* he **gets** a scholarship at an American university.	Use *unless* to mean *if not.* **Compare:** I won't go **unless** you **go.** I won't go **if** you **don't go.**
If I **think** about my native country, I **get** homesick. Children in America **learn** English *even if* their parents **speak** another language at home. You **can't come** to the U.S. *unless* you **have** a visa.	Sentences with *if, even if,* and *unless* can also be about the general present. In that case, the present tense is used in both clauses.

EXERCISE 13 Fill in the blanks with the correct form of the verb in parentheses ( ).

EXAMPLE   If the Hispanic population _____continues_____ to grow, 24 percent of the
                                              (continue)

U.S. population _____will be_____ Hispanic by the year 2050.
                         (be)

1. If the U.S. _____ almost 80 million people
                      (add)

   to the population in the next 50 years, it _____
                                                      (have to)

   build 30 million more housing units.

2. Even if the number of immigrants _____ down,
                                              (go)

   the population _____.
                         (increase)

3. If more children _____ born in the next 50 years,
    (be)

more schools _____.
    (passive: need)

4. The class size _____ if the number of school-age
    (increase)

children _____.
    (grow)

5. The U.S. population _____ over 400 million by
    (be)

2050 if immigration _____ at the same rate.
    (continue)

6. Immigrants _____ to come to the U.S. unless
    (continue)

there _____ a change in immigration policy.
    (be)

7. Children of immigrants _____ their native language
    (forget)

unless their parents _____ them to speak it.
    (encourage)

EXERCISE **14** **Change the *if* clause in the sentences below to an *unless* clause.**

EXAMPLE   You can't get on an airplane if you don't have a photo ID. <u>You can't get</u>
<u>on an airplane unless you have a photo ID.</u>

1. You can't enter the U.S. if you don't have a passport. _____

_____

2. Children of immigrants will forget their language if they don't use it.

_____

3. Immigrants will continue to come to the U.S. if conditions in their
    native countries don't improve. _____

_____

4. An American citizen can't be president of the U.S. if he or she was not
    born in the U.S. _____

_____

5. If the Hispanic birth rate doesn't change, Hispanics will be 24 percent
    of the U.S. population by the middle of the century. _____

_____

EXERCISE 15 **Fill in the blanks in this conversation between two Hispanic mothers. Use *if* or *unless*.**

CD 3, TR 20

A: My youngest daughter is seven years old, and she doesn't speak Spanish anymore. _____If_____ I say something to her in Spanish, she
    (example)
understands, but she answers in English.

B: _____ all her friends speak English, of course she's going to
        (1)
speak English.

A: My mother lives with us. She doesn't speak English. She can't understand

what my daughter is saying _____ I translate it for her.
                            (2)

B: I have the same problem. My son is 14 and he won't speak Spanish

_____ he has to. Last month he had to because my parents came
   (3)
to visit from Guatemala. But he mixes Spanish with English. My parents

had a hard time understanding him. There are a lot of Spanish words

he doesn't remember _____ I remind him.
                     (4)

A: Maybe we should put them in a bilingual program at school.

_____ they're in the bilingual program, they'll have to speak
   (5)
Spanish.

B: I don't think the school will put them in a bilingual program

_____ they're already fluent in English.
   (6)

A: We can't fight it. Our kids won't speak Spanish well _____
                                                            (7)
we go back to live in our native countries. And we're not going to do

that. We came to the U.S. as immigrants.

EXERCISE 16 **ABOUT YOU** **Complete each statement.**

EXAMPLES   I don't usually eat fast food _____unless I'm in a hurry_____ .

If I speak my native language all the time, _____I won't learn English quickly_____ .

1. If _____ I'll get a good grade.

2. _____ if I don't pass this course.

3. My English will improve if _____ .

4. If I have a serious problem _____ .

5. I study every day unless _____ .

6. I'm usually in a good mood unless _____.

7. I usually answer the phone unless _____.

8. I'll continue to study at this school unless _____.

9. I come to class even if _____.

10. Even if _____, people understand me.

11. _____ even if I'm sick.

12. _____ even if _____.

EXERCISE **17** **Fill in the blanks to complete this conversation between a Colombian woman who's going to immigrate to the U.S. and her friend. Answers may vary.**

A: I'm planning to go to Boston. I'm worried about the cold weather. What do people do in the winter? Aren't they afraid of the snow and the cold?

B: I'm sure people go out even if ___the weather is bad.___
                                    (example)

A: What if people won't understand me? My accent is not perfect.

B: Even if _____, people will probably understand you.
              (1)

A: But I make so many grammar mistakes.

B: Don't worry. People will understand you even if _____.
                                                      (2)
Are you planning to get a job there?

A: I don't think I'm going to need one. I'm going to live with my relatives and they said I can live there for free.

B: Even if _____, you'll need money for other things,
              (3)
like books, clothes, and transportation.

A: I know college is going to be expensive for me because I'm going to be an international student. I think college is free for American residents, isn't it?

B: No. Even if _____ you have to pay for college, but it's
                  (4)
cheaper for residents.

Adopting a Baby from Abroad

Before You Read

1. Do you know anyone who has adopted a child?

2. Is it important for parents to teach their children about their family histories?

CD 3, TR 21

Read the following Web article. Pay special attention to sentence connectors: *however, in addition, furthermore,* **and** *as a result.*

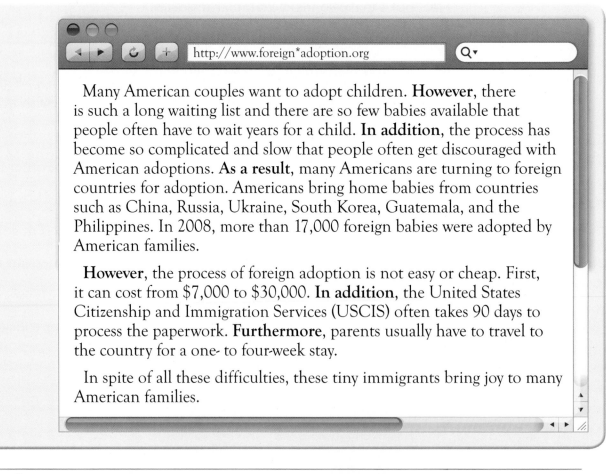

http://www.foreign*adoption.org

Many American couples want to adopt children. **However,** there is such a long waiting list and there are so few babies available that people often have to wait years for a child. **In addition,** the process has become so complicated and slow that people often get discouraged with American adoptions. **As a result,** many Americans are turning to foreign countries for adoption. Americans bring home babies from countries such as China, Russia, Ukraine, South Korea, Guatemala, and the Philippines. In 2008, more than 17,000 foreign babies were adopted by American families.

However, the process of foreign adoption is not easy or cheap. First, it can cost from $7,000 to $30,000. **In addition,** the United States Citizenship and Immigration Services (USCIS) often takes 90 days to process the paperwork. **Furthermore,** parents usually have to travel to the country for a one- to four-week stay.

In spite of all these difficulties, these tiny immigrants bring joy to many American families.

8.7 Sentence Connectors

Ideas can be connected by sentence connectors. These connectors show the relationship between ideas.

EXAMPLES	EXPLANATION
Many couples want to adopt American children. **However**, there are very few babies available. Many couples apply for adoption in a foreign country. **Nevertheless**, the process isn't cheap or easy.	Sentence connectors that show contrast are *however* and *nevertheless*. These words are similar in meaning to *but*.
Foreign adoption is not for everyone. It can be expensive. **In addition**, it can take a long time. Few American babies are available. **Furthermore**, the process has become complicated. The Hispanic population is growing for several reasons. **First**, immigration brings in a large number. **In addition**, the birth rate among Hispanics is high.	Sentence connectors that add more information to the same idea are *in addition*, *furthermore*, and *moreover*. These words are similar in meaning to *and*. Sometimes people order their thoughts using *first*, *second*, *third*, etc. These ordinal numbers can be replaced with *in addition*, *furthermore*, and *moreover*.
Many couples are frustrated with the adoption process in the U.S. **Therefore**, they go to other countries to adopt. Many couples in China prefer sons. **As a result**, the majority of adoptions from China are girls.	Sentence connectors that show result or conclusion are *therefore*, *as a result*, and *for this reason*. These words are similar in meaning to *so*.

Punctuation Note: Use either a period or a semicolon (;) before a sentence connector. Use a comma after a sentence connector.
> My friends couldn't adopt a baby here. **Therefore**, they went to another country to adopt.
> My friends couldn't adopt a baby here; **therefore**, they went to another country to adopt.

EXERCISE 18 Fill in the blanks with an appropriate connecting word. Answers may vary.

EXAMPLE The Lost Boys were happy living with their families in Sudan. __However__, a war forced them to leave.

1. The Lost Boys faced many problems when they left Sudan. They didn't know where to go. _____, they didn't have enough to eat.

2. Some of them couldn't swim. _____, some drowned when they had to cross a river in their escape.

3. Finally they found safety in a refugee camp in Kenya. _____, conditions in the camp were very poor.

(continued)

4. Many of the Lost Boys had never seen a gas stove before they came to the U.S. _____, they did not understand how to cook at first.

5. They faced problems in the U.S. They had to find jobs quickly. _____, they had to go to school to improve their English.

6. They are happy that they came to the U.S. _____, they still miss their family and friends back home.

7. Many immigrants came to America at the beginning of the twentieth century. _____, immigration slowed down during World War I.

8. Jews had a hard life in Eastern Europe. Many lived in poor conditions. _____, they were the victims of anti-Semitism.

9. My grandfather immigrated to the U.S. to find a job and make more money. _____, he wanted to be reunited with his relatives.

10. There was a big famine in Ireland. _____, many Irish people left and came to the U.S.

11. In 1924, Congress passed a law restricting the number of immigrants. _____, many people who wanted to come to the U.S. couldn't.

12. Many Cubans wanted to escape communism in the 1960s. _____, many of them couldn't get permission to leave Cuba.

13. Many Cubans tried to get permission to leave Cuba legally but couldn't. _____, many people found other ways of leaving. Some built or bought small boats and tried to reach Florida by sea.

14. Between 2000 and 2007, about 6.7 million immigrants arrived in the U.S. legally. _____, about 5.6 million illegal aliens arrived during this period of time.

15. A war broke out in Yugoslavia in 1992. _____, many people died or lost their homes.

16. Most immigrants came to the U.S. because they wanted to.

_____, Africans were brought to America against

their will to work as slaves.

17. In 1776, Thomas Jefferson wrote, "All men are created equal."

_____, Jefferson had 200 slaves at the time he wrote

these words.

18. Members of the same family were sent to different areas to work as

slaves. _____, African families were torn apart.

19. Slavery officially ended in 1865. _____, many

African families continued to suffer.

20. African-Americans had been the largest minority for many years.

_____, this changed in 2003 when the Hispanic

population became the largest minority.

21. Adopting a foreign baby is complicated. People have to pay a lot of

money. _____, they have to travel to the foreign

country to fill out forms and pick up the baby.

EXERCISE 19 **Complete each statement. Answers will vary.**

EXAMPLE The U.S. is a rich country. However, __it has many poor people.__

1. It is important for me to learn English. Therefore, _____

_____

2. It is important for me to learn English. However, _____

_____

3. Living in another country is difficult. Immigrants have to adjust to a

new language. In addition, _____

_____

4. Some children speak one language at home and another at school. As a

result, _____

5. To learn a new language, you must master the grammar. In addition,

_____

6. No one wants to leave friends and family. However, _____

_____

(continued)

7. If someone wants to come to the U.S. to visit, he or she must have a passport. In addition, _____

_____

8. It's important for a new immigrant to know English. Therefore, _____

_____

9. I may not speak English perfectly. However, _____

_____

EXERCISE 20 **Circle the correct words to complete this story.**

🔊
CD 3, TR 22

Many people have come to America (*because* / *(for)*) freedom. But
(example)
Africans lost their freedom and were brought to America against their
will (*for* / *to*) work in the fields. Africans were taken from their homes
(1)
and put on slave ships (*for* / *to*) cross the Atlantic. (*Because of* / *Since*)
(2)   (3)
hard conditions, many died along the way.

(*In spite of* / *In spite of the fact that*) they worked hard from morning
(4)
till night, they received no money. In fact, they were often beaten if they
didn't obey. They were forced to work hard (*so that* / *in order to*) white
(5)
plantation owners could become rich. (*Although* / *Unless*) many people
(6)
in the North were against slavery, slavery continued in the South
(*because of* / *since*) Southern slave owners did not want to give up their
(7)
cheap labor supply.

(*Even though* / *However,*) the law prohibited the importation of slaves,
(8)
slavery continued to increase. (*In spite of* / *In spite of the fact that*) the
(9)
difficulties of living under slavery, slaves formed strong communities.
They tried to keep their African cultural practices, which included music
and dance. (*Because* / *For*) people from the same regions in Africa
(10)
were separated from each other, they lost their native languages, used
English, and were given biblical names rather than African names.

Most of the African-Americans in the North were free.
(*In addition* / *However*), they didn't have an easy life. They couldn't
(11)

attend public schools. (*Furthermore / However*), they weren't allowed
(12)
to vote. Many slaves from the South tried to run away to the North.

(*However, / Although*) some were caught and sent back to their "owners."
(13)

(*Unless / Until*) the slaves were finally freed in 1865, they
(14)
faced many difficulties. (*In spite of the fact that / In spite of*) the
(15)
majority of Africans by that time were born in America, they suffered

discrimination (*because / because of*) the color of their skin.
(16)

Discrimination was still legal (*when / until*) 1965, when Congress
(17)
passed a law prohibiting discrimination in jobs and education.

(*Although / In spite of*) there has been progress toward equality for
(18)
all, there are still many inequalities in American life.

8.8 So . . . That / Such . . . That

We can show result with *so . . . that* and *such (a) . . . that*.

EXAMPLES	EXPLANATION
My grandparents had **such a hard life** in their country **that** they had to leave. The Lost Boys saw **such terrible things** in their life **that** they will never forget them.	We use: *such* + *a/an* + adjective + singular noun + *that* *such* + adjective + plural noun + *that*
Foreign adoption is **so expensive that** many people cannot afford it. Children of immigrants learn English **so easily that** they become fluent in a short time.	We use: *so* + adjective + *that* *so* + adverb + *that*
In Miami, there are **so many Spanish speakers that** you can hear Spanish wherever you go. Many American couples want to adopt a baby. However, there are **so few babies available** that many Americans adopt foreign babies.	We use: *so many* + plural count noun + *that* *so few* + plural count noun + *that*
There was **so much** poverty in Ireland in the 1800s **that** Irish people were forced to leave. The Lost Boys had **so little** food to eat **that** many of them died.	We use: *so much* + noncount noun + *that* *so little* + noncount noun + *that*

Language Note: *That* is often omitted in informal speech.
     John works **so hard** (*that*) he doesn't have time to rest.
     American life is **so strange** for him (*that*) it will take him time to understand it.	

EXERCISE 21 **Fill in the blanks with *so, so much, so many, so few, so little,* or *such (a/an)*.**

EXAMPLE We had _____ *so many* _____ problems in our country that we decided to leave.

1. I waited _____ long time that I thought I would never get permission.

2. When I got to the Miami airport, the security lines were _____ long that I had to wait for almost two hours. There were _____ people arriving at the same time.

3. I came to the U.S. by winning the Green Card Lottery. I was _____ happy when I got my letter that I started to cry.

4. The U.S. offers _____ freedom that people from all over the world want to come here.

5. I come from Mexico. There is _____ unemployment in Mexico that many people want to come to the U.S. for jobs.

6. Before I got my visa, I had to fill out _____ papers and answer _____ questions that I thought I would never be able to do it.

7. Our family has been in the U.S. for _____ long time that we hardly even speak our native language anymore.

8. My neighbor's baby was _____ young when she arrived from China that she doesn't remember anything about China at all.

9. There are _____ American babies to adopt that many families adopt babies from China, Russia, and other countries.

10. My uncle earned _____ money in Guatemala that he couldn't support his family, so he came to the U.S.

EXERCISE 22   **Fill in the blanks with *so, so much, so many, so little, so few*, or *such (a/an)*. Then complete each statement with a result. Answers will vary.**

EXAMPLES   Michael is _____ such a _____ good student _____ that he gets 100% _____ on all his tests.

Learning another language is _____ so _____ hard _____ it can take _____ a lifetime to do it.

1. My math class is _____ easy _____

   _____

2. Peter is taking _____ classes this semester _____

   _____

3. The teacher gives _____ homework _____

   _____

4. Sometimes the teacher talks _____ fast _____

   _____

5. My roommate is from India. She speaks English _____ well

   _____

6. My biology class is _____ boring _____

   _____

7. Ms. Stevens is _____ good teacher _____

   _____

8. English has _____ irregular verbs _____

   _____

9. We had _____ long test _____

   _____

10. I had _____ mistakes on my test _____

    _____

11. The teacher gave _____ confusing explanation _____

    _____

12. I was _____ tired in class yesterday _____

    _____

Summary of Lesson 8

1.

Words that connect a dependent clause or phrase to an independent clause:
(Abbreviations: C = Clause; NP = Noun Phrase; VP = Verb Phrase)

FUNCTION	CONNECTORS	EXAMPLES
Reason	*because* + C *since* + C *because of* + NP	**Because** he doesn't understand English, he can't find a job. **Since** he doesn't understand English, he can't find a job. **Because of** his poor English, he can't find a job.
Time	*when* *whenever* *until* *while* *for* *during* *since*	**When** I find a job, I'll buy a car. **Whenever** I work overtime, I make extra money. I worked **until** 8 P.M. I worked **until** the store closed. **While** I was slicing the bread, I cut my finger. I've been working **for** three hours. I worked **during** my summer vacation. I've been working **since** 9 A.M. I've been working **since** I woke up this morning.
Purpose	*(in order) to* + VP *so (that)* + C *for* + NP	He exercises **(in order) to** lose weight. He exercises **so (that)** he can lose weight. He exercises **for** his health.

Contrast	*even though* + C
	although + C
	in spite of the
	   fact that + C
	in spite of + NP
		Even though he's rich, he's not happy.
		Although he's rich, he's not happy.
		In spite of the fact that he's rich, he's
		   not happy.
		In spite of his wealth, he's not happy.

Condition	*if* *even if* *unless*	**If** it snows, we won't drive. We'll drive **even if** it rains. I won't go **unless** you go with me. I don't want to go alone.

2.

Words that connect two independent clauses:

FUNCTION	CONNECTORS	EXAMPLES
To add more to the same idea	*in addition* *furthermore* *moreover*	Adopting a baby from another country is not easy. Parents have to pay a lot of money. **In addition,** they have to get permission from U.S. Citizenship and Immigration Services.
To add a contrasting idea	*however* *nevertheless*	The law says that everyone is equal. **However,** inequalities still exist. The Lost Boys had a difficult childhood. **Nevertheless,** they are hopeful for their future.
To show a result	*therefore* *as a result* *for this reason*	It is difficult for an uneducated person to find a job that pays well. **Therefore,** I've decided to get a college degree. There was a war in Bosnia. **For this reason,** many people left.

3.

Words that introduce result clauses:

FUNCTION	CONNECTORS	EXAMPLES
Result with adjectives and adverbs	*so* + adjective + *that* *so* + adverb + *that*	I was **so tired that** I fell asleep in front of the TV. She speaks English **so fluently that** everyone thinks it's her first language.
Result with quantity words	*so many* + plural noun + *that* *so much* + noncount noun + *that* *so few* + plural noun + *that* *so little* + noncount noun + *that*	I received **so many letters that** I didn't have time to read them all. I received **so much mail that** I didn't have time to read it all. He has **so few friends that** he's lonely. She has **so little time that** she rarely takes a vacation.
Result with nouns	*such (a/an)* + adjective + singular noun + *that* *such* + adjective + plural noun + *that*	It was **such a good movie that** I watched it three times. These are **such good grapes that** I can't stop eating them.

Punctuation Note:
Compare:
He went home from work early because he was sick. (No comma)
Because he was sick, he went home from work early. (Comma)
He was sick. Therefore, he went home from work early. (Period before the connecting word, comma after *therefore*)
He had such a bad headache that he had to go to bed. (No comma)

Editing Advice

1. Use *to*, not *for*, with a verb when showing purpose.

                  to
She went to the doctor ~~for~~ get a checkup.

2. Don't combine *so* with *because*, or *but* with *even though*.

Because he was late, ~~so~~ he didn't hear the explanation.

Even though she speaks English well, ~~but~~ she can't write it.

3. Use *because of* when a noun phrase follows.

                  of
He came late because ^ bad traffic.

4. Don't use *even* without *though* or *if* to introduce a clause.

     though
Even ^ he's a poor man, he's happy.

                if
I won't call you even ^ I need your help.

5. Use the *-ing* form, not the base form, after a time word if the subject is deleted.

         going
Before ~~go~~ home, he bought some groceries.

6. Don't confuse *so that* (purpose) with *so* (result).

He wanted to learn to drive, so ~~that~~ he took driving lessons.

7. After *so that*, use a modal before the verb.

               could
I bought a DVD player so that I ^ watch all my favorite movies.

8. In a future sentence, use the simple present tense in the *if* clause or time clause.

If I ~~will~~ go back to my hometown, I will visit my best friend.

9. *However* connects two sentences. *Although* connects two parts of the same sentence.

                        However,
She was absent for three weeks. ~~Although~~ she did all the homework.

10. Use *so* + adjective/adverb. Use *such* when you include a noun.

             such a
My grandfather is ~~so~~ wise person that everyone goes to him for advice. OR *My grandfather is so wise that everyone goes to him for advice.*

Editing Quiz

Some of the shaded words and phrases have mistakes. Find the mistakes and correct them. If the shaded words are correct, write C.

I came to the U.S. five years ago ~~for~~ *to* study English. I chose to live in this

city because my sister was living here. Even I had studied grammar in my
(example) ... *(example)* ... *(1)*

country, I didn't have experience talking with Americans. I wanted to

prepare myself. Therefore, I took private lessons with an American in my
(2)

country for learn new American expressions. In addition, before coming
(3) ... *(4)* ... *(5)*

here, I read a lot about life in the U.S. so that I wouldn't be shocked.
(6) ... *(7)*

Although, I was surprised by so many things. First, I was surprised by
(8)

how cold it is in the winter in this city. Furthermore, I couldn't believe
(9)

that some students even call their teachers by their first names. Back home,

we always call our teachers "Professor" to show respect. I also miss
(10)

getting together with friends after class. Now I'm at a city college and most

students have jobs. In addition, most of them have families. As a result,
(11) ... *(12)*

everyone leaves so quickly after class that there's no time to make friends.
(13) ... *(14)*

I gave my phone number to some classmates so that we get together on
(15)

weekends, but no one ever calls me. Because my sister has a busy life, so
(16)

she doesn't have much time for me either. I had so hard time when I
(17)

arrived here that I wanted to go back. However, I got used to life here.
(18) ... *(19)*

I discovered that church is a good place to meet people, so that I joined
(20)

a church. When I will save more money, I'm going to get an apartment
(21)

with one of my new friends from church.

Even though life has become easier, but I still miss my family back
(22)

home.

Lesson 8 Test/Review

PART 1 Fill in the blanks with an appropriate time word: *when, whenever, while, for, during, since,* or *until.*

EXAMPLE   My friends were talking __during__ the whole movie. Everyone around them was annoyed.

1. They talk _____ they go to the movies. This happens every time.
2. They were talking _____ everyone else was trying to watch the movie.
3. They started talking _____ they sat down at the beginning of the movie.
4. They talked _____ two hours.
5. They didn't stop talking _____ they left.
6. _____ the movie was over, they left and went their separate ways.
7. I haven't seen them _____ we went to the movies last week.
8. I hate it when people talk to each other _____ a movie.

PART 2 Fill in the blanks with *because, because of, since, for, so that, in order to,* or *therefore.* In some cases, more than one answer is possible.

EXAMPLE   I came to this school __in order to__ learn English.

1. He came to the U.S. _____ he could learn English.
2. He came to the U.S. _____ find a better job.
3. He came to the U.S. _____ economic problems in his country.
4. He came to the U.S. _____ be with his family.
5. He came to the U.S. _____ a better future.
6. _____ the U.S. is a land of opportunity, many immigrants want to come here.
7. The U.S. is a land of opportunity. _____, many people from other countries want to immigrate here.
8. Irish people came to America in the 1800s _____ they didn't have enough to eat.

PART 3 Fill in the blanks with *even though, in spite of the fact that, in spite of,* or *however.* **In some cases, more than one answer is possible.**

EXAMPLE   _____Even though_____ there are many opportunities in the U.S., my cousin can't find a job.

1. _____ his fluency in English, he can't find a job.
2. He's fluent in English. _____, he can't find a job.
3. _____ he has lived here all his life, he can't find a job.
4. He can't find a job _____ he has good job skills.

PART 4 Fill in the blanks with *if, unless,* or *even if.*

EXAMPLE   _____If_____ you're absent, you should call the teacher to let him know.

1. You must do the homework _____ you're absent. Absence is no excuse for not doing the homework.
2. You should come to every class _____ you're sick. If you're sick, stay home.
3. _____ you don't have time to study, you should drop the course.
4. Some people go to work _____ they have a cold. They don't want to lose a day's pay.

PART 5 Fill in the blanks with *so, so many, so much,* or *such.*

EXAMPLE   I was _____so_____ late that I missed the meeting.

1. There were _____ people at the party that there wasn't anywhere to sit down.
2. The food was _____ delicious that I didn't want to stop eating.
3. I had _____ a hard day at work yesterday that I didn't have time for lunch.
4. My brother is _____ intelligent that he graduated from high school at the age of 15.
5. She spent _____ a long time on her composition that she didn't have time to do the grammar exercises.

PART 6 **Complete each sentence. Answers will vary.**

EXAMPLE   He didn't learn to drive until <u>he was 25 years old</u>.

1. I come to this school for _____.

2. I come to this school so that _____.

3. People sometimes don't understand me because of _____
_____.

4. Since _____, it is necessary
for immigrants to learn it.

5. She came to the U.S. to _____.

6. I don't watch much TV because _____.

7. I like to watch movies even though _____.

8. Many people like to live in big cities in spite of the fact that _____
_____.

9. Please don't call me after midnight unless _____.

10. I can usually understand the general meaning of a movie even if _____
_____.

11. I didn't speak much English until _____.

12. I fell asleep during _____.

13. Some students didn't study for the last test. As a result, _____
_____.

14. The teacher expects us to study before a test. However, _____
_____.

15. When applying for a job, you need to write a good résumé. In addition,
_____.

16. My mother has such a hard job that _____.

17. There are so many opportunities in the U.S. that _____
_____.

18. It was so cold outside last night that _____.

PART 7 Punctuate the following sentences. Some sentences are already correct and need no more punctuation. If the sentence is correct, write *C*. Make any other necessary changes.

EXAMPLES   When he met her, he fell in love with her immediately.

I'll help you if you need me.   *C*

1. The teacher will help you if you go to her office.
2. She always gets good grades because she studies hard.
3. Even though owning a dog has some disadvantages there are more advantages.
4. Because he didn't study he failed the test.
5. Before he got married his friends had a party for him.
6. She did all the homework and wrote all the compositions however she didn't pass the course.
7. Although I didn't do the homework I understood everything that the teacher said.
8. Even though he worked hard all weekend he wasn't tired.
9. I stayed home last night so that I wouldn't miss my favorite TV show.
10. I am unhappy with my job because I don't get paid enough furthermore my boss is an unpleasant person.
11. She was so emotional at her daughter's wedding that she started to cry.
12. My boss never showed any respect for the workers as a result many people quit.

Expansion

1 **Form a small group. Tell which one of each pair you think is better and why. Practice reason and contrast words.**

- owning a dog or owning a cat
- driving a big car or driving a small sports car
- sending an e-mail or writing a letter by hand
- watching a movie at home on a DVD player or watching a movie in a theater
- writing your compositions by hand or writing them on a computer
- studying at a small community college or studying at a large university
- living in the city or living in a suburb

EXAMPLE   Even though owning a cat is easier, I prefer dogs because they provide protection for the home.

2 **For each of the categories listed below, write a sentence with *even though* in the following pattern:**

    I like _____ even though _____.

Categories: food, exercise, movies, people, places, restaurants, hobbies, animals

EXAMPLES   I like to travel even though it's expensive.
                    I like to eat fast food even though I know it's not good for me.

Find a partner and compare your answers to your partner's answers.

3 **Write three sentences to complain about this city. Work with a small group. Practice *so/such . . . that*.**

EXAMPLE   There is so much traffic in the morning that it takes me over an hour to get to school.

4 **Write three sentences about this school. Try to convince someone that this is a good school.**

EXAMPLE   The teachers are so friendly that you can go to them whenever you need help.

❶ Frederick Douglass was an ex-slave who became a leader against slavery. In 1852, at a celebration of American Independence Day, Frederick Douglass gave a speech. He said, "This Fourth of July is yours, not mine. You may rejoice, I must mourn." Look up the words *rejoice* and *mourn*. Then tell what you think he meant by this.

❷ Besides the U.S., what other countries have large numbers of immigrants? Is the immigrant population accepted by the native population?

❸ When American parents adopt babies from other countries, should they try to teach them about their native countries? Why or why not?

Write

About It **❶** Write about how an agency or people you know have helped you and your family since you came to the U.S.

❷ Do you think a country is richer or poorer if it has a large number of immigrants? Write a short composition to explain your point of view.

❸ Write about the reasons you (or your family) came to the U.S.

❹ Write about the major reasons people immigrate to the U.S. from your native country.

EXAMPLE

Immigrants from Mexico

I come from Mexico. Many people from my country want to immigrate to the U.S. for economic reasons. Even though there is a lot of unemployment in the U.S., Mexicans can usually find jobs in a big American city. However, it is very difficult for Mexicans to get work authorization in the U.S. . . .

For more practice using grammar in context, please visit our Web site.

Adverbial Clauses and Phrases; Sentence Connectors; *So/Such . . . That* **365**

Grammar
Noun Clauses

Context
Caring for Children

9.1 Noun Clauses—An Overview

A clause is a group of words that has a subject and verb. A noun clause functions as a noun in a sentence. Compare:

Noun
He said **hello**.

Noun clause
He said **that he wanted to see the baby.**

EXAMPLES	EXPLANATION
I know **that you love children.** She didn't realize **that the baby was sick.** Do you think **that the kids are tired?**	We use a noun clause to include a *statement* within a statement or a question.
I don't know **how old the child is.** Do you know **if the babysitter is available?**	We use a noun clause to include a *question* within a statement or a question.
She said, **"I will pick up my son."** I asked, **"Where will you pick him up?"**	We use a noun clause to *repeat* someone's exact words.
She said **that she would pick up her son.** I asked her **where she would pick him up.**	We use a noun clause to *report* what someone has said or asked.

Bringing Up Baby

Before
You Read

1. Should employers provide maternity leave for new mothers? Why or why not?

2. Do you think grandparents should have a big part in raising children? Why or why not?

Read the following magazine article. Pay special attention to noun clauses.

Research shows **that a baby's early experiences influence his brain development.** What happens in the first three years of a baby's life affects his emotional development and learning abilities for the rest of his life. It is a well-known fact **that talking to infants increases their language ability** and **that reading to them is the most important thing parents can do to raise a good reader.** Some parents even think **that it's important to play Mozart to babies and show them famous works of art.** However, there is no scientific evidence to support this. It is known, however, **that babies whose parents rarely talk to them or hold them can be damaged for life.** One study shows **that kids who hardly play or who aren't touched very much develop brains 20 to 50 percent smaller than normal.**

Educators have known for a long time **that kids raised in poverty enter school at a disadvantage.** To prevent a gap[1] between the rich and the poor, they recommend early childhood education. A recent study at the University of North Carolina followed children from preschool to young adulthood. The results showed **that children who got high-quality preschool education from the time they were infants benefited in later life.** In this study, 35 percent of children who had preschool education graduated from college, compared with only 14 percent of children who did not have preschool education.

While it is important to give babies stimulating activities, experts warn **that parents shouldn't overstimulate them.**

---

[1]A *gap*, in this case, means a difference.

9.2 Noun Clauses after Verbs and Adjectives

EXAMPLES	EXPLANATION
Parents *know* (that) kids need a lot of attention. Some parents *think* (that) babies should listen to Mozart. Studies *show* (that) early childhood education is important.	A noun clause can follow certain **verbs**. *That* introduces a noun clause. *That* is often omitted, especially in conversation.
I am *sure* (that) children need a lot of attention. Are you *surprised* (that) some parents play classical music for their babies? Some parents are *worried* (that) they don't spend enough time with their kids.	A noun clause can be the complement of the sentence after certain **adjectives**.
It has been said **that it takes a village to raise a child.**	A noun clause can be used after certain verbs in the passive voice.
A: I hope **that our children will be successful.** **B:** I hope **so** too. **A:** Do you think **that the children are learning something**? **B:** Yes, I think **so.**	Noun clauses can be replaced by *so* after *think, hope, believe, suppose, expect,* and *know.* Do not include *so* if you include the noun clause. *Wrong:* I think **so** the children are learning something.
I realize that the child is tired **and that** he hasn't eaten lunch. I know that you are a loving parent **but that** you can't spend much time with your child.	Connect two noun clauses in the same sentence with *and that* or *but that.*

Language Notes:

1. A noun clause often follows one of these verbs:

believe	find out	notice	remember
complain	forget	predict	show
decide	hope	pretend	suppose
dream	know	realize	think
expect	learn	regret	understand
feel*			

2. A noun clause often follows *be* + an adjective:

be afraid	be clear	be obvious
be amazed	be disappointed	be sure
be aware	be glad	be surprised
be certain	be happy	be worried

*Feel followed by a noun clause means "believe" or "think." I *feel* that it's important for a mother to stay home with her baby. = I *believe/think* that it's important for a mother to stay home with her baby.

EXERCISE 1 Underline the noun clauses in the following conversation between two mothers.

EXAMPLE **A:** Do you know <u>that it's good to read to children when they're very young?</u>

B: Yes, I do. But I didn't realize that playing music was important too.

A: I'm not so sure that music is beneficial, but I suppose it can't hurt.

B: I think that it's good to give kids as much education as possible before they go to school.

A: I'm sure that's a good idea. But don't forget that they're just kids. They need to play too.

B: Of course they do. I hope my children will be successful one day.

A: I predict they will be very successful and happy.

EXERCISE 2 Fill in the blanks to complete the noun clause based on the reading on page 369. Answers may vary.

EXAMPLE Research shows that _____*a baby's early experiences*_____ influence his brain development.

1. Educators know that _____ enter school at a disadvantage.

2. Some parents think that _____ classical music for babies.

3. We all know that _____ to babies increases their language ability.

4. A study shows that _____ have smaller brains.

EXERCISE 3 Respond to each statistic about American families by beginning with *"I'm surprised that . . ."* or *"I'm not surprised that . . ."*

EXAMPLE Fifty percent of marriages in the U.S. end in divorce.
I'm not surprised that 50 percent of marriages in the U.S. end in divorce.

1. Only 25 percent of American households are made up of a mother, a father, and children.

2. About 7 million American children are home alone after school.

3. About 18 percent of American children live in poverty.

4. About 70 percent of married mothers work outside the home.

(continued)

5. Thirty-three percent of working wives with full-time jobs earn more than their husbands.

6. The average size of new American homes has increased as the size of the American family has decreased.

7. Twenty-six percent of households have only one person.

EXERCISE 4 **ABOUT YOU** Fill in the blanks with a noun clause to talk about your knowledge and impressions of the U.S.

EXAMPLES   I know ___that there are 50 states in the U.S.___

I'm surprised ___so many people live alone.___

1. I think _____

2. I'm disappointed _____

3. I know _____

4. I'm afraid _____

5. It's unfortunate _____

6. I'm surprised _____

7. I've noticed _____

8. I've learned _____

EXERCISE 5 What's your opinion? Answer the questions using *I think* and a noun clause. Discuss your answers.

EXAMPLE   Should mothers of small kids stay home to raise them?

I think mothers of small kids should stay home if their husbands can make enough money. But if they need the money, I think they should work.

1. Should the government pay for child care for all children?

2. Can children get the care and attention they need in day care?

3. Should fathers take a greater part in raising their kids?

4. Should grandparents help more in raising their grandchildren?

5. Should the government give new mothers maternity leave? For how long?

6. Should parents read books to babies before they learn to talk?

7. Should parents buy a lot of toys for their children?

Pediatricians' Recommendations

Before You Read

1. What are some good habits that children should develop? How can their parents encourage these habits?

2. What kind of influence does television have on children?

CD 4, TR 02

Read the following magazine article. Pay special attention to noun clauses.

Did You Know?

The average American child spends an average of 6.5 hours a day using some form of media (TV, computer, MP3 player, radio, etc.).

The American Academy of Pediatrics (AAP) is worried that American children spend too much time in front of the TV. The AAP suggests **that pediatricians help parents evaluate their children's entertainment habits.** Doctors are concerned that children who spend too much time in front of the TV don't get enough exercise. At least one in three children is overweight.

The AAP recommends **that children under two not watch any TV at all.** It is essential **that small children have direct interactions with parents for healthy brain growth.** The AAP advises **that parents offer children stimulating activities.**

The AAP recommends **that pediatricians be good role models** by not having TVs in their waiting rooms.

9.3 Noun Clauses after Expressions of Importance

EXAMPLES	EXPLANATION
The AAP *recommends* **that pediatricians <u>be</u> good role models.** The pediatrician *suggested* **that she <u>read</u> to her kids.**	A noun clause is used after verbs that show importance or urgency. The base form is used in the noun clause. The subject pronoun is used before the base form. **Compare pronouns:** He wants *her* to read. He suggested that *she* read.
It is essential **that a baby <u>have</u> stimulation.** *It is important* **that a father <u>spend</u> time with his children.**	A noun clause is used after expressions of importance beginning with *it*. The base form is used in the noun clause.
The AAP advises that children under two **not watch** any TV at all.	For negatives, put *not* before the base form.

Language Notes:

1. Some verbs that express importance or urgency are:

advise*	forbid*	request
ask*	insist	require*
beg*	order*	suggest
demand	recommend	

   *The starred verbs can also be followed by an object + infinitive.
   I advise *that she stay* home with her small children. =
   I advise *her to stay* home with her small children.

2. Some expressions that show importance or urgency are:

It is advisable	It is important
It is essential	It is necessary
It is imperative	It is urgent

   The above expressions can also be followed by *for* + object + infinitive.
   It is essential *that they play* with their children. =
   It is essential *for them to play* with their children.

EXERCISE **6**   **Rewrite these sentences as noun clauses.**

EXAMPLE   Kids should see a doctor regularly.

It is important that _____ *kids see a doctor* regularly. _____

1. Kids should eat a healthy diet.

   It is essential that _____

2. A child should exercise regularly.

   It is important that _____

3. A child must receive love.

It is essential that _____

4. Children shouldn't watch a lot of TV.

Doctors recommend that _____

5. Doctors want parents to give their children a healthy diet.

Doctors suggest that _____

6. Parents should talk to their babies and hold them.

It is essential that _____

7. Some parents tell their children to turn off the TV.

Some parents insist that _____

8. A child shouldn't eat a lot of candy.

Dentists recommend that _____

9. Parents should be good role models.

It is essential that _____

Day Care

Before
You Read

1. Do you think it's OK for mothers of small babies to work outside the home?

2. In your native culture, do women with babies work outside the home? If so, who takes care of the children?

CD 4, TR 03

Read the following Web article. Pay special attention to noun clauses as questions.

http://www.day*care*advice.com

Working parents often put their children in day care. While most parents interviewed say they are satisfied with the day care they use, experts believe that only about 12 percent of children receive high-quality care. Many parents really don't know **how good their day care service is**.

When choosing a day care center, of course parents want to know **how much it costs.** But there are many other questions parents should ask and observations they should make. Parents need to know **if the caregiver is loving and responds to the child's needs.** Does the caregiver hug the child, talk to the child, smile at the child, play with the child?

It is also important to know **if the day care center is clean and safe.** A parent should find out **how the caregiver takes care of sick children.** Is there a nurse or doctor available to help with medical care? Do caregivers know first aid?

Parents should ask **how many children there are per caregiver.** One caregiver for three babies is recommended.

Experts believe that parents should not put their babies in child care for the first four months. During this time, it is important for babies to form an attachment to their mothers.

Did You **Know?**

Twenty-five percent of preschoolers in married families are cared for by fathers, up from 17 percent in 1997.

9.4 Noun Clauses as Included Questions

A noun clause is used to include a question in a statement or another question.

EXAMPLES	EXPLANATION
Wh- Questions with auxiliaries or be	
Where is the mother? I don't know **where the mother is.** When will the children go home? Do you know **when the children will go home**?	Use statement word order in an included question—put the subject before the verb.
Wh- Questions with do/does/did	
What does the child want? Do you know **what the child wants**? Where did the child go? I wonder **where the child went.**	Remove *do/does/did* in the included question. The verb will show the **-s** ending for *he, she,* or *it,* or the past form for the past tense.
Wh- Questions about the subject	
Who takes care of the kids? I'd like to know **who takes care of the kids.** How many teachers work there? Please tell me **how many teachers work there.**	There is no change in word order in questions about the subject.
Yes/No Questions with auxiliaries or be	
Is the center clean? I'd like to know **if the center is clean.** Can the child play outside? I'm not sure **whether the child can play outside.**	Add the word *if* or *whether* before including a *yes/no* question. Use statement word order—put the subject before the verb.
Yes/No Questions with do/does/did	
Do the kids like their teacher? Can you tell me **whether the kids like their teacher**? Did your parents give you toys? I can't remember **if my parents gave me toys.**	Remove *do/does/did* in the included question. Add *if* or *whether* (. . . *or not*). The verb in the included question will show the **-s** ending for *he, she,* or *it,* or the past form for the past tense.
An included question is used after phrases such as these:	

I don't know	I'm not sure	Can you tell me
Please tell me	Nobody knows	Are you sure
I have no idea	I can't understand	Do you understand
I wonder	I'd like to know	Would you like to know
I don't remember	I can't tell you	Does anyone know
You need to decide	Do you remember	Do you know
It's important to ask		

(continued)

Language Note: You can add *or not* at the end of an included *yes/no* question.
  I'd like to know if the day care center is clean (**or not**).
  Do you know whether the teacher speaks Spanish (**or not**)?

Punctuation Note: Use a period at the end of the included question if the sentence is a statement. Use a question mark if the sentence begins with a question.
  I don't know what time it is.
  Do you know what time it is?

Usage Note: When asking for information, especially from a stranger, an included question sounds more polite than a direct question.
  Direct Question: Who is the director of the day care center?
  More Polite: Can you tell me who the director of the day care center is?

EXERCISE 7 **Fill in the blanks with an appropriate question word or phrase (*who, what, where, when, why, how, how many,* or *how much*), *if,* or *whether*.**

EXAMPLE Can you tell me _how much_ time the children spend watching TV?
  I'd like to know _if_ the day care center is expensive.

1. I don't know _____ my child's teacher's name is.

2. I can't remember _____ the class begins at 7:30 or 8:30.

3. You should ask _____ people take care of the children. It's good to have a lot of teachers.

4. I would like to know _____ the day care center is clean or not.

5. I would like to know _____ the caregivers do if the child gets sick.

6. Can you tell me _____ the director of the program is? I've never met her.

7. I have no idea _____ the day care charges.

8. Please tell me _____ the day care center is located.

EXERCISE 8 **Circle the correct words to complete the statement or question.**

EXAMPLE Please tell me how old (*is your child* / (*your child is*)).

1. I'd like to know when (*I have to* / *do I have to*) pick my child up.

2. Do you know what (*is the teacher's name* / *the teacher's name is*)?

3. Do you know (*is the center open* / *if the center is open*) on Saturday?

4. Can you tell me how much (*you paid* / *did you pay*) for the service?

5. I don't know where (*the day care center is located /*
   is located the day care center).

6. I want to know how old (*your son is / is your son*).

7. I'd like to know how much (*the service costs / does the service cost /*
   costs the service).

8. Can you tell me when (*the center closes / closes the center /*
   does the center close)?

9. I'd like to know (*the children watch TV / do the children watch TV /*
   if the children watch TV) at the center.

10. Please tell me (*if works a nurse / whether a nurse works / does a nurse work*)
    at the center.

11. I'd like to know (*the center has / has the center /*
    whether the center has) an outdoor playground or not.

12. I wonder (*if the teacher loves / does the teacher love / if loves the teacher*)
    her job.

EXERCISE 9 **Write these questions as included questions. (These are questions about the subject.)**

EXAMPLE Who wants to leave now?

I don't know ___*who wants to leave now.*_____

1. How many students in this class come from South America?
   I don't know _____

2. Who read the article about working mothers?
   I'd like to know _____

3. What happened in the last class?
   Can you tell me _____

4. Who brought a dictionary today?
   I don't know _____

5. Who failed the test?
   I wonder _____

EXERCISE 10 Write these questions as included questions. (These are *wh-* questions with *be* or an auxiliary verb.)

EXAMPLE   How many tests have we had?

I don't remember ___how many tests we have had.___

1. When will we have the final exam?

   I need to know _____

2. How many lessons are we going to finish?

   Can you tell me _____

3. Where is the teacher from?

   I wonder _____

4. Where will the final exam be?

   You should ask _____

5. When can the teacher see me?

   I need to know _____

EXERCISE 11 Write these questions as included questions. (These are *wh-* questions with *do, does,* or *did.*)

EXAMPLE   Where did you buy your books?

Can you tell me ___where you bought your books?___

1. When does the class begin?

   Can you tell me _____

2. What grade did I get on the last test?

   Can you tell me _____

3. How many mistakes did I make?

   I'd like to know _____

4. How many questions does the test have?

   It's not important to know _____

5. How many compositions does the teacher require?

   You should ask the teacher _____

EXERCISE 12   Write these questions as included questions. (These are *yes/no* questions with an auxiliary verb or *be*.)

EXAMPLE   Is the teacher American?

I'd like to know ___if the teacher is American.___

1. Is the test going to be hard?

   I don't know _____

2. Will you be our teacher next semester?

   I'd like to know _____

3. Can you help us with registration?

   I'd like to know _____

4. Have you been teaching here for a long time?

   Can you tell me _____

5. Are the students confused?

   I have no idea _____

EXERCISE 13   Write these questions as included questions. (These are *yes/no* questions with *do*, *does*, or *did*.)

EXAMPLE   Does your teacher give a lot of homework?

Can you tell me ___if your teacher gives a lot of homework?___

1. Does the school have a cafeteria?

   You should ask _____

2. Did everyone pass the last test?

   I don't know _____

3. Did you buy a dictionary?

   Please tell me _____

4. Does the teacher speak Spanish?

   I'm not sure _____

5. Do I need to write a composition?

   Can you tell me _____

EXERCISE 14 **These are some questions parents can ask before choosing day care for their children. Include each question after "I'd like to know."**

EXAMPLE How much does it cost?

I'd like to know ___how much it costs.___

1. Do the caregivers have a lot of experience?

I'd like to know _____

2. How does the caregiver discipline the children?

I'd like to know _____

3. Can the caregiver handle problems without getting angry or impatient?

I'd like to know _____

4. Am I welcome to drop in and visit?

I'd like to know _____

5. How does the caregiver take care of sick children?

I'd like to know _____

6. Is there a nurse or doctor to help with medical care?

I'd like to know _____

7. Are there smoke alarms in the building?

I'd like to know _____

8. How many caregivers are there?

I'd like to know _____

9. Does the caregiver hug the children?

I'd like to know _____

10. Who takes the children outside?

I'd like to know _____

11. Are the toys clean?

I'd like to know _____

12. Is the day care center licensed by the state?

I'd like to know _____

13. Do the children have stimulating activities?

I'd like to know _____

9.5 Question Words Followed by an Infinitive

EXAMPLES	EXPLANATION
What should I do? a. I don't know **what I should do.** b. I don't know **what to do.** Where can I find information? a. Please tell me **where I can find information.** b. Please tell me **where to find information.**	Some noun clauses with *can, could,* and *should* can be shortened to an infinitive phrase. Sentences (a) use a noun clause. Sentences (b) use an infinitive (phrase).
Should she work or stay home with her children? a. She can't decide **if she should work or stay home with her children.** b. She can't decide **whether to work or stay home with her children.**	Sentence (a) uses a noun clause. Sentence (b) uses an infinitive phrase. Use *whether,* not *if,* to introduce an infinitive phrase. *Wrong:* She can't decide *if* to work or stay home with her children.
How can I find a good day care center? I don't know **how to find a good day care center.**	An infinitive is used after *know how.*

EXERCISE **15** **Complete these sentences with an infinitive phrase.**

EXAMPLE   What should I do about my problem?

I don't know ___*what to do about* my problem._____

1. Where can I buy textbooks?

   I don't know _____

2. What classes should I register for?

   I can't decide _____

3. Should I take morning classes or evening classes?

   I don't know _____

4. What else should I do?

   I don't know _____

5. How can I use the computer in the library?

   I don't know _____

6. What can I do about cancelled classes?

   I don't know _____

7. Should I take biology or physics?

   I can't decide _____

8. Should I buy a new computer or a used one?

   I'm not sure _____

EXERCISE 16 **ABOUT YOU** Complete each statement with an infinitive phrase. Discuss your answers in a small group or with the entire class.

EXAMPLE   I can't decide _whether to stay in this city or move to another city._

1. When I came to this school, I didn't know _____

   _____

2. I can't decide _____

3. When I came to this city, I had to decide _____

   _____

4. There are so many choices of products in the stores. Sometimes I

   can't decide _____

EXERCISE 17 Two students are talking. Fill in the blanks to complete the included questions. Answers may vary.

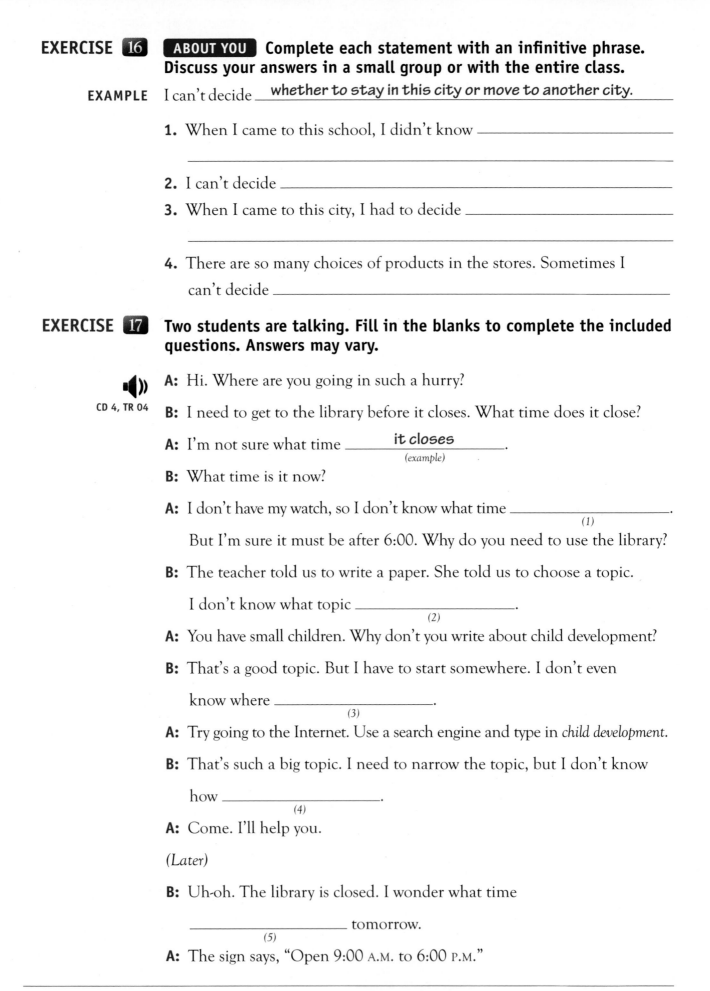

CD 4, TR 04

A: Hi. Where are you going in such a hurry?

B: I need to get to the library before it closes. What time does it close?

A: I'm not sure what time ____it closes____.
　　　　　　　　　　　　　(example)

B: What time is it now?

A: I don't have my watch, so I don't know what time _____.
　　　　　　　　　　　　　　　　　　　　　　　　　　　(1)

   But I'm sure it must be after 6:00. Why do you need to use the library?

B: The teacher told us to write a paper. She told us to choose a topic.

   I don't know what topic _____.
　　　　　　　　　　　　　　　(2)

A: You have small children. Why don't you write about child development?

B: That's a good topic. But I have to start somewhere. I don't even

   know where _____.
　　　　　　　　　　(3)

A: Try going to the Internet. Use a search engine and type in *child development*.

B: That's such a big topic. I need to narrow the topic, but I don't know

   how _____.
　　　　　　(4)

A: Come. I'll help you.

(Later)

B: Uh-oh. The library is closed. I wonder what time

   _____ tomorrow.
　　(5)

A: The sign says, "Open 9:00 A.M. to 6:00 P.M."

B: Can you meet me at the library at ten o'clock tomorrow and help me?

A: I'm not sure _____ or not. I have an appointment
(6)

at 8:30, and I don't know _____ by ten o'clock or not.
(7)

But don't worry; the librarian can show you how to do a search.

Dr. Benjamin Spock

Before
You Read

1. Have you ever heard of Dr. Benjamin Spock? What do you know about him?

2. What are some differences in the ways that children are raised in different cultures?

CD 4, TR 05

Read the following magazine article. Pay special attention to the words in quotation marks ("...") and other noun clauses.

Dr. Benjamin Spock, 1903–1998

New parents are always worried that they might be making a mistake with their new baby. The baby cries, and they don't know if they should let him cry or pick him up. The baby is sick, and they don't know what to do. **"Trust yourself. You know more than you think you do,"** wrote Benjamin Spock in his famous book *Dr. Spock's Baby and Child Care*, which first appeared in 1946. This book has sold over 50 million copies, making it the biggest-selling book after the Bible. In fact, many parents say **that it is the parents' bible for raising children.**

Before Dr. Spock's book appeared, John Watson was the leading child-care expert in the 1920s and 1930s. He wrote, **"Never hug or kiss your children; never let them sit in your lap."** He continued, **"If you must, kiss them once on the forehead when they say good night. Shake hands with them in the morning."** Also, he told parents **that it was necessary to feed children on a rigid schedule.** Dr. Spock disagreed with this strict manner of raising children and decided **that he would write a book. "I wanted to be supportive of parents rather than scold them,"** Dr. Spock said. **"Every baby needs to be smiled at, talked to, played with . . . gently and lovingly. Be natural and enjoy your baby."**

Dr. Spock never imagined **that his book would become so popular.** The last edition came out in 1998, a few months after his death at age 94. He will be remembered for his common sense advice. **"Respect children because they deserve respect, and they'll grow up to be better people."**

9.6 Noun Clauses as Exact Quotes of Notable Words

EXAMPLES	EXPLANATION
Dr. Spock said, **"Trust yourself."** John Watson said, **"Never hug or kiss your children."** Parents ask, **"What is the right way to take care of a baby?"**	An exact quote is used when the exact words are worth repeating and they are remembered because: • they have been recorded on video or audio. • they are a quote from a book, newspaper, or magazine.
a. **Dr. Spock said**, "Every baby needs to be smiled at." b. "Every baby needs to be smiled at," **Dr. Spock said.** c. "Every baby needs to be smiled at," **said Dr. Spock.**	The *said* or *asked* phrase can come at the beginning (a) or the end of a quote (b and c). If it comes at the end, the subject and the verb can be inverted (c).
"More than anything else," **said Dr. Spock,** "children want to help. It makes them feel grown up."	An exact quote can be split, with the *said* or *asked* phrase in the middle, separated from the quote by commas.

Punctuation Note:
Study the punctuation of sentences that contain an exact quote. Note that the first letter of an exact quote is a capital.

Dr. Spock said, "Trust yourself."

The mother asked, "Why is the baby crying?"

"Why is he crying?" asked the father.

"I'm going to feed him," said the mother.

"More than anything else," said Spock, "children want love."

EXERCISE 18 Read these quotes by Dr. Spock and Dr. Watson. Add quotation marks and capital letters where they are needed.

EXAMPLE   Watson said, ~~n~~ever kiss your child." *(with "N inserted)*

1. Watson said treat your children like small adults.

2. Too much love will harm your baby said Watson.

3. Spock said what good mothers and fathers instinctively feel like doing for their babies is usually best.

4. Spock said you know more than you think you do.

5. I wanted to be supportive of parents said Spock.

6. The most important value is to bring up children to help others, first in their family, and then other people said Spock.

7. To reduce violence in our society said Spock we must eliminate violence in the home and on television.

8. If children worship material success rather than truth or compassion Spock said it is because they have absorbed those values from others.

A Folk Tale

Before You Read

1. What kinds of stories or folk tales are popular for children in your native culture?

2. What stories do you remember your parents telling you when you were a child?

CD 4, TR 06

Nasreddin is a character in many folk tales throughout the world. Read this story about Nasreddin. Pay special attention to exact quotes.

One day a neighbor passed Nasreddin's house and saw him outside his barn on his hands and knees. He appeared to be looking for something.

"**What are you doing?**" the neighbor asked.

"**I'm looking for something,**" answered Nasreddin.

"**What are you looking for?**" the neighbor asked.

"**I'm looking for my ring. It's very valuable,**" Nasreddin replied.

"**I'll help you,**" said his neighbor. The neighbor got down on his hands and knees and started to help Nasreddin look for his ring. After searching for several hours, the neighbor finally asked, "**Do you remember where you were when you lost it?**"

"**Of course,**" replied Nasreddin. "**I was in the barn milking my cow.**"

"**If you lost your ring inside the barn, then why are we looking for it outside the barn?**" asked the neighbor.

"**Don't be a fool,**" said Nasreddin. "**It's too dark in the barn. But out here we have light.**"

9.7 Exact Quotes in Telling a Story

EXAMPLES	EXPLANATION
"What are you doing?" the neighbor asked. **"I'm looking for my ring,"** said Nasreddin.	Exact quotes are used in story telling to give words to the characters. Follow the same punctuation and word order rules as in Section 9.6.
"I will help you," said the neighbor, **"as soon as I can."**	An exact quote can be split, with the *said/asked* phrase in the middle.

EXERCISE 19 **Read the following fable[2] by Aesop. Insert quotation marks and correct punctuation and capitalization.**

A hungry wolf was looking for food when he met a house dog that was passing by. Cousin said the dog your life is much harder than mine. Why don't you come to work with me and get your food given to you regularly?

I would like that said the wolf. Do you know where I can find such a job?

I will easily arrange that for you said the dog. Come with me to my master's house and we will share my work.

So the wolf and the dog went towards the town together. On the way there, the wolf noticed that the hair on a certain part of the dog's neck was very much worn away, so he asked him how that had come about.

Oh, it is nothing said the dog. That is only the place where the collar is put on me every night to keep me chained up. It hurts a bit at first, but you will soon get used to it.

Then good-bye to you said the wolf. I would rather starve than be a fat slave.

9.8 Noun Clauses as Reported Speech

We use an *exact quote* when we want to write exactly what someone has said. Exact quotes are common in stories and news reports. We use *reported speech* when we want to report what someone has said.

Exact quote	Reported speech
Dr. Spock said, **"You know more than you think you do."**	Dr. Spock told parents **that they knew more than they thought they did.**
The dog said to the wolf, **"I will take you to my master's house."**	The dog told the wolf **that he would take him to his master's house.**
John Watson said, **"It is necessary to feed children on a rigid schedule."**	John Watson told parents **that it was necessary to feed children on a rigid schedule.**

[2]A *fable* is a short story that teaches a lesson. Often the characters of a fable are animals.

In the paragraph below, underline the noun clauses that show reported speech. Circle the verbs in the noun clauses. What tenses are used?

Last week my daughter's day care teacher called me at work and told me that my daughter had a fever and was resting in the nurse's office. I told my boss that I needed to leave work immediately. He said that it would be fine. As I was driving my car on the expressway to the school, a police officer stopped me. She said that I had been driving too fast. She said that I had been driving ten miles per hour over the limit. I told her that I was in a hurry because my daughter was sick. I said I needed to get to her school quickly. I told the police officer that I was sorry, that I hadn't realized I had been driving so fast. She said she wouldn't give me a ticket that time, but that I should be more careful in the future, whether my daughter was sick or not.

9.9 The Rule of Sequence of Tenses

After a past tense verb in the main clause (such as *said, told, reported*, etc.), the tense of the verb in the noun clause moves back one tense. This change in tense is called the rule of sequence of tenses. Observe the difference in verb tenses in the exact quotes on the left and the reported speech on the right.

Exact quote	Reported speech
He said, "I **know** you." (present)	He said (that) he **knew** me. (simple past)
He said, "I **am studying**." (present continuous)	He said (that) he **was studying**. (past continuous)
He said, "She **saw** me yesterday." (simple past)	He said (that) she **had seen** him the day before. (past perfect)
He said, "She **was helping** me." (past continuous)	He said (that) she **had been helping** him. (past perfect continuous)
He said, "I **have taken** the test." (present perfect)	He said (that) he **had taken** the test. (past perfect)
He said, "I **had** never **done** that." (past perfect)	He said (that) he **had** never **done** that. *(No change)* (past perfect)
Modals	
He said, "I **can** help you tomorrow."	He said (that) he **could** help me the next day.
He said, "She **may** leave early."	He said (that) she **might** leave early. *(possibility)*
He said, "You **may** go."	He said (that) **I could** go. *(permission)*
He said, "I **must** go."	He said (that) he **had to** go.
He said, "I **will** stay."	He said (that) he **would** stay.
Modals That Do Not Change Their Forms in Reported Speech	
He said, "You **should** leave."	He said (that) I **should** leave.
He said, "You **should have** told me."	He said (that) I **should have** told him.
He said, "You **must have** known."	He said (that) I **must have** known.
	Note: There is no change for modal + *have* + past participle.

(continued)

> **Observe all the differences between a sentence that has an exact quote and a sentence that uses reported speech.**

Sentence with Exact Quote:	**Sentence with Reported Speech:**
She said, "I will help you tomorrow."	She said that she would help me the next day.
• quotation marks	• no quotation marks
• comma after *said*	• no comma after *said*
• doesn't contain *that*	• contains *that* (optional)
• pronouns = *I, you*	• pronouns = *she, me*
• verb = *will help*	• verb = *would help*
• time = *tomorrow*	• time = *the next day*

Language Notes:

1. Time words change in reported speech.

   today → that day

   yesterday → the day before; the previous day

   tomorrow → the next day; the following day

   this morning → that morning

   tonight → that night

   now → at that time

2. We even change the tense in the following sentence:

   The teacher asked me what my name **was**.

   Even though your name is still the same, the tense shows that the conversation took place at a different time and place.

3. We often use reported speech when we want to paraphrase what someone has said. The exact words are not important or not remembered. The idea is more important than the exact words.

   Exact quote: Dr. Spock said, **"You know more than you think you do."**

   Paraphrase: Dr. Spock told parents **that they should trust their own instincts.**

EXERCISE 21 An adult is talking about things her parents and grandparents used to tell her when she was a little girl. Change to reported speech. Follow the rule of sequence of tenses.

EXAMPLE You are the love of my life.

My grandmother told me that ___I was the love of her life.___

1. You will always be my baby.

   My mother told me that _____

2. You have an easy life compared to mine.

   My father told me that _____

3. We had a much harder life.

My grandparents told me that _____

4. We want you to be happy.

My parents told me that _____

5. You have to listen to your teacher.

My father told me that _____

6. You can be anything you want if you study hard. (*Change all three verbs.*)

My parents told me that _____

7. We don't like to punish you, but sometimes it's necessary.

My parents told me that _____

8. Punishing you hurts me more than it hurts you.

My father told me that _____

9. We will always love you.

My grandparents told me that _____

10. You should wash your hands before meals.

My mother told me that _____

9.10 *Say* vs. *Tell*

EXAMPLES	EXPLANATION
a. She **said that** the children were happy.	a. In reported speech, we **say** that . . . .
b. She **told me that** the children were happy.	b. In reported speech, we **tell** <u>someone</u> that . . . . *Tell* is followed by an indirect object, but *said* is not.
c. She **added that** the day care center had 15 staff members.	c. Other common verbs used in reported speech that *do not* have an indirect object are: *add* *answer* *explain* *reply* } *that*
d. She **informed the parents that** the day care center would be closed for the holiday.	d. Other common verbs used in reported speech that have an indirect object are: *inform* *notify* *remind* *promise* } *someone that . . .*
Compare: She **said**, "I love you." She **said to her daughter**, "I love you."	In an exact quote, we use *say* or *say to someone*. We do not usually use *tell* for an exact quote.

EXERCISE 22   **Fill in the blanks with *said* or *told*.**

EXAMPLES   He _____*told*_____ his children that they should study hard.

I _____*said*_____ that I was a very happy child.

1. I _____ that I wanted to learn more about raising children.

2. Dr. Spock _____ parents that they should trust their instincts.

3. John Watson _____ that parents should not hug their children.

4. Dr. Spock _____, "You know more than you think you do."

5. The mother _____ to her son, "Eat your vegetables."

6. The mother _____ her son that she would pick him up after school.

7. My parents _____ me that they wanted me to get a good education.

8. I called my parents last week and _____ them about my new roommate.

9. The little girl _____ to her mother, "I want to grow up to be just like you."

10. Our parents _____ us to be honest.

EXERCISE 23   **Change each sentence to reported speech. Follow the rule of sequence of tenses.**

EXAMPLES   Lisa said, "I need to put the kids to bed."
Lisa said that she needed to put the kids to bed.

Lisa said to her son, "I'll read you a story."
Lisa told her son that she would read him a story.

1. Lisa said, "I have never read Dr. Spock's books."

_____

2. Lisa said to her friend, "I want to take my children to the zoo."

_____

3. Lisa said, "My children need to get exercise."

_____

4. Lisa and Paul said, "We will take our kids to the park tomorrow."

_____

5. Lisa said, "I forgot to give the kids their vitamins this morning."

_____

6. Lisa said, "The children went to bed early last night."

_____

7. Lisa said to her neighbor, "My son is in kindergarten."

_____

8. Lisa and Paul said, "Our son wants us to read him a story."

_____

9. Lisa said to Paul, "It's your turn to put the kids to bed."

_____

10. Lisa said to the teacher, "Our son's name is Tod."

_____

11. Tod said to his mother, "I don't want to go to bed."

_____

12. Tod said to his father, "I'm thirsty."

_____

13. Tod said to his friend, "I love my new bicycle."

_____

14. Tod said to his teacher, "I can write my name."

_____

15. Tod said to his friend, "My grandmother will buy me a toy."

_____

16. Lisa said to Tod, "You must go to bed."

_____

17. Tod said to his father, "I can't sleep."

_____

18. Tod said to his father, "I want to watch my favorite program on TV."

_____

19. Paul said to Tod, "You will not get enough sleep."

_____

20. Paul said to Tod, "I don't want to argue with you."

_____

9.11 Exceptions to the Rule of Sequence of Tenses

EXAMPLES	EXCEPTIONS TO THE RULE:
Parents **say** that Dr. Spock's book **is** their bible for raising children.	When the main verb is in the **present** tense, we do not change tenses.
Dr. Spock said that children **deserve** respect. Dr. Spock told parents that children **need** love.	In reporting a general truth, it is not necessary to follow the rule of sequence of tenses.
My brother has five children. He said that he **loves** (or **loved**) children. He said that he **wants** (or **wanted**) to have more children.	In reporting something that is still present, you can leave the tenses with no change or follow the rule of sequence of tenses.
Compare: a. Our teacher said that the test on Lesson 9 **will** (or **would**) be next week. b. My kindergarten teacher said that she **would** teach me to tie my shoes.	a. When the action has not happened yet, you can use *will* or *would*. b. When the action is **past**, use *would*.
A: I can't find my wallet. **B:** I didn't hear you. What did you say? **A:** I said I **can't** find my wallet.	When repeating speech immediately after it was said for someone who did not hear it, we do not usually follow the rule of sequence of tenses.
a. My mother said that she **was** born in 1948. b. My mother said that she **had** (or **had had**) a difficult childhood. c. She said that she **lived** (or **had lived**) in Poland when she was a child.	In reporting a statement about the past, it is not necessary to follow the rule of sequence of tenses if it is clear that the original verb was past. In sentence (a), it is clear that she said, "I **was** born in 1948" and not "I **am** born in 1948." It is rare to change *be* to past perfect if there is no confusion of time. In sentence (b), it is clear that she said, "I **had** a difficult childhood" not "I **have** a difficult childhood." In sentence (c), it is clear that she said, "I **lived** in Poland when I was a child."

EXERCISE **24** **Circle the correct verb to complete this composition. In a few cases, both answers are possible.**

I have two daughters, ages four and six. When I was a child, I said that I

(*want* / (*wanted*)) to have a large family. But now that I'm an adult, I see
   (example)

how hard it is to be married, work, and raise kids. Before we were married,

my husband said that he (*will* / *would*) help me with childcare 50/50.
         (1)

Yesterday it was his turn to take care of the kids. I told him that I

(*need* / *needed*) some time to be with my friends and that we (*are* / *were*)
   (2)   *(3)*

going out to lunch. After I left, he told the kids that they (*can / could*)
(4)
watch TV all day. I told him that the pediatrician always says that kids

(*watch / watched*) too much TV. I told my husband that he
(5)
(*needs / needed*) to take the kids out for exercise yesterday. But he told me
(6)
that he (*wants / wanted*) to work on his car. He said that he (*will / would*)
(7)   (8)
take them out next weekend. When I asked him about the lunch he gave

the kids, he said that they (*ate / had eaten*) a lot of popcorn while they were
(9)
watching TV so they weren't hungry for lunch. I always tell my husband

that the kids (*shouldn't eat / shouldn't have eaten*) snacks before they eat
(10)
a meal.

Sometimes I say that I really (*have / had*) three children: my two kids
(11)
and my husband!

9.12 Reporting an Imperative

EXAMPLES	EXPLANATION

"Trust yourself."
Spock **told** parents **to trust** themselves.
 	
"Sit down, please."
She **asked** me **to sit** down.
	To report an imperative, an infinitive is used. Use *ask* for an invitation or request. Use *tell* for a command or instruction. Don't use *say* to report an imperative.
	    Wrong: She *said me to sit* down.
	Use an object after *tell* or *ask*.
	    Wrong: He *told to close* the door.

"Don't watch TV." My father told me **not to watch** TV.	For a negative, put *not* before the infinitive.

Language Note: Don't forget to change the pronouns and possessive forms in the infinitive phrase.

"Show **your** children love."   "Give **me your** book."
He told us to show **our** children love.   He asked me to give **him my** book.

EXERCISE 25 Change these imperatives to reported speech. Use *asked* or *told* + an object pronoun.

EXAMPLE   The mother told her children, "Study for your test."

<u>The mother told them to study for their test.</u>

1. The son said to his mother, "Read me a story."

   _____

2. She told the babysitter, "Don't let the kids watch TV all day."

   _____

3. The girl said to her father, "Buy me a doll."

   _____

4. The mother said to her kids, "Eat your vegetables."

   _____

5. The father said to his daughter, "Help me in the garage."

   _____

6. The girl said to her parents, "Take me to the zoo."

   _____

7. The dentist said to the boy, "Brush your teeth after every meal."

   _____

8. I said to my parents, "Don't spoil your grandchildren."

   _____

9. The girl said to her mother, "Comb my hair."

   _____

10. The father said to his daughter, "Do your homework."

   _____

11. The father said to his teenage daughter, "Don't come home late."

   _____

12. The father said to his son, "Always be polite."

   _____

EXERCISE 26 Circle the correct word to complete this story about a babysitter. In some cases, both answers are possible.

CD 4, TR 07

Last month I babysat for a family that lives near me. It was my first

babysitting job. They (*said*/ *told*) that the children (*would* / *will*) sleep
          (example)   (1)

through the night and not cause any problems. But Danielle, the three-year-old

girl, woke up at 9:00 and (*said / told*) that (*I / she*) (*can't / couldn't*)
     (2)   (3)   (4)
sleep. I (*said / told*) her that I (*will / would*) read (*her / you*) a story. Every
          (5)   (6)   (7)
time I finished the story, she (*said / told*) me (*read / to read*) (*her / me*)
                                (8)   (9)   (10)
another one. She finally fell asleep at ten. Then Estelle, the five-year-old,

started crying. When I went to her room, she told me that (*I / she*)
                                                           (11)
(*has seen / had seen*) a monster in the closet. I tried to (*tell / say*) her that
     (12)   (13)
there (*aren't / weren't*) any monsters in her closet, but she didn't stop
        (14)
crying. I wanted to call the parents and tell them that Estelle (*is / was*)
                                                                 (15)
upset and that she (*is / was*) crying. They had given me their cell phone
                    (16)
number and told me (*call / to call*) (*us / them*) in case of any problem,
                    (17)   (18)
but when I called, there was no answer. Later they told me that they

(*must / had to*) turn off their cell phone because they were at a concert.
   (19)
     They said (*we / they*) (*would / will*) be home by eleven. But they didn't
                 (20)   (21)
come home till 1:00 A.M. They called and told me that the concert

(*has started / had started*) an hour late. I called my mother and told
     (22)
her that I (*can't / couldn't*) leave because the parents hadn't come home.
             (23)
She told me (*don't / not to*) worry. She said that it (*is / was*) my
             (24)   (25)
responsibility to stay with the kids until the parents came home. When they

finally got home, they told me that (*we / they*) (*don't / didn't*) have any
                                     (26)   (27)
money to pay (*you / me*) because they (*have forgotten / had forgotten*)
              (28)   (29)
to stop at a cash machine. They said that (*they / we*) (*would / will*)
                                           (30)   (31)
pay (*you / me*) (*next / the following*) week.
    (32)   (33)
     When I got home, my mother was waiting up for me. I told her that I

(*don't / didn't*) ever want to have children. She laughed and told me that
   (34)
the children's behavior (*wasn't / isn't*) unusual. She told me that (*you / I*)
                          (35)   (36)
(*will / would*) change (*my / your*) mind some day. I (*said / told*) her
   (37)   (38)   (39)
that I (*don't / didn't*) want to babysit ever again. She told me that I
        (40)
(*will / would*) get used to it.
   (41)

Being an Au Pair

1. Have you ever taken care of small children?

2. Do you know anyone who works in child care?

CD 4, TR 08

Read the following journal entry. Pay special attention to reported questions.

Five years ago, when I was 18 years old and living in my native Estonia, I read an article about an "au pair" program in the U.S. This is a program where young people, mostly women between the ages of 18 and 25, go to live in the U.S. with an American family for a year to take care of their small children. In the process, these young people can improve their English, learn about American culture, and travel in the U.S.

When I heard about it, I became very excited and asked my mother **if I could join**. At first she said, "Absolutely not." She asked me **why I wanted to leave our family for a year**. I told her that it would be an opportunity for me to improve my English. I have always wanted to be an English teacher in Estonia, but my English was far from perfect. My mother said she would talk it over with Dad, and they finally agreed to let me go.

After filling out the application, I had an interview. The interviewer asked **why I wanted to be an au pair**. She also asked me **whether I knew how to drive**. Sometimes an au pair has to drive kids to school and to play dates. I told her that I had just gotten my license. I asked her **how many hours a week I would have to work**, and she said 45. I wanted to know **if I would get paid**, and she said I would be paid about $200 a week. I also wanted to know **if I would have the opportunity to go to school in the U.S.**, and she said yes. She told me that the family would have to help pay for my schooling. I asked her **if I had to do housework**, and she said no, that my job was only to take care of the kids: wake them up, get them dressed, give them breakfast, take them to school, and help them with homework.

I was so excited when I was accepted.

My year in the U.S. (in Lansing, Michigan) was wonderful. The family treated me like a member of their family, taking me with them on trips and other family outings. I met other au pairs from around the world and have made many new friends. My English is 100 percent better now.

Friends often ask me **if I am happy that I spent a year in the U.S.**, and I say, "This was the opportunity of a lifetime."

9.13 Noun Clauses as Reported Questions

When we report a question, we follow the rule of sequence of tenses if the main verb is in the past tense (*asked, wanted to know, tried to understand*, etc.). Use statement word order—put the subject before the verb. Use a period at the end.

EXAMPLES	EXPLANATION
Wh- Questions with auxiliaries or be	
"How old are you?" She asked **me how old I was.** "Where will I go to school?" I asked **her where I would go to school.**	An object (*me, him, her,* etc.) can be added after *asked*.
Wh- Questions with do/does/did	
"Why do you want to be an au pair?" She asked me **why I wanted to be an au pair.** "How did you hear about the program?" She asked me **how I had heard about the program.**	Remove *do/does/did* in the noun clause.
Wh- Questions about the subject	
"Who taught you to drive?" She asked me **who had taught me to drive.** "What happened?" She asked me **what had happened.**	There is no change in word order in questions about the subject.
Yes/No Questions with auxiliaries or be	
"Will I have time to go to school?" I asked her **if I would have time to go to school.** "Can I take classes?" I asked her **whether I could take classes or not.**	Add the word *if* or *whether* before reporting a *yes/no* question. You can add *or not* at the end.
Yes/No Questions with do/does/did	
"Do I have to do housework?" I asked her **whether I had to do housework.** "Did you receive the application?" She asked me **if I had received the application.**	Remove *do/does/did.*

Language Notes:
1. If the *ask* phrase is in the present tense, do not follow the rule of sequence of tenses. Keep the same tenses as the original question.
    "**Are** you happy that you **spent** a year in the U.S.?"
    Friends often ask me if I **am** happy that I **spent** a year in the U.S.
2. Remember: Reported speech is often a paraphrase of what someone has said.
    She asked me, "Does your mother approve?"
    She asked me **if my mother was okay with it.**
3. For exceptions to the rule of sequence of tenses, see Section 9.11.
    She asked me if Estonia **is** in Europe.

EXERCISE **27** These are some questions the interviewer asked the au pair candidate. Change these questions to reported speech. Follow the rule of sequence of tenses.

EXAMPLE How old are you?

She asked me ___how old I was.___

1. Have you discussed this with your parents?

She asked me _____

2. Do you have experience with small children?

She asked me _____

3. When did you graduate from high school?

She asked me _____

4. Do you have younger sisters and brothers?

She asked me _____

5. How did you hear about the program?

She asked me _____

6. Have you ever traveled to another country before?

She asked me _____

7. Do you have a driver's license?

She asked me _____

8. How long have you had your driver's license?

She asked me _____

9. Did you receive our brochure?

She asked me _____

10. What are your plans for the future?

She asked me _____

11. Have you ever left your parents before?

She asked me _____

EXERCISE 28   These are some questions the au pair candidate asked the interviewer. Change these questions to reported speech. Follow the rule of sequence of tenses.

EXAMPLE   How much will I get paid?

She asked her ___*how much she would get paid.*___

1. Will I have my own room?

   She asked her _____

2. How many children does the family have?

   She asked her _____

3. How old are the children?

   She asked her _____

4. Are the children in school?

   She asked her _____

5. Should I get an international driver's license?

   She asked her _____

6. What is the climate like in Michigan?

   She asked her _____

7. Does the family have an extra bedroom?

   She asked her _____

8. Can I use the family's computer?

   She asked her _____

9. When will I get a vacation?

   She asked her _____

10. How much is the airfare?

    She asked her _____

11. Who will pay for the airfare?

    She asked her _____

12. Where can I study English?

    She asked her _____

EXERCISE 29   **Change these questions to reported speech. Follow the rule of sequence of tenses.**

EXAMPLE   The babysitter asked the child, "Do you feel sick?"

The babysitter asked the child ___if he felt sick.___

1. The babysitter asked the parents, "What time will you be home?"

   The babysitter asked the parents _____

2. The babysitter asked the parents, "Where are you going?"

   The babysitter asked the parents _____

3. The children asked the babysitter, "What's your name?"

   The children asked the babysitter _____

4. The babysitter asked the little boy, "How old are you?"

   The babysitter asked the little boy _____

5. The babysitter asked the parents, "Have the kids eaten dinner yet?"

   The babysitter asked the parents _____

6. The children asked the babysitter, "Do we have to go to bed at 8:00 p.m.?"

   The children asked the babysitter _____

   _____

7. The babysitter asked the parents, "Should I give the kids a snack

   before bed?"

   The babysitter asked the parents _____

   _____

8. The children asked the babysitter, "Do you want to play a game with us?"

   The children asked the babysitter _____

   _____

9. The children asked the babysitter, "Can we watch TV?"

   The children asked the babysitter _____

10. The parents asked the babysitter, "Have you ever taken care of an

    infant before?"

    The parents asked the babysitter _____

    _____

11. The babysitter asked the parents, "Do you have a phone number

    where I can reach you?"

    The babysitter asked the parents _____

    _____

9.14 Noun Clauses after Other Past Tense Verbs

EXAMPLES	EXPLANATION
Dr. Spock *decided* that **he would write a book.** He *thought* that **he could help parents feel more comfortable with their kids.** He *knew* **that he wanted to help parents.** The au pair *didn't know* **if she would be happy in the U.S.** She *wondered* **what her life would be like in the U.S.** Her mother *wasn't sure* **whether she should let her daughter go to the U.S. or not.**	If the verb in the main clause is past tense (*thought, knew, believed, wondered, realized, decided, imagined, understood, was sure,* etc.), follow the rule of sequence of tenses in Section 9.9.

EXERCISE 30 **Fill in the blanks to complete this story. Answers may vary.**

I'm from Romania. I never imagined that I _____**would be**_____ in
                                              (example)

the U.S. someday. But I heard about an au pair program and decided

to come here when I was 20 years old. I didn't think that my parents

_____ me permission to come here, but they did. They
        (1)

thought that living in another country _____ make me
                                              (2)

more independent and responsible. And they were right.

Before I came to the U.S. I wondered _____ my life
                                              (3)

_____ be like. I thought that I _____
        (4)   *(5)*

all the time and not have time for school and friends. But that's not true.

I've made a lot of good friends in my English class. I didn't realize that I

_____ people of different ages in a college class, but the
        (6)

students are as young as 17 and as old as 75! I was also surprised by how

many nationalities of people I _____. I've met students
                                       (7)

(continued)

from many countries, from Poland to Portugal to Peru! I thought that my

English _____ almost perfect because I had been studying
                (8)

it since I was a child. But I realized that I _____ a lot of
                                                        (9)

idiomatic expressions, like "It's a piece of cake" (it's easy).

I wondered _____ "my" American
                    (10)

family _____ be like. I didn't know that they
            (11)

_____ treat me like a member of the family. They have
        (12)

been so nice to me. Being an au pair has been an unforgettable experience

for me.

EXERCISE **31**   **ABOUT YOU** **Fill in the blanks and discuss your answers. Follow the rule of sequence of tenses.**

EXAMPLE Before I came to this city, I thought that ___*everybody here was unfriendly,*___
but it isn't true.

1. Before I came to this city (or the U.S.), I thought that _____
_____, but it isn't true.

2. Before I came to this city (or the U.S.), I didn't know that _____
_____.

3. Before I came to this city (or the U.S.), I was worried that _____
_____.

4. When I came to this school, I was surprised to learn that _____
_____.

5. When I came to this school, I realized that _____
_____.

6. When I was younger, I never imagined that _____
_____.

7. Before I came to the U.S. (or this city), I wondered _____
_____.

EXERCISE 32　**ABOUT YOU** Fill in the blanks to tell about you and your parents when you were a child. Follow the rule of sequence of tenses.

EXAMPLE　When I was a child, I dreamed that ___I would be a movie star.___

1. My parents told me that _____
2. My parents hoped that _____
3. My parents thought that _____
4. When I was a child, I dreamed that _____
5. When I was a child, I thought that _____
6. When I was a child, I didn't understand _____
7. When I was younger, I wondered _____
8. When I was younger, I didn't know _____
9. When I was younger, I couldn't decide _____

EXERCISE 33

🔊

CD 4, TR 09

The author of this book remembers this true story from her childhood. Change the words in parentheses to reported speech.

When I was about six years old, I

had the measles.[3] My mother told me

___to stay in the bedroom___
(example: "Stay in the bedroom.")

because it was dark in there. She said

_____.
(1 "I don't want the bright light to hurt your eyes.")

My bedroom was near the dining room

of the house. My mother told me _____

_____ because it was dark in
(2 "You can go into the dining room.")

there. She told me _____ because
(3 "Don't go into the living room.")

it was too light there. The TV was in the living room and she thought

_____.
(4 "The brightness of the TV can hurt your eyes.")

My sister Micki was three years older than I and liked to tease[4] me.

She had already had the measles, so she wasn't afraid of getting sick. She

---

[3]*Measles* is an illness that children often get. The medical name is rubeola.
[4]To *tease* means to make fun of.

(continued)

came to the door of my bedroom and asked me _____

_____. I told

(5 "Do you know why you can't go into the living room?")

her _____. She said, "The living room

(6 "I don't understand.")

is for living people. The dining room is for dying people, and you're

going to die." Of course I believed her because she was nine years old

and knew much more than I did. I didn't understand that

_____.

(7 " 'Dining' means 'eating,' not 'dying'.")

Today we can laugh about this story, but when I had the measles, I was

afraid that _____.

(8 "I will die.")

EXERCISE 34

🔊

CD 4, TR 10

This is a composition written by a former au pair. Change the words in parentheses ( ) to reported speech.

Two years ago, when I was 18 and living in my native Poland, I didn't

know exactly ___*what I should do*___ with my life. I had just graduated

(example: "What should I do?")

from high school and I couldn't decide _____.

(1 "Should I go to college or not?")

A neighbor of mine told me _____ and decided

(2 "I had the same problem when I was your age.")

to go to the U.S. for a year to work as an "au pair." She asked me

_____. I told her that

(3 "Have you ever heard of the au pair program in America?")

_____. She told me that _____,

(4 "I haven't.") *(5 "I lived with an American family for a year.")*

helping them take care of their two small children. I asked her

_____. She laughed and

(6 "How much will this program cost me?")

told me _____.

(7 "You will earn about $200 a week, get your own room, and get three meals a day.")

She also told me _____. I asked

(8 "You will have a chance to travel in the U.S.")

her _____, and she said _____.

(9 "Was it a good experience for you?") *(10 "It has changed my life.")*

She said _____ and

(11 "I have gained a new understanding of people.")

_____. I asked her _____

(12 "My English has improved a lot.") *(13 "Is the work very hard?")*

and she said _____ but that _____.

(14 "It is.") *(15 "It is very rewarding.")*

I looked up *au pair* on the Internet and found out how to apply. I

told my parents that _____. At first they
(16 *"I am thinking about going to America for a year."*)

told me _____. They thought that _____
(17 *"Don't go."*)   (18 *"You are too young."*)

and that _____. I reminded them
(19 *"You don't have any experience."*)

_____ and that by working in the U.S.
(20 *"I have babysat many times for our neighbors' kids."*)

_____. I also told them that
(21 *"I will get even more experience."*)

_____. My parents finally agreed
(22 *"My English will improve if I live with an American family."*)

to let me go. I filled out the application, had an interview, and was

accepted. I told my parents _____. I promised them
(23 *"Don't worry."*)

_____.
(24 *"I will keep in touch with you by e-mail almost every day."*)

When I arrived, my American family explained to me

_____. They had two small kids, and I had to wake them
(25 *"What do I have to do?"*)

up, make them breakfast, and take them to school in the morning. I asked

them _____, and they laughed. They told
(26 *"Do I have to wait for them at school?"*)

me _____.
(27 *"While the kids are in school, you can take English classes at a local college."*)

I told them _____,
(28 *"I don't have enough money to pay for school."*)

but they told me _____. So that's what I did. I met
(29 *"We will pay for your classes."*)

students from all over the world. I also had a chance to travel to many

American cities with other au pairs. When the year was over, I was very sad

to leave my new family, but we promised _____. They
(30 *"We will stay in touch."*)

told me _____.
(31 *"You will always be welcome in our house."*)

Now I am back home and in college, majoring in early childhood

education. My parents told me _____. They can
(32 *"We are happy we let you go to America."*)

see that I've become much more confident and mature. Becoming an au

pair in the U.S. was one of the best experiences of my life.

Summary of Lesson 9

Direct statement or question	Sentence with included statement or question	Use of noun clause or infinitive
She loves kids. She is patient.	I know **that she loves kids.** I'm sure **that she is patient.**	A noun clause is used as an included statement.
Talk to your children. Don't be so strict.	It is essential **that you talk to your children.** He recommends **that we not be so strict.**	A noun clause is used after expressions of importance. The base form is used in the noun clause.
Is the baby sick? What does the baby need?	I don't know **if the baby is sick.** I'm not sure **what the baby needs.**	A noun clause is used as an included question.
What should I do with the crying baby? Where can I get information about the "au pair" program?	I don't know **what to do with the crying baby.** Can you tell me **where to get information about the "au pair" program?**	An infinitive can replace *should* or *can.*
You know more than you think you do. Do you have children?	Dr. Spock said, **"You know more than you think you do."** **"Do you have children?"** asked the doctor.	A noun clause is used in an exact quote to report what someone has said or asked.
I will read a book about child care. Do you have experience with children?	She said **that she would read a book about child care.** She asked me **if I had experience with children.**	A noun clause is used in reported speech to report or paraphrase what someone has said.
Trust yourself. Don't give the child candy.	He told us **to trust ourselves.** He told me **not to give the child candy.**	An infinitive is used to report an imperative.

Punctuation with Noun Clauses	
I know where he lives.	Period at end. No comma before noun clause.
Do you know where he lives?	Question mark at end. No comma before noun clause.
He said, "I like you."	Comma after *said.* Quotation marks around quote. Period before final quotation mark.
"I like you," he said.	Quotation marks around quote. Comma before final quotation mark. Period at end.
He asked, "What do you want?"	Comma after *asked.* Quotation marks around quote. Question mark before final quotation mark.
"What do you want?" he asked.	Quotation marks around quote. Question mark before end of quote. Period at end.

Editing Advice

1. Use *that* or nothing to introduce an included statement. Don't use *what*.

   >   *that*
   > I know ~~what~~ she likes to swim.

2. Use statement word order in an included question.

   >   *it is*
   > I don't know what time ~~is it~~.

   > I don't know where ⟨lives⟩ your brother.

3. We *say* something. We *tell* someone something.

   >   *told*
   > He ~~said~~ me that he wanted to go home.
   >   *said*
   > He ~~told~~, "I want to go home."

4. Use *tell* or *ask*, not *say*, to report an imperative. Follow *tell* and *ask* with an object.

   >   *told*
   > I ~~said~~ you to wash your hands.

   >   *me*
   > She asked to show her my ID card.

5. Don't use *to* after *tell*.

   > He told ~~to~~ me that he wanted to go home.

6. Use *if* or *whether* to introduce an included *yes/no* question.

   >   *if*
   > I can't decide I should buy a car or not.
   >   *whether*
   > I don't know it's going to rain or not.

7. Use *would*, not *will*, to report something that is past.

   >   *would*
   > My father said that he ~~will~~ come to the U.S. in 2005.

8. Follow the rule of sequence of tenses when the main verb is in the past.

   >   *wanted*
   > When I was a child, my grandmother told me that she ~~wants~~ to travel.

9. Don't use *so* before a noun clause.

    He thinks ~~so~~ the U.S. is a beautiful country.

10. Use the base form after expressions showing importance or
    urgency.

    be
    It is urgent that you ~~are~~ on time for the meeting.

    review
    I suggested that the teacher ~~reviewed~~ the last lesson.

11. Use *not* + base form to form the negative after expressions
    showing importance or urgency.

    not
    Doctors recommend that small children ~~don't~~ watch TV.

12. *Don't* isn't used in reporting a negative imperative.

    not to
    He told me ~~don't~~ open the door.

Editing Quiz

**Some of the shaded words and phrases have mistakes. Find the
mistakes and correct them. If the shaded words are correct, write C.**

that
When I was fourteen years old, I told my parents ~~what~~ I wanted to work as
(example)

C
a babysitter, but they told me that I was too young. At that time, they told
(example)   (1)

me that they will pay me $1 an hour to help with my five-year-old brother.
(2)

A few times they asked me I could watch him when they went out for an
(3)

hour or so. They never left me alone with him for more than an hour. And

they always told me call them immediately in case of any problem. They
(4)

told me don't watch TV or talk on the phone with my friends while I was
(5)

working as a babysitter. When they came home, they always told me that I

have done a good job.
(6)

When I was fifteen, they gave me a few more responsibilities, like preparing a small meal for my brother. They always told me that it was (7) (8) important that he eat fruit, not candy, if he asked for something sweet. (9) I asked them whether I could get more money because I had more (10) responsibilities, and they agreed to give me $2 an hour. I saved my money and asked them if I can buy some new CDs with my earnings. My parents (11) said, "Of course. It's your money. You earned it." (12)

When I turned 17 two months ago, my parents let me work for other families. I started working for my neighbors, who have three children. The neighbors asked me had I gotten my driver's license yet. When I said yes, (13) (14) they were very pleased, because I could take their kids to the park or drive them to their tennis lessons. I never realized how hard was it to take care (15) of so many kids. Whenever I take the kids somewhere, they always ask, "Are we there yet?" as soon as we get in the car. They think so we should (16) (17) arrive as soon as we get in the car. When they're thirsty, they always ask me to buy them soda, but I say them what it is healthier to drink (18) (19) (20) water. But they always tell, "In our house we always drink soda." I don't (21) understand why do their parents always give them sweet things. In my (22) house, we always drink water. I didn't know whether to follow the rules of (23) my house or theirs. So I asked my parents what should I do. My parents (24) told me not to say anything about their parents' rules but that I should try (25) to encourage healthy habits by example.

Lesson 9 Test/Review

PART 1 Punctuate the following sentences.

EXAMPLE He said, "I can't help you."

1. I don't know what time it is
2. Do you know what time it is
3. I'm sure that you'll find a job soon
4. The teacher said I will return your tests on Monday
5. I didn't realize that you had seen the movie already
6. He asked me What are you doing here
7. What do you want he asked
8. I want to help you I said
9. I told him that I didn't need his help
10. Can you tell me where I can find the bookstore

PART 2 Fill in the blanks with an included question.

EXAMPLE How old is the president?

Do you know ___**how old the president is?**___

1. Where does Jack live?

   I don't know _____

2. Did she go home?

   I don't know _____

3. Why were they late?

   Nobody knows _____

4. Who ate the cake?

   I don't know _____

5. What does "liberty" mean?

   I don't know _____

6. Are they working now?

   Can you tell me _____

7. Should I buy the car?

   I don't know _____

8. Has she ever gone to Paris?

I'm not sure _____

9. Can we use our books during the test?

Do you know _____

10. What should I do?

I don't know _____

PART **3** **Change the following sentences to reported speech. Follow the rule of sequence of tenses or use the infinitive where necessary.**

EXAMPLE He said, "She is late."

He said that she was late. _____

1. They said, "We can help you."

_____

2. We said, "Don't go away."

_____

3. He said, "My mother left yesterday."

_____

4. You said, "I'm learning a lot."

_____

5. He said, "I've never heard of Dr. Spock."

_____

6. He said, "Give me the money."

_____

7. They said to me, "We finished the job."

_____

8. He said to us, "You may need some help."

_____

9. He said to her, "We were studying."

_____

10. You said to her, "I have your book."

_____

11. He said to us, "You should have called me."

_____

12. He said to his wife, "I will call you."

_____

Change the following questions to reported speech. Follow the rule of sequence of tenses.

EXAMPLES   He asked me, "What does she want?"
He asked me what she wanted.
_____

1. He asked me, "Do you have any children?"
_____

2. He asked me, "Where are you from?"
_____

3. He asked me, "What time is it?"
_____

4. He asked me, "Did your father come home?"
_____

5. He asked me, "Where have you been?"
_____

6. He asked me, "Will you leave tomorrow?"
_____

7. He asked me, "What do you need?"
_____

8. He asked me, "Are you a student?"
_____

9. He asked us, "Can you help me today?"
_____

10. He asked us, "Who needs my help?"
_____

Expansion

Classroom

Activities

❶ Write questions you have about the topics in the readings of this lesson. Express your questions with "I wonder . . . " Compare your questions in a small group.

EXAMPLES   I wonder why parents spend so much less time with their children than they used to.

I wonder why it is so hard to raise a child.

❷ **What advice did your parents, teachers, or other adults give you when you were younger? Write three sentences. Share them in a small group.**

EXAMPLES My mother told me to be honest.

My grandfather told me that I should always respect older people.

Talk
About It

❶ **How is your philosophy of raising children different from your parents' philosophy or methods?**

❷ **How do you think parents should punish children when they misbehave?**

❸ **Did your parents read to you when you were a child? Do you think reading to a child is important?**

❹ **Did you have a lot of toys when you were a child? Are toys important for children?**

❺ **Do you think children today behave differently from when you were a child?**

❻ **Is it hard to raise children? Why?**

❼ **Read the following poem. Discuss the meaning.**

Your children are not your children.
They are the sons and daughters of Life's longing for itself.
They come through you but not from you,
And though they are with you, yet they belong not to you.
You may give them your love but not your thoughts.
For they have their own thoughts.
You may house their bodies but not their souls,
For their souls dwell in the house of tomorrow, which you cannot
    visit, not even in your dreams.
You may strive to be like them, but seek not to make them like you.
For life goes not backward nor tarries with yesterday.
You are the bows from which your children as living arrows are
    sent forth.

. . .

Let your bending in the archer's hand be for gladness;
For even as he loves the arrow that flies, so he loves also the bow
    that is stable.

Kahlil Gibran (From *The Prophet*)

Write

About It

1 Write about a belief you used to have that you no longer have. Explain what this belief was and why you no longer believe it to be true.

2 Write a short fable or fairy tale that you remember. Include the characters' words in quotation marks. See the folk tale on page 387 for an example.

3 Write about an incident from your childhood, like the one in Exercise 33 on pages 405–406.

4 Write about some good advice your parents gave you when you were a child. Explain what the advice was and how this has helped you.

EXAMPLE

> ### My Parents' Advice
>
> When I was a child, my parents always told me that education was the most important thing in the world. They always told me to do my homework and to ask for help if I didn't understand something...

 For more practice using grammar in context, please visit our Web site.

Grammar

Unreal Conditions—Present

Real vs. Unreal Conditions

Unreal Conditions—Past

Wishes

Context

Science or Science Fiction?

Time Travel

Before You Read

1. Do you think time travel is a possibility for the future?

2. Can you name some changes in technology or medicine that have happened since you were a child?

CD 4, TR 11

Read the following magazine article. Pay special attention to unreal conditions.

If you **could travel** to the past or the future, which time period **would** you **visit**?

What would you like to see? If you **could travel** to the past and prevent your grandfather from meeting your grandmother, then you **wouldn't be** here, right?

Albert Einstein 1879–1955

About 100 years ago, Albert Einstein proved that the universe has not three dimensions but four—three of space and one of time. He proved that time changes with motion. Einstein believed that, theoretically, time travel is possible. The time on a clock in motion moves more slowly than the time on a clock that does not move. If you **wanted** to visit the Earth in the year 3000, you **would have to** get on a rocket ship going at almost the speed of light,[1] go to a star 500 light-years[2] away, turn around, and come back at that speed. While traveling, you **would age** more slowly. When you **got** back, the Earth **would be** 1,000 years older, but you **would** only **be** ten years older. You **would be** in the future.

However, using today's technologies, time travel would be impossible. If you **wanted** to travel to the nearest star, it **would take** 85,000 years to arrive. (This assumes the speed of today's rockets, which is 35,000 miles per hour.) According to Einstein, you can't travel faster than the speed of light.

Science and technology are evolving at a rapid pace. **Would** you **want** to travel to the future to see all the changes that will occur? **Would** you **come** back to the present and warn people of future earthquakes or accidents? Remember that if you **came** back 1000 years later, all the people you knew **would be** gone. These ideas, first presented in a novel called *The Time Machine*, written by H.G. Wells over 100 years ago, are the subject not only of fantasy but of serious scientific exploration. In fact, many of today's scientific discoveries and explorations, such as traveling to the moon, had their roots in science fiction novels and movies.

While most physicists believe that travel to the future is possible, many believe that travel to the past will never happen.

[1] The *speed of light* is 299,792,458 meters per second (or 186,000 miles per second).
[2] A *light-year* is the distance that light travels in a year through a vacuum (6 trillion miles or 9.46 trillion kilometers).

10.1 Unreal Conditions—Present

An unreal condition is used to talk about a hypothetical or imagined situation. An unreal condition in the present describes a situation that is not real now.

EXAMPLES	EXPLANATION

If we **had** a time machine, we **could travel** to the future or past.
    (Reality: We **don't have** a time machine.)
If I **could travel** to the past, I **would visit** my ancestors.
    (Reality: I **can't travel** to the past.)
If we **didn't have** computers, our lives **would be** different.
    (Reality: We **have** computers.)
	Use a past form in the *if* clause and *would* or *could* + base form in the main clause.

If we **could travel** at the speed of light, we**'d be able** to visit the future. If I **visited** my great-great-great-grandparents, they**'d be** very surprised to meet me.	All pronouns except *it* can contract with *would*: *I'd, you'd, he'd, she'd, we'd, they'd.*
If time travel **were** possible, some people **would do** it. If we **were** time travelers, we**'d see** the future.	*Were* is the correct form in the condition clause for all subjects, singular and plural. However, you will often hear native speakers use *was* with *I, he, she, it,* and singular nouns.
If I **were** in my native country now, I**'d be living** with my parents.	For a continuous result, use *would* + *be* + verb *-ing.*
I **wouldn't** travel to the past *unless* I **could** return to the present. *Even if* I **could** know my future, I **wouldn't** want to know it.	The condition can begin with *unless* or *even if.*
If I were you, I**'d study** more science.	We often give advice with the expression "*If I were you . . .*"
What if you **could travel** to the future? *What if* you **had** the brain of Einstein?	We use *what if* to propose a hypothetical situation.
If you **had** Einstein's brain, what **would** you **do**? If you **could** fly to another planet, **would** you **go**?	When we make a question with conditionals, the *if* clause uses statement word order. The main clause uses question word order.

Punctuation Note: When the *if* clause precedes the main clause, a comma is used to separate the two clauses. When the main clause precedes the *if* clause, a comma is not used.
    If I had Einstein's brain, I would be smarter. (Comma)
    I would be smarter if I had Einstein's brain. (No comma)

EXERCISE 1 **ABOUT YOU** Answer the following questions with *I would*. Give an explanation for your answers.

EXAMPLE   If you could meet any famous person, who would you meet?
I would meet Einstein. I would ask him how he discovered relativity.

  1. If you could travel to the past or the future, which direction would you go?
  _____

  2. If you could make a clone of yourself, would you do it? Why or why not?
  _____

  3. If you could travel to another planet, would you want to go?
  _____

  4. If you could change one thing about today's world, what would it be?
  _____

  5. If you could find a cure for only one disease, what would it be?
  _____

  6. If you could know the day of your death, would you want to know it?
  _____

  7. If you could have the brain of another person, whose brain would you want?
  _____

  8. If you could be a child again, what age would you be?
  _____

  9. If you could change one thing about yourself, what would it be?
  _____

  10. If you could meet any famous person, who would it be?
  _____

  11. If you could be any animal, what animal would you be?
  _____

EXERCISE 2 Fill in the blanks with the correct form of the verb in parentheses ( ) to complete these conversations. Use *would* + base form in the main clause. Use the past tense in the *if* clause.

EXAMPLE   A: What ___would you do___ if you ___were___ the mayor
                              (you/do)   (be)
            of this city?

            B: If I ___were___ the mayor, I ___would create___
                         (be)   (create)
            enough parking spaces for everyone.

1. **A:** If you _____ make a copy of yourself,
   (can)

   _____ it?
   (you/do)

   B: My mom says that one of me is

   enough. If she _____
   (have)

   two of me, it _____
   (drive)

   her crazy.

2. **A:** If you _____ come back to Earth in any form
   (can)

   after you die, how _____ back?
   (you/come)

   B: I _____ back as a dog. Dogs have such an easy life.
   (come)

   A: Not in my native country. There are many homeless dogs.

   B: I _____ as an American dog.
   (only/come back)

3. **A:** What _____ if you _____ a lot
   (you/do)   (have)

   of money?

   B: I _____ my family first. Then I
   (help)

   _____ a nice house and car.
   (buy)

4. **A:** If you _____ look like any movie star,
   (can)

   who _____?
   (you/look like)

   B: I _____ Brad Pitt.
   (look like)

5. **A:** If I _____ find a way to teach a person a
   (can)

   foreign language in a week, I _____ a million dollars.
   (make)

   B: And I _____ your first customer.
   (be)

6. **A:** If you _____ be invisible for a day,
   (can)

   what _____?
   (you/do)

   B: I _____ to my teacher's house the day she writes
   (go)

   the final exam.

7. **A:** Why are you writing your composition by hand?

   B: I don't know how to type. I _____ my
   (type)

   compositions on the computer if I _____ type fast.
   (can)

(continued)

A: If I _____ you, I _____ a class to
(be)   (take)
learn to type.

8. A: What _____ if you _____
          (you/do)   (can/travel)
to the past or future?

B: I _____ to the past.
      (go)

A: How far back _____?
              (you/go)

B: I _____ to the nineteenth century and stay there.
      (go)

A: Why?

B: If I _____ in the nineteenth century, I
          (live)

_____ work. My life _____ easy.
    (not/have to)   (be)

A: Yes, but if you _____ in the nineteenth century,
                (live)

you _____ vote. Women couldn't vote back then.
    (not/be able to)

9. A: It _____ nice if people _____
       (be)   (can)
live forever.

B: If people _____, the world
          (not/die)

_____ overpopulated. There
    (be)

_____ enough resources for everybody.
    (not/be)

A: I didn't think of that. If the world _____
                                   (be)

overpopulated, I _____ a parking space!
            (never/find)

EXERCISE 3 **Fill in the blanks with the correct form of the verb in parentheses ( ) to complete this conversation.**

🔊
CD 4, TR 12

A: If you _____ change one thing about yourself,
        could
      (example: can)

what _____?
       (1 it/be)

B: I _____ thinner. If I _____ about
      (2 be)   (3 can/lose)

30 pounds, I _____ much happier—and healthier.
          (4 be)

If I _____ so much, I _____ weight.
    (5 not/eat)   (6 lose)

A: Diet is not enough. You need to get exercise too. You can start right

now with exercise. Let's go jogging every day after work.

B: If I _____ so tired after work,
(7 be/not)

I _____ jogging with you. But I work nine hours
(8 go)

a day and it takes me two hours to commute³. So I'm too tired at the

end of the day.

A: Can't you get any exercise at your job?

B: If I _____ a different kind of job,
(9 have)

I _____ more exercise. But I sit at a desk all day.
(10 get)

A: How about going swimming with me on Saturdays? I go every Saturday.

Swimming is great exercise.

B: If I _____ how to swim, I _____
(11 know)   (12 go)

with you. The problem is I don't know how to swim.

A: You can take lessons. My gym has a pool and they give lessons on the

weekends. Why don't you sign up for lessons?

B: I'm too busy with the kids on the weekends. If I

_____ kids, I _____ much more
(13 not/have)   (14 have)

free time.

A: If I _____ you, I _____ to simplify
(15 be)   (16 try)

my life.

EXERCISE 4   **ABOUT YOU** **Make a list of things you would do if you had more free time. You may share your sentences in a small group or with the entire class.**

EXAMPLES   If I had more free time, I'd read more novels.

I'd visit my grandmother more often if I had more free time.

1. _____

2. _____

3. _____

4. _____

³To *commute* means to travel from home to work and back.

EXERCISE 5 **ABOUT YOU** Make a list of things you would do differently if you spoke or understood English better. You may share your sentences in a small group or with the entire class.

EXAMPLES   If I spoke English fluently, I wouldn't come to this class. _____

I wouldn't be so nervous when I talk on the telephone if I _____

understood English better. _____

1. _____

2. _____

3. _____

EXERCISE 6 **Fill in the blanks to tell what the following people are thinking.**

EXAMPLE   One-year-old: If I _____could_____ walk, I _____would walk_____
                              (can)   (walk)

into the kitchen and take a cookie out of the cookie jar.

1. Two-year-old: If I _____ talk, I _____
                          (can)   (tell)

my mother that I hate peas.

2. 14-year-old: I _____ happier if
                     (be)

I _____ drive.
     (can)

3. 16-year-old: If I _____ a car, my friends and
                       (have)

I _____ out every night.
     (go)

4. 19-year-old: I _____ a private university if
                     (attend)

I _____ a lot of money.
     (have)

5. 25-year-old: If I _____ married, my parents
                       (be)

_____ about me so much.
   (not/worry)

6. 35-year-old mother: I _____ more time for myself if
                            (have)

my kids _____ older.
          (be)

7. 60-year-old grandmother: If I _____ grandchildren,
                                   (not/have)

my life _____ so interesting.
          (not/be)

8. 90-year-old: If I _____ young today,
(be)

I _____ learn all about computers and other high-tech
(have to)

stuff.

9. 100-year-old: If I _____ you the story of my life,
(tell)

you _____ it.
(not/believe)

10. The dog: If I _____ talk, I _____
(can)   (say)

"Feed me a steak."

EXERCISE **7** **ABOUT YOU** Complete each statement.

EXAMPLES If I studied harder, _I would get better grades._

If I were the president, _I would lower taxes._

1. If I were the English teacher, _____

2. If I could live to be 200 years old, _____

3. If I could predict the future, _____

4. If I were rich, _____

5. If I could be a child again, _____

6. If I could change places with any other person in the world, _____

_____

7. My life would be better if _____

8. I'd be learning English much faster if _____

9. I'd study more if _____

10. I'd travel a lot if _____

11. I'd be very unhappy if _____

12. I wouldn't borrow money from a friend unless _____

_____

EXERCISE 8 **ABOUT YOU** **Answer each question with *yes* or *no*. Then make a statement with an unreal condition.**

EXAMPLES Do you have the textbook?

Yes. If I didn't have the textbook, I wouldn't be able to do this exercise.

Is this lesson easy?

No. If it were easy, we wouldn't have to spend so much time on it.

1. Are you an American citizen?

   _____

2. Do you have an e-mail address?

   _____

3. Do you work on Sundays?

   _____

4. Do all the students in this class speak the same language?

   _____

5. Does the teacher speak your native language?

   _____

6. Are you taking other courses this semester?

   _____

7. Do you have a high school diploma?

   _____

8. Do you have a cell phone?

   _____

9. Do you live far from school?

   _____

10. Do you have a job?

    _____

11. Do you speak English perfectly?

    _____

12. Do you have a computer?

    _____

10.2 Implied Conditions

EXAMPLES	EXPLANATION
I **would** do anything to meet my great-great-grandparents. Time travel **would** teach me a lot about life hundreds of years ago. I **would** never travel in a rocket, **would** you?	Sometimes the condition (the *if* clause) is implied, not stated. In the examples on the left, the implication is "if you had the opportunity" or "if the possibility presented itself."
Would you **want** to live without today's technologies? **Would** you **want** to travel to another planet? **Would** you **want** to have Einstein's brain? I **wouldn't want** to live for 500 years, **would** you?	*Would want* is used to present hypothetical situations. The *if* clause is implied.

EXERCISE 9 **ABOUT YOU** Answer these questions and discuss your answers.

1. Would you give money to a beggar?
2. Would you marry someone from another country?
3. Would you buy a used computer?
4. Would you lend a large amount of money to a friend?
5. Would you read someone else's mail?
6. Would you lie to protect a friend?
7. Would you tell a dying relative that he or she is dying?
8. Would you want to travel to the past or the future?
9. Would you want to live more than 100 years?
10. Would you want to visit another planet?
11. Would you want to live on the top floor of a hundred-story building?
12. Would you want to know how long you're going to live?

EXERCISE 10 **ABOUT YOU** Answer these questions.

EXAMPLE What would you do if a stranger on the street asked you for money?
I would say, "I'm sorry. I can't give you any."

1. What would you do if you found a wallet in the street with a name and phone number in it?

(continued)

2. What would you do if you lost your money and didn't have enough money to get home by public transportation?

   _____

3. What would you do if you saw a person in a public park picking flowers?

   _____

4. What would you do if a cashier in a supermarket gave you a ten-dollar bill in change instead of a one-dollar bill?

   _____

5. What would you do if you hit a car in a parking lot and no one saw you?

   _____

6. What would you do if you saw another student cheating on a test?

   _____

7. What would you do if your doctor told you that you had six months left to live?

   _____

8. What would you do or say if you could meet the president?

   _____

9. What would you do if your best friend borrowed money from you and didn't pay you back?

   _____

10. What would you do if your best friend told your secret to another person?

   _____

Traveling to Mars

Before You Read

1. Are you interested in exploration of different planets?

2. Do you think there is life on other planets?

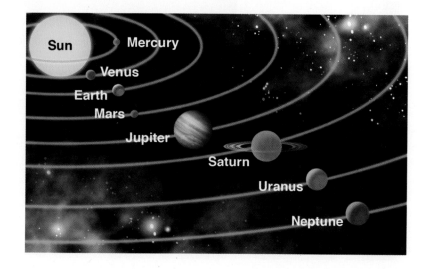

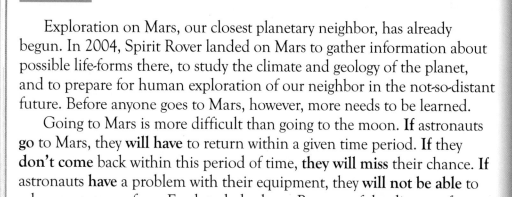

CD 4, TR 13

Read the following textbook article. Pay special attention to conditions beginning with *if*.

Exploration on Mars, our closest planetary neighbor, has already begun. In 2004, Spirit Rover landed on Mars to gather information about possible life-forms there, to study the climate and geology of the planet, and to prepare for human exploration of our neighbor in the not-so-distant future. Before anyone goes to Mars, however, more needs to be learned.

Going to Mars is more difficult than going to the moon. **If** astronauts **go** to Mars, they **will have** to return within a given time period. **If** they **don't come** back within this period of time, **they will miss** their chance. **If** astronauts **have** a problem with their equipment, they **will not be able** to rely on a message from Earth to help them. Because of the distance from Earth, it can take about 40 minutes from the time a message goes out from Earth until it is received on Mars. Also, a visitor to Mars will have to be gone for at least three years because of the distance and time necessary to travel. But one of the biggest problems with traveling to Mars is the danger of radiation. **If** a person **goes** to Mars, he or she **will be exposed** to much more radiation than someone traveling to the moon.

(continued)

According to Charles Cockell, a British microbiologist, humans could go to Mars now. "Technically, we **could** go today **if** we **wanted** to," he says. "As time goes on, we're going to be more and more ready to go as technology gets better and life support systems improve."

If you **had** the chance to go to Mars, **would** you go?

Spirit Rover

10.3 Real Conditions vs. Unreal Conditions

EXAMPLES	EXPLANATION
If astronauts **go** to Mars, they **will have** to return within a given time period. **If** they **have** problems, they **will have** to solve them by themselves. **If** a person **goes** to Mars, he **will be** gone for three years.	The sentences on the left describe a real possibility for the **future**. Notice that for real possibilities, we use the present tense in the *if* clause and the future tense in the main clause.

If you **were** on Mars, you **would weigh** about one-third of what you weigh on Earth.
If you **could** go to Mars, **would** you **go**?
	The statements to the left are about hypothetical or imaginary situations in the **present**. They are not plans for the future.
	
	    Reality: You are not on Mars now.
	    Reality: You can't go to Mars today.
	
	Notice that we use the past tense in the *if* clause and *would* or *could* in the main clause.

EXERCISE 11 Fill in the blanks with the correct form of the verb in parentheses ( ).
Both real conditions and unreal conditions are used.

A: Do you think that astronauts will travel to Mars soon?

B: Not so soon. I read that there's too much radiation.

A: Is that a problem?

B: Yes. If a person _____ **is** _____ exposed to too much
(example: be)

radiation, it _____ his bones. And it will probably
(1 damage)

cause cancer. Scientists are trying to build a spacecraft that can

minimize radiation to the astronauts. If they _____
(2 solve)

the radiation problem, probably travel to Mars _____
(3 happen)

in our lifetime. _____ you _____
(4)   (5 want)

to go to Mars?

A: Of course. If I _____ to Mars today,
(6 go)

I _____ back a rock as a souvenir.
(7 bring)

B: If you _____ for Mars today, you
(8 leave)

_____ back for at least three years.
(9 not/come)

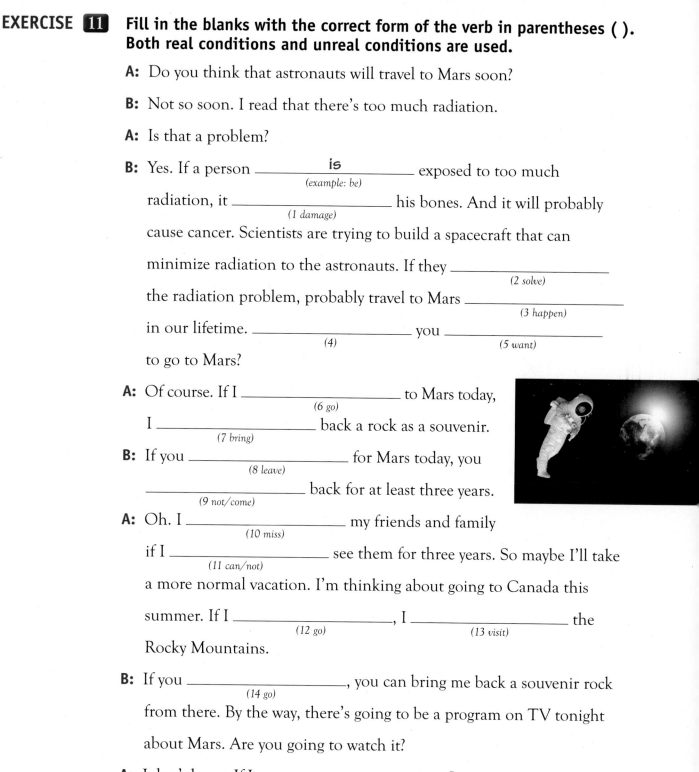

A: Oh. I _____ my friends and family
(10 miss)

if I _____ see them for three years. So maybe I'll take
(11 can/not)

a more normal vacation. I'm thinking about going to Canada this

summer. If I _____, I _____ the
(12 go)   (13 visit)

Rocky Mountains.

B: If you _____, you can bring me back a souvenir rock
(14 go)

from there. By the way, there's going to be a program on TV tonight

about Mars. Are you going to watch it?

A: I don't know. If I _____ time, I _____ it.
(15 have)   (16 watch)

B: If you _____ it, you _____ a lot about
(17 watch)   (18 learn)

space travel.

EXERCISE **12** Fill in the blanks with the correct form of the verb in parentheses ( ).
Unreal conditions are used.

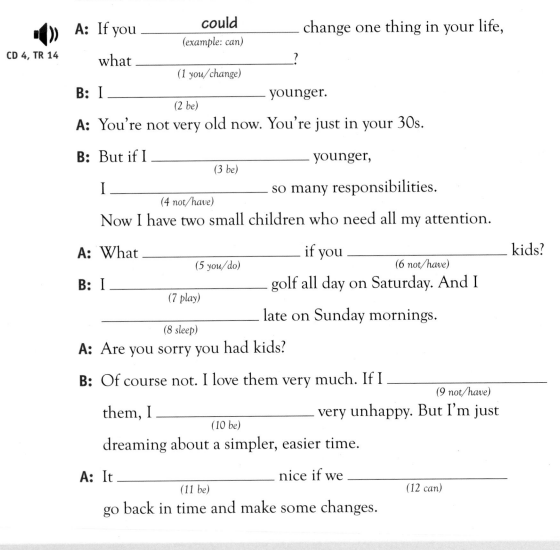

CD 4, TR 14

A: If you _____could_____ change one thing in your life,
(example: can)

what _____?
(1 you/change)

B: I _____ younger.
(2 be)

A: You're not very old now. You're just in your 30s.

B: But if I _____ younger,
(3 be)

I _____ so many responsibilities.
(4 not/have)

Now I have two small children who need all my attention.

A: What _____ if you _____ kids?
(5 you/do)   (6 not/have)

B: I _____ golf all day on Saturday. And I
(7 play)

_____ late on Sunday mornings.
(8 sleep)

A: Are you sorry you had kids?

B: Of course not. I love them very much. If I _____
(9 not/have)

them, I _____ very unhappy. But I'm just
(10 be)

dreaming about a simpler, easier time.

A: It _____ nice if we _____
(11 be)   (12 can)

go back in time and make some changes.

Life 100 Years Ago

Before You Read

1. Can you imagine what life was like 100 years ago? 1,000 years ago?

2. Would you want to visit a different time in history? What period in history would you want to visit?

Read the following magazine article. Pay special attention to unreal conditions in the past.

Most of us are amazed by the rapid pace of technology at the beginning of the twenty-first century. We often wonder what life will be like 20 or 50 or 100 years from now. But do you ever wonder what your life **would have been** like if you **had been** alive 100 years ago?

If you **had lived** around 1900 in the U.S., you **would have earned** about $200–$400 a year. You probably **wouldn't have graduated** from high school. Only 6 percent of Americans had a high school diploma at that time. If you **had been** a dentist or an accountant, you **would have made** $2,500 a year. If you **had been** a child living in a city, you **might have had** to work in a factory for 12–16 hours a day.

If you **had gone** to a doctor, he probably **would not have had** a college education. Only 10 percent of doctors at that time had a college degree. And if you **had had** a baby at that time, it **would have been** born at home. If you **had gotten** an infection at that time, you probably **would have died** because antibiotics had not yet been discovered. The leading causes of death at that time were pneumonia, influenza, and tuberculosis.

What about your home? If you **had been living** 100 years ago, you probably **wouldn't have had** a bathtub or a telephone. You **would have washed** your hair about once a month.

Do you think you **would have been** happy with life 100 years ago?

Did You Know?

The average life expectancy for someone born in the U.S. in the year 1900 was 47 years. For someone born in the year 2000, it was 75.

10.4 Unreal Conditions—Past

An unreal condition can describe a situation that was not real in the past.

EXAMPLES	EXPLANATION
If you **had been** alive 100 years ago, you **would have made** about $200 a year. If you **had lived** 100 years ago, you probably **wouldn't have graduated** from high school.	Use the past perfect in the *if* clause and *would have* + past participle in the main clause.
If you **had gotten** an infection, you **could have died**. If you **had had** a baby, it **might have died** young.	*Could* or *might* can be used in the main clause instead of *would*.
If I **had known** that learning English *was going* to be so hard, I **would have studied** it in my country. If **I had realized** how hard I *would have to* work as a waitperson, I **would have gone** to college.	A noun clause can be used within an *if* clause (after *know, realize,* etc.). Follow the rule of sequence of tenses in the noun clause. (See Section 9.9.)
If my great-grandparents **had been able to** come to the U.S. 100 years ago, I **would have been** born here and my life **would have been** easier.	In the *if* clause, use *had been able to* for the past perfect of *could*.
a. If you **were** born 100 years ago, your life **would have been** different. <div align="center">OR</div>b. If you **had been** born 100 years ago, your life **would have been** different.	Sometimes we don't change to the past perfect, especially with the verb *be*, if it is clear that the action is past. It is clear that you *were* born in the past. Sentences (a) and (b) have the same meaning.

Language Notes:

1. In relaxed speech, *have* after *could, would,* or *might* is pronounced like *of* or /ə/. Listen to your teacher pronounce the sentences above with relaxed pronunciation.
2. In very informal conversational English, you often hear *would have* in both clauses.
    If I *would have known* about the problem, I *would have told* you. (Informal)
    If I *had known* about the problem, I *would have told* you. (Formal)
3. Sometimes we mix a past condition with a present result.
    If my mother **had** never **met** my father, I **wouldn't be** here today.
4. Sometimes we mix a present condition with a past result.
    If I **had** a car, I **would have driven** you to the airport last week.

EXERCISE 13 Fill in the blanks with the correct form of the verb about life in the U.S. 100 years ago.

EXAMPLE If you _____had been_____ a doctor 100 years ago, you
                              (be)

_____wouldn't have been_____ rich.
                  (not/be)

1. If you _____ a baby 100 years ago, it probably
                          (have)

_____ at home.
        (be/born)

2. If you _____ an infection, you
(get)

probably _____.
(die)

3. If you _____ around 1900,
(live)

you probably _____ high school.
(not/finish)

4. You _____ a car if you
(not/have)

_____ at the beginning of the last century.
(live)

5. Your president _____ Theodore Roosevelt if you
(be)

_____ in the U.S. at the beginning of the last century.
(live)

6. If you _____ to travel to another city,
(need)

you _____ by train.
(travel)

7. You probably _____ if you
(work)

_____ a child 100 years ago.
(be)

EXERCISE `14` **A middle-aged woman is telling her daughter how the young lady's life would have been different if she had grown up in the late 1950s. Fill in the blanks with the correct form of the verb in parentheses ( ) to complete the story.**

🔊
CD 4, TR 16

It's great that you're thinking about becoming a doctor or astronaut.

When I was your age, I didn't have the opportunity you have today.

You can be anything you want, but if you ___**had been**___ a woman
(example: be)

growing up in the fifties, your opportunities _____ limited.
(1 be)

If you _____ to college, you probably
(2 go)

_____ in nursing or education,
(3 major)

or you _____ a secretarial course.
(4 take)

You probably _____ married in
(5 get)

your early twenties. If you _____
(6 get)

pregnant, you probably _____ your job.
(7 quit)

(continued)

You probably _____ (8 have) two or more children. Your husband

_____ (9 work) to support you and the children. But today,

you have the opportunity to continue working after you have children.

Technology _____ (10 be) different too. Your house

_____ (11 have) one TV and one phone. Because we had only

one TV, the family spent more time together. You _____ (12 not/have)

a computer or a cell phone.

If you _____ (13 grow) up in the fifties, your life

_____ (14 be) completely different.

EXERCISE 15 **ABOUT YOU** Complete each statement.

EXAMPLE If I had taken the TOEFL test last year, __I wouldn't have passed it.__

1. If I hadn't taken beginning English, _____

2. If I hadn't come to class today, _____

3. If I hadn't studied for the last test, _____

4. If I had been born 200 years ago, _____

5. If I had known how important English was going to be in my life, _____

_____

EXERCISE 16 **ABOUT YOU** Complete each statement.

EXAMPLE I would have saved money if __I had bought a used laptop.__

1. I would have done better on the last test if _____

_____

2. I would have taken an easier course if _____

_____

3. I would have studied English when I was a child if _____

_____

4. My parents would have been disappointed in me if _____

_____

5. I wouldn't have learned about time travel if _____

_____

Science or Wishful Thinking?

Before You Read

1. Do you wish for things you don't have in your life?

2. Would you want to live for 150 years?

CD 4, TR 17

Read the science news articles and the conversation that follows. Pay special attention to *wish* and the verbs that follow it.

In laboratory experiments, scientists at the University of Connecticut have been able to double the life span of fruit flies from 70 days to 140 days. They have been able to produce mice that live 30 percent longer than the average mouse. If these experiments worked in humans, it would mean that we would be able to live up to 150 years.

A 63-year-old California woman gave birth to a baby. The woman is believed to be the oldest woman in the United States ever to give birth. She went through a program of in-vitro fertilization[4] at the University of Southern California.

If you wish your loving cat had nine lives, you can make your dream come true. A U.S. company announced the start of its cat-cloning service. For $32,000 you can have your darling cat cloned.

A: I **wish** I **were** younger. I **wish** I **didn't have to** get old and sick. Science can do so much these days. I **wish** they **could find** a way to keep us young.

B: I read an article about how scientists are working to extend our lives. It's possible that soon people will be able to live 150 years.

A: I wouldn't want to be 150 years old and sick. I **wish** I **could be** 21 forever.

B: I don't think scientists will ever find a way to make us any younger than we are now. The best they can do is extend our lives and keep us healthier longer. What would you do differently if you were 21?

A: I would be going to parties on weekends. I wouldn't have so many responsibilities. I wouldn't have to take care of children. I started to have my children when I was in my early twenties. I **wish** I **had waited** until I was older.

[4]*In-vitro fertilization* is a surgical procedure to help a woman conceive a baby.

(*continued*)

B: My aunt is 55 and just got married for the first time a few years ago. She **wishes** she **had gotten** married when she was young and she **wishes** she **had had** children. But now she's too old.

A: I'm not so sure about that. I read an article about a 63-year-old woman who gave birth to a baby with the help of science.

B: That's amazing! What will science do for us next?

A: Scientists have started to clone animals.

B: I used to have a wonderful dog. I miss her. I **wish** I **could have** cloned her. But it's too late. She died 10 years ago.

A: Technology in the twenty-first century is moving so fast, isn't it? Don't you **wish** you **could come** back in 1,000 years and see all the changes in the world after that period of time?

B: I read an article that says that if we could travel at almost the speed of light, we could leave the Earth and come back a thousand years from now.

A: I wouldn't want to live in the future. I just **wish** I **could visit** the future. All our friends and relatives would be long dead if we left the present and returned 1,000 years later.

10.5 Wishes

We often wish for things that are not real or true in the present.

EXAMPLES	EXPLANATION
Present **Reality:** I **don't have** a dog. **Wish:** I wish (that) I **had** a dog. **Reality:** We **have** to get old. **Wish:** I wish (that) we **didn't have** to get old. **Reality:** I **can't live** 150 years. **Wish:** I wish I **could live** 150 years.	Use a **past** tense verb to wish for something in the **present**. After *wish*, you can use *that* to introduce the clause, but it is usually omitted.
Formal: I wish I **were** younger. **Informal:** I wish I **was** younger. **Formal:** I wish it **were** Sunday. **Informal:** I wish it **was** Sunday.	With *be*, *were* is the correct form for all subjects. In conversation, however, you will often hear native speakers use *was* with *I*, *he*, *she*, and *it*.

EXAMPLES	EXPLANATION
I'm not young, but I wish I **were**. I don't have a car, but I wish I **did**.	We can use an auxiliary verb (*were*, *did*, *could*, etc.) to shorten the *wish* clause.

We often wish for things that are not real or true in the past.

EXAMPLES	EXPLANATION

Past
  Reality: I **didn't know** my grandparents.
   Wish: I wish I **had known** them.
 	
  Reality: My aunt **didn't have** kids when she was young.
   Wish: She wishes she **had had** kids when she was young.
 	
  Reality: My favorite dog died years ago. I **couldn't clone** my dog.
   Wish: I wish I **could have cloned** her.
	Use a **past perfect** verb to wish for something in the **past**.
	
	If the real situation uses *could*, use *could have* + past participle after *wish*.

I didn't bring my photo album to the U.S., but I wish I **had**.	We can use the auxiliary verb *had* to shorten the *wish* clause.
Usage Note: In conversation, you often hear Americans use *would have* + past participle for past wishes. Formal: I wish you *had told* me the truth. Informal: I wish you *would have told* me the truth.	

EXERCISE 17 **Fill in the blanks to complete this conversation about wishes in the present.**

A: I wish we ___could___ stay young forever. Don't you?
    (example)

B: I just read a book called *You: Staying Young.*[5]

A: Is it about some new scientific discovery?

B: Not at all. The authors are doctors. They write about things you can do to live a longer, healthier life.

A: Really? I wish I _____ live to be at least 100 years old.
    (1)

B: According to the book, there are a lot of things you could do to live longer.

A: Like what?

B: For one thing, the doctors recommend walking 30 minutes a day.

[5]The full title is *You: Staying Young: The Owner's Manual for Extending Your Warranty,* by Michael Roizen and Mehmet Oz (Free Press, 2007).

(continued)

A: I wish I _____ time for a 30-minute walk. I work so many hours
that I'm too tired to exercise when I get home.

B: Maybe you can walk to work.

A: No. I live too far. I wish I _____ closer to my job.
_(3)_

B: How about walking on the weekend?

A: I have too many other things to do on the weekends, like laundry and

shopping. I wish I _____ so many things to do. When it's
_(4)_

Monday and I start work, I wish it _____ Friday. But when it's
_(5)_

Friday and I have so many things to do on the weekend, sometimes

I wish it _____ Monday. What other advice does this book give?
_(6)_

B: The authors recommend that we sleep seven to eight hours a night.

A: I wish I _____ so many hours, but I can't. I have too many
_(7)_

things to do. It sounds like you have to work hard to live longer.

There's no magic pill. I wish there _____ a magic pill.
_(8)_

B: Me too.

EXERCISE 18   **ABOUT YOU** **Fill in the blanks to complete each statement.**

EXAMPLE I wish I had __more time to spend with my family.__

1. I wish I were _____
2. I wish I knew how to _____
3. I wish I didn't have to _____
4. I wish I had _____
5. I wish I could _____

EXERCISE 19   **Fill in the blanks with a past wish.**

A: I didn't bring my photo album to the U.S. I wish I __had brought__
(example)

it with me to see the pictures of my family and friends back home. And

I brought too many unnecessary books to the U.S. I wish I

_____ them back home. I don't need them anymore.
_(1)_

What about you? Did you bring the right things?

B: More or less. But I didn't know how cold it was going to be in the winter here. I wish I _____. We arrived in December
(2)
and I wasn't prepared for a Boston winter.

A: I started to study English when I got to the U.S. I wish I

_____ it when I was younger. But my school back home
(3)
only offered German. I wish they _____ English too.
(4)

B: So are you fluent in German?

A: Not really. I wasn't a good student when I was young. I wish

I _____ a better student. I didn't realize how important
(5)
education was.

B: I wish I _____ that my parents were planning to
(6)
immigrate to the U.S. But they didn't tell me until a few months before
the move. I had studied English for many years, but I didn't have practice
with native speakers. I wish I _____ more practice with
(7)
native speakers. There was an American school near my house, and I
wish I _____ classes there.
(8)

A: There are so many new discoveries in science. Maybe they'll figure out a
way for us to learn a foreign language faster.

B: That would be great. It's so tough to learn a new language.

EXERCISE **20** **Name something.**

EXAMPLE Name something you wish had never happened.
I wish the war had never happened.

1. Name something you wish you had done when you were younger.
2. Name something you wish you had studied when you were younger.
3. Name something your family wishes you had done differently.
4. Name something you wish you had known before you came to this city.
5. Name something you wish your parents had done or told you.
6. Name something you wish you had never done.
7. Name something you wish had never happened.

EXERCISE 21 Fill in the blanks with the correct form of the verb in parentheses ( ) in each of the conversations below. Some wishes are about the present, some are about the past.

EXAMPLE

🔊
CD 4, TR 18

A: I wish I _____had_____ good vision.
(have)

B: You can have perfect or near perfect vision. Why don't you try laser surgery?

A: What can that do for me?

B: A lot. I had it two years ago, and I don't need glasses anymore. I had worn glasses since I was a child. I wish they ____had had____ this
(have)
surgery years ago. Now I can see first thing in the morning, read, drive, and play sports without wondering where my glasses are.

1. A: I wish I _____ thin.
(be)

B: Why don't you try a diet?

A: I've tried every diet. Nothing works.

B: You need to exercise every day.

A: I'm too tired when I get home from work. I wish scientists

_____ find a pill that would make me thin
(can)
with no effort on my part.

2. A: I've been bald since I was 25 years old. I wish I

_____ bald.
(be/not)

B: They say bald men are very manly.

A: I don't care what they say. I wish I _____ hair.
(have)
I wish someone _____ find a cure for baldness.
(can)

3. A: It's so expensive to call my country. I wish I

_____ talk to my family every day.
(can)

B: You can. Just get a microphone for your computer and you can chat with them online for free.

A: I wish I _____ how to do that.
(know)

B: Don't worry. I'll show you.

4. **A:** I wish I _____ older.
        (be)

   B: Why? No one wants to get old.

   A: I didn't say "old." I just said "older." Older people have more experience and wisdom.

   B: I wish we _____ have the wisdom of old
          (can)
   people and the bodies of young people.

   A: If everyone stayed young and no one died, where would we find space on the Earth for all the new babies born every day?

   B: We could colonize Mars.

5. **A:** I wish I _____ travel to the future.
        (can)

   B: Why?

   A: I would be able to see future problems and then come back and warn people about them.

   B: I wish I _____ go to the past.
          (can)

   A: Why?

   B: I would like to meet my grandparents. I never knew them. I wish
          I _____ them, but they died before I was born.
            (knew)

6. **A:** We saw a great movie last night about time travel.

   B: I wish I _____ with you, but I had to study
            (can/go)
   for my biology test.

7. **A:** I studied Italian when I was a child. I wish I
          _____ English.
              (study)

   B: I wish I _____ born in the U.S. Then English
            (be)
   would be easy for me.

8. **A:** I wish I _____ college before getting married.
            (finish)

   B: But you have a great husband.

   A: I know. But I wish I _____ a few years. Now
              (wait)
   I have no education and a lot of responsibilities.

(continued)

B: You can finish college now.

A: I wish I _____, but with my two kids, there's no time.
  (can)

9. **A:** I'm an only child. I wish I _____ a sister or brother.
  (have)

 B: Maybe you will someday.

 A: I don't think so. My mom is in her fifties already.

 B: With today's biological technologies, older women can still have kids.

 A: Maybe so. But she doesn't have the energy to raise a small child.

10.6 Wishing for a Desired Change

EXAMPLES	EXPLANATION
My parents wish I **wouldn't watch** so many science fiction movies. They wish I **would study** harder. They wish I **would be** more serious about my education.	*Would* + base form is used after *wish* to show that a person wants something different to happen in the **future**. It shows a desire for change.
I wish I **could** travel to the past. (I can't travel to the past.) I wish I **were** young. (I'm not young.)	*Wish* without *would* is not a desire for change but an expression of discontent with the present situation.

EXERCISE 22 **A father (F) is complaining to his teenage son (S). Fill in the blanks to show a desire that the person do something differently.**

F: Your hair's so long. I wish you ____would cut____ it.

S: But, Dad, I like long hair. All my friends have long hair.

F: And I wish you _____ your room. It's so dirty.
  (1)

S: I cleaned it two weeks ago.

F: Well, it's dirty again. Your clothes are on the closet floor. I wish you

 _____ them up.
  (2)

S: I'll do it when I get back tonight. I'm going with my friends to a movie.

F: I wish you _____ it now. And I wish you
  (3)

 _____ out on a weeknight. You have school tomorrow
  (4)

 morning. You need to study and do your homework.

S: I'll study when I get back.

F: But it'll be late. I wish you _____ home instead of
(5)

going out with your friends all the time.

S: Dad, I'm 18. I wish you _____ me like a baby.
(6)

F: And I wish you _____ like a baby. Try to be more
(7)

responsible.

EXERCISE 23 A man is complaining about his apartment situation. Fill in the
blanks with the correct form of the verb in parentheses ( ). Include
would if you think he is hoping for a change. Don't include *would* if
you think there is no possibility of change.

EXAMPLES I wish my neighbors _____*would be*_____ more quiet.
(be)

I wish the walls _____*were*_____ thicker.
(be)

1. I wish my landlord _____ more heat.
(provide)

2. I wish the building _____ an elevator.
(have)

3. I wish there _____ more trees and flowers around
(be)

the building, but there is concrete all around.

4. I wish my kitchen _____ larger.
(be)

5. I wish I _____ a gas stove, not an electric stove.
(have)

6. I wish the landlord _____ my rent every year.
(not/raise)

7. I wish the apartment _____ sunnier.
(be)

8. I wish the landlord _____ the hallways more often.
(clean)

9. I wish the people upstairs from me _____ around
(not/walk)

so much at night.

10. I wish I _____ rich enough to buy a house.
(be)

11. I wish I _____ air-conditioning.
(have)

12. I wish I _____ move, but I can't.
(can)

EXERCISE 24 **ABOUT YOU** Fill in the blanks to complete these statements. Your wish can include a desire for a change (by using *would*) or it can simply state that you're unhappy with the way things are right now.

EXAMPLES I wish the class _didn't have so many students._

I wish my parents _would let me go out with my friends._

1. I wish my family _____

2. I wish the teacher _____

3. I wish my neighbors _____

4. I wish the government _____

5. I wish more people _____

6. I wish my apartment _____

EXERCISE 25 A student is complaining about her class. Fill in the blanks with the correct form of the verb. Include *would* if you think she hopes for a change. Don't include *would* if you think that she believes there is no possibility of change. Both present, past, and future wishes are included.

EXAMPLES I wish I ____spoke____ English as well as the teacher.
                    (speak)

I wish the teacher ____would spend____ more time on conditionals.
                         (spend)

1. I wish I _____ skip ESL and go into regular English.
                (can)

2. I wish the book _____ the answers in the back.
                      (have)

3. I wish I _____ more attention to learning
              (pay)

   English when I was in my native country.

4. I wish I _____ a dictionary in my native country.
              (buy)

   Dictionaries are much cheaper there.

5. I wish I _____ my counselor's advice and
              (take)

   registered early. I couldn't get into the biology class I wanted.

6. I wish I _____ my dictionary to class today.
              (bring)

   We're going to write a composition, and I need to check my spelling.

7. I wish the teacher _____ us use our books
   (let)

   during a test.

8. I wish we _____ write so many compositions.
   (not/have to)

9. I wish the students in the back _____ quiet.
   (be)

   They're always making so much noise.

10. I wish I _____ the teacher's brain. Then I would
    (have)

    know English perfectly.

EXERCISE 26   **A mother (M) is complaining to her adult son (S). Fill in the blanks with the correct form of the words in parentheses ( ) to express their wishes.**

CD 4, TR 19

M: You never visit. I wish you ____**would visit**____ me more
   (example: visit)

   often. I'm not going to live forever, you know.

S: I *do* visit you often. Isn't once a week often enough?

M: Some day I won't be here, and you'll say to yourself, "I wish I

   _____ my mom more often."
   (1 visit)

S: Mom, you're only 48 years old.

M: Who knows how long I'll be here? There are no guarantees

   in life. My own mother died when I was a teenager. I wish she

   _____ to see you and your sister.
   (2 live)

S: I do too. But what can we do?

M: I wish you _____ married already.
   (3 be)

S: Mom, I'm only 25 years old. There's plenty of time to get married.

M: Well, your sister's only 23, and she's already married.

S: I wish you _____ comparing me to my sister.
   (4 stop)

   She has different goals in life. Besides, you don't like Shari's husband.

M: You're right. I wish she _____ a different man.
   (5 marry)

S: There's nothing wrong with Paul. He's a good husband to her.

(continued)

M: We'll see. You know, you're too thin. I wish you

_____ more.
(6 eat)

S: I eat enough. When I was a teenager, you said I was too fat.

M: I'm still your mother. I wish you _____ to me.
(7 listen)

S: I *do* listen to you. But I've got to live my own life.

M: Sometimes you act like a child and tell me you're old enough to make

your own decisions. Then you tell me you're too young to get married.

S: I'm not too young to get married. I just don't want to now. I want to be

a rock musician.

M: I wish you _____ a real job.
(8 find)

S: It *is* a real job.

M: You didn't finish college. I wish you _____ your
(9 get)

degree. How are you ever going to find a real job?

S: You don't need a college degree to be a rock musician.

M: Well, I hope I live long enough to see you married, with a good job.

S: With today's technologies, you'll probably live to be 150 years old

and not only see me married, but also see your great-great-great-

grandchildren married.

M: I wouldn't want to live so long.

S: You wouldn't? Just think, you'll be 150 years old and I'll be 127.

You'll still be telling me how to live my life. That would make you

happy, wouldn't it?

Summary of Lesson 10

1.

Unreal Conditions—Present

Verb ——→ Past	Verb ——→ *Would / Might / Could* + Base Form
If I **were** an astronaut,	I **would go** to Mars.
If I **could** live to be 150 years old,	I **would know** my great-great-grandchildren.
If my parents **spoke** better English,	they **might have** more opportunities.
If you **could** travel to the past,	you **could meet** your ancestors.
If she **didn't have** children,	she **would have** more free time.
If we **didn't have** advanced technology,	we **wouldn't be** able to explore space.

2.

Unreal Conditions—Past

Verb ——→ Past Perfect	Verb ——→ *Would / Might / Could* + Have + Past Participle
If you **had lived** 100 years ago,	you **wouldn't have had** a computer.
If a doctor **had lived** 100 years ago,	he **could have practiced** medicine without a college degree.
If you **had gotten** an infection,	you **might have died**.
If my father **had** not **met** my mother,	I **wouldn't have been** born.

3.

Real Possibilities for the Future

Condition	Future Result
If we **explore** Mars,	we **will learn** a lot.
If I **go** to New York,	I **will send** you a postcard.
If she **is** late,	she **will miss** the meeting.

4.

Wishes

Present	Future	Past
I wish my grandparents **were** here.	I wish you **would cut** your hair.	I wish I **had studied** English when I was younger.
I wish I **could speak** English fluently.	I wish he **would turn** off the TV.	I wish you **could have seen** the movie.

Editing Advice

1. Don't use *will* with an unreal condition.

   If I ~~will be~~ *were* rich, I would buy a house.

2. Always use the base form after a modal.

   She would ~~has~~ *have* called you if she hadn't lost your phone number.

3. Use the past perfect, not the present perfect, for unreal conditions and wishes.

   If she ~~has~~ *had* studied harder, she wouldn't have failed the test.

   I wish I ~~have~~ *had* seen that movie.

4. For a real condition, use the simple present tense in the *if* clause.

   If I ~~will~~ have time tomorrow, I will write my composition.

Editing Quiz

Some of the shaded words and phrases have mistakes. Find the mistakes and correct them. If the shaded words are correct, write C.

There are a few things in my life that I wish were *(C)* different. First, I wish
(example)

I ~~have~~ *had* a better job and made more money. Unfortunately, I don't have
(example)   *(1)*

the skills for a better job. When I was in high school, I wasn't interested

in college. My parents always said, "We wish you would continued
                           (2)

your education," but I was foolish and didn't listen to them. If I have
                (3)

gone to college, I will be making much more money now. And if I had
     (4)   *(5)*

more money, I could help my family back home. And, if I have a good
    (6)   *(7)*

education, my parents would be very proud of me. I wish I can convince
        (8)   *(9)*

my younger brothers and sister about the importance of an education, but they'll have to make their own decisions.

Another thing I'm not happy about is my living situation. I have a roommate because I can't afford to pay the rent alone. I wish I don't have (10) a roommate. My roommate always watches TV, and the TV is too loud. I wish he would (11) turn off the TV at night and let me sleep. My parents have told me, "If I were (12) you, I will (13) get a better roommate." But we signed a one-year lease together and I can't do anything about it until next May. If I had known (14) that he was going to be so inconsiderate, I never would had (15) roomed with him. I wish it was (16) May already! I prefer to live alone rather than live with a stranger. I'm saving my money now. If I will have (17) enough money, I'll get my own apartment next May. Another possibility is to room with my cousin, who's planning to come here soon. If he comes (18) to the U.S. by May, I'll share (19) an apartment with him. He's very responsible. I wish he has come (20) to the U.S. with me last year, but he didn't get his visa at that time.

I realize that we all make mistakes in life, but we learn from them. If I could (21) give advice to every young person in the world, I'd (22) say, "Look before you leap." And I will say, (23) "Listen to your parents. They've lived longer than you have, and you can learn from their experience."

Lesson 10 Test/Review

PART 1   **Fill in the blanks to express an unreal condition about the present.**

EXAMPLE   If I _____ *spoke* _____ English perfectly, I _____ *wouldn't be* _____ in this class.

1. We can't travel to the past. If we _____ to the past, we _____ our ancestors. Wouldn't you like to visit yours?

2. She doesn't have enough time to read. She _____ more books if she _____ more time.

3. You're sick. You need to see a doctor. If I _____ you, I _____ an appointment with the doctor immediately.

4. The weather is terrible today, so we're going to stay home. We _____ out if the weather _____ nice today.

5. My neighbor offered to buy my dog. I love my dog. I _____ my dog even if my neighbor _____ me a million dollars.

6. You have a lot of responsibilities. You're not a child. If you _____ a child, you _____ so many responsibilities.

7. If you _____ any animal, what animal _____ you _____?

PART 2   **Fill in the blanks to express an unreal condition about the past.**

EXAMPLES   I took a wrong turn on the highway. I arrived at the meeting one hour late.
If I _____ *hadn't taken* _____ a wrong turn on the highway,
I _____ *would have arrived* _____ at the meeting on time.

1. I forgot to set my alarm clock, so I didn't wake up on time.
I _____ on time if I _____ my alarm clock.

2. She didn't pass the final exam, so she didn't pass the course. If she _____ the final exam, she _____ the course.

3. She didn't hear the phone ring, so she didn't answer it. She

_____ the phone if she

_____ it ring.

4. He left his keys at the office, so he couldn't get into the house. If he

_____ his keys at the office,

he _____ into the house.

5. He didn't take the medicine, so his condition didn't improve. If he

_____ the medicine, his

condition _____.

6. I didn't have my credit card with me, so I didn't buy the computer I

saw last week. I _____ the computer

if I _____ my credit card with me.

PART ❸ **Fill in the blanks in the conversations to express present or past wishes.**

1. A: We went to see a great movie last night. I wish you

___ **had come** ___ with us.
(example)

B: You didn't tell me about it. I wish you _____ me.
What was it about?

A: It was about a man who wishes he _____ rich. And
his wish comes true. He's suddenly very rich, and he starts to have
all kinds of problems.

B: I wish I _____ those kinds of problems!

2. A: Do your parents live near you?

B: No. They live far away. I wish they _____ so far
from me.

3. A: I don't have a car. I wish I _____ a car. I have to
take the bus to work.

B: I have a car and drive to work. Traffic is horrible. I wish I

_____ to drive to work. I wish I

_____ near a train station so I could ride a train to

work. But I live far from the train station.

(continued)

4. A: I came to the U.S. last year. I wish I _____ here 15 years ago.

B: Me too. I didn't study English as a child. I wish I _____ it as a child.

A: It's too bad we can't go back and start our lives again. I wish I _____ back and make some changes in the past.

5. A: Do you have any sisters and brothers?

B: No. I'm an only child. I wish I _____ a brother or a sister.

6. A: Why do you eat while you drive?

B: I don't have enough time to stop and eat.

A: I wish you _____ that. People who do that sometimes have an accident.

7. A: Do you want to go to a party with us on Saturday night?

B: I can't. I have to work every night. I wish I _____ to work at night. I wish I _____ with you.

PART 4 **Some of the following sentences contain real conditions; some contain unreal conditions. Write the letter of the correct words to fill in the blanks.**

1. I _____ drive to Canada if I had a car.

    a. were   **b.** will   **c.** would   **d.** would be

2. I might go shopping next Saturday. If I _____ shopping next Saturday, I'll buy you a scarf.

    a. will go   **b.** went   **c.** would go   **d.** go

3. If I _____ you, I'd move to a different apartment.

    a. were   **b.** am   **c.** will be   **d.** would be

4. I can't help you. I would help you if I _____.

    a. can   **b.** could   **c.** would   **d.** will be able to

5. I might have to work next Monday. If I have to work, I _____ be able to come to class.

    a. wouldn't   **b.** won't   **c.** weren't   **d.** wasn't

6. My life would be easier if I _____ more English.

    a. knew   **b.** know   **c.** will know   **d.** would know

7. She has three children. She has no time to study. If she

    _____ children, she would have more time to study.

    a. doesn't have   **c.** wouldn't have

    b. weren't have   **d.** didn't have

8. It's raining now. If it _____ now, I'd go for a walk.

    a. isn't raining   **c.** weren't raining

    b. doesn't raining   **d.** wouldn't raining

9. She wouldn't tell you the secret even if you _____ her a

    million dollars.

    a. pay   **b.** paid   **c.** will pay   **d.** would be pay

10. If I could live in any city in the world, I _____ in Paris.

    a. will live   **c.** would live

    b. live   **d.** would have lived

11. I don't have a house. I wish I _____ a house.

    a. had   **b.** will have   **c.** have had   **d.** have

12. I can't drive a car. I wish I _____ a car.

    a. could drive   **c.** would drive

    b. can drive   **d.** will drive

13. If I had known how difficult it was to learn English,

    I _____ it when I was young.

    a. would study   **c.** would had studied

    b. would studied   **d.** would have studied

14. My uncle never exercised and was overweight. He had a heart attack

    and died when he was 50 years old. If he _____ better care of

    himself, he might have lived much longer.

    a. would take   **c.** had taken

    b. took   **d.** will take

(continued)

15. My brother needs more driving lessons before he can take the driver's

license test. If he _____ the test last week, he would have failed it.

    a. were taken   **c.** has taken

    b. would take   **d.** had taken

16. I didn't have time to call you yesterday. I _____ you if I had had

more free time.

    a. would call   **c.** would have called

    b. will call   **d.** would called

17. He was driving without a seat belt and had a car accident. He

was seriously injured. If he had been wearing his seat belt, he

_____ such a serious injury.

    a. might not have had   **c.** didn't have

    b. wouldn't had   **d.** hadn't had

18. Nobody told me we were going to have a test today. I wish someone

_____ me.

    a. would tell   **c.** would told

    b. had told   **d.** were told

19. Why didn't you tell me about your move last week? If you had told

me, I _____ you.

    a. could have helped   **c.** could helped

    b. could help   **d.** could had helped

20. My roommate talks on the phone all the time. I wish he

_____ on the phone so much.

    a. won't talk   **c.** doesn't talk

    b. wouldn't talk   **d.** wouldn't have talked

Expansion

Classroom Activities

❶ Do you think the world would be better or worse if . . . ? Form a small group and discuss your reasons.

a. there were no computers?
b. everyone were the same religion or race?
c. everyone spoke the same language?
d. we could live to be about 150 years old?
e. people didn't have to work?
f. families were allowed to have only one child?
g. every job paid the same salary?

❷ Fill in the blanks. Share your sentences in a small group.

a. If I could change one thing about myself (or my life), I'd change

_____.

b. If I lost my _____, I'd be very upset.

c. Most people would be happier if _____.

d. If I could travel to the past, _____.

e. If I could travel to the future, _____.

f. The world would be a better place if _____.

g. I wish I were _____ years old.

❸ Fill in the blanks and explain your answers.

If I had known _____,
I would (not) have _____.

EXAMPLE   If I had known that I needed computer skills in the U.S.,
I would have studied computers in my native country.

❹ Fill in the blanks and explain your answers.

a. I didn't _____, but I wish I had.
b. I _____, but I wish I hadn't.

❺ Write some sentences about your job, your school, your apartment, or your family. What do you wish were different? Share your answers in a small group.

EXAMPLES   I have to work on Saturdays. I wish I didn't have to work on Saturdays.

My brother watches TV all day. I wish he would play with his friends more.

❻ On a piece of paper or index card, finish this sentence:

I would be happier if _____.

The teacher will collect the cards or papers and read each statement. The rest of the class has to guess who wrote it. (Many people will write "if I were rich," or "if I knew more English," so try to think of something else.)

Talk
About It

❶ If you could meet anyone in the world, who would you want to meet?

❷ If you had the brain of another person, who would you be?

❸ Since Albert Einstein's death in 1955, his brain has been kept in a jar for study. If it were possible to create a new Einstein from a brain cell, would it be a good idea to do so? Why or why not?

❹ If you had the possibility of making a clone of yourself or a member of your family, would you do it? Why or why not?

❺ If you could live 200 years, would you want to?

❻ If we could eliminate all diseases, would the Earth be overpopulated?

❼ In Lesson 6, we read about Tim Berners-Lee, the creator of the World Wide Web. He has never made any money from the Web. Do you think he would have tried to make money on his idea if he had known how popular the Web was going to become?

❽ What entirely new things do you think might be possible in the future?

9 Read the following poem and discuss its meaning.

> There was a young lady named Bright,
> Who traveled far faster than light.
> She left one day
> In a relative way
> And returned the previous night.

10 Read what people have said in the past about the future. Discuss in small groups.

- "Heavier-than-air flying machines are impossible."
  (Lord Kelvin, president, Royal Society, 1895)
- "There is no reason for any individual to have a computer in their home."
  (Ken Olsen, president, chairman, and founder of Digital Equipment Corp., 1977)
- "The telephone has too many shortcomings to be seriously considered as a means of communication. The device is inherently of no value to us."
  (Western Union internal memo, 1876)
- "Airplanes are interesting toys but of no military value."
  (Marshal Ferdinand Foch, French commander of Allied forces during the closing months of World War I, 1918)
- "Who . . . wants to hear actors talk?"
  (Harry M. Warner, Warner Brothers, 1927)
- "Everything that can be invented has been invented."
  (Charles H. Duell, commissioner, U.S. Office of Patents, 1899)

Write
About It

1 Write about personality traits or bad habits you have. Write how your life would be different if you didn't have these traits or habits. (Or you can write about the habits or traits of another person you know well.)

2 Write about an important event in history. Tell what the result would or might have been if this event hadn't happened.

3 Write about how your life would have been different if you had stayed in the same place your whole life.

4 **Write about some things in your life that you are not happy about. How would you want to change your life?**

EXAMPLE

> ### My Wishes
>
> There are a few things I wish were different in my life.
> First, I wish my parents had come to the U.S. with me.
> But they are old now, and they didn't want to make a big
> change…

 For more practice using grammar in context, please visit our Web site.

Appendices

Noncount Nouns

There are several types of noncount nouns.

Group A: Nouns that have no distinct, separate parts. We look at the whole.

milk	juice	bread	electricity
oil	yogurt	meat	lightning
water	pork	butter	thunder
coffee	poultry	paper	cholesterol
tea	soup	air	blood

Group B: Nouns that have parts that are too small or insignificant to count.

rice	hair	sand
sugar	popcorn	corn
salt	snow	grass

Group C: Nouns that are classes or categories of things. The members of the category are not the same.

money or cash (nickels, dimes, dollars)	mail (letters, packages, postcards, flyers)
furniture (chairs, tables, beds)	homework (compositions, exercises, readings)
clothing (sweaters, pants, dresses)	jewelry (necklaces, bracelets, rings)

Group D: Nouns that are abstractions.

love	happiness	nutrition	patience	work	nature
truth	education	intelligence	poverty	health	help
beauty	advice	unemployment	music	fun	energy
luck/fortune	knowledge	pollution	art	information	friendship

Group E: Subjects of study.

history	grammar	biology
chemistry	geometry	math (mathematics*)

*Note: Even though *mathematics* ends with *s*, it is not plural.

(continued)

Notice the quantity words used with count and noncount nouns.

Singular Count	Plural Count	Noncount
a tomato	tomatoes	coffee
one tomato	**two** tomatoes	**two cups of** coffee
	some tomatoes	**some** coffee
no tomato	**no** tomatoes	**no** coffee
	any tomatoes (with questions and negatives)	**any** coffee (with questions and negatives)
	a lot of tomatoes	**a lot of** coffee
	many tomatoes	**much** coffee (with questions and negatives)
	a few tomatoes	**a little** coffee
	several tomatoes	**several** cups of coffee
	How many tomatoes?	**How much** coffee?

The following words can be used as either count nouns or noncount nouns. However, the meaning changes according to the way the nouns are used.

Count	Noncount
Oranges and grapefruit are **fruits** that contain a lot of vitamin C.	I bought some **fruit** at the fruit store.
Ice cream and butter are **foods** that contain cholesterol.	We don't need to go shopping today. We have a lot of **food** at home.
He wrote a **paper** about hypnosis.	I need some **paper** to write my composition.
He committed three **crimes** last year.	There is a lot of **crime** in a big city.
I have 200 **chickens** on my farm.	We ate some **chicken** for dinner.
I don't want to bore you with all my **troubles**.	I have some **trouble** with my car.
She went to Puerto Rico three **times**.	She spent a lot of **time** on her project.
She drank three **glasses** of water.	The window is made of bulletproof **glass**.
I had a bad **experience** during my trip to Paris.	She has some **experience** with computer programming.
I don't know much about the **lives** of my grandparents.	**Life** is sometimes happy, sometimes sad.
I heard a **noise** outside my window.	Those children are making a lot of **noise**.

Appendix B

Uses of Articles

Overview of Articles

Articles tell us if a noun is definite or indefinite.

	Count		Noncount
	Singular	**Plural**	
Definite	**the** book	**the** books	**the** coffee
Indefinite	**a** book	**(some/any)** books	**(some/any)** coffee

Part 1. Uses of the Indefinite Article

A. To classify a subject

Examples	Explanation
Chicago is **a** city. Illinois is **a** state. Abraham Lincoln was **an** American president. What's that? It's **a** tall building.	• Use *a* before a consonant sound. • Use *an* before a vowel sound. • You can put an adjective before the noun.
Chicago and Los Angeles are cities. Lincoln and Washington were American presidents. What are those? They're tall buildings.	Do not use an article before a plural noun.

B. To make a generalization about a noun

Examples	Explanation
A dog has sharp teeth. **Dogs** have sharp teeth. **An elephant** has big ears. **Elephants** have big ears.	Use the indefinite article (*a/an*) + a singular count noun or no article with a plural noun. Both the singular and plural forms have the same meaning.
Coffee contains caffeine. **Milk** is white. **Love** makes people happy. **Money** can't buy **happiness**.	Do not use an article to make a generalization about a noncount noun.

(continued)

C. To introduce a new noun into the conversation

Examples	Explanation
I have **a cell phone.** I have **an umbrella.**	Use the indefinite article *a/an* with singular count nouns.
Count: I have **(some) dishes.** Do you have **(any) cups?** I don't have **(any) forks.** **Noncount:** I have **(some) money** with me. Do you have **(any) cash** with you? I don't have **(any) time.**	Use *some* or *any* with plural nouns and noncount nouns. Use *any* in questions and negatives. *Some* and *any* can be omitted.
There's **an elevator** in the building. Are there **any restrooms** on this floor? There isn't **any money** in my checking account.	*There* + a form of *be* can introduce an indefinite noun into a conversation.

Part 2. Uses of the Definite Article

A. To refer to a previously mentioned noun

Examples	Explanation
There's **a dog** in the next apartment. **The dog** barks all the time.	We start by saying a *dog*. We continue by saying *the dog*.
We bought **some grapes.** We ate **the grapes** this morning.	We start by saying *some grapes*. We continue by saying *the grapes*.
I need **some sugar.** I'm going to use **the sugar** to bake a cake.	We start by saying *some sugar*. We continue by saying *the sugar*.
Did you buy **any coffee?** Yes. **The coffee** is in the cabinet.	We start by saying *any coffee*. We continue by saying *the coffee*.

B. When the speaker and the listener have the same reference

Examples	Explanation
The boy is shoveling snow. **The toys** are broken. **The money** on the table is mine.	The object is present, so the speaker and listener have the same object in mind.
a. **The teacher** is writing **on the board** in **the classroom**. b. **The president** is talking about taxes. c. Please turn off **the lights** and shut **the door** and **the windows** before you leave **the house**.	a. Students in the same class have things in common. b. People who live in the same country have things in common. c. People who live in the same house have things in common.
The house on the corner is beautiful. I spent **the money you gave me**.	The listener knows exactly which one because the speaker defines or specifies which one.

C. When there is only one in our experience

Examples	Explanation
The sun is bigger than **the moon**. There are many problems in **the world**.	The *sun*, the *moon*, and the *world* are unique objects. There is only one in our immediate experience.
Write your name on **the top** of the page. Sign your name on **the back** of the check.	The page has only one top. The check has only one back.
The Amazon is **the longest** river in the world. Alaska is **the biggest** state in the U.S.	A superlative indicates that there is only one.

(continued)

D. With familiar places

Examples	Explanation
I'm going to **the store** after work. Do you need anything? **The bank** is closed now. I'll go tomorrow.	We use *the* with certain familiar places and people—*the bank, the zoo, the park, the store, the movies, the beach, the post office, the bus, the train, the doctor, the dentist*—when we refer to the one that we habitually visit or use.

Language Notes:
1. Omit *the* after a preposition with the words *church, school, work,* and *bed.*
   He's **in church.**
   I'm going **to school.**
   They're **at work.**
   I'm going **to bed.**
2. Omit *to* and *the* with *home* and *downtown.*
   I'm going **home.**
   Are you going **downtown** after class?

E. To make a formal generalization

Examples	Explanation
The shark is the oldest and most primitive fish. **The bat** is a nocturnal animal.	To say that something is true of all members of a group, use *the* with singular count nouns.
The computer has changed the way people deal with information. **The cell phone** uses radio waves.	To talk about a class of inventions, use *the*.
The heart is a muscle that pumps blood to the rest of the body. **The ear** has three parts: outer, middle, and inner.	To talk about an organ of the body in a general sense, use *the*.

Language Note:
For informal generalizations, use *a* + a singular noun or no article with a plural noun.

Compare:
   The computer has changed the way we deal with information.
   A computer is expensive.
   Computers are expensive.

Part 3. Special Uses of Articles

No Article	Article
Personal names: John Kennedy George Bush	The whole family: the Kennedys the Bushes
Title and name: Queen Elizabeth Pope Benedict	Title without name: the Queen the Pope
Cities, states, countries, continents: Cleveland Ohio Mexico South America	Places that are considered a union: the United States the former Soviet Union Place names: the _____ of _____ the Republic of China the District of Columbia
Mountains: Mount Everest Mount McKinley	Mountain ranges: the Himalayas the Rocky Mountains
Islands: Coney Island Staten Island	Collectives of islands: the Hawaiian Islands the Philippines
Lakes: Lake Superior Lake Michigan	Collectives of lakes: the Great Lakes the Finger Lakes
Beaches: Palm Beach Pebble Beach	Rivers, oceans, seas, canals: the Mississippi River the Atlantic Ocean the Dead Sea the Panama Canal
Streets and avenues: Madison Avenue Wall Street	Well-known buildings: the Willis Tower the Empire State Building
Parks: Central Park Hyde Park	Zoos: the San Diego Zoo the Milwaukee Zoo
Seasons: summer fall spring winter Summer is my favorite season. **Note:** After a preposition, *the* may be used. In (the) winter, my car runs badly.	Deserts: the Mojave Desert the Sahara Desert

(continued)

No Article	Article

Directions:
    north   south
    east   west
	Sections of a piece of land:
	    the Southwest (of the U.S.)
	    the West Side (of New York)

School subjects:
    history   math
	Unique geographical points:
	    the North Pole the Vatican

Name + *college* or *university:*
    Northwestern University
    Bradford College
	The University/College of _____
	    the University of Michigan
	    the College of DuPage County

Magazines:
    Time   *Sports Illustrated*
	Newspapers:
	    the *Tribune* the *Wall Street Journal*

Months and days:
    September
    Monday
	Ships:
	    the *Titanic*
	    the *Queen Elizabeth II*

Holidays and dates:
    Mother's Day
    July 4 (month + day)
	The day of month:
	    the fifth of May
	    the Fourth of July

Diseases:
    cancer   AIDS
    polio   malaria
	Ailments:
	    a cold a toothache
	    a headache the flu

Games and sports:
    poker
    soccer
	Musical instruments, after *play:*
	    the drums the piano
	Note: Sometimes *the* is omitted.
	    She plays (the) drums.

Languages:
    French
    English
	The _____ language:
	    the French language
	    the English language

Last month, year, week, etc. = the one
before this one:
    I forgot to pay my rent last month.
    The teacher gave us a test last week.
	The last month, the last year, the last
	week, etc. = the last in a series:
	    December is the last month of the year.
	    Summer vacation begins the last
	    week in May.

In office = in an elected position:
    The president is in office for four years.
	In the office = in a specific room:
	    The teacher is in the office.

In back/in front:
    She's in back
    of the car.
	In the back/in the front:
	    He's in the back of the bus.

Appendix C

The Verb *GET*

Get has many meanings. Here is a list of the most common ones:

- get something = receive
  I got a letter from my father.

- get + (to) place = arrive
  I got home at six. What time do you get to school?

- get + object + infinitive = persuade
  She got him to wash the dishes.

- get + past participle = become

get acquainted	get worried	get hurt	get engaged
get lost	get bored	get married	get accustomed to
get confused	get divorced	get used to	get scared
get tired	get dressed		

  They got married in 1989.

- get + adjective = become

get hungry	get sleepy	get rich	get dark	get nervous
get angry	get well	get old	get upset	get fat

  It gets dark at 6:30.

- get an illness = catch
  While she was traveling, she got malaria.

- get a joke or an idea = understand
  Everybody except Tom laughed at the joke. He didn't get it.
  The boss explained the project to us, but I didn't get it.

- get ahead = advance
  He works very hard because he wants to get ahead in his job.

- get along (well) (with someone) = have a good relationship
  She doesn't get along with her mother-in-law.
  Do you and your roommate get along well?

- get around to something = find the time to do something
  I wanted to write my brother a letter yesterday, but I didn't get around to it.

- get away = escape
  The police chased the thief, but he got away.

- get away with something = escape punishment
  He cheated on his taxes and got away with it.

(continued)

- get back = return
  He got back from his vacation last Saturday.

- get back at someone = get revenge
  My brother wants to get back at me for stealing his girlfriend.

- get back to someone = communicate with someone at a later time
  The boss can't talk to you today. Can she get back to you tomorrow?

- get by = have just enough but nothing more
  On her salary, she's just getting by. She can't afford a car or a vacation.

- get in trouble = be caught and punished for doing something wrong
  They got in trouble for cheating on the test.

- get in(to) = enter a car
  She got in the car and drove away quickly.

- get out (of) = leave a car
  When the taxi arrived at the theater, everyone got out.

- get on = seat yourself on a bicycle, motorcycle, horse
  She got on the motorcycle and left.

- get on = enter a train, bus, airplane
  She got on the bus and took a seat in the back.

- get off = leave a bicycle, motorcycle, horse, train, bus, airplane
  They will get off the train at the next stop.

- get out of something = escape responsibility
  My boss wants me to help him on Saturday, but I'm going to try to get out of it.

- get over something = recover from an illness or disappointment
  She has the flu this week. I hope she gets over it soon.

- get rid of someone or something = free oneself of someone or something undesirable
  My apartment has roaches, and I can't get rid of them.

- get through (to someone) = communicate, often by telephone
  She tried to explain the harm of eating fast food to her son, but she couldn't get through to him.
  I tried to call my mother many times, but her line was busy. I couldn't get through.

- get through (with something) = finish
  I can meet you after I get through with my homework.

- get together = meet with another person
  I'd like to see you again. When can we get together?

- get up = arise from bed
  He woke up at six o'clock, but he didn't get up until 6:30.

Appendix D

Gerund and Infinitive Patterns

1. Verb + Infinitive

> They need **to leave**.
> I learned **to speak** English.

agree	claim	know how	seem
appear	consent	learn	swear
arrange	decide	manage	tend
ask	demand	need	threaten
attempt	deserve	offer	try
be able	expect	plan	volunteer
beg	fail	prepare	want
can afford	forget	pretend	wish
care	hope	promise	would like
choose	intend	refuse	

2. Verb + Noun/Object Pronoun + Infinitive

> I want you **to leave**.
> He expects me **to call** him.

advise	convince	hire	require
allow	dare	instruct	select
appoint	enable	invite	teach
ask	encourage	need	tell
beg	expect	order	urge
cause	forbid	permit	want
challenge	force	persuade	warn
choose	get	remind	would like
command	help*		

*Note: After *help*, *to* is often omitted: "He helped me (to) move."

(continued)

3. Adjective + Infinitive

They are happy **to be** here.
We're willing **to help** you.

afraid	disturbed	lucky	sorry
ashamed	eager	pleased	surprised
amazed	foolish	prepared	upset
careful	fortunate	proud	willing
content	free	ready	wrong
delighted	glad	reluctant	
determined	happy	sad	
disappointed	likely	shocked	

4. Verb + Gerund

I enjoy **dancing**.
She delayed **going** to the doctor.

admit	detest	miss	resent
advise	discuss	permit	resist
anticipate	dislike	postpone	risk
appreciate	enjoy	practice	stop
avoid	finish	put off	suggest
can't help	forbid	quit	tolerate
complete	imagine	recall	understand
consider	keep (on)	recommend	
delay	mention	regret	
deny	mind	remember	

5. Expressions with *Go* + Gerund

He **goes fishing** every Saturday.
They **went shopping** yesterday.

go boating	go hiking	go sightseeing
go bowling	go hunting	go skating
go camping	go jogging	go skiing
go dancing	go sailing	go swimming
go fishing	go shopping	

6. Preposition + Gerund

Verb + Preposition + Gerund
We talked about **moving**.
I look forward to **having** my own apartment.

adjust to	concentrate on	forget about	refrain from
argue about	depend on	insist on	succeed in
believe in	(dis)approve of	look forward to	talk about
care about	dream about	object to	think about
complain about	feel like	plan on	worry about

Adjective + Preposition + Gerund
I'm fond of **traveling**.
She's not accustomed to **eating** alone.

accustomed to	famous for	interested in	sure of
afraid of	fond of	lazy about	surprised at
appropriate for	good at	proud of	tired of
ashamed of	grateful to . . . for	responsible for	upset about
concerned about	guilty of	sorry about	used to
excited about	(in)capable of	suitable for	worried about

Verb + Object + Preposition + Gerund
I thanked him for **helping** me.
I apologized to him for **forgetting** his birthday.

accuse . . . of	devote . . . to	prevent . . . from	suspect . . . of
apologize to . . . for	forgive . . . for	prohibit . . . from	thank . . . for
blame . . . for	keep . . . from	stop . . . from	warn . . . about

(continued)

Gerund After Preposition in Certain Expressions

Who's in charge of **collecting** the papers?
What is your reason for **coming** late?

impression of	in favor of	in the middle of	requirement for
in charge of	instead of	need for	technique for
in danger of	interest in	reason for	the point of

7. Noun + Gerund

He has difficulty **speaking** English.
She had a problem **finding** a job.
She spent three weeks **looking** for an apartment.

Use a gerund after the noun in these expressions:

have a difficult time	have a hard time
have difficulty	have a problem
have experience	have trouble
have fun	spend time/money
have a good time	there's no use

8. Verb + Gerund or Infinitive (with little or no difference in meaning)

They like **to sing**.   I started **to read**.
They like **singing**.   I started **reading**.

attempt	intend
begin	like
can't stand	love
continue	neglect
deserve	prefer
hate	start
hesitate	

Verbs and Adjectives Followed by a Preposition

Many verbs and adjectives are followed by a preposition.

accuse someone of	(be) familiar with	(be) prepared for/to
(be) accustomed to	(be) famous for	prevent (someone) from
adjust to	feel like	prohibit (someone) from
(be) afraid of	(be) fond of	protect (someone) from
agree with	forget about	(be) proud of
(be) amazed at/by	forgive someone for	recover from
(be) angry about	(be) glad about	(be) related to
(be) angry at/with	(be) good at	rely on/upon
apologize for	(be) grateful to someone for	(be) responsible for
approve of	(be) guilty of	(be) sad about
argue about	(be) happy about	(be) satisfied with
argue with	hear about	(be) scared of
(be) ashamed of	hear of	(be) sick of
(be) aware of	hope for	(be) sorry about
believe in	(be) incapable of	(be) sorry for
blame someone for	insist on/upon	speak about
(be) bored with/by	(be) interested in	speak to/with
(be) capable of	(be) involved in	succeed in
care about	(be) jealous of	(be) sure of/about
care for	(be) known for	(be) surprised at
compare to/with	(be) lazy about	take care of
complain about	listen to	talk about
concentrate on	look at	talk to/with
(be) concerned about	look for	thank (someone) for
consist of	look forward to	(be) thankful (to someone) for
count on	(be) mad about	think about/of
deal with	(be) mad at	(be) tired of
decide on	(be) made from/of	(be) upset about
depend on/upon	(be) married to	(be) upset with
(be) different from	object to	(be) used to
disapprove of	(be) opposed to	wait for
(be) divorced from	participate in	warn (someone) about
dream about/of	plan on	(be) worried about
(be) engaged to	pray to	worry about
(be) excited about	pray for	

Direct and Indirect Objects

> **The order of direct and indirect objects depends on the verb you use. It also can depend on whether you use a noun or a pronoun as the object.**

Group 1	Pronouns affect word order. The preposition used is *to*.

Patterns: He gave a present to his wife. (DO to IO)
He gave his wife a present. (IO/DO)
He gave it to his wife. (DO to IO)
He gave her a present. (IO/DO)
He gave it to her. (DO to IO)

Verbs:	bring	lend	pass	sell	show	teach
	give	offer	pay	send	sing	tell
	hand	owe	read	serve	take	write

Group 2	Pronouns affect word order. The preposition used is *for*.

Patterns: He bought a car for his daughter. (DO for IO)
He bought his daughter a car. (IO/DO)
He bought it for his daughter. (DO for IO)
He bought her a car. (IO/DO)
He bought it for her. (DO for IO)

Verbs:	bake	buy	draw	get	make
	build	do	find	knit	reserve

Group 3	Pronouns don't affect word order. The preposition used is *to*.

Patterns: He explained the problem to his friend. (DO to IO)
He explained it to her. (DO to IO)

Verbs:	admit	introduce	recommend	say
	announce	mention	repeat	speak
	describe	prove	report	suggest
	explain			

Group 4	Pronouns don't affect word order. The preposition used is *for*.

Patterns: He cashed a check for his friend. (DO for IO)
He cashed it for her. (DO for IO)

Verbs:	answer	change	design	open	prescribe
	cash	close	fix	prepare	pronounce

Group 5	Pronouns don't affect word order. No preposition is used.

Patterns: She asked the teacher a question. (IO/DO)
She asked him a question. (IO/DO)

Verbs:	ask	charge	cost	wish	take (with time)

Appendix G

Spelling and Pronunciation of Verbs

Spelling of the -s Form of Verbs

Rule	Base Form	-s Form
Add -s to most verbs to make the -s form.	hope eat	hopes eats
When the base form ends in ss, zz, sh, ch, or x, add -es and pronounce an extra syllable, /əz/.	miss buzz wash catch fix	misses buzzes washes catches fixes
When the base form ends in a consonant + y, change the y to i and add -es.	carry worry	carries worries
When the base form ends in a vowel + y, do not change the y.	pay obey	pays obeys
Add -es to go and do.	go do	goes does

Three Pronunciations of the -s Form		
We pronounce /s/ if the verb ends in these voiceless sounds: /p t k f/.	hope—hopes eat—eats	pick—picks laugh—laughs
We pronounce /z/ if the verb ends in most voiced sounds.	live—lives grab—grabs read—reads	run—runs sing—sings borrow—borrows
When the base form ends in ss, zz, sh, ch, x, se, ge, or ce, we pronounce an extra syllable, /əz/.	miss—misses buzz—buzzes wash—washes watch—watches	fix—fixes use—uses change—changes dance—dances
These verbs have a change in the vowel sound.	do/**du**/—does/**dʌz**/	say/**sei**/—says/**sɛz**/

(continued)

Spelling of the *-ing* Form of Verbs

Rule	Base Form	-*ing* Form
Add -*ing* to most verbs. **Note:** Do not remove the *y* for the -*ing* form.	eat go study carry	eating going studying carrying
For a one-syllable verb that ends in a consonant + vowel + consonant (CVC), double the final consonant and add -*ing*.	p l a n C V C s t o p C V C s i t C V C g r a b C V C	planning stopping sitting grabbing
Do not double the final *w*, *x*, or *y*.	show mix stay	showing mixing staying
For a two-syllable word that ends in CVC, double the final consonant only if the last syllable is stressed.	refér admít begín rebél	referring admitting beginning rebelling
When the last syllable of a multi-syllable word is not stressed, do not double the final consonant.	lísten ópen óffer límit devélop	listening opening offering limiting developing
If the word ends in a consonant + *e*, drop the *e* before adding -*ing*.	live take write arrive	living taking writing arriving

Spelling of the Past Tense of Regular Verbs

Rule	Base Form	-ed Form
Add -ed to the base form to make the past tense of most regular verbs.	start kick	started kicked
When the base form ends in e, add -d only.	die live	died lived
When the base form ends in a consonant + y, change the y to i and add -ed.	carry worry	carried worried
When the base form ends in a vowel + y, do not change the y.	destroy stay	destroyed stayed
For a one-syllable word that ends in a consonant + vowel + consonant (CVC), double the final consonant and add -ed.	s t o p | | | C V C p l u g | | | C V C	stopped plugged
Do not double the final w or x.	sew fix	sewed fixed
For a two-syllable word that ends in CVC, double the final consonant only if the last syllable is stressed.	occúr permít	occurred permitted
When the last syllable of a multi-syllable word is not stressed, do not double the final consonant.	ópen háppen devélop	opened happened developed

Pronunciation of Past Forms that End in -ed

The past tense with -ed has three pronunciations.			
We pronounce a /t/ if the base form ends in these voiceless sounds: /p, k, f, s, š, č/.	jump—jumped cook—cooked	cough—coughed kiss—kissed	wash—washed watch—watched
We pronounce a /d/ if the base form ends in most voiced sounds.	rub—rubbed drag—dragged love—loved bathe—bathed use—used	charge—charged glue—glued massage—massaged name—named learn—learned	bang—banged call—called fear—feared free—freed stay—stayed
We pronounce an extra syllable /əd/ if the base form ends in a /t/ or /d/ sound.	wait—waited hate—hated	want—wanted add—added	need—needed decide—decided

Capitalization Rules

- The first word in a sentence: **My** friends are helpful.

- The word "I": My sister and **I** took a trip together.

- Names of people: **Julia Roberts**; **George Washington**

- Titles preceding names of people: **Doctor** (**Dr.**) **Smith**; **President Lincoln**; **Queen Elizabeth**; **Mr. Rogers**; **Mrs. Carter**

- Geographic names: the **United States**; **Lake Superior**; **California**; the **Rocky Mountains**; the **Mississippi River**

  NOTE: The word "the" in a geographic name is not capitalized.

- Street names: **Pennsylvania Avenue** (**Ave.**); **Wall Street** (**St.**); **Abbey Road** (**Rd.**)

- Names of organizations, companies, colleges, buildings, stores, hotels: the **Republican Party**; **Heinle Cengage**; **Dartmouth College**; the **University of Wisconsin**; the **White House**; **Bloomingdale's**; the **Hilton Hotel**

- Nationalities and ethnic groups: **Mexicans**; **Canadians**; **Spaniards**; **Americans**; **Jews**; **Kurds**; **Eskimos**

- Languages: **English**; **Spanish**; **Polish**; **Vietnamese**; **Russian**

- Months: **January**; **February**

- Days: **Sunday**; **Monday**

- Holidays: **Christmas**; **Independence Day**

- Important words in a title: ***G**rammar in **C**ontext*; ***T**he **O**ld **M**an and the **S**ea*; ***R**omeo and **J**uliet*; ***T**he **S**ound of **M**usic*

  NOTE: Capitalize "the" as the first word of a title.

Appendix I

Plural Forms of Nouns

REGULAR NOUN PLURALS

Word Ending	Example Noun	Plural Addition	Plural Form	Pronunciation
Vowel	bee banana	+ s	bees bananas	/z/
ch, sh, x, s, ss	church dish box bus class	+ es	churches dishes boxes buses classes	/əz/
Voiceless consonants	cat lip month	+ s	cats lips months	/s/
Voiced consonants	card pin	+ s	cards pins	/z/
Vowel + *y*	boy day	+ s	boys days	/z/
Consonant + *y*	lady story	y̶ + ies	ladies stories	/z/
Vowel + *o*	video radio	+ s	videos radios	/z/
Consonant + *o*	potato hero	+ es	potatoes heroes	/z/
Exceptions: photos, pianos, solos, altos, sopranos, autos, and avocados			
f or *fe*	leaf knife	f̶ + ves	leaves knives	/z/
Exceptions: beliefs, chiefs, roofs, cliffs, chefs, and sheriffs			

(continued)

IRREGULAR NOUN PLURALS

Singular	Plural	Explanation
man woman tooth foot goose	men women teeth feet geese	Vowel change (**Note:** The first vowel in *women* is pronounced /I/.)
sheep fish deer	sheep fish deer	No change
child person mouse	children people (OR persons) mice	Different word form
	(eye)glasses jeans belongings pajamas clothes pants/slacks goods scissors groceries shorts	No singular form
alumnus cactus radius stimulus syllabus	alumni cacti (OR cactuses) radii stimuli syllabi (OR syllabuses)	*us → i*
analysis crisis hypothesis oasis parenthesis thesis	analyses crises hypotheses oases parentheses theses	*is → es*
appendix index	appendices (OR appendixes) indices (OR indexes)	*ix → ices* OR *→ ixes* *ex → ices* OR *→ exes*
bacterium curriculum datum medium memorandum criterion phenomenon	bacteria curricula data media memoranda criteria phenomena	*um → a* *ion → a* *on → a*
alga formula vertebra	algae formulae (OR formulas) vertebrae	*a → ae*

Metric Conversion Chart

Length

When You Know	Symbol	Multiply by	To Find	Symbol
inches	in	2.54	centimeters	cm
feet	ft	30.5	centimeters	cm
feet	ft	0.3	meters	m
yards	yd	0.91	meters	m
miles	mi	1.6	kilometers	km
Metric:				
centimeters	cm	0.39	inches	in
centimeters	cm	0.03	feet	ft
meters	m	3.28	feet	ft
meters	m	1.09	yards	yd
kilometers	km	0.62	miles	mi

Note:
12 inches = 1 foot
3 feet / 36 inches = 1 yard

Area

When You Know	Symbol	Multiply by	To Find	Symbol
square inches	in²	6.5	square centimeters	cm²
square feet	ft²	0.09	square meters	m²
square yards	yd²	0.8	square meters	m²
square miles	mi²	2.6	square kilometers	km²
Metric:				
square centimeters	cm²	0.16	square inches	in²
square meters	m²	10.76	square feet	ft²
square meters	m²	1.2	square yards	yd²
square kilometers	km²	0.39	square miles	mi²

(continued)

Weight (Mass)

When You Know	Symbol	Multiply by	To Find	Symbol
ounces	oz	28.35	grams	g
pounds	lb	0.45	kilograms	kg
Metric:				
grams	g	0.04	ounces	oz
kilograms	kg	2.2	pounds	lb
Note: 1 pound = 16 ounces				

Volume

When You Know	Symbol	Multiply by	To Find	Symbol
fluid ounces	fl oz	30.0	milliliters	mL
pints	pt	0.47	liters	L
quarts	qt	0.95	liters	L
gallons	gal	3.8	liters	L
Metric:				
milliliters	mL	0.03	fluid ounces	fl oz
liters	L	2.11	pints	pt
liters	L	1.05	quarts	qt
liters	L	0.26	gallons	gal

Temperature

When You Know	Symbol	Do this	To Find	Symbol
degrees Fahrenheit	°F	Subtract 32, then multiply by $5/9$	degrees Celsius	°C
Metric:				
degrees Celsius	°C	Multiply by $9/5$, then add 32	degrees Fahrenheit	°F

Sample temperatures

Fahrenheit	Celsius
0	– 18
10	–12
20	–7
32	0
40	4
50	10
60	16
70	21
80	27
90	32
100	38
212	100

Comparative and Superlative Forms

Comparative and Superlative Forms

	Simple	Comparative	Superlative
One-syllable adjectives and adverbs*	tall fast	taller faster	the tallest the fastest
Two-syllable adjectives that end in y	easy happy	easier happier	the easiest the happiest
Other two-syllable adjectives	frequent active	more frequent more active	the most frequent the most active
Some two-syllable adjectives have two forms.**	simple common	simpler more simple commoner more common	the simplest the most simple the commonest the most common
Adjectives with three or more syllables	important difficult	more important more difficult	the most important the most difficult
-ly adverbs	quickly brightly	more quickly more brightly	the most quickly the most brightly
Irregular adjectives and adverbs	good/well bad/badly far little a lot	better worse farther less more	the best the worst the farthest the least the most

Language Notes:

1.*Exceptions to one-syllable adjectives:

bored	more bored	the most bored
tired	more tired	the most tired

2.**Other two-syllable adjectives that have two forms:
handsome, quiet, gentle, narrow, clever, friendly, angry, polite, stupid

The Superlative Form

Subject	Verb	Superlative Form + Noun	Prepositional Phrase
Alaska	is	the biggest state	in the U.S.
California	is	the most populated state	in the U.S.

The Comparative Form

Subject	Linking Verb[1]	Comparative Adjective	*Than*	Noun/Pronoun
She	is	taller	than	her sister (is).
She	seems	more intelligent	than	her sister.
Subject	**Verb Phrase**	**Comparative Adverb**	***Than***	**Noun/Pronoun**
I	speak English	more fluently	than	my sister (does).
I	sleep	less	than	you (do).

Comparisons with Nouns

Subject	Verb	Comparative Word + Noun	*Than*	Noun/Pronoun
I	work	fewer hours	than	you (do).
I	have	more time	than	you (do).

Equality or Inequality with Adjectives and Adverbs

Subject	Linking Verb	*As*	Adjective	*As*	Noun/Pronoun
She	isn't	as	old	as	her husband (is).
She	looks	as	pretty	as	a picture.
Subject	**Verb Phrase**	***As***	**Adverb**	***As***	**Noun/Pronoun**
She	speaks English	as	fluently	as	her husband (does).
He	doesn't work	as	hard	as	his wife (does).

[1]The linking verbs include *be, look, seem, feel, taste, sound,* and *seem.*

(continued)

Equality or Inequality with Quantities

Subject	Verb	*As Many/Much*	Noun	*As*	Noun/Pronoun
She	works	as many	hours	as	her husband (does).
Milk	doesn't have	as much	fat	as	cream (does).

Subject	Verb	*As Much As*	Noun/Pronoun		
Chicken	doesn't cost	as much as	meat (does).		
I	don't drive	as much as	you (do).		

Equality or Inequality with Nouns

Pattern A Subject	Verb	*The Same*	Noun	*As*	Noun/Pronoun
She	wears	the same	size	as	her mother (does).
She	isn't	the same	height	as	her brother (is).

Pattern B Subject & Subject	Verb		*The Same*	Noun
She and her mother	wear		the same	size.
She and her brother	aren't		the same	height.

Similarities Using *Like/Alike*

Pattern A Subject	Linking Verb	*Like*	Noun/Pronoun
Sugar	looks	like	salt.
Regular coffee	tastes	like	decaf.

Pattern B Subject & Subject	Linking Verb	*Alike*	
Sugar and salt	look	alike.	
Regular coffee and decaf	taste	alike.	

Glossary of Grammatical Terms

- **Adjective** An adjective gives a description of a noun.

  It's a *tall* tree.   He's an *old* man.   My neighbors are *nice*.

- **Adverb** An adverb describes the action of a verb, an adjective, or another adverb.

  She speaks English *fluently*.   I drive *carefully*.
  She speaks English *extremely* well.   She is *very* intelligent.

- **Adverb of Frequency** An adverb of frequency tells how often the action happens.

  I *never* drink coffee.   They *usually* take the bus.

- **Affirmative** means *yes*.

- **Apostrophe** ' We use the apostrophe for possession and contractions.

  My *sister's* friend is beautiful.   Today *isn't* Sunday.

- **Article** The definite article is *the*. The indefinite articles are *a* and *an*.

  I have *a* cat.   I ate *an* apple.   *The* teacher came late.

- **Auxiliary Verb** Some verbs have two parts: an auxiliary verb and a main verb.

  He *can't* study.   We *will* return.

- **Base Form** The base form, sometimes called the "simple" form, of the verb has no tense. It has no ending (*-s* or *-ed*): *be, go, eat, take, write*.

  I didn't *go* out.   We don't *know* you.   He can't *drive*.

- **Capital Letter** A B C D E F G . . .

- **Clause** A clause is a group of words that has a subject and a verb. Some sentences have only one clause.

  She speaks Spanish.

  Some sentences have **a main clause** and a **dependent clause**.

MAIN CLAUSE	DEPENDENT CLAUSE **(reason clause)**
She found a good job	because she has computer skills.

MAIN CLAUSE	DEPENDENT CLAUSE **(time clause)**
She'll turn off the light	before she goes to bed.

MAIN CLAUSE	DEPENDENT CLAUSE **(if clause)**
I'll take you to the doctor	if you don't have your car on Saturday.

(continued)

- **Colon :**

- **Comma ,**

- **Comparative Form** A comparative form of an adjective or adverb is used to compare two things.

  > My house is *bigger* than your house.
  > Her husband drives *faster* than she does.

- **Complement** The complement of the sentence is the information after the verb. It completes the verb phrase.

  > He works *hard.*   I slept *for five hours.*   They are *late.*

- **Consonant** The following letters are consonants: *b, c, d, f, g, h, j, k, l, m, n, p, q, r, s, t, v, w, x, y, z.*

  > NOTE: *y* is sometimes considered a vowel, as in the world *syllable.*

- **Contraction** A contraction is made up of two words put together with an apostrophe.

  > *He's* my brother.   *You're* late.   They *won't* talk to me.
  > (*He's* = he is)   (*You're* = you are)   (*won't* = will not)

- **Count Noun** Count nouns are nouns that we can count. They have a singular and a plural form.

  > 1 pen – 3 pens   1 table – 4 tables

- **Dependent Clause** See **Clause.**

- **Direct Object** A direct object is a noun (phrase) or pronoun that receives the action of the verb.

  > We saw *the movie.*   You have *a nice car.*   I love *you.*

- **Exclamation Mark !**

- **Frequency Words** Frequency words are *always, usually, generally, often, sometimes, rarely, seldom, hardly ever, never.*

  > I *never* drink coffee.   We *always* do our homework.

- **Hyphen –**

- **Imperative** An imperative sentence gives a command or instructions. An imperative sentence omits the word *you.*

  > *Come* here.   *Don't be* late.   Please *sit* down.

- **Infinitive** An infinitive is *to* + base form.

  > I want *to leave.*   You need *to be* here on time.

- **Linking Verb** A linking verb is a verb that links the subject to the noun or adjective after it. Linking verbs include *be, seem, feel, smell, sound, look, appear, taste.*

  > She *is* a doctor.   She *seems* very intelligent.   She *looks* tired.

- **Modal** The modal verbs are *can, could, shall, should, will, would, may, might, must.*

    They *should* leave.   I *must* go.

- **Negative** means no.

- **Nonaction Verb** A nonaction verb has no action. We do not use a continuous tense (*be* + verb *-ing*) with a nonaction verb. The nonaction verbs are: *believe, cost, care, have, hear, know, like, love, matter, mean, need, own, prefer, remember, see, seem, think, understand, want,* and sense-perception verbs.

    She *has* a laptop.   We *love* our mother.   You *look* great.

- **Noncount Noun** A noncount noun is a noun that we don't count. It has no plural form.

    She drank some *water.*   He prepared some *rice.*
    Do you need any *money?*   We had a lot of *homework.*

- **Noun** A noun is a person (*brother*), a place (*kitchen*), or a thing (*table*). Nouns can be either count (*1 table, 2 tables*) or noncount (*money, water*).

    My *brother* lives in California.   My *sisters* live in New York.
    I get *advice* from them.   I drink *coffee* every day.

- **Noun Modifier** A noun modifier makes a noun more specific.

    fire department   *Independence* Day   *can* opener

- **Noun Phrase** A noun phrase is a group of words that form the subject or object of the sentence.

    A *very nice woman* helped me at registration.
    I bought *a big box of cereal.*

- **Object** The object of the sentence follows the verb. It receives the action of the verb.

    He bought *a car.*   I saw *a movie.*   I met *your brother.*

- **Object Pronoun** Use object pronouns (*me, you, him, her, it, us, them*) after the verb or preposition.

    He likes *her.*   I saw the movie. Let's talk about *it.*

- **Parentheses** ( )

- **Paragraph** A paragraph is a group of sentences about one topic.

- **Participle, Present** The present participle is verb + *-ing.*

    She is *sleeping.*   They were *laughing.*

- **Period** .

- **Phrase** A group of words that go together.

    Last month my sister came to visit.
    There is a strange car *in front of my house.*

(continued)

- **Plural** Plural means more than one. A plural noun usually ends with *-s*.

     She has beautiful *eyes*.   My *feet* are big.

- **Possessive Form** Possessive forms show ownership or relationship.

     Mary's coat is in the closet.   *My brother* lives in Miami.

- **Preposition** A preposition is a short connecting word: *about, above, across, after, around, as, at, away, back, before, behind, below, by, down, for, from, in, into, like, of, off, on, out, over, to, under, up, with.*

     The book is *on* the table.   She studies *with* her friends.

- **Pronoun** A pronoun takes the place of a noun.

     I have a new car. I bought *it* last week.
     John likes Mary, but *she* doesn't like *him*.

- **Punctuation** Period . Comma , Colon : Semicolon ; Question Mark ? Exclamation Mark !

- **Question Mark** ?

- **Quotation Marks** " "

- **Regular Verb** A regular verb forms its past tense with *-ed*.

     He *worked* yesterday.   I *laughed* at the joke.

- **-s Form** A present tense verb that ends in *-s* or *-es*.

     He *lives* in New York.   She *watches* TV a lot.

- **Sense-Perception Verb** A sense-perception verb has no action. It describes a sense. The sense-perception verbs are: *look, feel, taste, sound, smell.*

     She *feels* fine.   The coffee *smells* fresh.   The milk *tastes* sour.

- **Sentence** A sentence is a group of words that contains a subject[2] and a verb (at least) and gives a complete thought.

     SENTENCE: She came home.
     NOT A SENTENCE: When she came home

- **Simple Form of Verb** The simple form of the verb, also called the base form, has no tense; it never has an *-s*, *-ed*, or *-ing* ending.

     Did you *see* the movie?   I couldn't *find* your phone number.

- **Singular** Singular means one.

     She ate a *sandwich*.   I have one *television*.

- **Subject** The subject of the sentence tells who or what the sentence is about.

     My sister got married last April. *The wedding* was beautiful.

---

[2]In an imperative sentence, the subject *you* is omitted: *Sit down. Come here.*

- **Subject Pronouns** Use subject pronouns (*I, you, he, she, it, we, you, they*) before a verb.

  They speak Japanese.   *We* speak Spanish.

- **Superlative Form** A superlative form of an adjective or adverb shows the number one item in a group of three or more.

  January is the *coldest* month of the year.
  My brother speaks English the *best* in my family.

- **Syllable** A syllable is a part of a word that has only one vowel sound. (Some words have only one syllable.)

  change (one syllable)   after (af·ter = two syllables)
  look (one syllable)   responsible (re·spon·si·ble = four syllables)

- **Tag Question** A tag question is a short question at the end of a sentence. It is used in conversation.

  You speak Spanish, *don't you?*   He's not happy, *is he?*

- **Tense** A verb has tense. Tense shows when the action of the sentence happened.

  SIMPLE PRESENT: She usually *works* hard.
  FUTURE: She *will work* tomorrow.
  PRESENT CONTINUOUS: She *is working* now.
  SIMPLE PAST: She *worked* yesterday.

- **Verb** A verb is the action of the sentence.

  He *runs* fast.   I *speak* English.

  Some verbs have no action. They are linking verbs. They connect the subject to the rest of the sentence.

  He *is* tall.   She *looks* beautiful.   You *seem* tired.

- **Vowel** The following letters are vowels: *a, e, i, o, u.* Y is sometimes considered a vowel (for example, in the word *mystery).*

Alphabetical List of Irregular Verb Forms

Base Form	Past Form	Past Participle	Base Form	Past Form	Past Participle
be	was/were	been	find	found	found
bear	bore	born/borne	fit	fit	fit
beat	beat	beaten	flee	fled	fled
become	became	become	fly	flew	flown
begin	began	begun	forbid	forbade	forbidden
bend	bent	bent	forget	forgot	forgotten
bet	bet	bet	forgive	forgave	forgiven
bid	bid	bid	freeze	froze	frozen
bind	bound	bound	get	got	gotten
bite	bit	bitten	give	gave	given
bleed	bled	bled	go	went	gone
blow	blew	blown	grind	ground	ground
break	broke	broken	grow	grew	grown
breed	bred	bred	hang	hung	hung[3]
bring	brought	brought	have	had	had
broadcast	broadcast	broadcast	hear	heard	heard
build	built	built	hide	hid	hidden
burst	burst	burst	hit	hit	hit
buy	bought	bought	hold	held	held
cast	cast	cast	hurt	hurt	hurt
catch	caught	caught	keep	kept	kept
choose	chose	chosen	know	knew	known
cling	clung	clung	lay	laid	laid
come	came	come	lead	led	led
cost	cost	cost	leave	left	left
creep	crept	crept	lend	lent	lent
cut	cut	cut	let	let	let
deal	dealt	dealt	lie	lay	lain
dig	dug	dug	light	lit/lighted	lit/lighted
dive	dove/dived	dove/dived	lose	lost	lost
do	did	done	make	made	made
draw	drew	drawn	mean	meant	meant
drink	drank	drunk	meet	met	met
drive	drove	driven	mistake	mistook	mistaken
eat	ate	eaten	overcome	overcame	overcome
fall	fell	fallen	overdo	overdid	overdone
feed	fed	fed	overtake	overtook	overtaken
feel	felt	felt	overthrow	overthrew	overthrown
fight	fought	fought	pay	paid	paid

[3]*Hanged* is used as the past form to refer to punishment by death. *Hung* is used in other situations: She *hung* the picture on the wall.

Base Form	Past Form	Past Participle	Base Form	Past Form	Past Participle
plead	pled/pleaded	pled/pleaded	sting	stung	stung
prove	proved	proven/proved	stink	stank	stunk
put	put	put	strike	struck	struck/stricken
quit	quit	quit	strive	strove	striven
read	read	read	swear	swore	sworn
ride	rode	ridden	sweep	swept	swept
ring	rang	rung	swell	swelled	swelled/swollen
rise	rose	risen	swim	swam	swum
run	ran	run	swing	swung	swung
say	said	said	take	took	taken
see	saw	seen	teach	taught	taught
seek	sought	sought	tear	tore	torn
sell	sold	sold	tell	told	told
send	sent	sent	think	thought	thought
set	set	set	throw	threw	thrown
sew	sewed	sewn/sewed	understand	understood	understood
shake	shook	shaken	uphold	upheld	upheld
shed	shed	shed	upset	upset	upset
shine	shone/shined	shone/shined	wake	woke	woken
shoot	shot	shot	wear	wore	worn
show	showed	shown/showed	weave	wove	woven
shrink	shrank/shrunk	shrunk/shrunken	wed	wedded/wed	wedded/wed
shut	shut	shut	weep	wept	wept
sing	sang	sung	win	won	won
sink	sank	sunk	wind	wound	wound
sit	sat	sat	withdraw	withdrew	withdrawn
sleep	slept	slept	withhold	withheld	withheld
slide	slid	slid	withstand	withstood	withstood
slit	slit	slit	wring	wrung	wrung
speak	spoke	spoken	write	wrote	written
speed	sped	sped			
spend	spent	spent			
spin	spun	spun			
spit	spit	spit			
split	split	split			
spread	spread	spread			
spring	sprang	sprung			
stand	stood	stood			
steal	stole	stolen			
stick	stuck	stuck			

Note:

The past and past participle of some verbs can end in -ed or -t.

burn	burned or burnt
dream	dreamed or dreamt
kneel	kneeled or knelt
learn	learned or learnt
leap	leaped or leapt
spill	spilled or spilt
spoil	spoiled or spoilt

Map of the United States of America

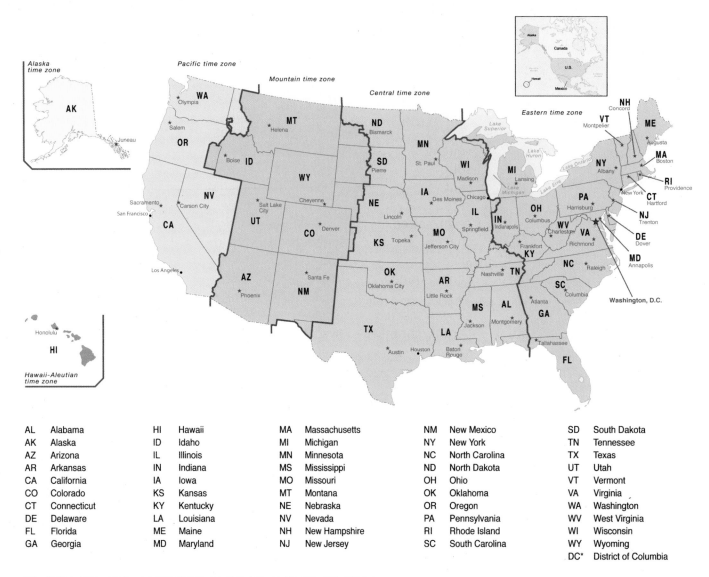

AL	Alabama	HI	Hawaii	MA	Massachusetts	NM	New Mexico	SD	South Dakota
AK	Alaska	ID	Idaho	MI	Michigan	NY	New York	TN	Tennessee
AZ	Arizona	IL	Illinois	MN	Minnesota	NC	North Carolina	TX	Texas
AR	Arkansas	IN	Indiana	MS	Mississippi	ND	North Dakota	UT	Utah
CA	California	IA	Iowa	MO	Missouri	OH	Ohio	VT	Vermont
CO	Colorado	KS	Kansas	MT	Montana	OK	Oklahoma	VA	Virginia
CT	Connecticut	KY	Kentucky	NE	Nebraska	OR	Oregon	WA	Washington
DE	Delaware	LA	Louisiana	NV	Nevada	PA	Pennsylvania	WV	West Virginia
FL	Florida	ME	Maine	NH	New Hampshire	RI	Rhode Island	WI	Wisconsin
GA	Georgia	MD	Maryland	NJ	New Jersey	SC	South Carolina	WY	Wyoming
								DC*	District of Columbia

*The District of Columbia is not a state. Washington, D.C., is the capital of the United States.
Note: Washington, D.C., and Washington state are not the same.

Index

Photo Credits